# DATE DUE

| | | | |
|---|---|---|---|
| | | | |
| | | | |
| | | | |
| | | | |
| | | | |
| | | | |
| | | | |
| | | | |
| | | | |
| | | | |
| | | | |
| | | | |
| | | | |
| | | | |
| | | | |
| | | | |
| | | | |
| | | | |

DEMCO 38-296

# Havana

**World Cities Series**

Edited by
Professor R. J. Johnston and Professor P. Knox

Published titles in the series:

Forthcoming titles in the series:

Other titles are in preparation

# Havana

## Two Faces of the Antillean Metropolis

**Roberto Segre**
*Universidade Federal do Rio de Janeiro, Brazil*
*and*
*Instituto Politécnico José Antonio Echeverría, Havana, Cuba*

**Mario Coyula**
*Instituto Politécnico José Antonio Echeverría, Havana, Cuba*

*and*

**Joseph L. Scarpaci**
*Virginia Tech, Blacksburg, Virginia, USA*

JOHN WILEY & SONS

Chichester • New York • Weinheim • Brisbane • Singapore • Toronto

Copyright © 1997 by Roberto Segre, Mario Coyula & Joseph L. Scarpaci

'r,
), England

)1243 779777
+44) 1243 779777
customer service enquiries):

n http://www.wiley.co.uk
r http://www.wiley.com

Reprinted March 1998

*Other Wiley Editorial Offices*

John Wiley & Sons, Inc., 605 Third Avenue,
New York, NY 10158-0012, USA

WILEY-VCH Verlag GmbH, Pappelallee 3,
D-69469 Weinheim, Germany

Jacaranda Wiley Ltd, 33 Park Road, Milton,
Queensland 4064, Australia

John Wiley & Sons (Asia) Pte Ltd, 2 Clementi Loop #02-01,
Jin Xing Distripark, Singapore 129809

John Wiley & Sons (Canada) Ltd, 22 Worcester Road,
Rexdale, Ontario M9W 1L1, Canada

*Library of Congress Cataloging-in-Publication Data*

Segre, Roberto, 1934–
    Havana: two faces of the Antillean Metropolis / Roberto Segre, Mario Coyula, and Joseph L. Scarpaci.
        p.  cm.—(World cities series)
    Includes bibliographical references and index.
    ISBN 0–471–94979–5
    1. Urbanization—Cuba—Havana—History.  2. City planning—Cuba—Havana—History.  3. Havana (Cuba)—Economic conditions.  4. Havana (Cuba)—Social conditions.  I. Coyula, Mario.  II. Scarpaci, Joseph L.  III. Title.  IV. Series.
    HT384.C92H387  1997                                                                          96-50142
    307.76´09729´23—dc21                                                                              CIP

*British Library Cataloguing in Publication Data*

A catalogue record for this book is available from the British Library

ISBN 0-471-94979-5
Typeset in 10/12 Palatino by Poole Typesetting Ltd, Bournemouth
Printed and bound in Great Britain from PostScript files by Biddles Ltd, Guildford and King's Lynn

This book is printed on acid-free paper responsibly manufactured from sustainable forestation, for which at least two trees are planted for each one used for paper production.

# Contents

# List of figures

# List of tables

# Preface

This book is a work of love. As with all amorous encounters, it has been titillating and taxing, uplifting and unnerving, and fulfilling and frustrating. It grew out of a deep appreciation for one of the truly great cities of the world. Regrettably, little has been written in English recently about Havana. Forces beyond our control have made that so. Nonetheless, scholars and residents enamored with *San Cristóbal de la Habana* have been writing about its complex beauties in Spanish and other Romance languages. We trust that one of this book's modest contributions will be to assemble these voices into a single tome, spun, inevitably, into a perspective conceived by its authors. At the outset, we realize that some readers will attempt to pigeon-hole our epistemological, philosophical and political approach before reading a word further. Anything written about Cuba, it seems, creates predetermined positions. To those skeptics, we ask that you read on with an open mind and heart.

Our perspectives are informed by vastly different life experiences. Roberto Segre was born in Milan, Italy, reared in Buenos Aires, Argentina, and has worked most of his professional life in Havana. His writings about architecture in Revolutionary Cuba – translated into many languages – are benchmarks about the transformation of socialist Cuba as expressed in the island's built environment. Mario Coyula is the native-born author in this project. His voice surfaces in these pages stemming from a 40-plus-year involvement in the revolutionary struggle since his days as a student at Havana University during the mid-1950s. His professional experience as an architect, planner, and professor gives continuity and authority to the work while sometimes confronting his co-authors in the assessment of undergoing issues in present Cuba. Thus, Havana's 'two faces' show even in gentle tensions among the authors of this book.

Joseph L. Scarpaci, a native of Pittsburgh, Pennsylvania, came to Cuba late in his life. He has tried to make up for that handicap by visiting Havana 10 times over the past 6 years. The only social scientist on the team, his training in human geography and his work in social policy and urban planning in other parts of Latin America (Puerto Rico, Chile, Argentina, Colombia) seek to provide a comparative perspective in the study of Havana.

The cast of co-authors formally entered into this project with John Wiley in 1993, arguably the most difficult economic time in recent Cuban history. To complicate matters, Segre assumed a visiting professorship in Brazil immediately thereafter. The chilling winds of the cold war between Washington, DC and Havana made Scarpaci's trips to Cuba more difficult. In the midst of this, Coyula managed to work in a city burdened with power blackouts and in a worsening protocol situation that made travel to the US more difficult than normal for Cubans.

For a city referred to as a 'living museum', for better or worse, we chose a busy time in Cuban history to write about its capital city. No sooner would we have a contemporary aspect of Havana down in writing, when something would change; a new law, an investment scheme, or forecast led to a revision and updating. Despite this modification, we managed to exchange manuscripts, diskettes, photographs, and slides through the usual assortment of 'gee-whiz technologies': e-mail, FAX, next-day courier, and the like (though countless friends also lugged our pages as carry-on baggage). We have savored those all too infrequent times when we could bridge time and space, and pour over our one-hundred thousand plus words in the same room. Through it all, we have learned much from each other. We trust our professional and personal backgrounds will cast a net that is broad enough to attract those who do not know Havana and, in turn, urge them to do so. And to those who are old friends of the city, we hope you reacquaint yourselves with this marvelous place.

Roberto Segre, Rio de Janeiro
Mario Coyula, La Habana
Joseph L. Scarpaci, Blacksburg, Virginia

# Acknowledgments

The idea for this book project first grew out of conversations that one of the Series Editors, Paul Knox, began with Roberto Segre back in 1985. Roberto Segre held a Guggenheim Fellowship that year, and lectured briefly at Virginia Tech. Over the past decade Knox has done much so that this book be written, despite the changing composition of the research team. In Cuba, Gina Rey, Director of the *Grupo para el Desarrollo Integral de la Capital*, was instrumental in providing resources and encouragement so that the project took flight. Jill Hamberg in New York has also supported its publication. She has offered thoughtful and extensive comments on the project at various times. The errors and misrepresentations, however, are ours alone. In what follows we each give special thanks to those who were helpful along the way.

**Roberto Segre,** *Rio de Janeiro*

The documentation gathered for the historical analysis of this work was made possible by the position I held as Director of GIHAU (*Grupo de Investigaciones Históricas de la Arquitectura y del Urbanismo*, 1972–1982), at the School of Architecture the Instituto Superior Politécnico 'José Antonio Echeverría'. I also wish to thank Dr. Denise Pinheiro Machado, DPUR, FAU (*Faculdade do Arquitectura e Urbanismo*) of the *Universidade Federal de Rio de Janeiro*, for the generous time she granted me for writing this book. The *Conselho Nacional de Pesquisa* (CNPq) in Brasilia awarded me a grant to carry out a multimedia project which was related to the work contained in this book. I was also able to complete a study under this grant, Evolution of Latin American Cities in the 20th Century. A comparative study of transformations in urban space and its cultural meaning: Rio de Janeiro/Havana. I carried out this research between 1994 and 1996.

My wife, Licenciada Concepción Pedrosa Morgado helped in the compilation of the bibliography. In Cuba, I received support from architects Dr. Eliana Cárdenas, Dr. Rita Yebra, the Director of CENCREM, Isabel Rigol, and Francisco Bedoya.

At Rice University, Houston, Texas, Professor Stephen Fox commented on drafts of this text, as did Halley Margon and Professor José Kós, both collaborators on my research team in Río de Janeiro.

**Mario Coyula,** *La Habana*

Thanks to my grandfather
a forgotten icon to be reborn one day
To my elder son, uprooted before harvest
whose void is refilled with rage and tenderness
Thanks to those old-fashioned abstractions
family   honor   courage
fidelity   decency
To enduring loves and to others that have faded
To those who back me and those in front
Thanks to the Revolution
for expanding two-thirds of my time
with successes and flaws, which are also mine
To this salty island, long-suffering and rebellious
the homeland sculpted by my ancestors
broken and reshaped again and again
And thanks to my Havana, graceful and crumbling
waiting for this body, already fulfilled
meant to breed new lives
and mourn the same deaths

**Joseph L. Scarpaci,** *Blacksburg, Virginia*

My children Cristina Alessandra and Michael Joseph graciously tolerated the interruptions of this project. They treated the writing of this book as a younger sibling competing for their father's attention. My wife, Gilda de los Angeles Machín, a *camagüeyana*, naturally looked with suspicion on the attention that Havana consumed. She nurtured, cajoled and – at times – tolerated the disruptions caused by the book's unusually long gestation period.

The College of Architecture and Urban Studies at Virginia Tech provided financial support for production of many of the illustrations. Cathy Gorman of Virginia Tech's Photographic Services produced several illustrations with patience and good cheer. My graduate assistants – Mary Ellen Carroll, Robert Moore, and Scott Sincavage – commented on segments of the manuscript. Jill Hamberg, Wendy Prentice, Amparo Avella, and Felípe Préstamo reviewed the entire manuscript.

The Acosta, Hernández, Berríos-Niz, Sosa and Vargas families were characteristically gracious and supportive over 5 years of research in and out of Havana.

*A todos, nuestro profundo agradecimiento.*

# 1

# History, geography and society

Yet it was something else to stroll through the city. Behind those formidable and sad walls was a world of color and gaiety. A kaleidoscopic juxtaposition of races and ethnic shades, of historical stages. In brief, there lay the riches and misery of the capital's face, where foreigners could find what they had left behind in their countries, plus the entertainment and universal vices that characterized Havana's infamous lifestyle.

Julio Le Riverend, *La Habana, Biografía de una Provincia*, 1961

*San Cristóbal de la Habana* is a beautiful world city where history's hand has left a mark on every corner. For nearly half a millennium its built environment has shown capitalist grandeur and plunder, as well as the mediating successes and failures of socialist planning. Havana is unique in many ways and this book explores those defining features.

The city defies most of the conventional schema that classify cities by their shape or skylines. Urban geographers, for instance, are intrigued by its polycentric structure. Its lack of a discernible center, central business district, or some semblance of a core is noteworthy, as are the many changes in the location of the center over time. *Habaneros* lack a consensus about where *el centro* might be; references to it form part of the daily parlance among commuters, cyclists, and bus riders. More perplexing is that while the debate over defining Havana's central region is relatively new in the city's historical geography – arising only this century – the wandering of the city's former centers has left vestiges of an urban landscape, rich in architecture and social history, making it easy even for a novice to 'read' the built environment as if it were text (Segre *et al.* 1981). Havana was on its way to developing a skyline of steel-and-glass towers, but that process ended abruptly. Understanding why that is so speaks volumes about the history of both Havana and Cuba.

## 2   Havana

The discourse about Havana, like Cuba in general, is often emotionally and intellectually charged, depending on the 'lenses' one uses to interpret the city. Marxist students of the city, for instance, claim that public spaces had become 'decommodified' under socialist rule; that is, Havana was isolated from market forces that produce non-essential consumer goods and prestigious private shops, restaurants, and clubs. That characterization was accurate from the early 1960s until the 1990s. In response to the collapse of the former USSR, however, the Cuban government legalized the circulation of US currency and limited private markets. This new direction of economic development is called the 'Special Period in a Time of Peace' (*El Período Especial en el Tiempo de Paz*) (or simply, 'Special Period') and is changing the face of Havana significantly. Despite the reintroduction of a market economy, many architects and urbanists consider Havana to be a city of eclectic and decentralized neighborhoods that are joined by roads, public services, and urban culture. Regardless of the perspective, San Cristóbal de la Habana is undeniably a modern, world-class city whose cultural landscapes, arts, theaters, universities, public institutions, and Afro-European roots make it special when compared to the world cities of Europe, Latin America, and North America. The urban historical geography of Havana invites the reader to experience the delights and intrigues of its spaces, buildings, natural settings, and the transformation of its social content.

The aims of this chapter are modest considering the arduous task implied by its title: to identify the forces behind nearly 500 years of urbanization in Havana. Accordingly, the approach is broad, selecting key points in history and urban geography to anchor the chapters that follow. It begins with a survey of pre-Columbian Cuba and the level of material culture that Columbus may have seen in 1492. The settlement of Havana over the next three centuries follows, calling attention to significant historic events that tied Havana to the Spanish colonial economy.

A central argument is that Havana served first as a transfer point for wealth coming from other Spanish colonies, and subsequently from the rest of the island. Generating little wealth of its own, it was not until the sugar boom of the nineteenth century that the island developed a formidable resource base. Although Havana has always had a large service economy (today it has just one sugar mill), it benefited from the wealth generated by sugar barons throughout the island (Marrero 1975a, b).

In the latter half of the chapter, attention turns to the spread of the city. Havana's fortifications included a vast network of forts, castles, and watchtowers (Segre 1968a). Ultimately, a wall was erected between the seventeenth and eighteenth centuries, only to be torn down in the middle of the nineteenth century. The rise and fall of the walled city marked both

Havana's urban growth and its political challenge to Spain about serving as its American warehouse. In the first half of the nineteenth century Havana no longer grew at a leisurely pace that could be contained in the colonial core. The city spilled over the crumbling walls and pushed west and south. A service economy tied to agriculture, not industry, filled Havana's coffers and enabled an ambitious governor, Miguel Tacón, to lay out a template of public buildings and a street plan that ushered Havana's urbanization into the present century. Lastly, this chapter offers a glimpse of twentieth century Havana, enticing readers to pursue those themes more fully in the chapters ahead. In brief, the urban historical geography of Havana identifies the nuanced transitions of a city originally designed and ruled by the Spanish, modernized by the United States and, ultimately, governed by a centrally-planned Cuban government. We begin with the physical backdrop and the dawn of European conquest.

**The physical context**

Cuba is the largest island (114 524 square kilometers) in the Antilles archipelago. It is three times as large as Hispaniola, nine times larger than Jamaica, and 12 times the size of Puerto Rico. Straddled to the north by the Florida Straits, to the south by the Caribbean Sea, to the east by the Windward Passage, and to the west by the Gulf of Mexico, Cuba's main island is complemented by more than 1600 small islands and keys. Cuba spans 1250 kilometers from east to west at its maximum and has median width of roughly 100 kilometers.

More than half of the island's topography is plain while the balance is in mountains and hills. Cuba, like the entire 2400 kilometers stretch of the Greater Antilles, is linked tectonically with the eastern flank of the Yucatan peninsula. Mountain-building processes from the Cretaceous period were associated with the plate tectonic movements of North and South America and produced Cuba's mountains. Eastern Cuba is both the most rugged area of Cuba and the oldest core region in the Caribbean. Its deeply folded and dissected Sierra Maestra mountain range is in the southeastern corner of the island. West of the city of Santiago de Cuba is the highest elevation of the island, Turquino Peak, at 2005 meters (6570 feet). Other orographic features include the Escambray Mountains in south-central Cuba, near the colonial city of Trinidad. Another range, the Sierra de los Organos in the western part of the island, can be seen from western points of the Province of Havana and on a clear day from Havana City when arriving by airplane.

Western Cuba and the areas surrounding Havana are composed mostly of Cretaceous limestone that has produced a karstic topography of caves, caverns, underground streams, and resistant surface remnants known technically as monondocks (called *mogotes*, locally). Despite more than 200 bays and 5746 kilometers of coastline along the main island, the bays of Havana, Matanzas, Mariel, Nuevitas, Santiago de Cuba, Cienfuegos, and Nipe are the only major deep-water ports. The preponderance of the island's limestone base makes for acidic soils which, coupled with heavy precipitation, can lead to the leaching of valuable soil minerals and nutrients. In addition, Cuba is well endowed with extensive nickel reserves, discovered in the twentieth century. Nickel ranks as Cuba's fourth or fifth export, depending on prevailing market conditions. Copper, iron, cobalt and manganese are also found, but in smaller quantities. Although in 1993 a record of 1.1 million tons of oil were extracted in Cuba – some 22 times larger than production levels of the late 1950s – the island only satisfies about 10% of its consumption demands (Portela 1994, p. 6; Rivero 1994, p. 7).

Located just within the northern limit of the Tropic of Cancer, Cuba exhibits a classical wet–dry tropical climate. Average monthly temperatures always exceed 18°C (72°F) with heavy summer rains produced from convection. The maximum temperature ever registered officially in Havana by the National Observatory reached 35.8°C in May 1923, although there was an unofficial reading of 42°C in Sagua de Tánamo in 1927. The minimum temperatures for Havana hover about 10°C in the winter months, although Rancho Boyeros in southern Havana registered 0°C (32°F) during a cold wave in 1939. A long dry period ensues in the winter months and a short dry season prevails in the summer. These pronounced wet–dry periods produce a savanna landscape with distinct drought-resistant (xerophylic) species (Marrero 1981a, pp. 70–73).

Havana receives an average of 45 inches of rain per year, with pronounced convectional downpours in the warmer months (May–October) and dry weather between December and April. Havana's location (23°N, 82°W) on the Straits of Florida exposes it to the prevailing northeast trade winds. Havana's average monthly temperatures range from 27°C (81°F) in July and August to 22°C (71°F) in January and February, with an annual average of 24.5°C (76°F) (Wernstedt 1961, p. 33).

The coastal plain surrounding Havana yields to rolling hills as one moves inland. Enhanced with large water supplies, the city of Havana is drained by two principal rivers: the Almendares, between Vedado and Miramar municipalities on the north shore, and the Luyanó, draining much of the southeastern corner of the city before emptying into Havana Bay. Numerous freshwater reservoirs (*embalses*) provide the city with most of its water. New wells are sought in a large aquifer, El Gato, lying

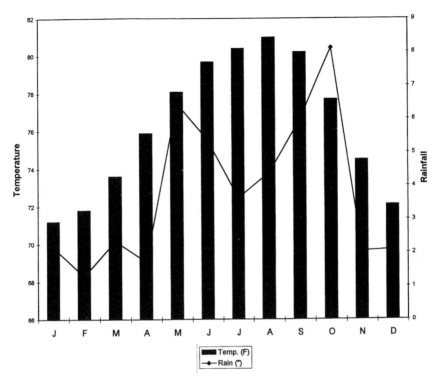

**Figure 1.1** Havana rainfall and temperature

outside the city proper. Other minor water resources only provide Havana and the rest of the island with limited hydroelectric energy.

Because it is a long and narrow island with rapid precipitation runoff, Cuba's water resources are threatened by saltwater intrusion. Of the hundreds of catchments for fresh water, only about 15% are larger than 200 square kilometers (77 square miles). As a result, one of Cuba's gravest environmental concerns is the provision of fresh water for cities, industry and farms. Non-cyclical periods of drought brought devastating consequences to cities and agriculture in 1964–1966, 1970–1971, 1973–1976, and 1986–87. Cuba's extensive underground water resources, however, compensate for rapid runoff and supplied 6.5 billion cubic meters (1.7 trillion gallons) in 1994. Underground water lies in basins and requires pumps and costly fossil fuels so it can be distributed. Overuse of these underground sources aggravates salinization conditions.

The island's total water resources appear to be underutilized because of the high relative energy costs in pumping the water. Perhaps as much as half of Cuba's water may be polluted though the industrial downturn in the 1990s may have limited sources of pollution. The gravest environmental threat to their drinking water in Havana comes from the saltwater intrusion in the South Havana Aquifer, the city's main source of drinking water. Estimates are that the water table has fallen about 30% and seawater has invaded some well fields (*CubaNews*, April 1995, Cuba's water resources, p. 9). As if these problems were not sufficiently daunting, an estimated 55% of the water pumped through Havana is lost through leakage (Pérez and Fernández 1996). We discuss water problems more fully in Chapters 5 and 10.

Geologists describe the northernmost shores of Cuba, including those around Havana, a region that is in a 'process of emergence.' This means that between Mariel harbor 30 kilometers west of Havana, to Matanzas harbor, some 100 kilometers east, a gradual rising of the landmass has contributed to small, sandy beaches. Differential erosion produced from the rise and fall of water levels during the last ice ages has carved out a moderately scarped coastline, characterized by marine erosion that leaves rock outcrops and fine-sand beaches. For centuries, these rocks have provided the city's builders with readily available limestone that could be crushed and used for making *mampostería*, a building technique using rubble. Quarries operated at many of these sites until as recently as the early twentieth century (Figure 1.2), and the remnants of one are still visible at the base of the Hotel Nacional and the Malecón (Havana's oceanfront promenade) in the Vedado section of Havana. A series of well defined marine terraces from which these outcrops derive is evident along this stretch of shoreline (Marrero 1981b, p. 59).

The marine terraces produced by the sea's recent rising and falling has shaped the layout and settlement of Havana. A series of capes and escarpments – still quite visible despite landscape modification – characterizes the main settlements, neighborhoods and roads of contemporary Havana (Tingle and Montenegro 1923). Old Havana (Habana Vieja) sets on a cape on the western side of the bay. The cape is a structural remnant of a marine terrace. In Vedado, one can easily walk inland (e.g., south) from the ocean front along the Malecón – preferably along Paseo Avenue or Presidentes Avenue because of their gardened pedestrian medians – and encounter a series of these gentle platforms. Línea Street, about five blocks from the Malecón, marks the first separation between the coastal level and the first prominent escarpment. Seven blocks farther along, one arrives at Calle 23 which marks the beginning of yet another marine terrace (Figure 1.3). In fact, the entire city's irregular grid twists and turns to accommodate the marine terraces, resistant outcrops, and low-lying areas prone to flooding and occupied by swamps. Habana Vieja's oval shape stems from the curvature of the bay and the construction of roads running parallel to

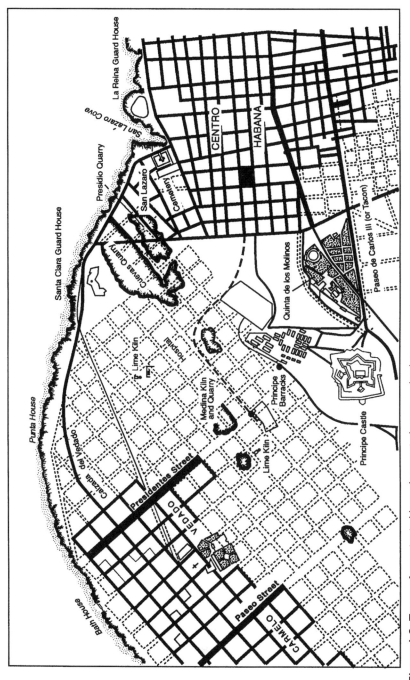

**Figure 1.2** Traces of quarries in Havana's twentieth century landscape

the shore. While the 'grid' of the old city resembles the perpendicular principles of modern street design, the curvilinear imprint imposed by the waterfront has endured nearly 500 years of urbanization (Figure 1.4). The original roads of the city – called *calzadas* – still exist and guided nineteenth century expansion. The *calzadas* of Infanta, Monte, Luyanó, Cerro and Diez de Octubre follow either the hilltop ridges or lowlands of the marine terraces. It is precisely this irregular grid depicted in Figure 1.4 which Carpentier (1966, p. 51) attributes 'the primordial, tropical necessity of playing hide-and-seek with the sun, laughing at its surfaces, exposing shaded areas, and fleeing from the torrid announcements of twilight, with an ingenious proliferation of awnings draped across the streets'. Such an irregular design of early Havana represented a victory of medieval ideas held by the colonizers over the abstract theories of the Renaissance that had not yet made their way to the city planning guidelines of the Laws of the Indies.

**The pre-Columbian setting**

On October 28, 1492, Christopher Columbus allegedly remarked when he saw Cuba that it was 'the loveliest land ever beheld by human eyes.' Like most of the indigenous peoples in the Caribbean, the early inhabitants of Cuba had not developed the high material culture of large cities or the monumental structures found in Meso-America or in the Andes. Columbus found three culturally distinct indigenous groups in Cuba: Guanajatabeyes, Siboneyes, and Taínos. The Guanajatabeyes represented about 10% of Cuba's indigenous population, located in the western part of the island – ethnically related to natives on Hispaniola – and were perhaps the oldest population (ICGC 1979, p. 9). They were cave dwellers, hunters and gatherers, and exhibited the lowest level of material culture. Sustenance derived from turtles, fish and plants found in the natural landscape. Of a notably higher material level, the Siboneyes were scattered about all parts of the island. However, they were not agriculturists and lived in caves until the arrival of the Taínos who forced them into servitude. Originally nomadic when they arrived in Cuba, the Siboneyes later established small villages along the coast and rivers (Portuondo 1965).

   The indigenous population clustered mainly in the eastern central portions of the island and resided in straw and palm-thatched dwellings called *bohíos*, a term still used today to describe small huts and shacks in the Cuban countryside. Taíno settlements were structured around a central plaza and they preferred higher elevations with fertile soils and potable water near by. Although they were not numerous, the Taíno modi-

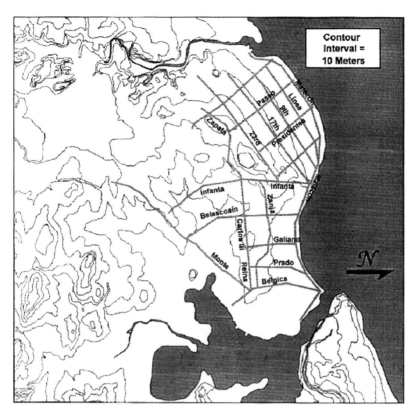

Contour
Interval =
10 Meters

**Figure 1.3** Imprint of marine terraces on selected main streets in Vedado

fied the pre-Columbian landscape more than other indigenous groups, and left the Spaniards with numerous place, flora and fauna names that form part of contemporary Cuban culture (West and Augelli 1966; Rallo and Segre 1978; Marrero 1981a, pp. 143–144).

Details on the pattern and process of Amerindian settlement and culture defy easy reconstruction. None of the indigenous cultures had a written language and the European conquest decimated most of them quickly. Archeological review of middens, village sites, burial caves, as well as scattered writings from early settlers and explorers, provide most of what we know about these people. Alexander von Humboldt, the German naturalist who visited Cuba in the early nineteenth century, placed the native population of Cuba at one million. West and Augelli (1966), however, argue that such a figure must have included Hispaniola, Cuba and Puerto Rico. Rallo and Segre (1978) reviewed contemporary anthropological and historical records in Cuba and give a much smaller figure. Given the swamps, mountains, and dense vegetation in certain parts, it is unlikely

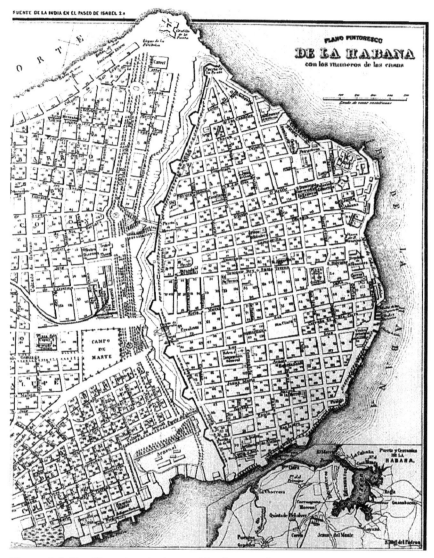

**Figure 1.4** Curvilinear imprint imposed by the waterfront on street pattern of Habana Vieja, c. 1849

that more than 300 000 persons occupied the island in 1492, and the minimum was probably 50 000. This range is corroborated by the *Atlas Demográfico de Cuba*, which estimated about 112 000 aborigines on the island at the time of conquest (ICGC 1979, p. 9).

The native population clustered in villages, called *bateyes*, that were concentrated on the coast, near the mouths of rivers, and in the hills rising above swampy areas. The style of native architecture was determined by social, climatic and technological factors. Huts were erected on stilts using palm-tree leafs as building materials. Structures not on wooden stilts had earthen floors. The *batey* was not laid out on a strict grid system as were most Incan, Mayan and Aztec settlements in Meso-America and Andean-America. Although the use of the palm leaf in building construction protected them from intense tropical heat and torrential downpours, early settlers soon learned that it transferred many parasitic diseases (Rallo and Segre 1978, p. 10).

## The settlement of Havana: 'a lemon not worth squeezing'

Between 1500 and 1515 an expedition of about 300 men, headed by explorer and Governor, Diego Velázquez de Cuéllar, searched the island for mineral wealth. They founded seven original settlements – military outposts actually – called *villas*: Baracoa (1512), Bayamo (1513), Trinidad (1514), Sancti Spíritus (1514), San Cristóbal de la Habana (1514 on the southern coast, and then in 1519 on the northern coast), Santiago de Cuba (1515), and Puerto Príncipe (1514 but later moved inland to Camagüey in 1528). The *villas* would determine in good measure the subsequent urbanization of the island by controlling trade and production in their hinterlands (Figure 1.5). Each received a loosely defined area of jurisdiction. At the time of settlement, however, their relative locations were less than desirable in many respects. In some cases, the *villas* were settled because there was a small indigenous settlement that could be evangelized. In others, the existence of a navigable river or a deep harbor proved attractive, as did proximity to fertile soils, healthy sites (i.e., removed from swamps) and potable water. Only two of the original settlements –

**Figure 1.5** Settlement of *villas* in Cuba (1512–1528)

Camagüey and Santiago – were founded on good harbors, and the former's location on the Nuevitas Bay later shifted inland. Baracoa and Trinidad were situated on small bays that were actually next to much deeper and navigable harbors that were overlooked at the time. The historical resiliency of these original settlements is noteworthy because they have survived into the present (Díaz Briquets 1994, p. 173). In 1509, Sebastián de Ocampo docked in what is now Havana Bay to repair his small fleet while circumnavigating the island. His expedition dispelled Columbus' contention that Cuba was a continent. However, he did not settle there and two false starts would mark the path to Havana's present site.

Havana was first located on the Broa Inlet, just off the Gulf of Batabanó, on the southern coast of Cuba, on the Caribbean Sea. The fifth of the seven *villas*, the settlement on the Broa Inlet was directed by Pánfilo de Narváez, who was acting on the orders of Governor Velázquez. It is believed that this was Hernán Cortés' last stop in the Caribbean on his first voyage to conquer Mexico. However, the unhealthy environs and the shallow port forced the settlers to relocate. In 1519 the *villa* of Havana moved to the northeastern shore of the island, almost due north, on the Florida Straits. Although the precise location of this original settlement is unknown, it is believed to have been founded along the shore of a small river that the Indians called *Casiguagua* (later renamed Almendares by the Spanish). Reasonable estimates place the settlement near the mouth of the Almendares, along the Ensenada de la Chorrera. The location was considered ideal because of the fresh water of the Almendares, but that advantage was outweighed by its vulnerability to rising seas and the lack of a sheltered harbor. Shortly thereafter, in late 1519, the *villa* was again relocated, this time to the western side of a large, deep-water bay, a few kilometers east of the Almendares site. There, on a flat cape adjacent to a large deep-water bay, Havana Bay (Bahía de la Habana), is where the city of Havana has been for nearly 500 years. Legend has it that the location of the young *villa* was sanctioned when both a mass and a town-council meeting were held under a large *ceiba* tree (kapok or silk-cotton, g. *Bombax*). A commemorative neoclassical monument, *El Templete*, was built in 1828 to commemorate the city's founding and still stands on the southern side of the Plaza de Armas in Habana Vieja.

Obscurity surrounds the origin of the city's name. Some claim that it is a derivative of the Spanish word *sabana* (savanna or prairie). Others speculate that it comes from a defunct northern European port, Havana, a name possibly derived from the Anglo-Saxon word 'haven'. The refuge that the bay affords residents from tropical cyclones lends credence to that interpretation. Still others contend that western Cuba was ruled by an indigenous *cacique*, Habaguanex. The Spanish spelling muddles the term further because the letters *v* and *b* are pronounced similarly. Regardless of its etymology, all that is certain is that the city's patron saint, Christopher, remains the guardian of travelers.

The discovery of the Bahamian Channel made San Cristóbal de la Habana a key transshipment point in the commerce between the Old and New Worlds. This new and important city refurbished Spanish ships carrying gold and silver originating from Mexico and South America. Ships sailing in either direction naturally called there for supplies or sought refuge if followed by enemies. Although Havana became a mere temporary holding place for the Spanish fleet, it nonetheless brought the city both geomilitary significance and modest wealth. The Spanish-Caribbean route staked out by the Spanish fleet was called the *Carrera de Indias* (Indies Route) which was actually a set of maritime routes that united Spain with her colonies (Marrero 1976; Segre 1990).

In 1561 Spain issued a royal decree that sanctioned and regulated with great precision the movement of its fleet. Two fleets carrying goods from Seville (via the port of Cádiz, Spain) would leave each year. The first would set sail for Mexico in April and would include ships stopping in the Greater and Lesser Antilles as well as Honduras. A second convoy would depart Seville in August, bound for Nombre de Dios (Panama), Cartagena and Santa Marta (Colombia), and other ports on the mainland (*terra firme*). Havana was clearly privileged by its relative location in this hemispheric trade pattern, earning the name *Llave del Nuevo Mundo y Antemural de las Indias Occidentales* (Key to the New World and Bulwark of the West Indies). Transshipments from Cartagena and Portobelo, Trujillo and Puerto Cortés, and Veracruz carried wealth extracted from South America, Central America and Mexico, respectively (Marrero 1956).

Havana's role in assisting Spain to fight the forces of nature and pirates became essential to the motherland's economic and political might. Jacques de Sores attacked and burned Havana in 1555. Spain authorized Havana to function as the sole port to engage in commerce in 1558. It was then decided to build the La Fuerza fortress (1558–1577), the first military stone building in Latin America. The Italian engineer, Juan Bautista Antonelli, designed the coastal defensive system. Two main fortresses still flank the entrance of the bay: Tres Reyes del Morro (1589–1610) and San Salvador de la Punta (1589–1600). The network also includes a series of small sentry towers between La Chorrera and Bacuranao (Weiss 1972). The Cuban port could both harbor and supply ships with essential provisions during their 1700-league and at least 75-day journey between Seville and Nombre de Dios (Panama) and Veracruz (Mexico). The fleet took advantage of the shifting Trade Winds between winter and summer.

No major port was as close to the Gulf Stream – the major force carrying ships eastward – than Havana. The fleet would try to leave the New World between April and June to avoid hurricanes, and they would often dock in Havana to wait out bad weather (Sánchez-Albornoz 1974, pp. 82–83). One description of the armed convoy that would accompany Spain's merchant ships comes from Bartolomé Carreño who, in 1552, set out for the Antilles from Seville. He documented four large boats with a 250–300 ton capacity, and two smaller ships with an 80–100 ton capacity, that could carry 360 soldiers. The convoy would escort the merchants to the Caribbean, at which point the ships would disperse to their various destinations. In the meantime, the bulk of the convoy would head off to Havana were it would dock and use the colonial port as general head-quarters for combing adjacent waters in pursuit of pirates and corsairs (Marrero 1956, p. 123).

In the early sixteenth century, gold deposits in Cuba had proved more bountiful than in Puerto Rico (Wright 1927; Hardoy and Aronovich 1969). Local Indians in Cuba were forced to pan for gold and work the few oper-ating mines. Spanish treatment was brutal and the constant insurrections by the Amerindians, coupled with infectious diseases, led to the rapid demise of the natives. Panned gold came out of the Arimao, Escambray, and Holguín rivers. Important gold mines were La Mina, close to Havana, and one near Bayamo. Following the general wave of Spanish settlement from east to west throughout the Greater Antilles, the search for gold and settlement in Cuba also moved from the eastern to western ends of the island. Havana remained subordinate to Santiago de Cuba as a political and economic power until the locus of Spanish power shifted from the Caribbean to Mexico. In doing so, Havana's importance grew as a strate-gic gateway between the continent and the Caribbean settlements. The initial number of Spaniards in Cuba probably hovered at about 300, but then reached a maximum of 3000 between 1518 and 1520; these were the early years of gold exploration and settlement in the hinterlands sur-rounding the seven *villas*. However, the population 'dropped sharply as the colonists followed Cortés and others to the greener pastures of the mainland' (West and Augelli 1966, p. 66).

When Cortés left Cuba en route to Mexico in 1519, he took the largest collection of gold ever mined and processed in a single year in Cuba: $104 000 pesos (Marrero 1956, p. 232). By 1547, gold production had vir-tually ceased in Cuba (Wright 1916a). The island of Hispaniola supplied Spain with most of its Caribbean sugar. In response to its poor terms of trade, colonists in Cuba sought out alternative markets, including clan-destine trade with French, Dutch, and English ships. In the mid-sixteenth century, when authorities in the Canary Islands received permission from the Royal Crown to dispatch ships directly to the Indies, maritime commerce between Havana and the Canaries increased dramatically. Records show Canarian wine was in great demand in Havana because of the scores of ships that would dock there. Still, the influence of the Sevillan monopoly over Cuba's sixteenth century island was great, and the island's economy was, in the words of Wright (1916b), 'a lemon not worth squeezing'.

If eastern Cuba possessed the economic and political clout of the island during the first half of the sixteenth century, changing political and economic winds moved westward during the balance of the century. Santo Domingo would lose some of its importance as Mexico and other economies on *terra firma* gained in importance. Havana benefited from this shift in economic power, and its ample bay protected merchant ships from menacing northerly winds (*los nortes*). Havana dominated maritime routes among the Gulf of Mexico, the Straits of Florida, and the Yucatán Channel, and was akin to Tangier which guarded the Straits of Gibraltar in the Mediterranean Sea. Although the concentration of gold-laden ships passing by the northern shores of Cuba would create a breeding ground for corsairs and pirates, Havana would become the 'Key to the Indies' and a collection point for ships carrying American treasures to Spain. Havana's significance in Antillean maritime trade led the Audience of Santo Domingo in 1553 to transfer Cuba's governor's office from Santiago de Cuba in the east, to Havana in the west (Marrero 1956, pp. 118–121).

The swift elimination of the indigenous people of Cuba created a demand for slave labor. Slavery in Cuba dates from 1513 when Amador de Lares obtained permission to bring four Africans from neighboring Hispaniola. Within a decade some 300 'prisoners' began working the Jagua gold mine in Cuba (Williams 1994, p. 22). Carabalí and Bantu peoples along the Congo River comprised the largest share of Africans in Cuba, but they would not occupy a strategic role in the island's economy until the eighteenth century. Even though sugar cane was introduced in Cuba in 1523, it lacked export value and was not pursued as a major crop for another two centuries (Rallo and Segre 1978, p. 17).

In contrast to the more casual style of the French, English and Dutch who came to the Caribbean a century later, the *conquistadores* evolved a unique system of land usage, land tenure and colonial administration (Peyrerea 1929). The first Audiencia (colonial administrative region) in the New World was that of Santo Domingo, founded in 1511. It consisted of a rosary of islands: Puerto Rico, Hispaniola, Jamaica (until 1655), Cumaná and Margarita. By 1574 the dispersed territory claimed only 32 settlements, comprising about 1654 residents or *vecinos* (García-Saiz 1990, p. 261). Although Havana remained the principal settlement of Cuba in

**Table 1.1** Population of selected major villages in the Antillian section of the Audiencia of Santo Domingo, 1574

| Hispaniola | | Puerto Rico | |
|---|---|---|---|
| Santo Domingo | 500 | San Juan | 200 |
| Santiago | 70 | San German | 50 |
| Concepción de la Vega | 60 | Arecibo | 30 |
| Monte Christi | 30 | | |
| Puerto Príncipe | 46 | Cuba | |
| El Cotuy | 17 | La Habana | 60 |
| Azua | 15 | Santiago | 3 |
| Puerto Plata | 15 | Baracoa | 80 |
| | | Bayamo | 80 |
| Jamaica | | Higüey | 19 |
| Puerto Príncipe | 46 | | |
| Vega | 11 | | |

*Data source*: García-Saiz (1990, p. 261). Note: Early census figures counted only adult Spanish males, and discounted women, children, Indians and Negro slaves as well as transient merchants and sailors.

1574, it was an intermediate-sized settlement compared with the rest of the Spanish Antilles (Table 1.1).

Havana developed a few essential public works to sustain its development. Its key position in supplying the crews and passengers of the Spanish fleet introduced new pressures to satisfy the fleet demand for fresh water. Originally, the small *villa* met its fresh water needs with a small cistern replenished by rain water. In 1550, the Havana *cabildo* (town council) issued a proclamation to increase Havana's water supply by bringing water from the Almendares River, 9 kilometers to the west. Such a grand public works project dominated civic and political discourse in Havana throughout most of the late sixteenth century.

The main problem, though, was how to finance the project. Original estimates placed the cost of the project at 5000 pesos, then later at 8000 ducats (gold coins). In a novel move, the Havana *cabildo* requested special permission to establish a local tax (*echar sisa*). In addition, Philip II authorized an 'anchoring fee' in Havana Bay to finance the construction of a canal (*zanja*, and called the Zanja Real or 'Royal Canal') connecting the small *villa* to the Almendares River (Zanja Street running through Vedado and Centro Habana retraces much of the original course). This ambitious project marked the first major water supply built by Europeans in the New World. By 1562, however, records showed that many ships were reluctant to dock at Havana's port because of the high fee and, instead, opted for the port of Matanzas, 100 kilometers east. Havana lost out not only on the anchoring fee, but on the economic multipliers of supplying the ships.

In late 1562, the fee was lifted and a novel municipal fund-raising venture ensued on two fronts. One was a sliding tax scale based on personal income; the wealthiest *habaneros* paid 50 ducats while the most destitute paid a single ducat. A second way was a 'sin tax' levied against three basic products: wine, soap, and meat. In truth, two-thirds of the 'canal tax' (*sisa de la zanja*) derived from the sale of wine. The project opened in 1592 and by 1600 its construction costs had been fully recovered (Marrero 1956, p. 152).

The cumulative effect of completing this major aqueduct in 1592, coupled with Havana's transshipment functions, convinced Spanish King Philip II to grant Havana its official title as a 'city.' Havana had already completed many of the requirements of the standard Spanish grid layout settlement as carefully documented by the planning guide, the Law of the Indies. As a 'legitimate' city in the Spanish Empire, Havana thus qualified to adopt a coat of arms as part of its new status. Characteristically, the coat of arms reflected the significance of the city's absolute and relative location. Three castles in the official city seal denote the city's great fortresses and garrisons – Fuerza, Morro and Punta – under which lies a golden key. The key represented Havana's ability to 'unlock' lands and seas in the Caribbean, continental America and the Old World. Colonial rulers in Mexico welcomed Havana's status as a royal city. Veracruz was the only decent Gulf port available to the Spanish in Mexico, but its harbor entrance was marred by a series of islets described by mariners as 'a pocket full of holes.' Thus Mexico welcomed Spanish investment in Havana which, to some extent, served as a port for all of Mexico. In fact, so important was Havana to Mexico's prosperity that it provided Cuba with a permanent and open credit line which was especially useful when the island lacked minted coins or required provisions and *matériel* for naval and military defense (Santovenia 1943).

Havana would become the most heavily fortified city in the Americas even though for most of its first century it was just a small frontier port town. Its unlit streets were perilous at night. Harlotry flourished and with that came syphilis. It ranked as one of the most nefarious towns in the West Indies despite its impressive forts and veneer of military discipline. Along with youth came styles of design and governance adopted from other kingdoms. Spain was a new political entity when Havana was established. Only three decades earlier had it managed to shake off the yoke of Moorish domination which had ebbed and flowed across the Iberian peninsula since the eighth century. Moorish influence as well as Italian, Greek and Roman styles influenced the early Spanish towns throughout the Americas, and Havana was no exception. However, it would take centuries before a distinctively Cuban or Havanan architecture and urban design could be identified, and then those origins would be subject to great intellectual debate (Weiss 1966; Amaral 1994).

A systematic effort to circumscribe the city with a protective wall did not begin until 1674. In 1767, the entire wall was finally completed. As discussed in Chapter 9, the walls were torn down in the 1860s, and today only scattered remains of the walls can be seen along the periphery of Habana Vieja. The largest stretch is the Puerta de la Tenaza (built between 1674 and 1740), on Egido Street, one block south of the train station (Estación Central de Ferrocarriles), in the southern part of the old town. The contemporary traveler cannot avoid seeing the vestiges of Havana's fortresses situated on prominent hills and points in the center of the city. Except for Cartagena de las Indias, Colombia – with its colonial wall and well-preserved buildings still intact – perhaps no other city in the New World holds so many relics of a past military landscape.

The second paradox is that Havana kept few of those riches it fought so hard to protect; wealth merely passed through its ports. Only a small elite manifested any semblance of affluence. The relative location of Havana gave salience to its role as colonial entrepôt and would continue to exert powerful influences for centuries to come.

To compensate for its role as an intermediary agent in foreign trade, colonial Havana turned to the land for its survival. Spanish authorities established a land-distribution system (*mercedazgo*) to their loyal servants. The land (*mercedes*) was defined by first establishing a central point which was used to delineate a radius. This became the loosely defined circular border for each *merced*. Over time and with the subdivision of property, these circular land plots would overlap and leave a distinct imprint in the Cuban landscape. The Havana *cabildo* granted 148 mercedes between 1552 and 1601 in order to satisfy the port's demand for meat and produce. Havana was, moreover, the only Cuban settlement that registered the granting of *mercedes* during this period, thus underscoring its importance in the local and inter-hemispheric contexts (Pérez de la Riva 1946).

## Havana in the colonial hierarchy

The geopolitical organization of the Audiencia de Santo Domingo was subdivided into archdioceses. The Archdiocese of Santo Domingo (1511) covered the entire island of Hispaniola (1511), San Juan (1511) encompassed the island of Puerto Rico. Cuba's Archdiocese (1522) was divided between Santiago in the east and Havana in the west, and Venezuela (1531) was split between Coro on the coast and Caracas in the mountains. The Atlantic coast of Florida held scattered fortresses with the exception of the formidable castle in Saint Augustine. The dominant classes in the archdioceses imported wine, oil, wheat, tools, arms, furniture, and utensils from Spain. Only the poor Spanish settlers used such indigenous tools as wooden chairs, clay and wooden utensils, hammocks, and poorly spun cotton clothing. Horses were used and became a valued commodity for expeditions and armed warfare, even though the settlement was evidently less engaged in warfare than elsewhere in Spanish America.

The seven original *villas* in Cuba reflected the authority of the Church, the army and the *cabildos*. Although each of the *villas* had a main plaza, the original town design was irregular and sporadic, obeying more the whims of the topography or the original settlers than any guidelines that would come with the Law of the Indies, or planning and zoning ordinances promulgated by the Spanish government during the sixteenth century. Coastal *villas* such as Havana built their plazas on the waterfront, while the land-based *villas* situated the plazas in the middle of the buildings and houses (Duverger 1993b). The only type of residential segregation was between the white Spanish population, settled around the *plaza*, and the indigenous population, who settled behind the Spanish.

The Audiencia de Santo Domingo suffered endemic problems between 1573 and 1750. It was beleaguered by pirate raids and hurricanes. As gateway to Spanish America, the Audiencia was less interested in preventing the Lesser Antilles from being occupied by non-Spanish powers and more concerned with refurbishing ships coming and going from Seville and *terra firme* in Mexico and South America. Thus by the late sixteenth century the Caribbean Sea was no longer a 'Spanish Lake' but a commercial body of water traversed by African slaves, French, English, Dutch, and Danes engaged in business transactions, most of them illicit and 'dirty' in nature (García-Saiz 1990, p. 262).

Santo Domingo was by most accounts the 'first' city of Spanish America, at least until the latter part of the sixteenth century. Havana lacked the institutional structures and ceremonial buildings that colonial towns of importance boasted. Santo Domingo, however, showcased a cathedral, a hospital, and convents and churches run by the most important religious orders.

By the 1600s, primacy in the Spanish Antilles had shifted to Cuba. Its main urban center, Havana, became a commercial and defensive enclave as well as a crucial node in trade between the 'metropolis' (Spain and the rest of western Europe) and territories in the New World. Sir Francis Drake's sacking of Santo Domingo left in its wake a path of ruin and burnt buildings. Palm (1955) contends that Drake's looting of Santo Domingo in 1586 sealed its fatal demise and cast it merely as a provincial city, despite its status as capital of the Audiencia and its university. Drake later postured offensively at the entrance to Havana Bay, but decided not to attack. Instead, he sailed to St. Augustine, Florida, which he destroyed, and then on to Roanoke Island, North Carolina to rescue survivors of Sir Walter

Raleigh's ill-fated colony (Roberts 1953). Havana's rising prominence was not reflected by the city's stately buildings until the eighteenth century. A Jesuit church located on the old Plaza de la Ciénaga (now Plaza de la Catedral) was built in 1749. The original cathedral, Parroquial Mayor, situated on the Plaza de Armas, was demolished.

While San Cristóbal de la Habana prospered from Santo Domingo's loss of political and economic power, it was never characterized in the sixteenth to eighteenth centuries as a city of great splendor. (Havana would have to wait until sugar profits in the late eighteenth century found their way into the city's *calzadas*, parks, promenades, and the new elite neighborhood of Cerro. Only then would wealth situate Havana among the truly beautiful cities of the Americas. Indeed, by the second decade of the twentieth century, Havana's attractiveness was perhaps only exceeded by Buenos Aires in Latin America.) British threats on Havana were a decisive factor in the city's development, and they placed great demands on the island's mines. Artillery for Morro and Punta castles were forged from Cuban copper mines, and most of it was supplied from the Bacuranao copper mine near Havana. After 2000 *quintales* (92 000 kg) of copper was forged from the Bacuranao mines, newer deposits were sought out in eastern Cuba, near Santiago de Cuba.

Emphasis on Havana's economic and geopolitical significance did little to stimulate the arts in the sixteenth century. It was not the official capital of the island (Santiago was) and thus lacked the few privileges that came with such status. During most of the first quarter of the sixteenth century governors would divide their time between Santiago and Havana, 'while the Crown in its dilatory way refused to admit that the new town was becoming the real center of Cuba's activities. On the broader stage of the Antilles, [Havana] played the role in the west that Santo Domingo still played in the middle' (Roberts 1953, p. 11).

Tropical heat and humidity were unkind to the relatively small collections of oil paintings and outdoor sculptures in colonial Cuba. Insects, particularly termites, took their toll on picture frames, wooden crucifixes, wooden carvings, and other colonial artwork. Even though many fine woods native to the island withstood termite damage, those woods are now rare. Contemporary Havana homes have imported furniture made from non-termite resistant wood that show the consequences of using exotic woods.

Wood products contributed much to Havana's early colonial economy before the demand for sugar led to quick deforestation in the early nineteenth century. The shipbuilding trades figured among some of the first industrial activity in Cuba, and Havana was an ideal location because of its maritime traffic. In the latter half of the sixteenth century, shipbuilders in Havana sought out *ácana, guayacán*, oaks and mahogany for their strength and water resistance. So strategic was Havana's shipbuilding industry to the Spanish Crown that a Royal Decree was enacted in 1620 that authorized the free cutting of all trees in Cuba whose wood would be destined for shipbuilding. The governors of the island (Menéndez de Avilés 1568–1573; Texeda 1589–1594; Valdés 1602–1608) took pride in both the size and quality of galleons built at the Machina shipyard located at Alameda de Paula Street along the waterfront of Havana Bay (Marrero 1956, p. 308). The Spaniards also used these hardwoods for carving ornamental keepsakes, termite-resistant building construction, and furniture making. Even today one can appreciate the likeness between the colonial ceilings of Santa Clara Convent in Habana Vieja and in the ceilings of other historic structures, and an inverted ship hull. Unfortunately, as Havana's role increased as a major refurbishing port for Spanish fleets, so too mounted pressures on the island's resources. Deforestation around Havana resulted from farming, lumbering, ranching and urban sprawl (Marrero 1981a, p. 165).

Havana, like most colonial Spanish cities, has a semi-regular grid related to the subsequent Law of the Indies. Sartor (1993) describes the irregular layout as 'organic' and closer to the medieval towns of Europe than the formal grid plan found in most Latin American cities. Placing La Fuerza fortress on the Plaza de Armas disrupted the usual pattern of locating important buildings of the church (*iglesia*) and government (*cabildo*, or town council) on a single town square. As we will discuss in the following chapter, this dispersed city functions to other town squares, and characterized Havana's polycentric nature. Plaza de Armas held the major military institutions, Plaza de la Catedral was home to the church, and the commercial activities concentrated around Plaza Vieja, while Plaza de San Francisco handled mainly foreign trade (Segre 1994a).

If the sixteenth century in the economic history of the European conquest of the New World was 'Spain's century' (Herring 1966; Pendle 1978), then Havana played no small part in helping the Iberians secure that position. France, Holland and England would not seriously erode Spain's power until the defeat of the Spanish Armada in 1588 and the sacking of Cádiz by the English in 1596. Those three European powers had secured colonies in the Caribbean, and they would use them to launch raids against Cuba. Cuba's bilateral relations with non-Spanish powers in the Caribbean swung from illegal contraband trade at one extreme, to sustained naval and land warfare at the other. The vicissitudes of prosperity and warfare have led Pichardo-Moya (1943) to refer to the seventeenth century as Cuba's 'Middle Ages.' Under the last of the Hapsburg kings (Philip III, 1598–1621; Philip IV, 1621–1665; and Charles

II, 1665–1700) who ruled Spain in the seventeenth century, Cuba was subjected to the mercantilist policy of a closed sea and trade (*mare clausum*). This meant the island could not receive foreign ships, merchants or colonists (Barnou 1951). Spain's three hostile maritime rivals – Holland, France, and England – drew up a 'Friendship Line' which consisted of the meridian of longitude running through the Azores (28°W) and the parallel of latitude noted by the Tropic of Cancer (23.5°N).

On January 4, 1762 George III of England declared war on Spain and the strategic data gathered by Knowles, recast in a military plan drawn up by the Duke of Cumberland, would be used to gain control of Havana. Advances in munitions and artillery made El Morro vulnerable. A fleet of British ships – possibly the largest that had ever sailed into the Caribbean at that time – easily outmaneuvered the Havana militia which counted on nearly 27 000 soldiers and sailors and nearly as many residents. Part of the British fleet sailed to the west of the city and feigned a landing near the Almendares River. The Spanish dispatched a goodly number of men to that point. Meanwhile, the other part of the British fleet – acting on the keen data of Admiral Knowles – landed east of El Morro. They gambled on securing the ridge above the eastern side of the bay, across from the walled city. The logic here was that Havana would be rendered useless if the ridge above it was not secured. The gamble paid off handsomely for the British. Within six weeks the 'Key to the New World' had been finally unlocked by a non-Spanish power.

The flag of St. George flew over the island of Cuba for the next six months during which time the *habaneros* proved to be ornery and uncooperative. Sir George Keppel, Earl of Albermarle, headed the British occupation. A normal amount of war booty was extracted and a fair amount of tithes were taken from the *cabildo*, the Church, merchants and the elite. On February 10, 1763, France, Spain and England signed a peace treaty in Paris. In what has been considered one of the most curious deals struck during the colonial wars in the Americas, Cuba was exchanged for Florida. Back in England, William Pitt the Elder argued fiercely against the treaty, contending that with Havana, 'all the riches and treasures of the Indies lay at our feet' (Williams 1994, p. 94). Pressure from sugar-cane growers in what was then an 'English' Jamaica, and who disdained competition, led to the swap. Florida, though, was little more than a low-lying sandy peninsula that only afforded the British a contiguous colony along the American Atlantic seaboard (Kuethe 1986).

The fall of Havana to the English and a natural disaster brought four notable accomplishments to Havana's city planning and design. First, there was an official designation of neighborhoods in Havana following a particularly late-arriving hurricane in October 1768. The storm, Hurricane

Santa Teresa, revealed the vulnerability of many residential structures. Two quarters resulted: La Punta in the northern section of the walled city and Campeche in the south. Each quarter held four *barrios* (neighborhoods or districts). La Punta contained Estrella, Monserrate, Dragones and Angel *barrios*. Campeche contained Santa Teresa (named after the storm), San Francisco, Paula and San Isidro. Physical inspections of roofs were carried out and royal-palm bark thatching was ordered to be replaced by flat Moorish masonry roofs or tiles. Second, a public street-lighting system was established. Third, modest changes to the colonial design followed. After the wall was completed in 1740, traffic from within became a problem. Only two gates to the city existed: one connecting La Punta and a second near the center of the rampart. By 1773 five additional gates had been constructed, much to the relief of local merchants. Last, to remedy the city's strategic vulnerability shown from the war with England, a fortress was built on La Cabaña ridge and construction of Atarés and Príncipe fortresses began at about 1774. But it was not Spain that would finance this project. Instead, the viceroyalty of Mexico donated some 14 million dollars to the project (Roberts 1953, p. 55).

The island's defeat at the hands of the British led indirectly to a sugar boom after 1763 (Moreno Fraginals 1964). A strict system of militia recruitment and training went into effect, and planter-officers exacted commercial privileges in exchange for their military services. The combined effect was to establish institutional structures conducive to capitalist expansion and production. Reform programs put in place by Charles III facilitated the growth of the sugar industry, and Havana served as a major center for exports, banking and commercial services. When in 1791 a slave revolt led by Toussaint l'Ouverture in Saint Dominique (Haiti) threw the French colony into a devastating 12-year war against the homeland, Haiti lost its position as the world leader in sugar production.

Cuba profited from Haiti's economic decline. From 1793 onward, Cuba prospered from unrestricted commerce with all countries except enemy nations. Neutral trade lent access to the profitable markets of the United States which was positioning itself as a leading shipping power that traded wood (for packing crates) and fuel with Cuba, as well as flour from its bountiful milling operations. By 1815, an island population of 600 000 placed Cuba 'on the threshold of world leadership in sugar production' (Kuethe 1986, p. 175), and Havana had become the locus of power in this rising sugar empire.

Sugar, though, could not reign mighty without abundant and cheap labor. Until the late 1700s, the ratio of African slaves was relatively low in Cuba compared with Jamaica, Haiti, Trinidad and Curacao. However, the collapse of the French colony Saint Dominique in 1791 placed Cuba in a position to increase sugar revenues for the Royal Crown, and the rate of slave importation rose markedly in the following decades. Wealthy French immigrants emigrated to Cuba and exerted strong influences in coffee and sugar production around Cienfuegos, Nipe, Banes, and Nuevitas, all of which were all founded about this time.

In the closing years of the eighteenth century and the start of the nineteenth, Cuba was poised to receive immigrants who wished to visit or move to Cuba. Nearly 30 000 people came from Santo Domingo following a slave insurrection there. When Louisiana was transferred to France in 1803, many Spaniards left, and Havana was their port of entry into Cuba. The Spanish colonial government issued a decree in 1817 that greatly encouraged land ownership by foreigners. South America sent forth thousands of Spanish-speaking peoples to Havana who fled the devastation of the Independence Wars that swept the continent. The first census of Cuba conducted by the Marquis de la Torre in 1774 showed an island population (probably greatly undercounting slaves) of only 171 620 inhabitants – 1.5 habitants per square kilometer – after two and a half centuries. By 1861, though, Cuba's sugar production had spread and the population had grown by 816% to 1.4 million. During its peak years of growth following the Haitian revolution and the immigration of French and Haitians, Cuba averaged an annual rate of growth of 3.4% between 1792 and 1817 (Marrero 1981b, pp. 144–145). Population increase driven by agricultural production meant an increase in the immigration of African slaves and, in the middle of the nineteenth century, Chinese indentured workers. Thus, the white population, constituting 56% of the island's total in 1774, dropped to 42% in 1841. An 1845 decree that ended the importation of slaves caused a rise in the white population to 54% in 1861.

Cuba's expanding sugar industry unleashed a new demand for labor. Slavery was becoming increasingly difficult as Britain attempted to interrupt slave shipments between Africa and the New World. Cuban sugarcane growers, however, were always in search of slaves to replace their exhausted labor. A relatively unpopulated island that had been settled by Europeans and African slaves for three centuries began to increase its population steadily. The Cuban government even tried buying Indians from the Yucatan peninsula as slaves. Spanish regulations also included a campaign to promote Chinese immigration. Between 1847 and 1860 nearly 48 000 Chinese entered Cuba (Niddrie 1971, p. 98).

The Havana Asiatic Company (*Compañía Asiática de La Habana*) brought over most of the Chinese coolies who settled among the sugarcane communities between Havana and Matanzas, and around the towns of Cárdenas and Colón. Contract labor of Chinese workers in Cuba, as in

**Table 1.2** Population of Cuba, selected years, late nineteenth century

| Year | Population |
|------|------------|
| 1861 | 1 396 530 |
| 1877 | 1 521 684 |
| 1887 | 1 631 687 |
| 1899 | 1 572 797 |

*Source*: *Censo de Población*. Havana, 1899.

Peru and Mexico, was 'hardly distinguishable from slavery' (Sánchez-Albornoz 1974, p. 150). Havana today still has vestiges of a small Chinatown near the Capitolio building, though intermarriage and out-migration since then have left a relatively small population of pure Chinese in Havana. A small though well preserved Chinese cemetery remains in Havana, near the large Colón Cemetery in Vedado. Although some Native Americans from the Yucatan peninsula also immigrated in the mid-nineteenth century, their contribution to the national population stock was minor. The 1899 census classified 67% of the population as white and 33% as 'colored', including Chinese (Gobierno de Cuba 1899).

Cuba's national population fluctuated greatly during the latter half of the nineteenth century because of the long periods of war between Cuba and Spain (Table 1.2). While the first half of the nineteenth century registered rapid population growth, Cuba actually lost population during the latter half of the century. In 1887, Cuba registered 1.63 million residents, but by the end of the Independence Wars (discussed in Chapter 2) in 1898, the island had 60 000 fewer inhabitants. Marrero (1981b, p. 149) calculates an annual loss of 0.3% during the warring 1887–1899 period.

Rapid population growth in early nineteenth century Cuba meant a larger labor pool for Cuba's agricultural production, and more wealth for Havana. The slave trade in the Caribbean was largely concentrated in Cuba, and more than 387 000 Negro slaves entered the island between 1800 and 1865, despite Spain's abolition laws of 1845. It was common among even modest white, Creole, middle-class *habaneros* to have several slaves. Bells were not used in summoning slaves within the home. Rather, the master's family would merely yell, for the slaves lived conveniently in entresols. White Creoles (Cuban-born Spaniards) and *peninsulares* (Spaniards born in Spain) were expected to maintain a Negro mistress within the home, and the men were not all that concerned about hiding these sexual antics. Bastards from Creole fathers and Negro mistresses usually were granted freedom and the family surname when they reached adulthood.

## The rise and fall of the walled city

The walling of colonial Havana was a long process, not only for the great amount of labor and raw materials required for the public work, but because of the decision-making process leading up to its approval. It seems to have become a key point of public discussion following the attack of the French pirate, Jacques de Sores, in 1555. Alternatives to encasing the city included placing barricades at the ends of the streets. Juan Bautista Antonelli's nephew, Cristóbal de Roda, argued against the walls, claiming that the city was sufficiently protected by the network of fortresses.

The building of the wall sealed Havana's status as a link in Spain's mercantile system. An erratic flow of funds from Spain delayed construction and systematic building did not commence until in 1663 and ended some eight decades later. Havana's bulwark fortress consisted of walls set in a polygon made up of nine bastions. Parapets and escarpments pulled the walls together with an exterior moat. The nothern end of the walled city was anchored by La Punta Castle while San Francisco de Paula grounded the southern end. When construction began, the ramparts encased a larger area than had been settled. Well before the completion of the wall, the town exceeded its limits. When the final stone was laid in 1740, the original design had not been faithfully erected. It failed to include a covered passageway and a moat around the entire wall. In the end, the walled city consisted of 56 streets, 179 blocks, five plazas (Catedral, Armas, Vieja, San Francisco and del Cristo), 14 churches and convents, two hospitals, six military barracks, and one jail (Roberts 1953, p. 41).

The elite of colonial Havana used key social spaces to flaunt their status. One prominent display was the outing in the family coach just beyond the walled city. This was particularly important for the well-off women of Havana. At the end of the eighteenth century, the Alameda de Paula along the bay was *the* place with the greatest amount of street life, especially on days when dances and *retretas* (impressive displays, musical bands, and evening military parades) were held. Although some men strolled there, women almost always remained in the *carruajes*. The *paseo en carruaje* for carriages had acquired greater importance than the *paseo a pie* for pedestrians. With the creation of the Tacón Theater and the widening of the Paseo Extramural in the 1830s, the coach *paseos* became more common as the elite sought recreation outside the crowded conditions of the walled city. New customs such as theater, cafés, traveling carnivals, and the carriage stroll brought the well-off *habaneros* outside the confines of the walled city. It served, furthermore, as a creation of popular space where rich and poor could see the differences between Spanish life-styles and those of the island (Le Riverend 1992).

Ways of life and land uses in Havana in the early nineteenth century were at cross-purposes. On the one hand, provisions, animals, and light industries that were essential to the survival of the *villa* when it was a frontier town, held less importance in the 1800s. Beasts of burden and all kinds of carts and carriages made the streets of the walled city nearly impassable. Public hygiene suffered greatly from the more than 2000 horses and mules kept in Habana Vieja. Street congestion resulted from the more than 2000 two-wheel carriages (*volantas*), open horse-drawn carriages (*quitrines*), and other passenger and cargo carts and wagons (Chateloin 1989). On the other hand, much of the city had grown beyond the old ramparts as the fear of corsair and pirate attacks waned, and the livelihood of the city's residents moved into services outside the original core (Pérez Beato 1936). Epidemics and infectious diseases compounded the misery in parts of the walled city, and the cholera outbreak of 1833, which took 3000 lives, was particularly tragic. Water quality was also poor, noting that between 1592 and 1835, the potable water came from the Zanja Real which required constant upgrading and maintenance (Marrero 1956, 1981b).

By 1860, Havana's role in the world economy had changed its land use and urban morphology, giving rise to a well defined commercial district outside the walled city. New elite neighborhoods, more thoroughly discussed in Chapters 2 and 3, originated from sugar wealth. At that time there existed outside the walled city 10 furniture stores, six clothing stores, five leather shops, five cafés, six hardware stores, four china shops, three pharmacies, and a handful of tailor shops, tea shops and restaurants, barber shops, print shops, and even a store devoted exclusively to Asian merchandise. When the walls came down in the early 1860s, Havana had outlived its role as a mere warehouse of Mexican and Peruvian wealth; it had emerged as an economic power in its own right.

## Design and style in colonial Havana

The classic elements of Spanish architecture of cut stone and lumber arrived relatively late to the Cuban economy. Abundant clay soils favored the use of brick and adobe construction materials. Even the first public buildings in the *villas* used the indigenous construction method of thatched leafs and stalk covered with a layer of mud and clay. When 'Spanish' architecture did take hold, it reflected a strong Moorish influence. Interior patios remain today in Havana that are similar to designs found in Tunis, Alger, Seville, Granada, and Cádiz.

The transition from Baroque to Neoclassicism also arrived relatively late in Cuba, and there is even some dispute about whether it even took hold (Sánchez Agusti 1984). Even though Baroque was beginning to decline in Europe in the 1740s, it did not arrive in Cuba in full force until the beginning of the nineteenth century. Local stone, with its wide grain and hollow cavity, did not lend itself easily to Baroque decoration. Another factor impeding the transfer of European building styles in Cuba was that military engineers were responsible for most of the major projects in Havana. By training, they were unaccustomed to the decorative ways of civilian architects. Perhaps more significant, though, was that Cuban craftsmen were not trained in the Baroque style, limiting their talents to the smooth curves of the Segundo Cabo (Intendente) Palace. (A similar problem is discussed in Chapter 9 regarding the loss of building trade skills because of twentieth century prefabrication.) Thus the type of stone was a determining factor in the predominant style of architecture of the nineteenth century (Weiss 1972).

Other political and ideological factors also interfered with the transition from Baroque to Neoclassical. Neoclassicism was associated with rationality and the French Revolution, at least in its early phase. Cuba, though, was relatively conservative as a Spanish colony, at least until the late eighteenth and early nineteenth century awakenings brought on by the stirrings of a Cuban independence movement, and the example set by Haiti. Havana's entrance into Neoclassical design was facilitated by Bishop Espada, the influential organization The Economic Society of Friends of the Country (*Sociedad Económica de Amigos del País*), French immigration to Cuba via Haiti, and the intelligent government of Carlos III in Spain. The outlying suburb of Cerro received the bulk of this new, Neoclassical design in the first half of the nineteenth century. Iron was used in versatile and whimsical ways typical of the Baroque, and made the use of wood obsolete in verandahs and balustrades. Greco-Roman styles were also used widely in Havana through Neoclassical buildings and homes. Neo-Gothic ornaments also appeared and the Villanueva Station was perhaps the city's finest example.

Colonial residential structures were equally simple. Habana Vieja's initial homes were merely huts (*bohíos*) structured with wooden slats, wattle and guano. These structures were later improved with walls of broken stone cemented by plaster (*mampostería*) or a combination of buttresses, mud walls and tiles (Weiss 1972, 1978). Such precarious structures were highly susceptible to fire, which swept through colonial Havana often. *Habaneros* built more stone structures after the French torched Havana in 1538. Even in the nineteenth century, most buildings were only of one story, and in cases of two-story buildings, the ground floor was most often used for retailing. Windows did not have glass and instead were covered by heavy iron bars on the street side, and wooden shutters on the inside.

Few houses had basements because of the miry soil, which was polluted by sewage. Wood, not stone, characterized the sixteenth century city. Buttresses, beams, doors, joists, trusses, and railings were made of high-quality wood which covered the island.

Havana is remarkable today because of its broad *portales* (arcade or arched colonnades), which reflect the influence of Spanish immigrants. In the era of the *villas*, retail trade took place in the plazas, near the coast, in open-air markets and in makeshift wooden kiosks. In the seventeenth century houses were built out of various block mixtures (*albañilería*, which used cementing materials such as crushed limestone, fruit juices, and oxen blood, mixed with brick or shattered stone), wooden roofs and tiles, and formed one- or two-story structures. The owner of the house occasionally used or rented out the street-level floor for retail trade and often lived on the second floor. The Laws of the Indies proclaimed that the colonial cities of Latin America would 'surround the plaza and the four main streets emanating out from them, will have *portales* for the comfort of passer-bys' (Aruca 1985, p. 25, our translation). The *portales* were added on to the Havana buildings located on town squares around the beginning of the seventeenth century. In the eighteenth century, so important were the *portales*, that homes were classified as either having or lacking them (Aruca 1985, p. 25).

In the early nineteenth century, Havana's elite looked to France for ideas and models to emulate (López Segrera 1972). *Habaneros* danced and dressed like the French elite even before the immigration of French and Spanish residents who had resided in Haiti and Louisiana. The minuet, moreover, was danced only by the aristocracy in Cuba. With the arrival of these new immigrants and their servants, French music became so popular that Spanish and Cuban music were played with a distinguishing French touch.

One venue for disseminating this French influence was the *Academia de Música de Santa Cecilia* which was founded in 1816 with the financial support of the *Sociedad Económica de Amigos del País*. French artists arrived in Havana and influenced local painters. They included Garneray (1807) and Vermay (1817). The latter founded the San Alejandro Painting Academy in 1818. In literature the romanticism of Heredia illuminated local readers and writers. The surge in elite admiration of the French could even be seen in the interiors of Havana's upper-class houses which were decorated in French style. The Aldama Palace, which was the most important Neoclassical residential building in Cuba, illustrates this. Even the quintessential Cuban habit of drinking coffee derived from the French.[1] The slave rebellion in Haiti was a major catalyst in bringing the practice of coffee drinking to Cuba.

## Tacón: the Neoclassical appeal of Washington, DC

The nineteenth century marked a watershed period of independence movements and change in Latin America. In the Caribbean, however, the sugar-oriented economies remained fairly isolated from the *independentista* fervor on Mexican, Central and South American soil. While the Creoles in Cuba strongly resented the disproportionate power exercised by the *peninsulares*, they feared even more the winds of change that might sweep over the growing sugar economy. Haiti's independence movement unleashed violent uprisings of Negro slaves against plantation owners, the reports of which were fresh in the minds of white Cubans. Thus, 'they considered a Spanish colony preferable to a black republic', even though Spanish rule was 'appallingly corrupt' (Pendle 1978, p. 119).

Governor Miguel Tacón's main charge from 1834 to 1838 was to keep Cuba a Spanish colony, and improving Cuba's economy and image was one way to achieve that goal. Tacón wished to make Havana a symbol of urban modernity, which at the time was identified with Neoclassicism. This modern drive embraced sobriety, order, righteousness, strait avenues, and open spaces for the new middle class. Tacón's elder brother, Francisco, was the Spanish ambassador in Washington, D.C., and there is speculation that the young capital's layout by L'Enfant might have influenced Governor Tacón's urban reforms (Chateloin 1989). Governor Tacón had a rivalry with the influential Creole Count of Villa nueva (Pérez de la Riva 1963), which greatly benefited Havana.

Tacón also wanted to bring law and order to the Cuban capital. His police force had to meet minimum weekly arrest quotas. Illegal slave trade was allegedly snuffed out, even though he is said to have profited from kickbacks and direct revenues for certain slave trading which he

---

[1]Culture and economy in Havana were interwoven in essential ways. The social value placed on coffee consumption led to an increase in coffee production. At the beginning of the nineteenth century Cuba was exporting 50 000 arrobas (Spanish weight of 25 lbs) of coffee beans, and by 1830, production reached 2 million. Half of that production was consumed on the island and half was exported. By 1840, the railroad precipitated the substitution of coffee around Havana for sugar cane. But the production and consumption of coffee increased. Drinking coffee replaced the practice of sipping chocolate among the well off, and cafés like those found in Europe appeared. The first café was opened on the Plaza Vieja within the walled city in 1772, and it would become an important gathering place in the nineteenth century. It was originally called Café de Tavern but was renamed Café de la Taverna. Other cafés followed: in 1804 the Café de los Franceses opened on the Campo de Marte (just outside the walled quarters) and the Café de las Copas was opened on Oficios Street (within the walled city). This is where early separatist thinkers met. The Café de la Dominica on Obispo Street (1812) and Café de la Paloma (1825) were also popular meeting places for the elite, foreign travelers, and the early revolutionaries who sought independence from Spain (Chateloin 1989, pp. 31–32). The role of cafés as public gathering places has all but disappeared in contemporary Havana.

condoned. In Havana, though, he began an erstwhile beautification process. Beginning with renovating the Captain's General Palace in the Plaza de Armas, he added a neoclassical marble *pórtico* over the main entrance door which faced the town square. Tacón recognized that the town jail – a locally unwanted land use in today's vocabulary – was not desirable in its location, so he moved it to a less central position near the Punta Castle, where a small portion still remains.

The Prado boulevard, at that time called the *Alameda* (literally, a poplar-lined street), was redesigned with trees on both sides. It was renamed Paseo de Isabel II and became the principal avenue for afternoon rides in thickly decorated carriages (*volantas*) carrying rich women. The *volantas* were elaborately designed with leather hoods, brass buckles, and the insides were decorated with imported fabrics and even small Persian rugs (Figure 1.6). Such outings in carriages were of great social value among upper-class women (Barclay 1993, p. 179).

Although these carriage outings lasted just 2 hours, it was often the only time aristocratic women could get out of the house. As 'their only means of escape', it contributed to a distinctly gendered, spatially defined, and class-specific use of space in nineteenth century Havana.

THE VOLANTE.

**Figure 1.6** Typical elite carriage (*volanta*) in Habana Vieja, early nineteenth century. Courtesy of the Library of Congress

Tacón's chief contribution to altering the urban shape of Havana was yet to come. The western suburbs during his reign were little more than a few scattered houses outside the city walls. He built a wide boulevard running directly west of the walled city, naming the main section Carlos III. This broad extension (Figure 1.7) was the continuation of Paseo de la Reina which was later renamed Avenida de Bolívar. This new monumental avenue commissioned by Tacón took on his name (Paseo de Tacón) which later became Carlos III and ultimately, to Salvador Allende under the Castro government. Carlos III ran to Príncipe Castle and passed the beautiful grounds of the Spanish Governor's summer residence, called La Quinta de los Molinos. Even today, remnants of the city's first aqueduct – the Zanja Real of 1592 – trickle through the botanical gardens on those grounds where stone mills (*molinos*) used to grind tobacco leaves into *rapé*.

Tacón set out to clean up much of the riffraff – thieves, assassins, vagrants – and generally ruled with an iron hand. Clamping down on gambling led him to raid illegal gaming houses, especially in the small town in the southeastern corner of the bay, Regla. The backwater village

**Figure 1.7**   A view of the boulevard Alameda de Isabel II, with the Tacón Theater to the left and the Paseo del Prado in the background. This series of broad monumental roads, beginning with the Paseo de Tacón was designed by Ramón de la Sagra. According to Pérez de la Riva (1946), it was the first monumental boulevard in the Americas, pre-dating the Paseo de la Reforma, carried out by Maximiliano in Mexico City, which connected the Chapultepec Castle with the city

had become notorious for cockfighting, smugglers and illicit gambling (Barclay 1993, p. 172). He censored many of the presses permitted by his predecessors and did his utmost to exclude Creoles from sources of power. The colonial governor understood all too well the value of maintaining a slave-driven sugar economy and would not tolerate any of the revolutionary fervor spreading throughout Spanish America.[2]

A favorable sugar market financed public works and city beautification programs during Tacón's administration. When he took office in the 1830s, sugar was selling for eight reales per arroba; 5 years later it had risen to 11.25. In 1832 a steam-powered barge with four huge nets reaching a depth of 30 feet were used to clean debris in Havana Bay. In 1830, just 5 years after the invention of the steam locomotive, formal proposals were launched in one of the island's colonial government branches to finance a railroad project. Tacón would mediate between aristocratic Creole factions who wanted English capital and technology to finance the project, and Tacón's council of advisors who were pressured by the sugar aristocracy (Moreno Fraginals 1976). It is now clear that Tacón's short administration in the 1830s was part of a larger set of historic 'firsts' in Havana in the nineteenth century that gave the city a special place in Cuba, the Caribbean and Latin America (Table 1.3).

If Havana owed her fortune in the nineteenth century to her port and relative geographic location, then surely the second most essential factor was the railroad. Its construction permitted the expanse of sugar-cane planting without fear of losing precious sugar content while cut cane lay waiting for horse-cart transport to sugar mills. The railroad compressed both time and space, and in so doing contributed to the wealth of the capital city. Appropriately, then, train stations mirrored the forms common in the United States and England where train technology had originated. The Villanueva Station in Havana had a classic, symmetrical appearance. Two curved beams were supported by six Doric columns. And though the railroad was of English construction, the planners, stock brokers, engineers, and superintendents were American (James 1959).

With growing coffers under his control and a prosperous economy before him, Governor Miguel Tacón turned his gaze towards the city of Havana. For nearly 300 years Havana had been designed, planned, built and lived in strictly for the perspectives of military strategists and power-

---

[2]Yet despite his seeming penchant for law and order, Tacón was not above barter and negotiation. A well known tale of his administration includes the establishment of a fish market by Francisco Marty, by all accounts a crafty merchant. In exchange for showing Tacón how contraband was run through the island, Marty won exclusive rights to build and operate the fish market. Similar 'deals' were struck with other entrepreneurs.

**Table 1.3** Historic nineteenth century 'firsts' in Havana

| Year | Historic 'First' |
| --- | --- |
| 1794 | Use of first steam engine |
| 1818 | McAdam road-paving system employed |
| 1819 | First regular steam-engine maritime route in Latin America established between Havana and Matanzas |
| 1834–1838 | Urban planning reforms under Governor Miguel Tacón |
| 1837 | Rail service between Havana and Bejucal, 35 kilometers south of Havana. Cuba becomes seventh country – even before Spain – to establish railroad |
| 1837 | Ferry service in Havana Bay between Habana Vieja and Regla |
| 1848 | Gas-fired public lighting system employed |
| 1849–1850 | Italian Antonio Meucci invents the telephone (he called it the 'talking telegraph', or *telégrafo parlante*) in Havana. He later works with Alexander Graham Bell. US Supreme Court recognizes Meucci as inventor after his death |
| 1851–1855 | Telegraph service established |
| 1862 | Animal drawn tram car service begun |
| 1874–1893 | Albear Aqueduct |
| 1881 | Telephone service developed in Havana |
| 1890 | Electric public street lighting |
| 1897 | Cinema arrives. First short feature film shot in Havana, 1898–1902 |
| 1898–1902 | First automobiles arrive. Malecón expansion begins |
| 1901 | Electric street-car system inaugurated |

*Source*: *Estrategia* (1990). Havana: *Grupo para el Desarrollo Integral de la Capital*

ful religious orders. Tacón admired the works of Pierre L'Enfant and used them as a model for his Havana. While L'Enfant used the topography of Washington, DC to locate key monuments on prominent hills that served as pedestals for his monuments (e.g., the Capitol building on Jenkins Hill and the White House at a right angle from there), Tacón failed to consider the role of local topography in Havana. Indeed, his idea for Havana was merely to adopt the axes that L'Enfant had used to connect Washington. In doing so, Tacón has been criticized for 'breaking out of the urban scale . . .' and 'perpetuating not only isolated Havana architectural works, but also [for] being a redesigner of urbanism' (Chateloin 1989, p. 92, our translation). Unlike L'Enfant who used open spaces as 'state squares' throughout Washington, DC, Tacón used them as places to display military prowess.

Some of Tacón's projects were ostentatious and symbolic. For example, a magnificent theater house with a beautiful Doric exterior carried both his name and a 1000-light chandelier. There was also a notable increase in shantytowns on the city's outskirts which held the indigent, thieves, assassins, army deserters, freed slaves and beggars. Many urban improvements had mixed results politically and pragmatically. On the one hand, numerous streets were widened or resurfaced. Obispo and O'Reilly Streets were paved from the port to Monserrate. On the other hand, some of the improvements were ineffective. The thoroughfare just outside the wall to the west of the city – now Monserrate–Egido Avenues – could only accommodate about 10% of the nearly 2700 carriages in the city in the late 1820s (Chateloin 1989, p. 95).

His grandest project advanced the Parisian example of straight and wide boulevards like those later built under Napoleon III and his prefect, Baron Haussmann. It entailed the widening and extension of Carlos III westward. The project was resented by the Creoles of Cuba, more for its symbolism than its practicality. It marked an authoritarian stamp of colonial power across the Havana landscape, and its maximum utility would not fully be realized as a transportation artery until decades later. Tacón's other accomplishments included a slaughterhouse, public lighting, fire squad, siren system, sinkhole filling, and street sign campaign, among many others (Table 1.4).

## Sugar is king: nineteenth century Havana

When the walls came down in the 1860s, Havana had already broken out of the confines of the walled city, even though most of the commerce clustered around the old plazas. Some commercial activity was evident outside the walled city as were residential areas, warehousing, and some retail shops. The economic hub of Havana, though, was concentrated along the streets of Ricla (now Muralla), Teniente Rey, San Ignacio, Obispo and O'Reilly. This retail activity grew thanks to the sugar trade which had made the port of Havana, already a major harbor, one of the most important in the world. Muralla Street served as a major warehousing center, displaying silks, china, silverware and other goods. Only the street of Jesús del Monte had any significant retail trade beyond the colonial core (Aruca 1985).

Nineteenth century Havana was greeted with relative prosperity and even splendor. By 1790, Havana and its suburbs held about 44 000 residents on an island of 273 000 (Roberts 1953, p. 61). That same year marked the printing of the first newspaper in the colony, *Papel Periódico de La Habana*. Sugar destined for the United States filled city coffers with unprecedented tax revenues, some of which went to public works projects. In 1845, for instance, El Morro Castle received its present-day beacon which is perhaps the most widely recognized symbol of the city. For many years it bore the name 'O'Donnell 1845' in honor of the Spanish governor,

**Table 1.4** Public-works projects in Havana, commissioned by Miguel Tacón, Governor of Cuba, 1834–1838

| Year(s) | Project | Location | Present status |
|---|---|---|---|
| 1834–1835 | Santo Cristo market | Inside wall on Teniente Rey street | No longer exists. |
| | Tacón Market | Outside wall, on Plaza de Vapor, between Aguila, Dragones, San Luis Gonzaga and Galiano | No longer exists. A park stands there today. |
| | Fish Market | Walled city on Desembocadura del Puerto, near the Cathedral | No longer exists. Land occupied by other works on Avenida del Puerto. |
| 1835 | Road paving, street signs, sewer lines, sinkhole filling | Inside and outside walled city | Some street signs still visible. |
| | Repairs to San Juan de Dios Hospital | Walled city, on block flanked by Aguilar, Habana, Empedrado and San Juan de Dios | No longer exists. |
| | Remodeling Governor's House | Walled city, facing *Plaza de Armas* | Museum of the City today. |
| 1836 | Campo de Marte | Outside walls near Paseo Extramural | Part of Fraternity Park near Capitolio. |
| | Tacón Jail | Outside walls, at end of Paso Extramural (Prado, today) | Demolished in 1939 though chapel remains. |
| 1836–1837 | Enhancing Galiano Bridge | Outside walls | Does not exist. |
| | Tacón's rest home and gardens | Outside walls | Known today as Quinta de los Molinos and Botanical Gardens on Salvador Allende Street. |
| | Neptune Fountain and dock repairs | Walled city | Fountain moved to Vedado, in Gonzalo de Quesada Park, but was recently removed. |
| | Widening of Paseo Extramural | Outside walls. In 1840 renamed Isabel II | Officially 'Paseo José Martí' bur popularly called 'El Prado'. |
| | Paseo de Tacón | Outside walls | Called Carlos III later. |

Table 1.4 continued

| Year(s) | Project | Location | Present status |
|---------|---------|----------|----------------|
| | San Luis Gonzaga Street | Outside walls | Known later as Reina. |
| 1837–38 | Carabineros' Jail | Walled city | No longer exists. |
| | Monserrate Gate | Entrance through wall | Walls torn down. |
| | Tacón Theater | Outside wall | On corner of Prado and San Rafael, next to Hotel Inglaterra. |

*Data source*: Greatly modified after Chateloin (1989, pp. 209–212)

Leopoldo O'Donnell. Prosperity from sugar also led to urban sprawl, and in 1862, the inevitable happened: the city government authorized the piecemeal destruction of the colonial walls which had outlived their utility. In their place stood new buildings, streets, and city blocks, but at the cost of destroying colonial buildings.

Moreno Fraginals (1976, pp. 172–173) offers one interpretation of Cuba's nineteenth century economic history which situates Havana's growth in national and international frameworks. He dismisses the notion that Cuba was exclusively a monocultural and dependent sugar-cane producer for the external market. Instead, he contends that between 1815 and 1842, Cuba distributed its exports among the USA, Spain, England, Germany, France, Russia, and the Low Countries, as well as smaller markets. Cuba's economy grew by 4.0% per annum between 1815 and 1842 while the value of sugar exports rose by only 2.6%. This meant a relative increase in the island's overall economic performance, and suggests that Cuba was not the monocultural sugar-cane exporter as many have claimed.

Cuba alone could not exercise decisive political pressure to produce economic advantages for itself. In the latter half of the nineteenth century, however, Cuba increased its sugar exports to the USA. The USA also increased its imports of processed honey, rum, coffee, leaf and processed tobacco, copper, wax, and precious woods. The core of Cuba's export economy, though, was comprised of sugar, honey and rum, and it passed mainly through the port of Havana. Not only was the island the leading exporter of sugar and coffee during this period but it also led the world in copper exports. The three key agricultural export goods – sugar, molasses and rum – originated on slave-worked plantations.

Underlying Moreno Fraginals' theorization of the sugar-driven stages of economic development during the nineteenth century is the precept that slavery was incompatible with mechanization. The traditional sugar-

**Figure 1.8** Calzada de Vives (Avenida España), c. 1954. In Jesús María neighborhood, southwest of Havana Vieja. Covered sidewalks (*portales*) straddle both sides of Havana's *calzadas*. *Portales*, dating back to the nineteenth century, are a feature of the contemporary city

mill complex (*ingenio*) representing early sugar-processing techniques and traditional technology, was greatly challenged in the late nineteenth and early twentieth centuries by the new *centrales*, most of which were built by US investors. Bergad (1989) disagrees with the basic tenet of Moreno Fraginals, arguing instead that economic dependence and monoculture were controlled mainly by Cubans. In his study of sugar production in Matanzas Province (sharing its western border with Havana Province), Bergad (1989, pp. 336 and 338) concludes that: 'There were no foreign villains here, ransacking the local economy and repatriating profits to their countries of origin . . . [D]ependence was created by Cubans responding to their own carefully defined class interests.'

The introduction of new technology aided Cuba's insertion in the world economy as a producer of tropical agricultural products. In 1837, a rail line connected Havana and the town of Bejucal, just south of the city. In so doing, Cuba laid claim to the first Spanish-speaking nation in the world to introduce the railroad. Modest improvements in technology facilitated Cuba's trade with the rest of the world. Sugar plantings spread throughout Havana's hinterland in the early 1800s. Rail connections spread beyond the first Havana–Bejucal line, and enabled Cuban planters to settle in provinces adjacent to Havana (Le Riverend 1960). The first generation of Havana sugar growers entered Matanzas in the early nineteenth century because 'the exhaustion of soil and forest reserves in Havana province led them to seek new territory for sugar production' (Chomsky 1994, p. 226).

The Ten Years' War (1868–1878) between the Cuban colony and Spain interrupted the importation of legal (contract labor with Haitians and Jamaicans) and illegal (African slaves) workers in the sugar economy, which remained essentially labor-intensive. Abolition in 1878 threatened traditional sugar-cane production in Cuba, as did competition from European beet sugar. Many old planters gave up or sold their *ingenios* and sought new investment opportunities in Havana and Santiago de Cuba (Moreno Fraginals 1964). Just as this new economic restructuring was unfolding, the War of Independence in 1895–1898 shattered it. US investors would move in later and build large *centrales* (modern steam-fired mills), shape the Cuban economy well into the next century (Chomsky 1994, p. 227), and solidify Havana's role as the island's service center and gateway to the world economy.

Like most Latin American cities, the planning and zoning of colonial Havana was satisfactory until the mid-nineteenth century (Hardoy 1992, p. 21), but proved to be too restrictive to accommodate rapid urbanization. The building codes laid out in the *Ordenanzas de la Construcción de 1861* (Building Codes of 1861) gave the colonial city a unique look. This meant carefully monitoring even the smallest design of new buildings and road networks. As a major building code and planning mandate, the *Ordenanzas* were quite progressive for its day and left an indelible mark on Havana. Roads were classified in a hierarchy, and a Neoclassical style was imposed on the *pórticos*, which contrasted with the commanding baroque style of the walled city. First-order roads were called *calzadas*, whose width could not be less than 25 meters (90 feet). *Calzadas* Zapata, Puentes Grandes, Güines, Cristina, Monte, Cerro, Galiano, Belascoaín, and Jesús del Monte (later called Diez de Octubre) and Infanta still exist today, adding *calzada* to the roadway nomenclature of *calle* (street) and *avenida* (avenue) that form part of contemporary Havana's road names. These *calzadas* were typically lined with porticated public corridors called *portales* (Figure 1.8). These *portales* gave access to stores at the ground level, with dwellings above. Such a pattern was key in shaping the look of the city beyond the old-walled city (the *extramuros*), but in the old-walled historic core, *portales* were confined to the buildings surrounding the main plazas. Secondary roads, deemed the *Ordenanzas*, would also have *portales* at the expense of land lots if necessary. Covered sidewalks and promenades outside the walled city were wider and longer, and recommended for a pedestrian's protection from the tropical sun.

The columned *portales* is Havana's trademark. By the late 1880s, Vedado designed its building fronts with deep setbacks and the rhythmically positioned colonnades (Livingston 1996). So pronounced was the construction of these *portales* in neighborhoods like San Lorenzo, Cerro, Diez de Octubre, and Centro Habana that the entire city has been referred to as the 'City of Columns' (Carpentier 1982). Not all primary and secondary roads, however, were shaded by *portales*. When used, however, they joined visual elements above the sidewalks and symbolized the economic power and social position of merchants in the city.

### Population density and land area: 1519–1958

Havana's growth over four and a half centuries of urbanization is closely tied to the availability of land through annexation or new settlements. If we assume that population density averages are inversely linked to the quality of life, we can then infer about general patterns related to the quality of urban life over time. Two distinct patterns can be gleaned from the six historical periods shown in Figure 1.9. First, as discussed in Chapter 2, the end of Cuba's Independence Wars increased the available land in metropolitan Havana appreciably. Between 1899 and 1924. Havana's land area – through annexation and the opening up of new lands to the west and south – increased nearly fourfold from 800 to 3000 hectares. By 1958, the land area nearly doubled to 5000 hectares.

A second discernible pattern shows widely ranging population density, defined here as the number of persons per hectare. Curiously, the peak periods of high-density settlement emerged in the seventeenth (1601–1750) and nineteenth (1831–1899) centuries, when persons per hectare reached 330 and 312, respectively. These data complement the

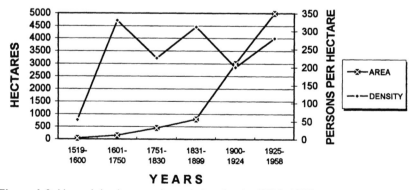

**Figure 1.9** Havana's land area and population density (1519–1958)

narrative descriptions of the very crowded conditions (for animals and people) discussed previously. With the tearing down of the colonial walls in the 1860s, the expanse of new suburban additions and the relocation of the city center to Centro Habana, the population density fell by 35%, from 312 persons per hectare (1831–1899) to 200 (1900–1924).

Between 1924 and 1958 the population density increased to 280 persons per hectare, yet it was still below both the seventeenth and nineteenth century peak periods. The overall pattern points to a fairly low population density over time where massive densification in the city center was replaced by a slow, low-density suburbanization at the urban edge. The low-density amenity of contemporary Havana has prevailed in the 1990s and has given the city a quality of life uncommon in other Latin American world cities including Mexico City, Lima, Río de Janeiro and Buenos Aires.

## A glimpse into the twentieth century

With the end of Spanish colonial rule in 1898, the old city fell into severe decay. US authorities embarked on several projects during their occupation of the island between 1898 and 1902. Perhaps the most influential in the planning and design fields was starting the Malecón – the waterfront boulevard now passing through Vedado and linking Habana Vieja with Miramar – from the northern edge of the Old City (González 1993). This eased the establishment of summer homes for the elite in points west of San Lázaro neighborhood, and allowed automobiles easier access into the sparsely settled bedroom communities of Vedado and Miramar. If the suburbanization of the city to the west and the south marked the gradual decay of the old city, this turn-of-the-century construction continued the linear network of *portales*, so characteristic of nineteenth century Havana.

Independence from Spain in 1898 replaced one second-class world power (Spain) with a first-class power (USA). The island was lightly populated with only 1.5 million inhabitants in 1900, about the size of Havana in 1970. One-fifth of the nation's sugar production was concentrated in 19 sugar mills owned by US businesses, where some 13 000 tenant farmers labored. The long period between harvest and planting, on the one hand, and the lengthy growing season, on the other hand, left thousands of seasonally unemployed rural workers throughout most of the year. Urban migration – especially to Havana – would spring from this idle labor and create slums and shanties around the city edge. The urban poor also sought housing in the more dilapidated structures of the old walled city. In classic fashion, the low-income 'invasion' of the colonial core produced a 'succession' of migrant groups who would occupy the housing stock of the generation before them (Park *et al.* 1925).

On the eve of the twentieth century, Havana was, as at so many times in its past, a paradox (Le Riverend 1992). Pockets of great wealth contrasted with abject penury and environmental ruin. General Leonard Wood of the US occupation forces remarked that Cuba was the 'new California . . . a brand new country' and set out to open up investment there (Pérez 1988, p. 121). At the same time, though, Havana had all of the decadence that the Revolution would find half a century later; more than 200 brothels were registered in Havana, most in the old city and in the industrial sectors near immigrant neighborhoods.

By 1898, Spain had made few improvements in the city's infrastructure beyond the accomplishments of Governor Tacón six decades earlier. Havana Bay was especially polluted: 'Between Morro Castle and its neighbor across the way, La Punta, the vessels steam into that bay, foul with four hundred years of Spanish misrule and filth, where three hundred years of the slave trade centered, and into which the sewers of a great city poured their filth' (White 1898, p. 134). Raw sewage pouring into the harbor was not diluted, and became most unpleasant during the summer months, producing a 'festering mass . . . fronting the whole sea wall and throwing a stench into the air which must be breathed by everyone on shipboard' (White 1898, pp. 134–135). If it was this bad for the tourists, then the residents of Regla, Habana Vieja and those downwind from the trade winds were constantly exposed to the bay's wrath.

The twentieth century would not significantly modify the look of the city, nor the Afro-Spanish imprint of its population. Chapter 3 argues that the city's most significant buildings both qualitatively and quantitatively were constructed in the twentieth century, but for the most part would blend into the city's beige, low-lying skyline. The early decades of the twentieth century would also vary the ethnic composition of Havana as the city accepted refugees and migrants fleeing war-torn Europe and the breaking up of colonial empires. The dissolution of the Ottoman Empire, for instance, sent thousands of *Turcos* into the major Atlantic seaports of Latin America. Havana was no exception, and it accepted thousands of Jews, Greek Orthodox, and Arabs.

Cuba had been one of the friendliest and most welcoming host countries for Jews in the Americas (Levine 1993, p. 7). Perhaps because Cuba had a small indigenous population, foreigners had always been prominent on the island. In 1900 fewer than 1000 non-Spanish Europeans lived in Cuba, but by 1917 there were 5619 (Levine 1993, p. 2). Jews were authorized to enter Cuba in large numbers for the first time in 1881, but they could not practice their faith openly until after the Spanish–American War. Moreover, some American Jews who fought in the war remained in Cuba as part of an expatriate community. They founded the first synagogue in 1906, the United Hebrew Congregation. Some Jewish peddlers – Ashkenazic and Sephardic – acquired enough capital to set up shops along Sol, Muralla, Bernaza and Teniente Rey Streets. Both East European and Sephardic Jews ghettoized themselves in these Habana Vieja neighborhoods at least until the Second World War, and they rarely interacted, except at the Jewish market (Levine 1993, pp. 293–94). Muralla and Sol Streets housed many Jewish retail activities during much of the twentieth century.

By 1900, Habana Vieja had developed a special residential flavor that went beyond the traditional breakdown of Spaniard, White Creole, Mulatto, and Black. Historically, Andalucians, Castillians, and Extremeños were the regional Spanish groups that predominated during the founding of Cuba. After the first century of conquest, they became a minor migration stream to Cuba. Instead, Galicians (*gallegos*), Asturians (*asturianos*), Basques (*vascos*) and Canary Islanders (*isleños*) prevailed, especially in the eighteenth and nineteenth centuries. Popularly, Cubans tended to simplify the various Spanish immigrant groups by referring to all of them as *gallegos*. Even though Europeans north of the Pyrenees who migrated to the island were not numerous, Cubans referred to all central Europeans and Jews as *polacos*, all Turks, Lebanese, and Syrians were called *turcos*, and all Asians were referred to as *chinos*. Americans were simply called *americanos*; *gringo* was not commonly used in Cuba (Johnson 1920).

The Havana of 1900 contained three distinct parts: 'Old' Havana (the old quarters behind the walls), 'New' Havana (parts of Centro Habana, Vedado and Cerro) and 'Suburban' Havana (new developments in points west and south). Old Havana consisted of tightly packed structures of adobe, mortar, rubble, stone and plaster construction. Streets remain narrow there as a carry over from the days of needing to defend against attackers, and to keep the streets cool by stretching awnings above them (Figure 1.10). Habana Vieja may not have looked much like Andalucía in Spain, but it was clearly the daughter of Sevilla, Málaga, Cádiz, and Córdoba. The effect was enhanced by the yellowish umber and related pastel shades adorning its walls.

The demarcation of an 'Old' from a 'New' Havana depended both on form and function. Older quarters held less desirable attributes: low-lying, prone to flooding, close to industrial zones, and overwhelmed by the stench of the bay. These less desirable neighborhoods include parts of Regla, Habana Vieja, Cerro, and Atarés. If social distinctions characterize the old from the new, so does the location of economic activity. The amount and location of commercial establishments before and after 1900 changed significantly (Llanes 1988). In about 1880, nearly two of three commercial establishments were located in the area that had previously

**Figure 1.10** Obispo Street with awnings (*toldos*) (c. 1906). Courtesy Library of Congress

been walled. Forty years later, nearly that same percentage of commercial establishments (70%) had shifted to areas beyond the walls (Aruca 1985, p. 26).

During the first decades of the twentieth century, Havana expanded more rapidly than at any time in its history (Santovenia and Shelton 1964) (Figure 1.11). Outside the old town lay 'New' Havana with regularly laid out and wider streets than its colonial predecessor. Designed for the automobile though still retaining Mediterranean Spanish style of light colored buildings (mostly khaki), New Havana (or Centro Habana) spreads westward (Figure 1.12). It begins along the Prado where fine mansions from the turn of the century still remain. When the city crept into this part a hundred years ago, it left behind the colonial administrative buildings and churches. In their place were built modest middle-income housing, schools, retailing and convent hospitals. New Havana moves along the Malecón up to the Vedado district. Its western boundary ends with the University of Havana on Aróstegui Hill. Built between 1908 and 1932, the university is flanked by the Quinta de los Molinos. Príncipe Castle and Atarés Castle mark respectively the western edge of New Havana and denote the historic limit of the city's archaic defense system.

Suburban Havana would become more American than Spanish, leaving behind an Old World architectural style (see Chapter 3). The wealthy

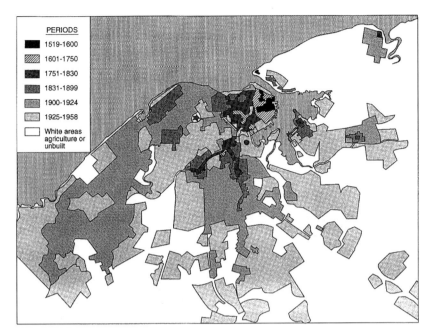

PERIODS
■ 1519-1600
▨ 1601-1750
▧ 1751-1830
▨ 1831-1899
▨ 1900-1924
▨ 1925-1958
□ White areas
agriculture or
unbuilt

**Figure 1.11** Territorial expansion of Havana: 1519–1958

**Figure 1.12** Looking westward across Centro Habana (foreground) which is mostly of uniform, nineteenth century construction and design. In the horizon lies 'New' Havana, with the Habana Libre Hotel (1958, left), Focsa apartment building (1957, middle), and Hotel Nacional (1930, twin towers at far right). Photograph by Roberto Segre

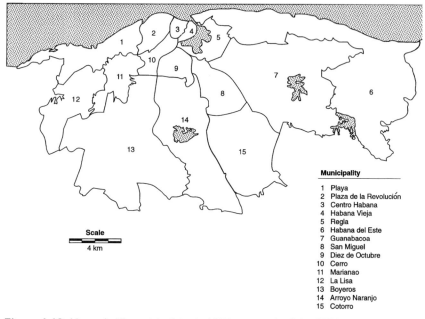

**Municipality**

1  Playa
2  Plaza de la Revolución
3  Centro Habana
4  Habana Vieja
5  Regla
6  Habana del Este
7  Guanabacoa
8  San Miguel
9  Diez de Octubre
10 Cerro
11 Marianao
12 La Lisa
13 Boyeros
14 Arroyo Naranjo
15 Cotorro

Scale
4 km

**Figure 1.13** Havana's 15 municipalities in 1997 as a result of the 1976 political administrative division

and the middle class would stake out neighborhoods in the west and the south, respectively. First Miramar and then Miramar in the west would house the twentieth century elite while the middle-income groups staked out Víbora, Luyanó, and Santos Suárez as their claim (Figure 1.13). As Chapters 2 and 3 will show, these areas were designed to accommodate automobile travel for the city's middle- and upper-income groups, who commuted from Miramar, Country Club, and Nuevo Vedado prior to the Revolution. The city's new suburban landscape would hold a few modern buildings that stand out like high-rise curios, but the overall effect of Havana's charm softens these iron and glass intrusions.

Twentieth century Havana would acquiesce to US economic powers. But not all of its planners and designers would hail from the north. The influence of Beaux Artes in the 1920s came with Forestier and the modern movement (1940s and 1950s) arrived in Cuba through Le Corbusier and the CIAM (*Congrés Internationale d'Architecture Moderne*) (Duverger 1994). Currents of avant garde surfaced among scores of Cuban architects and planners. Not all twentieth century public officials were corrupt, but the pre-Revolutionary city would dote on ceremonial projects at the expense of essential sites and services (Chapters 4–6 and 8). The USA would invest heavily in areas formerly coveted by the Spanish, and they would meddle often behind the scenes in political dealings. Both its economic prowess and political shenanigans would keep the Cuban people from attaining the sovereignty they had sought during the long wars of independence in the nineteenth century. The twentieth century would also be a time of preservation – a time of accommodating urban growth with the built environments of the past – not always by design, and more often by default.

# 2

## The first half century: the rise of an Antillean metropolis

Havana is a city of unfinished works, of the feeble, the asymmetrical, and the abandoned. Since the time we were kids, we've been coming across tenement houses daily where cans are piling up and the garbage is becoming increasingly worldly and more diverse.

Alejo Carpentier, 1939

### Postwar modernity in the colonial city

The US army that occupied Cuba in 1898 snatched victory from the Cuban patriots. Seen from a reconnaissance air balloon over the city (Figure 2.1), they found a dispersed city made up of a central core (Habana Vieja) surrounded by small, suburban and rural settlements. Havana was depressed and lackluster, vastly different from its heyday of the sugar booms before the colonial wars. As the century drew to a close, Havana was being pulled in two opposing directions. One was shaped by social and economic powers that wanted to make Havana a modern city. The other was an attempt to slow down the quest for political power that accompanies economic might. Spain had long been preoccupied with a useless and fratricidal Cuban war. It sought to preserve its last colony in the Americas, 'The Pearl of the Caribbean' (*La Perla del Caribe*), or at least cling to an antiquated vision of what they thought that might be.

Cuba's Independence Wars (1868–1878, 1879–1880, 1895–1898) had paralyzed virtually all building construction and destroyed an economy that had flourished since the end of the eighteenth century. Unlike other

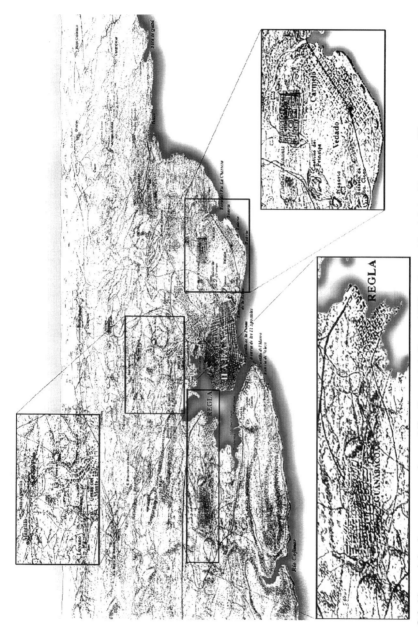

**Figure 2.1** Havana's landscape as seen from a US military air balloon, 1899, enhanced by Adobe Photoshop™

independence wars in the Americas, Cuban patriots were vastly outnumbered by Spanish troops. The 'enemy' had been equipped with the most modern means of communications, transportation and weapons. Adding to the regular forces, the paramilitary troops – Spanish volunteers and Cuban guerrillas – Spain unleashed some 600 000 soldiers against the Cuban troops (*mambises*) on an island with 1.5 million inhabitants. By comparison, Spain sent less than 100 000 soldiers and militiamen against the 14 Spanish colonies during the first part of the nineteenth century. General Simón Bolívar, moreover, warred with only 25 000 Spaniards. As well, the former 13 colonies of the United States fought against just 50 000 British soldiers.

These wars devastated Havana in several ways. Wealthy Creole landowners and Spanish merchants had tried to forge new construction on a monumental scale beyond the old walled city along Monserrate Street in the last half of the nineteenth century (Venegas Fornias 1990). Such projects included palatial residences, theaters and huge cigar factories that rivaled contemporary models found in mainland Latin America: Mexico, Lima and Buenos Aires. A few isolated new buildings, however, could not undo the precarious living conditions of the city's almost one-quarter million residents, most of whom were crowded within 10 square kilometers (Duverger 1993a). Squalor, unhealthy living conditions, and deficient roads and infrastructure characterized the setting of the masses (Le Riverend 1992).

Urban poverty was exacerbated by the settlement efforts of the Spanish Army. Under the charge of Captain General Valeriano Weyler, the Spanish tried to force the rebelling rural population into designated towns (a process that was known as *reconcentración*) and cities where they could be more easily contained. Nearly 100 000 persons were resettled in Havana where they lived in improvised shelters called *yaguas*. Clustered at the city edge, these shantytowns were ravaged by epidemics of typhus, dysentery, cholera and German measles (Poumier 1975). Rural uprooting and forced urban migration quite possibly marked the beginning of contemporary urban marginality in Latin America (Alvarez Estévez 1988).

The first measures taken by the US administration in Cuba between 1898 and 1902 were to establish basic infrastructure to ensure the growth of a modern city. The United States introduced at least five major public works projects. First, they completed a network of water mains throughout the city. Second, they expanded the networks of electric street lights, telephones and natural gas. Third, comprehensive systems of sewage and garbage collection were established. Fourth, extended street paving ended many pitted dirt roads and would later satisfy the demands of a small number of automobile owners. Fifth, the electric streetcar replaced the horse-drawn tram running through the new neighborhood of Vedado, and was gradually extended through the inner city and some suburbs (Bens Arrarte 1956). At the same time, there were advances in building materials. Tile, cement and architectural adornment factories were developed to accommodate the building frenzy during the early years of the Republic (De las Cuevas Toraya 1993). Havana, introverted and drawn towards the bay and *terra firma*, increased its potential to develop more of the ocean front through the extension of the Malecón. Curiously, though the seaside promenade has come to symbolize Havana, it was introduced fairly recently in the city's history.

Following the war, US business interests moved quickly to monopolize urban services. Cubans and Spaniards set aside the rancor of the bloody Independence Wars and delved into real-estate development and land speculation. More than a half-million immigrants arrived in Cuba during the first three decades of the twentieth century. Real-estate markets absorbed the growing numbers of new immigrants and their businesses. Almost one out of three (29.6%) of the 660 958 immigrants – mostly from Spain – settled in Havana. As a result, the city doubled in size by 1925 with a population of just over a half million (Roig de Leuchsenring 1952). Its land base increased to 116 square kilometers in 1923 from 95 square kilometers only 4 years earlier (Le Riverend 1992, p. 243). In the face of changing times, the confining colonial shell of the city was left behind.

### Havana expands its borders

The 1898 map of Havana (Martín and Rodríguez 1992, 1993) shows the compact yet successive rings of expansion by the nineteenth-century city. At the century's end, Havana's western edge reached Calzada de Infanta Street. New growth stretched between the bay to the east and the ocean shoreline to the north, forming a semi-regular grid plan of city blocks and streets. The traditional main arteries of the city – the *calzadas* – connected Havana to a broad hinterland to the south where new neighborhoods developed. The districts of Cerro, Jesús del Monte and Puentes Grandes were more loosely defined and dispersed than the confining colonial core. It was only a matter of time before outlying villages and towns would be drawn into Havana's metropolis: Guanabacoa, Regla and Casablanca to the east, Santiago de las Vegas and San Francisco de Paula in the south, and Marianao to the west (see Figure 2.1).

Urbanization to the east of the colonial core of Havana had long been impeded by the Havana Bay. Several proposals were put forth to link the eastern areas of Havana, including one to build a massive iron bridge across the bay (Valladares 1947). That plan was discarded in 1914 and road networks fanned out elsewhere, especially to the west and southeast. Their courses were determined by the preexisting transportation lines – the railroad and electric streetcar paths – and the location of social groups which were becoming increasingly segregated and stratified. Residential segregation was particularly acute along the sea breeze-filled oceanfront districts of Vedado, Miramar and Country Club. Here is where the wealthiest *habaneros* resided while the surrounding hills served as territory to the small bourgeoisie and a nascent proletariat.

Even though Havana's building codes and regulations were unevenly enforced, they helped to preserve a fairly homogeneous style of new construction during the first decades of the twentieth century. As noted in Chapter 1, the Building Codes of 1861 dictated the use of columnar *portales* in both central and residential areas. This ensured uniformity of construction well into the present century. Many master plans for the city were put forth, including those by Raúl Otero (1905), Camilo García de Castro (1916), Walfrido de Fuentes (1916) and Pedro Martínez Inclán (1919). However, these plans were rendered defenseless against crude land speculation by landowners who held on to large tracts of land, or sold them off in piecemeal fashion. Wealthy Cubans and Spaniards controlled the housing market through the sale of spacious suburban estates which, later, would be converted to compact *repartos* (subdivisions).

Not all landowners at the city's edge sold out immediately: Dionisio Velasco y Sarrá, owner of several kilometers of eastern shoreline property, waited until the 1950s for building new 'bedroom communities' (Análisis del Mercado de la Vivienda 1955; see Chapter 3). A good number of landowners, though, made a name for themselves through large-scale suburban expansion. These included the entrepreneur Zaldo y Salmón who promoted *Ensanche de la Habana* (the Almendares district, in 1914); José Manuel Cortina initiated recreational facilities at Playa de Marianao (Marianao Beach) in 1916; Antonio González de Mendoza and Pedro Pablo Kohly established Ampliación de Almendares (Almendares Heights) in Marianao; and lastly Enrique Conill reserved a strategic tract of land in the southwest which covered the area from Príncipe Castle at the edge of Vedado, to the mechanic shops of Ciénaga. Conill's holdings enabled him to get an edge on the ambitious residential project at Loma de los Catalanes where the Plaza de la Revolución is presently located.

### Housing styles and social diversity

Havana is one of the most architecturally diverse cities in Latin America. Its variations range from the housing stock of the wealthy to the many functions of its central districts. The first decades of this century witnessed distinct settlement patterns that would shape the evolution of Havana's neighborhoods. The upper bourgeoisie of Spanish origin would gradually abandon the pre-Baroque and Baroque colonial mansions in the compact core to take up residences at the summer homes of Cerro (Quintana 1974). Housing tastes and construction changed with this move to the suburbs. No longer would the Creole elite opt for the *casa–almacén* (warehouse–mansion) which consisted of a sugar, tobacco or coffee warehouse on the ground floor; a middle floor (entresol or mezzanine) held the offices or slave quarters, and the top floor was occupied by the master and his family. The layout centered on a large interior courtyard. In place of the *casa–almacén* stood lighter, modern housing with its characteristic colonnade: a gallery of Neoclassical columns surrounding the house. The architectural origin of this design can be traced to the *portales* found on mansions located in town squares or facing open spaces, typified by the monumental Aldama Palace. Another new feature of the nineteenth century home was a generous green space between the building and both the street and neighbors' houses. Architectural individuality nestled within a natural landscape marked the end of the Neoclassical Spanish style of a large home occupying an entire city block.

Spanish heritage also meant an aversion to waterfront construction, leaving an abundance of shoreline properties for future residential development. Such a disdain for waterfront properties, to paraphrase Juan Pérez de la Riva (1946, 1975), stemmed from Cuba being surrounded by 'enemy waters' on all sides throughout its history. The wealthy Creoles preferred placing their mansions in the district of Cerro. However, working-class intrusion diluted the social 'purity' of Cerro. Residents in clusters of working-class neighborhoods who worked in the nearby arsenal, factories, and the port also sought housing in Cerro. Another drawback of Cerro was that its undulating landscape produced an irregular pattern of streets and blocks. Many Cerro merchants and landowners who suffered economically during the Independence Wars were forced to sell their lands to offset losses. Parceling lands created small lots for non-elites, thereby interrupting Havana's urban and social geography.

Two large country farms in the western edge of the city were subdivided in 1859. These farms ran along the coast from the city's edge at Calzada de Infanta to the Almendares River (Roig de Leuchsenring 1963, 1964). Engineer Luis Iboleón Bosque surveyed these two farms – El Carmelo and Vedado – which were owned by Domingo Trigo, Juan Espino and the Count of Pozos Dulces (Izquierdo and Quevedo 1972; see also Figure 1.2). Approximately 400 city blocks comprised of 100 meter sides marked the first broad and systematic layout of Havana's grid pattern. Unlike the irregular colonial pattern, the residential streets of the western suburbs were 16 meters wide. Spacious tree-lined boulevards of Paseo, Línea, Calle 23, and Avenida de los Presidentes served as major thoroughfares through the new district (see Figures 1.2 and 1.3).

These new boulevards gave distinction to neighborhoods and were anchored by a public square. Zoning laws mandated 5-meter building set-backs (mostly for houses) from the street, creating a buffer of green space called the *carmen*. Buildings had to meet the 4-meter wide portal require-ment on the ground floor. The new grid pattern standardized lot sizes which, in turn, facilitated the orderly sale of suburban houses. Street-sign nomenclature consisting of letters and numbers reinforced this geometric pattern (Rama 1985) with its design elements borrowed from the sub-urban garden city style. Perhaps coincidentally, it wove green spaces into the city's traditional fabric as Ildefons Cerdá had proposed for Barcelona (Coyula 1991a). Through the balance of the nineteenth century, these lands were gradually settled and wooden gingerbread-style bungalows dotted the landscape. By 1894, only 30% of these lots had houses on them (González Manet 1976). Later, roughly from the time of the Republic (post-1902) until the 1930s, luxurious houses filled in the remainder of the neighborhood. Most of the residences were built by the *nouveau riche* during the prosperous 'fat-cow' (*vacas gordas*, or prosperous) years (1914–1920) when sugar prices soared.[1]

Great wealth in Cuba prompted a surprising outpouring of architec-tural styles by professionals such as Leonardo Morales, Raúl Otero, Eugenio Rayneri, and Govantes y Cabarrocas (Alvarez-Tabío 1989). Several con-tributing factors ushered in this flurry of design and construction. One was the return of Cuban capital that had been temporarily deposited in the United States for safe-keeping during the Independence Wars. Placed back into circulation on the island, this capital found its most profitable outlets in real estate and building construction. Another factor was that the US government required repayment on its war loan that was used to pay the salaries of Cuban officials, many of whom built spacious houses in Vedado (Ibarra 1985, 1992). Property was subdivided and sold by cash-strapped landowners. Rises in sugar prices on the world markets during the First World War also increased the circulation of hard currency on the island. These factors led to a building boom.

---

[1]During this time powerful entrepreneurs and socialites such as the Marquises de Avilés, Josefina García de Mesa, Ernesto Sarrá, Juan Gelats, José Ramón del Cueto, Catalina Lasa, Juan Pedro Baró, Condesa de Revilla-Camargo, and Pablo González de Mendoza built mag-nificent homes in what is today called Vedado (Martín and Rodríguez 1992).

Once Vedado filled up and the Almendares River was bridged at Quinta Avenida and Calle 23, the private automobile entered into wide use. Suburbanization spread to Marianao, particularly the district of Miramar. New construction in this corner of Havana become more segregated. It was influenced by design features from within and outside the island. City building codes were greatly relaxed. The Anglo-Saxon concept of the garden city exerted a strong appeal at this time. The city's fabric opened up and spread out to Country Club which resembled the winding layout of Riverside in suburban Chicago. These new places embraced the garden city ideas of Frederick Law Olmsted and his work in Illinois that allowed the affluent to live in neatly landscaped suburban enclaves. These became the defining features of Havana's wealthy outskirts.

Unlike its sister Caribbean cities of San Juan, Puerto Rico and Santo Domingo, Dominican Republic, Havana's urban growth in the early century did not relinquish its compact nature (Segre 1994a). Newcomers to Havana did not settle in unspoiled areas. Spanish immigrants, a new urban proletariat, and the lower-middle-class workers, for example, settled in the well-established Centro Habana, the Calzada de Monte, and Jesús María neighborhoods. Houses were modest in scope, typically two-story structures called 'twins' (*gemelas*). The house was set deep inside the block along a narrow gallery. It marked a stylistic transition from the colonial-style to the Republican home era. Long gone were the massive unadorned walls of the colonial core with its limited entrances and exits. In their place were windows and doors framed by highly decorative classical ornamentation that combined with the vibrant façades of houses. The fronts of these buildings blended together by means of the filigree ironworks covering doors and windows. This design spread to the neighborhoods of Santos Suárez, Luyanó and Víbora in a process that disrupted the look of residential structures from the compact block model of the traditional grid pattern, to the free-standing cottage-style home (Llanes 1985, 1988, 1993).

The first apartment buildings appeared in the center of the city as well by 1910. Interspersed within these new styles came tenement houses, slums, and shantytowns. According to Diego Tamayo in 1904, there were 2839 *solares* (older subdivided houses converted into tenements for the poor) that housed 86 000 people in a city of about a quarter-million inhabitants (Llanes 1978). *Solares* lacked the most elementary of conveniences and suffered greatly from overcrowding (Bay Sevilla 1924).

The government acted slowly and superficially when housing the urban poor. As the administration of President José Miguel Gómez set out to build workers' housing, it proved to be more of a publicity stunt than a real solution. For example, of the 2000 houses planned for Pogolotti neighborhood in Marianao, only 950 units were completed in 1913 after three years of construction. Each unit was to be a semidetached house (two homes per structure) with a wooden covered porch at the front. The final construction lacked storm sewers and used flimsy materials. Not surprisingly, the housing stock deteriorated quickly and Pogolotti soon turned into a slum, notorious for outbreaks of infectious diseases (De Armas 1975; De Armas and Robert 1975).

## Symbols and allegories of political and economic power

The new Republic displayed its prowess and made its presence felt through the functions it executed. The two decades spanning the administrations of Presidents Tomás Estrada Palma (1902–1906) and Mario G. Menocal (1913–1921) defined the location of government offices of the young Republic. Other prominent forces were vying for strategic locations to represent their constituents. These included new economic actors: banks, insurance companies, and firms in the hands of United States, Spanish and Cuban investors. Old peninsular elites held on to the more traditional cultural symbols of power but only temporarily. Early Republican governments set up their offices at the Captain-General's Palace on the Plaza de la Catedral, but later abandoned the site because the quarters became cramped. Beyond the old 'ring' of Habana Vieja, the administrations of the new Republic diffused national icons through the construction of prominent landmarks: the Fire Station (*Cuartel de los Bomberos*, 1910), the Presidential Palace (*Palacio Presidencial*, 1919), the National Capitol (*Capitolio*, 1929), and the High School (*Instituto de Segunda Enseñanza*, 1929). 'Functional' buildings built by US engineers included the Central Train Station (*Estación Central de Ferrocarriles*) in 1912 and the Customs House (*Aduanas*) in 1914, bringing closure to the distinctive ring of buildings around Habana Vieja that is visible today.

Early this century, the compact layout of the narrow colonial streets and the old-fashioned and quiet interior courtyards of the Habana Vieja houses were slowly replaced by modern buildings that rose above the prevailing building heights of just a few stories (Anónimo 1919). Within just 20 years, high-rise government office buildings, warehouses, shops, and even a stock-market building called the Lonja de Comercio (1910) broke through the sleepy landscape of the historic core (Rallo and Segre 1978). The automobile was especially unkind to the city's old quarters. The atmosphere was described this way:

> Traffic is bedlam . . . and overflows and crashes against the walls and

smashes into doors and bludgeons the street corners. It is invasive and noisy like a fat and disgusting river spilling over its banks and sweeping every-thing away . . . it feels like we are entering a savage beehive (Mediz Bolio 1916, p. 42; our translation).

Since the end of the nineteenth century, the social life of the Creole elite tended to concentrate on an axis defined by the Campo Marte (to the west of the 'old city') where the Prado (originally known as Isabel II) meet and the Aldama Palace was built. The nation's main theaters (Nacional, Payret, Irijoa, Politeama, Alhambra) and the nation's first tourist hotels (Inglaterra, Plaza, Telégrafo, Sevilla Biltmore) were located in this area. With the advent of the Republic, the axis acquired a key spatial dimension for socializing: Parque Central (Central Park) held the new monumental buildings tied to the competition between the state, private initiatives and Spanish communities. In this setting emerged the Manzana de Gómez (1894–1917), the first shopping arcade of European style with offices on the upper floors. Of course, the politicians and the Spanish community could not miss out on this social setting. Along the Prado, like in Vedado, majestic mansions were built including the homes of the US Consul Frank Steinhart (1908) and President José Miguel Gómez (1915) (Alvarez-Tabío 1989).

Despite the disappearance of colonial power, the *peninsulares* (Spaniards born in Spain) held on to significant economic power until the crisis of 1920, which definitively sealed the hegemony of US capital (Ibarra 1992). Havana's urban scale revealed itself at two territorial dimensions: the center and periphery. Areas adjacent to Parque Central held cultural and recreational centers of regional Spanish groups. Not to be outdone by the classic monuments of government, these Spanish ethnic groups erected the *Centro de Dependientes* (1907; Figure 2.2), *Centro Gallego* (Galician Center) (1909), *Casino Español* (Spanish Country Club) (1914), and the *Centro Asturiano* (Asturian Center) (1924). Buildings with neo-Baroque interior spaces of uncommon dimensions gave definition to a public life dominated by rituals handed down from the ostentatious practices of the motherland. Hospitals and medical clinics of mutual-aid societies prolonged the Neoclassical repertoire of buildings with colonnades. Spaniards from different regions formed mutual-aid clinics such as Benéfica, Covadonga, Dependientes, and Purísima Concepción (Presno 1952). They took up residence on the edge of Havana on what were once neighboring farms that were let go by the local aristocracy during the Independence Wars.

If Havana's primary commercial center functioned in neighborhoods adjacent to the colonial town squares, then its second one was close by. Large tobacco factories such as La Meridiana (1880), Barces y López

**Figure 2.2** Centro de Dependientes (c. 1910) at Prado and Trocadero Streets. Built in 1907, the large (3871 square meters) social club contained a gym, library, billiard hall, as well as drawing, music and dance schools. It could accommodate 5000 couples and was typical of the grandiose social clubs built during the early years of the Republic.
Courtesy of the University of Havana, Department of the History of Art

(1886), José Gener (1882), and Calixto López appeared on the outskirts of the original colonial ring. Tobacco factories employed thousands of manual laborers from adjacent neighborhoods just beyond the confines of the old city walls. This light industry peaked during the first decade of the century, and reaffirmed its prominence by occupying such a central place.

**Figure 2.3** Tobacco factories from the nineteenth century still operating today, behind the Capitolio building. Photograph by Roberto Segre

Behind the Capitolio building there existed from the nineteenth century the Partagás Tobacco Factory, and in front of the Presidential Palace (*Palacio Presidencial*) just off Prado avenue was La Corona (built by the American Tobacco Company, in 1902) (see Figure 2.3; Venegas Fornias 1989).

Palatial residences representing Cuba's bourgeois power located so close to these factories that it made Havana unique in Latin American urban planning and design circles (Bühler–Oppenheim 1949). However, the symbolic axis of Republican power was interrupted by working-class neighborhoods in Habana Vieja and Centro Habana. By the turn of the century, it was too late to use radical slum eradication measures as were taken in Paris a half century before. Those plans would have expelled the poor from these areas as was done by Haussmann in Paris. They would have also wiped out the 'gray' spaces of the 'non-existent' city and convert them, as was done in Paris, to income-stratified neighborhoods (Aymonino 1965). It became indispensable for wealthy *habaneros*, on the one hand, to seek refuge in the exclusive suburbs and, on the other hand, to grant the poor proximity to key landmarks in the city center.

### The mirror of progress in the Caribbean's Nice: Havana, 1920–1935

The economic crisis of the late 1920s paralyzed building construction in Havana. Sugar fell from 20 cents to 3 cents a pound (Le Riverend 1960, 1965). This downfall introduced the 'lean cow' (*vacas flacas*) days of Cuba's economic history. While the recession forced many Spanish and Cuban firms into bankruptcy, it marked a decided upturn for US businesses. From 1925 until the world stock-market crash of 1929, US businesses invested $1.5 billion in Cuba, equaling just over one-quarter of all investment in Latin America during that period (Acosta and Hardoy 1971). This was the era when the great 'sugar barons' emerged in the eastern provinces of the island. Foreigners controlled 78% of the island's arable land, and the United States consumed 50% of Cuban sugar (Le Riverend 1966). It was in this setting that the 1925 unveiling of the monument honoring the sunken SS Maine took on symbolic meaning. The SS Maine mysteriously exploded in Havana Bay in 1898 and helped the United States justify its 'intervention' in the final days of the Cuban independence war against Spain. The dictator Gerardo Machado, closely tied to foreign economic interests, also took power in 1925.

Until Machado's overthrow in 1933, and with the enthusiastic help of the Minister of Public Works, Carlos Miguel de Céspedes (known as the Tropical Haussmann), the Cuban government invested its own money, as well as loans drawn on US banks, to modernize Havana. In doing so, Cuba's economy became even more closely tied to the United States than in the past, as did a growing number of Latin American countries at that time. Cuba's unique Latin American role, however, was consecrated with the holding of the Sixth Pan-American Conference in Havana in 1928. President Calvin Coolidge's attendance at the conference highlighted the significance the meeting held for both US foreign policy and business interests. At that time Havana possessed half a million residents, covered

102 square kilometers, received 70% of Cuba's imported items, and welcomed 250 000 tourists per year (Soto 1977). This is why Pedro Martínez Inclán sought to make Havana the 'Nice of America', even if it meant first becoming the 'perverse Pompeii of the Caribbean'.

In the *années folles* of more prosperous and earlier decades, the city center offered many first-rate hotels: the Plaza (1908), Sevilla Biltmore (1908–1923), Saratoga, Lincoln, Central, and Isla de Cuba, as well as the older 'classic' hotels (Inglaterra, Plaza, and Pasaje). In the 1920s, though, more luxurious and sophisticated ones were being built in Vedado. These included three landmark properties: (i) the Hotel Nacional (built by McKim, Mead and White in 1930) located on the Malecón, which would stand as the insignia hotel of Havana; (ii) the Palace (1928); and (iii) Presidente (1927); the latter two situated on the gardened Avenida de los Presidentes.

Havana in the 1920s was rife with contradiction. Part of its street plan was fragmented and disorderly. Its building stock consisted of deteriorating colonial structures and a precarious infrastructure as well as a new wealthy class (in Vedado and Miramar), a petite bourgeoisie (Víbora and Lawton) and a proletariat (Jesús María and Cayo Hueso). Solid masonry houses contrasted with light wooden structures in different neighborhoods. Few wooden structures withstood the terrible hurricane of 1926. Yet this was an image of Havana far removed from the ostentatious Caribbean capital envisioned by Céspedes and Machado.

Some of the main problems identified by urban planners were the lack of green areas and a poor road network incapable of handling the increasing automobile traffic. At least since the late nineteenth century an idea circulated that would make Serrano Avenue a limited-access road to link the Captain General's Palace at the Plaza de la Catedral with the periphery (Roig de Leuchsenring 1952, 1963, 1964). Walfrido de Fuentes (1916) also argued for the widening of some main streets in Habana Vieja – Cuba and Lamparilla – to relieve vehicular congestion. In the 1920s the engineer Amado Montenegro revived the idea of 'The Great Havana Road' (*La Gran vía de La Habana*) in expectation of the imminent population increase. Finally, Martínez Inclán, in his book, *La Habana Actual* (1925), envisioned a network of 26 avenues to resolve the city's transportation problems.

The problems of the city's center were foremost in the urban planning debates of the day. Even though Martínez Inclán supported strengthening the complex of monuments around *Parque Central*, it became clear that government buildings needed to be relocated in the suburbs. In so doing, it would provide an impetus for subsequent urbanization. Deliberating on land use and determining the location of new public buildings were internal affairs; only a small cadre of politicians and professionals debated the advantages and disadvantages of different sites and designs. The Cuban people, of course, had little say in the matter.

In 1923, a group of engineers (Raúl Otero, Camilo García de Castro, Enrique J. Montoulieu, and Martínez Inclán) concluded that properties around Loma de los Catalanes (Catalans' Hill), which belonged to Enrique Conill, would be designated for a government buildings complex. By late 1925, the Chief of Parks and Streets of Paris, J.C.N. Forestier, had arrived in Havana to assess the site development. His entourage included a team of French designers (Beaudoin, Labatut, Leveau, Hietzler, Sorugue) who were contracted by the Cuban Minister of Public Works to draft the city's master plan (Segre 1992b). Forestier, who had visited Buenos Aires only a few years before to consult on green spaces (Novick 1991), was already well known in Cuba. Both the government and Cuban elite had made the acquaintance of Forestier in 1918 when President Mario G. Menocal appointed him to design the park around La Punta fort at the northern edge of the old city. Wealthy landowner Enrique Conill – who sponsored Forestier's visit to the island – had also introduced him to his circle of friends and business associates. Beginning in 1925, Forestier and his associates worked with a group of architects for the next 5 years. Their objective was to link metropolitan Havana's dispersed places into a harmonious land-use plan. Although Forestier's team of Cuban architects Raúl Otero, Emilio Vasconcelos, and J.I. del Alamo were not completely successful in reaching their goals, their master plan helped to define the unique classical and tropical beauty of Havana.

One aspect that set Forestier apart from the practice of urban planning was that he belonged to the Parisian school of civic art headed by the core of designers Marcel Poéte, Henri Prost and Eugéne Hénad. Theirs was not necessarily a rigid academic approach to urban design that entailed merely applying preconceived schema. Rather, it embraced some of Haussmann's ideas about the importance of road networks. This meant connecting the Ship Terminal, the Central Train Station, the Plaza Cívica and the Hotel Nacional by a network of diagonal streets and round points. This road plan emphasized functional needs (integrating the city's road system) and symbolic iconography (accentuating prominent landmarks). To carry out this plan, Forestier and the Minister of Public Works flew over the city in a small aircraft, just as Le Corbusier had done. This air reconnaissance confirmed the thesis posited by the Cuban team: the new monumental center – Plaza Cívica – should be located at the Loma de los Catalanes, because it lay mid-way between the old and new middle-class neighborhoods (Figure 2.4).

The new master plan executed by the binational team emphasized Havana's natural setting. It incorporated the rolling topography, the lush

**Figure 2.4** Present-day Plaza de la Revolución looking south-southeast on Avenida Paseo. Parades and key public ceremonies are held in this area. It is anchored by the obelisk José Martí Monument (center), and flanked by government ministries and other public buildings. The Ministry of the Armed Forces Building (MINFAR) is visible to the left (east). Photograph by Joseph L. Scarpaci

tropical vegetation and the enduring presence of the ocean. The French master perceived both the present and future dimensions of the city in his beltways, traffic circles and spoke-like road networks. He even sensed that Havana Bay would only temporarily impede the city's spread eastward. Perhaps due to his European training, Forestier was unwilling to give attention to the automobile if it meant sacrificing tree-lined pedestrian spaces. Instead, he accentuated the roles of royal-palm lined avenues and pedestrian malls to protect *habaneros* from the scorching tropical sun. Promenades adorned with flower beds and thick shade trees were used wherever possible. The Prado best illustrated these landscape architecture principles. Forestier, however, did not have a crystal ball. Just as he could not anticipate the role of the automobile, neither could he foresee the role of the bus or truck, the introductions of which were encouraged by US sugar interests. Thus, he gave considerable importance to the railroad station at the expense of these newer modes of transportation. President Machado's approval of the Central Highway (*Carretera Central*) to link provincial capitals was as much to satisfy US commerce in Cuba as it was for national businesses. In the end, Forestier's plans were cut short by the depression of 1929 and the popular uprising of 1933 that toppled Machado, followed by the 1935 popular movement led by Sergeant Fulgencio Batista (who would return as self-appointed President in the 1950s). Graft and strong-arm tactics ultimately pushed through the central highway project, with little concern about the costs or consequences for the Cuban people (Bens Arrarte 1931). Despite all of this, Forestier's work in landscape architecture left an indelible mark on the city.

## Tropical landscapes and classical monuments

Havana's image can be characterized by four successive architectural languages whose synthesis contributes to the city's personality. They include: (i) popular architecture; (ii) early Baroque styles in the colonial monuments of Habana Vieja; (iii) academic codes of design imposed during the first three decades of this century; and (iv) the International Style built in the new central areas (La Rampa in Vedado) and the suburban neighborhoods. Nevertheless, the greatest visual presence in Havana is the widespread classical structures used as much by modest and anonymous builders as by name designers on some of the city's landmarks. Alejo Carpentier devised a separate classification system, and enlisted what he called, a 'Third Style': that which has no style. This 'Third Style' is 'the process of symbiosis, of amalgams, of transmutations, both in the architectural and the human' (Carpentier 1974b, p. 12). We must add to that the ecological conscience of Forestier and his associates who were determined to strike a balance between nature and the built form. In the 1930s, these designs would become the capital's defining features (Duverger 1994).

In the first two decades of the twentieth century, Havana strengthened its Caribbean character by the compactness of its center, evidenced by the relationship between the building grid and the light building façades. Towards the end of the 1930s, the classical designs had become 'tropicalized' by the colonnade passages along the streets and avenues of Havana. The social life of the bustling city enlivened as neighborhoods became racially and socioeconomically integrated except, of course, in the elite quarters. Recognizable design features made their mark, including the gable, spire, entablature, talamon, and caryatid. Even today these elements are visible along the central streets of San Lázaro, Galiano, Belascoaín, Reina and Infanta. They even surfaced in what was then the remote settlements along the *calzadas* of Monte, Cerro, Diez de Octubre, Puentes Grandes, Luyanó and Güines (Fernández 1990; Cárdenas 1991; Llanes 1993; Martín and Rodríguez 1993). The *portales* that first appeared in the nineteenth century became an integral part of the city. Even today, city dwellers circulate under the shade of the *portales* and street vendors huddle there to sell their wares. The latter foreshadowed the rise of the 'informal' economy that would spawn in these same places (Chailloux 1945). Adjacent to these shaded corridors were the retail stores and the corner grocery stores (*bodegas*) frequented by mixed social classes.

The French landscape architect understood well the different social spaces of the city and the ways in which Habana Vieja and the rest of the city contrasted. If the small scale of the colonial core represented an introverted segment cut off from the rest of Havana – the solitude and silence imposed by the walls – then the expanding metropolis required broad new perspectives (Kavafis 1978). Forestier was sensitive to the meaning of open spaces as a means of framing the city's monuments and also as a stage for the casual stroller who could ponder the aesthetic beauty created by the tropical landscape (Labatut 1957; Benjamin 1962). The interaction between classical beauty and the encompassing natural landscape constituted one of the essential premises in redesigning the social areas in the city center (Forestier 1928). Landmarks, argued Forestier and his disciples, were not to be autonomous and isolated objects but rather should interact with spaces near and far. This premise is verified in Havana with the concentration of six essential focal points built in the late 1930s.

1. Parque de la Fraternidad, a rhythmic expansion of the Ionic order of the Capitolio building.
2. Avenida de las Palmas (or Avenida de las Misiones), which frames the Presidential Palace.
3. La Avenida de la Universidad, which was supposed to be a nexus between the Plaza Cívica and Colina, but which was never executed. Such a union would have been important because the university's design atop a hill parallels the Acropolis in Athens as a temple of knowledge, although filtered through the model of Valhalla by Von Klenze (Gelabert-Navia 1994).
4. The gardens surrounding Príncipe Castle which are terraced from the tops of the hills down to Carlos III street.
5. The Maine Monument, whose property extends the gardens of the Hotel Nacional down towards the Malecón (Otero 1940).
6. The Prado, the city's 'living room' with its green 'roof' creating a serene space for the casual stroller who can appreciate such symbolic historical structures as the dome on the Capitolio and the composed and colossal Morro Castle (Cabrera Infante 1992).

The streets and avenues configure the fabric of the city's central districts and blend its identity into a collective unit. Forestier's work defined the city's edge that separated architecture from nature. The first element valued in diverting the two was the waterfront and the creation of an exterior 'side' of the city that would renew Havana's long-standing look within, away from the ocean. This meant allowing a sizable setback of buildings away from the water. Beginning with the port – the 'reception hall' for tourists arriving by ship – this waterfront edge of the city winded along the Malecón. From there it passed successive parks and monuments. Several kilometers west of the port, the water edge meets the Avenida de los Presidentes and Avenida Paseo in the Vedado. Forestier envisioned the city's 'water edge' to continue westward until the beaches of Marianao, and the Malecón would serve as the city's seaside thoroughfare.

Having just returned from Buenos Aires, Forestier envisioned the Malecón as the same grand boulevard that he built in the Argentine capital in 1924, the Costanera. The Costanera is a wide shore-walk avenue running along the River Plate extending from downtown Buenos Aires to the northern suburbs of Palermo. It is adorned with gardens, parks and tree-lined promenades in the classic landscape design so typical of Forestier. However, crude land speculation and environmental disregard made the extension of the Malecón beyond the Vedado impossible. The Almendares River, separating Miramar from Vedado, marked an edge to the city and forced urbanization to points south. As we discuss in Chapter 3, the festive beer gardens of the two large breweries along the banks of the Almendares served as the city's 'green lungs'. By the 1950s, twentieth century urbanization, partly shaped by the French master's work decades before, had left an indelible stamp on Havana (Figure 2.5).

Forestier's plan faithfully followed the attributes of the Beaux Arts styles. It also shared in less pronounced ways the features of the Garden City, the English and German hygienists, the US City Beautiful movement, and the functionalist theories of Le Corbusier. His plan was perhaps the last attempt to safeguard the 'human' dimension of Havana and achieve an equilibrium among practical needs, private initiative, and state control, while maintaining continuity and coherence in the built environment. Even though only isolated remnants of Forestier's designs survived, they helped Havana to come of age and assume the expressive codes of modernity (Segre 1994c, d).

While the designs of Forestier did much to beautify the city, there were still plenty of neglected pockets. State policies directed mostly to the wealthy did little to alleviate the precarious living conditions of the poor, most of whom were devastated by the 1926 hurricane. A succession of misfortunes aggravated the welfare of Havana's poor in rapid succession: the 1929 stock-market crash, the ensuing Great Depression, and the decline of sugar exports to the United States. US exports dropped from 50% of the

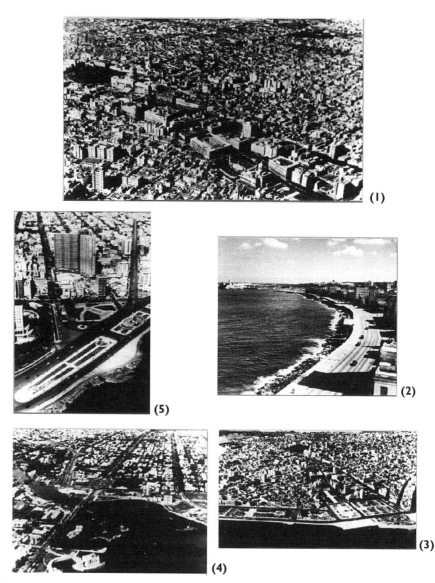

**Figure 2.5** Five aerial views of Havana (c. 1950). Clockwise from top: (1) The 'ring' of Havana between Habana Vieja and Centro Habana seen from the north-northeast looking south-southeast; (2) the Malecón in Centro Habana seen from the west looking east; (3) aerial view of the 'ring' of Havana from the entrance to the bay, seen from the northeast looking southwest; (4) mouth of the Almendares River between Vedado and Miramar, before the tunnel connected Línea Street with Fifth Avenue (*Quinta Avenida*) in Vedado and Miramar, respectively. Note the presence of the old bridge, with still-standing 'Iron Bridge' (Puente de Hierro) upstream (south, at left of bridge); and (5) view of the Malecón in Vedado looking southwest with Focsa building upper center, Maine Monument on Malecón, middle right, and part of Hotel Nacional visible, middle left

island's production in 1925 to 28.6% in 1932 (Le Riverend 1966). Both urban unemployment and migration to Havana shot up in response to the global crisis. The latter led to a dramatic increase in squatter settlements on the outskirts of Havana.

In light of this crisis, all the government did was extol a single, public funded, proletariat housing project. The project, Lutgardita, was constructed in the midst of light industries such as paint, tannery, and oil factories. Although this working-class housing project designed by Evelio Govantes and Félix Cabarrocas was only half-heartedly received by the dictator Machado in 1929, it marked one of the first experiments of its kind in Latin America (Fernández 1987). The workers' housing complex was situated near Rancho Boyeros Avenue on the road to the airport and consisted of 100 free-standing residences. The units were comparable to the models proposed by the European and Latin American 'Commissions of Low-cost Housing' and were well endowed with sites and services. Lutgardita, built in 1929, clustered at the city's southern edge, included a school, kindergarten, hospital, theater, and shops. Its Spanish colonial architectural style conferred a romantic populist image that suggested balance and social well-being, aspects far from the reality of the urban poor (Segre 1994a).

## Breaking up the urban image: 1935–1950

*The expansion of the periphery*

Until the 1930s, the state's role in urban planning concentrated on building classical monuments and landmarks. Government authorities had uncritically adopted a model of urban planning which was based on defining and constructing a hierarchy of monuments that symbolized middle-class power. These attributes molded Havana's image as a cosmopolitan city ready to be launched into modernity. More important, such symbolism covered up the very real and precarious conditions of its past. Neither the millions of dollars of loans from US banks nor the radiant shine of its granite and marble buildings could hide the age of Havana's old plastered walls. The growth of the urban poor, moreover, increasingly encroached upon Havana's exclusive suburban neighborhoods. With the overthrow of Machado in 1933 and the ensuing political crisis that lasted until the 1940s, so too ended the good old days of Cuba's *belle époque*.

This convulsive political and economic situation would limit Havana's growth until 1940 when the Second World War produced a windfall of profits for Cuban sugar. Two presidential administrations benefited from strong sugar prices: Fulgencio Batista (1940–1944) and Ramón Grau San Martín (1944–1948). President Grau San Martín established the Sugar Differential, a tax added to sugar sales to help finance public-works projects. US interests invested heavily in light industry at a time when most of Latin America was experimenting with import-substitution industrialization. In Cuba, light industry was located on the outskirts of Havana. Sugar-derived prosperity and burgeoning new industries demanded an increase of labor in Havana. The need for labor, moreover, made suburban areas grow faster than the central city. While Havana's population grew 45% from 837 670 inhabitants in 1943 to 1 216 762 ten years later (Pérez de la Riva 1965), the core urban counties within the city (*municipios*) increased by only 17% during the same period, from 676 376 to 787 765 (Roig de Leuchsenring 1963/1964).

Forestier's plan had enhanced internal road traffic among the city's residential districts and also improved local and regional tourist routes. The central highway facilitated the spread of the metropolitan area towards the southeast and the suburban neighborhoods of Diezmero, San Francisco de Paula, Cotorro, and San José de las Lajas. The highway also promoted westward expansion through Marianao, La Lisa, Arroyo Arenas, Punta Brava, and Bauta. These westward and southeastern throughways served as sites for new industries and working-class residences. The new airport to the south of Havana and the extension of Rancho Boyeros Avenue brought the development of small factories throughout Calabazar, El Cano and Santiago de las Vegas (Le Riverend 1992). Besides these radial axes, peripheral beltways to get around the city also became necessary. Avenida del Puerto facilitated the shipping of imported goods towards Vía Blanca and the Central Highway with further connections to Rancho Boyeros through Santa Catalina, Lacret and Avenida de Acosta.

Emphasis on transportation networks also had an international counterpart during this time. Cuba participated in the Pan-American Highway projects by running a ferry service from Florida and the Yucatan. The Habana–Pinar del Río Highway marked Cuba's contribution to the Atlantic–Caribbean branch of the Pan-American Highway.

Within this flurry of road building and economic activity, local professionals returned to plans of action focusing on fragmented and isolated patches of the city. José Luis Sert's whirlwind tour through Havana en route to the United States in 1939 served as a rallying point for vanguard architecture and debates in urban planning. The 1940 Constitution came in the first year of the elected Batista government and included articles concerning urban and regional planning, industrial zones and low-cost public and private housing. In 1942, Pedro Martínez Inclán headed up an academic and policy forum concerned about urban affairs and planning (*Patronato Pro-Urbanismo*). As a precursor to a national commission on similar issues, the forum's impetus came from the works of such luminaries as the Frenchman Gastón Bardet, who lectured throughout Latin

America and the Austrian Karl Brunner, who resided for a long time in Chile and Colombia, respectively (Violich 1987; Eliash and Moreno 1989). On the heels of these initiatives, the Ministry of Public Works created a number of work groups in 1943. Their task was to modernize the obsolete urban laws and define the limits of the growth of the city. Proposing urban dispersion and establishing satellite cities in metropolitan Havana received support from the Anglo-Saxon notions of the garden city (Bens Arrarte 1959, 1960a–c). Finally, Pedro Martínez Inclán introduced for the first time his 'Havana Charter' (*Carta de La Habana*) at the 1948 First National Architecture Conference. Martínez Inclán's plan was a direct transposition of the 'Athens Charter',[2] but his version included the peculiarities of the Caribbean city which had previously been ignored (Rossi 1966).

Ramón Grau San Martín's government (1944–1948) carried out the largest urban plan by the state in the first half of the century (San Martín 1947). For the first time ever, urban and regional planning authorities designed a pragmatic master plan for Havana and the provincial capitals of Pinar del Río, Matanzas, Cienfuegos, and Santiago de Cuba. After long and heated debate, the academic project of Forestier was finally put to rest. In its place, rose the executors of the new master plan: the architects José R. San Martín, Minister of Public Works, and Luis Dauval Guerra, General Director of Architecture. Drawing on Franklin Delano Roosevelt's New Deal, their efforts absorbed idle rural laborers who were unemployed in dead time (*el tiempo muerto*, that period between planting sugar cane and harvest). Despite the habitual detouring of funds and the deals struck by politicians in office, the public works projects that materialized did modernize the city, especially at the outskirts. Other key works entailed modernizing the port facilities, upgrading the water and sewage systems, building new roads, creating parks and gardens, and building houses, schools and hospitals. Bens Arrarte (1956) estimated that city public-works projects averaged $80 million annually during the government of Grau San Martín.

This first wave of modernizing Havana left the major features of the city undisturbed. In fact, expansion at the city's edge merely continued some of the city's defining traits. This is evident in the types of housing and public buildings designed by the state architectural offices. The use of such styles as Monumental-modern, Spanish Colonial, Proto-rationalist and Art Deco merely echoed in the suburbs many of the designs of the city

---

[2]The Athens Charter was a seminal document resulting from the 4th International Congress of Modern Architecture (CIAM in French) held in 1933 on a boat that traveled from Marseilles to Athens. It was dedicated to town planning and included the experiences of 33 cities. Standards identified in its pages became the driving force behind the modern movement, up to the 1960s.

center (Rossi 1966). The proliferation of apartment buildings was not associated with the huge isolated complexes of the CIAM (*Congrés International d'Architecture Moderne*). Instead, Havana's flurry of construction conserved the homogeneous layout of city blocks, limited building heights to four stories, and continued the *portales* along the city's main thoroughfares. The traditional Spanish interior courtyard (patio) reappears in the form of the *cortijo* model, evident throughout the Caribbean by means of the Spanish colonial style used widely in California and Florida. The small single-family houses in the suburban neighborhoods, with their flat Mediterranean-style roofs, front porches and simple Art-Deco decorative details, have little in common with the central-city landmarks.

## The brevity of the welfare state

The government began addressing the lack of basic social services in squatter settlements without neglecting ongoing projects of a 'loftier' nature. Projects concerned with defining central Havana continued, including works tied to the Plaza Cívica, and the Pro-José Martí Central Commission initiated at an inter-American design competition. Despite difficulty in finding support for the project, the architect Aquiles Maza and the sculptor Juan José Sicre won the design competition in 1942 (Pereira 1985). In 1953, a year after he led the military *coup d'etat*, Fulgencio Batista started building the monument, but replaced the first-prize winner's design with that of the second place finalists: Jean Labatut, Raúl Otero, and Enrique Luis Varela (Noceda 1984).

Identifying the backgrounds of the social and political groups that define the landmarks of Havana reflects broader structural profiles of Cuba. When Machado fell in 1933, the generation of soldiers headed by Sergeant Batista, himself from a modest background, managed things from behind the scenes. These officers had little interest in a national monument, which was, from its inception, a project supported and valued by Havana's core elite. Rather, from that moment of support for a new multifunctional core, the army focused on the Columbia military base in Marianao. Several housing projects and public monuments to be built at the periphery of this military stronghold supported this new multifunctional core: Plaza Finlay (1944), the Military Hospital (1940), and the maternity hospital *Maternidad Obrera* (1939). These works expressed notions of a peripheral centrality compared to the standing built hegemonic structures. Future master plans would neglect this kind of peripheral centrality.

Cuba pulled out of the depression of the 1930s thanks to a rise in sugar prices which in turn steered private construction into a strong phase. In 1939, investment in private housing stood at $9 million but by 1946 had risen to $36 million (De Armas and Robert 1975). A rent-control law was passed in 1939. It favored landlords and addressed the demand for more housing brought on by migration into Havana. These new communities required hospitals and schools. Even today, most of the schools and hospitals in the city date back to the 1940s. Other larger projects of the late 1930s and 1940s included the children's anti-tuberculosis sanitarium, *La Esperanza*, *La Benéfica* clinic, *Las Ánimas* hospital, and the high schools *Institutos de Segunda Enseñanza* which were located in Víbora, Marianao and Vedado (Weiss 1947, 1966, 1973). A zoo was also built in Nuevo Vedado. Architectural styles of the day were influenced by prominent foreign styles: the functionalism of New Deal public buildings from the United States coupled with Rationalism and Art Deco from Europe.

Although Havana experienced a spate of public construction, it did little to enhance the condition of housing among the neediest *habaneros*. The quality and quantity of low-income housing progressively worsened as shown by the proliferation of tenement houses (*casas de vecindad, solares*, and *ciudadelas*).[3] Infamous squatter settlements of the era were Las Yaguas, La Timba, Cueva del Humo, and La Tambora, among others. Unevenly dispersed throughout the city, this destitute population – the majority of them Black or mulatto – reached upwards of 300 000 *habaneros*, or about one-third of the city's residents.

The first appearance of a popular housing complex, built according to the features of European Rationalism, emerged. However, as with two previous state-funded demonstration projects – Pogolotti (1910–1913) and Lutgardita (1929) – it was a token showing of public welfare. In 1944, the government of Grau San Martín developed the *Barrio Residencial Obrero de Luyanó* (Luyanó Workers' Residential Neighborhood) pilot project in Reparto Aranguren. Using lands just south of the bay that were sandwiched in between industrial complexes, architects Pedro Martínez Inclán, Mario Romañach and Antonio Quintana worked on the project which originally entailed 1500 houses, eight four-story apartment complexes and sites and services that included a market, school, sports field, and senior-citizen center. This was a significant project because the architects involved were pioneers in the Cuban Modern Movement. Generous

---

[3]Of the many variables that go into classifying the collective housing for the poor in Cuba, the number of rooms per structure is perhaps the least controversial. A *casa de vecindad* consists of homes or buildings with 12 rooms; the *solar* held about 20–30 rooms, and *ciudadelas* more than 100. Precarious housing is discussed in more detail in the next chapter.

amounts of green spaces were interspersed throughout the complex. At the 1947 official inauguration of the complex, however, only 177 houses and some of the sites and services had been completed (López 1987). *Barrio Residencial Obrero de Luyanó* represented the only example of working-class housing built during the first half of the century under Republican governments, and it was designed according to the canonical principles of the Modern Movement.

## The sad joys of tourism in Havana

Havana in the 1950s, with its paradoxical effervescence, marked a time of intense adherence to modern architecture and planning. Most professionals acritically adopted the International Style disseminated from the United States. There remained, however, a group of professionals who questioned the loss of Cuban identity and experimented with new ways to express the country's cultural legacy of urbanism (Quintana 1974). The venue for this new voice surfaced in the 1953 public debate, The Plaza Cívica Forum. It served as a sounding board for a broad range of politicians, intellectuals, urban planners, and architects about the present and future of Havana (López Segrera 1972, 1980, 1989; Segre 1975).

The United States invested heavily in Cuba throughout the 1950s. Le Riverend (1966) estimated an average annual investment of $713 million during the decade. Most of the US monies were targeted for light industry and the service sector. The products and brand names in Havana at that time read like a list from any US telephone directory or stock sheet: soft drink bottlers (Coca Cola, Pepsi Cola, Canada Dry, Royal Crown), pharmaceutical companies (Abbott, Parke-Davis, Squibb), paint manufacturers (Sherwin Williams, Glidden, duPont), and tire makers (US Rubber, Good Year, Firestone) (Gutelman 1967; Aranda 1968). US retail chain stores of the day: Ten Cents, Sears and Roebuck, and Woolworth (Pino-Santos 1973; Pérez 1975) appeared throughout Cuba's major cities.

Internationally renowned as a tourist destination since at least the 1930s, Havana's image was heightened in the 1950s. Since the fall of Machado, organized crime from the United States increased its operations in Havana. Notorious figures such as Charles 'Lucky' Luciano, Santos Trafficante and Meyer Lansky were perhaps the most well known as were their commercial dealings in Havana after the Second World War. Representatives of the large organized 'families' divided themselves among the zones of influence along a strategic triangle of US tourist and gambling centers: Las Vegas, Miami and Havana. Organized crime also controlled gambling (legal and illegal), narcotics and prostitution. As we discuss in Chapter 3, the Batista government of the 1950s participated in these lucrative businesses through its approval of concessions and licenses and the construction of multimillion dollar tourist complexes. Tourism in the Caribbean, established by multinational firms along the Miami–Havana–San Juan axis, centered around Havana's unique features. In the early stage of modernity, the central business district reaffirmed the compact form and retained the centrality of its residential areas (Fernández 1990). However, the unitary image of Havana began to unravel in the 1950s[4]. High-rise office buildings and apartment complexes located in high-rent areas permanently transformed the city's landscape (Segre 1985a).

The Hispanic flavor of the Antillean capital city became progressively diluted through the spread of US-like single-family houses, increasingly located farther away from the city center as the result of improved roads. A fictitious aura of rapid progress invaded the life-style and replaced the slow Caribbean rhythm of Havana. Street-life diminished and even disappeared in some quarters as air-conditioning beckoned folks into cooler buildings. Department stores proliferated in the city center – Fin de Siglo, El Encanto and Flogar – and quickened the decline in street vendors and traditional store-front retailing. Although the traditional bodega (small, 'mom & pop' corner grocer) remained in working-class neighborhoods, supermarkets and shopping centers began to appear in the more affluent sections of Vedado and Miramar. These included La Rampa and La Copa, as well as the Ekloh chain on the main thoroughfares of 42nd and 41st Streets in Miramar, 17th Street in Vedado, and 26th Avenue in Nuevo Vedado.

These new retail centers offered economies of scale and variety in high-income neighborhoods. The more contemplative way of life found in open-air bars and outdoor cafes, protected by the shade of large trees or under the awnings of downtown shopping galleries, was offset by the counters of bars and fast-food corners of department stores. Boogie, Fox Trot and Feeling (filin, an assimilated American influence) displaced the traditional rhythms of the danzones and cha-cha-cha that had sounded in public spaces. Much of the impromptu local music and dancing under the sun faded into the crimson darkness of night clubs and cabarets. At the city's edge there survived a smattering of local culture and theater,

---

[4]Until the 1940s, Cuban architecture and city planning vacillated between the dynamics of the European vanguard and the functional efficiency of the United States. A cast of European maestros flocked to the United States before the Second World War: Ludwig Mies van der Rohe, Walter Gropius, Richard Neutra, Marcel Breuer, and José Luis Sert. Their influence directly and indirectly led to many international style and post-Rationalist buildings and developments in Havana's city centers and suburbs.

designed mainly for the nighttime entertainment of US tourists. There the Tropicana cabaret and its 'fiery mulattas' (*mulatas de fuego*) became the lewd symbol of Havana in the 1950s.

## A metropolis of three million

By the 1950s the great Antillean city had reached its long sought dream. The nation's 1958 population stood at 6 548 300 while Greater Havana registered 1 361 600, Metropolitan Havana held 1 272 300, and the City of Havana housed 813 300. Growth rates between 1950 and 1958 for the three areas registered 20.8%, 19.4%, and 12.4%, respectively. Although the city occupied only 0.3% of the total area of the country (47 846 hectares or 478 square kilometers) and 8.5% of the Province of Havana, one of five Cubans and one of every three urban dwellers were *habaneros*. Havana in the 1950s, therefore, exhibited the classic features of a primate city (whereby the largest city is several times larger than the second city). It was 6.4 times larger than Santiago de Cuba, the nation's second largest city and 9.4 times larger than Camagüey, the third largest city. While Metropolitan Havana constituted 76.1% of the provincial total, Santiago de Cuba contained only 9.2% of its provincial population, Oriente.

The spatial differentiation of Havana varied considerably. The symbolic administrative and commercial center occupied 4.9% of the metropolitan area (2350 hectares) and possessed the greatest population density, ranging from an average of 399 persons per hectare to a maximum of 800 per hectare. This latter high-density area comprised the blocks between Belascoaín, Galiano and the Malecón. The remainder of the urban agglomeration consisted of 15 000 hectares (32% of the city's area) and the peripheral zones with close to 13 000 hectares. Here at the city's edge the population densities dropped off dramatically to 40–54 hectares in Marianao and 7 hectares in Boyeros and La Coronela. Such irregularity in the population distribution meant maladjustment in several functional relationships in the city such as the location of housing to services, work and recreational areas. A crude translation of this spatial irregularity is that more than a million hours daily were 'lost' in commuting time within the city. The clustering of great concentrations of industries and services led to disparities among municipalities. The municipality of 10 de Octubre, for example, with 391 342 residents lacked industrial and service installations while Boyeros (120 000) was equipped with industries, factories, laboratories, hospitals, and services that were at a metropolitan scale (Segre 1974).

Havana's primacy also surfaced in statistical tabulations other than population data. The city generated 52.8% of the nation's industrial output – including the processing of sugar – and 75% of the national total without sugar's contribution. Eighty percent of Cuba's imports came through the Port of Havana as did 60.7% of its everyday consumer goods. The 1953 breakdown of the labor force revealed a prevalence of tertiary-sector workers: 41.9% worked in services, 20% in industry, and 17.9% in commerce (see also Chapter 7). Primarily a city of consumption, Havana absorbed 38% of all wages, 35% of domestic commerce, and 49% of services. Practically every sector of the economy revealed the concentration of the nation's services and functions in Havana. The capital held 40.7% of all hospital beds and 45% of all public health personnel. There were 13.9 beds per 1000 residents in Havana while Matanzas had only 5.9 beds per 1000 (see Chapter 8). Nearly two-thirds of the nation's hotel beds, university students, and high schools were concentrated in the capital, as were three-quarters of Cuba's professional labor force and 90% of its architects.

Despite the concentration of the building trades in Havana, the housing conditions of the poor and the overall urban services of the city were quite tenuous. Almost half of the housing stock was in bad condition and 6% of the population lived in shantytowns (see Chapter 6). Havana had only 1.1 square meters of green areas per inhabitant even though standards based on its climate recommended 18 square meters (see Chapter 8). Havana lacked about one-third of the water required daily; about 80 million gallons which would have complied with the normative guideline of 140 gallons per person needed to meet all domestic and industrial needs (Rallo and Segre 1978). Like other Latin American cities (López Rangel and Segre 1986), two mirrors reflected the urban image. The wealthy one showed the daily glow of a beautiful seaside landscape defined by the Malecón and the thick vegetation of the houses, parks and gardens along Quinta Avenida (Fifth Avenue in Miramar, see Figure 2.6). The poor reflection was opaque and somber as evidenced by the growing deterioration and crowding of Habana Vieja, *solares* and *cuarterías*. It included the squalor of the port area and the industrial back-bay quarters as well as the precarious houses of the proletariat located along the winding roads that linked Havana with the center of the island (Garnier 1973).

A group of professionals took measures to solve these visible and

---

[5]Among the many we note Alberto Prieto, Eduardo Montoulieu, Manuel de Tapia Ruano, Eduardo Cañas Abril, and Nicolás Quintana. The visit of José Luis Sert to Havana in 1939 created a contingent of Cuban loyalists to the CIAM and opened contacts between Cubans and European *maestros*; Walter Gropius, Richard Neutra (1945) and Joseph Albers (1952) passed through Havana and gave lectures. In the wake of this interest arose a series of meetings debating urban problems: the First National Conference of Architects (1948), the celebration as of 1950 of the World Day of Urbanism (November 8), the Eighth Pan-American Conference of Architects (1954), and the First National Planning Conference (1956).

**Figure 2.6** View of Fifth Avenue (Quinta Avenida), in Reparto Miramar, taken from Clock Tower (c. 1921). From American Photo Studios, Havana, *The Tropical Paradise of the West Indies*

mounting contradictions. Never before had urban affairs and planning been so intensely debated in Havana. The pioneer work of Pedro Martínez Inclán (1883–1957) is noteworthy. He became the Chair of Urban Planning at the University of Havana (Martínez Inclán 1925, 1946, 1949). Since 1925 he had argued forcefully for the need to use a master plan leading to balanced growth for Havana. His doctrine, at first connected to the French academic tradition and later attached to the Le Corbusier School of the CIAM, was furthered by colleagues and students who played an active role in the theoretical formulations of this interdisciplinary group.[5]

The decision of the government of Fulgencio Batista to build the José Martí Monument in the Plaza Cívica in Havana generated bitter controversy. Personal and political motives made Batista award the design to the second-place team headed by Enrique Luis Varela (Tejeira-Davis 1987).

---

[6]This group was made up of architects such as Eduardo Montoulieu, Mario Romañach, Nicolás Quintana and Jorge Mantilla, all of whom were connected with Sert, Gropius and Neutra. They joined the workings of the government in the Planning Board (*Junta de Planificación*) established in 1955. The Board would oversee the development of multimillion dollar tourist projects in Havana, the beach resort of Varadero, the colonial town of Trinidad, and *Isla de Pinos* (Isle of Pines, today Isle of Youth, *Isla de la Juventud*).

Their design was exhibited and provoked heated discussion in a forum organized by the Institute of Architects (*Colegio de Arquitectos*), the principal professional organization of Cuban architects. Despite the triumph of the traditionalists who finalized the academic and monumental image of the Plaza Cívica through such structures as the Martí Monument, Palacio de Justicia and the National Library, a new group of professionals arrived on the scene.[6]

Multinational interests in the hospitality industry were addressed by preparing countries for massive international tourism throughout the Caribbean. Once the tunnel was completed underneath Havana Bay, the city could begin expanding to lands east of the city that for four centuries had remained inaccessible. To accommodate the perceived image of a new metropolis of three million inhabitants, the Planning Board (*Junta Nacional de Planificación*) contracted the office of Town Planning Associates that included José Luis Sert, Paul Lester Wiener and Paul Schulz (Bastlund and Sert 1967).

Latin America in the 1950s was one of the last bastions left untouched by the urban planning theorists of the CIAM. Significant projects related to CIAM ideas were launched throughout the region: Sert and Le Corbusier's plan for Bogotá (1951), Lucio Costa's idea for Brasilia (1957), and Antonio Bonet's project (1957) for the Barrio Sur neighborhood of Buenos Aires (Gutiérrez 1983). Havana's project of 1956 joined this list with each of these plans sharing the Le Corbusieran models associated with the Athens Charter. In general, these models emphasized a hierarchy as the guiding component in urban projects, as shown by:

1. the five principal roads used by Le Corbusier in Chandigarh, India;
2. the presence of a hegemonic political-administrative center;
3. the separation of social functions (residential areas, government complexes, industrial zones); and
4. the breadth of green areas, and the layout of housing in strips and isolated clusters.

Nonetheless, Havana exhibited several unique characteristics that were defined not by theory or concepts, but by dominant economic forces. These powers revealed themselves through landowners, major 'Mafia' projects, and politicians backing certain businesses (Ramón 1967).

This blend of economic might shaping Havana in the 1950s appeared in the treatment of political-administrative spaces. It culminated with the design of the 'modern' enclave, the Plaza Cívica, which interrupted the road system established by the Martí Monument and the imposing Palacio de Justicia. Towards the Quinta de los Molinos (the former summer retreat of the colonial governor located between Vedado and the Plaza) and the Colina Universitaria (University Hill, home of the University of Havana in Vedado), a series of new buildings was constructed: National Theater (1958), General Comptroller's Office (Tribunal de Cuentas) (1953), Ministry of Communications (1954), Ministry of Public Works (1960), Bus Station (1949), and Havana City Hall (Ayuntamiento de la Habana) (1960). Another complex of government structures or a presidential palace would not have been necessary because the 1950 arrangement was adequate.

Batista, however, sought refuge from the political and social tensions of the city, especially, perhaps, because of the attack on the Presidential Palace that nearly cost him his life in 1957. He supported the idea of creating a new governmental growth pole near Habana del Este which, if completed, would have marked the fourth and final 'center' of Havana's polycentric design. Land between the Morro Castle and the Cabaña fortress would have afforded him space that was distant from the latent aggressiveness of the city, yet allow him direct contact with the exclusive areas of the bourgeoisie who would soon settle in Habana del Este. With the recent inauguration of the tunnel under Havana Bay came an expected boom in residential areas along the coast. In this context surfaced a potential real-estate bonanza for the powerful landowner Dionisio Velasco y Sarrá who subdivided his land and placed Miguel Gastón in charge of its development. Gastón, in turn, solicited alternative development and design proposals from the US firm of Skidmore, Owings and Merrill and the Italian architect Franco Albini.

José Luis Sert's plan under review by the Batista government anticipated considerable population growth. The most widely criticized aspect of Sert's plan for Havana centered around changes in the Malecón and the transformation of the city's historic old town. In this plan he contradicted the basic concepts of his book, *Heart of the City*, in which the traditions of people and their life-styles, and the use of styles that conform to the social history of a city, were paramount. For example, substituting the homogeneous waterfront with its low-lying buildings, colonnades and Eclectic architecture, for a series of high-rise hotels and apartments, would have violated premises of harmonious and historically-sensitive design. City blocks in the old quarters would have been reconfigured with parking lots (Figure 2.7). Although Havana would ultimately be spared this assault, San Juan, Puerto Rico and Santo Domingo, Dominican Republic did not fare as well. The proposal for redesigning Havana was even more audacious than its Caribbean sisters because it contemplated building in the Straits of Florida an 'artificial island' of hotels, casinos and businesses (Figure 2.8). The design was a banal parody of the *Cité des Affaires* in the Río de la Plata as envisioned by Le Corbusier in the Master Plan of Buenos

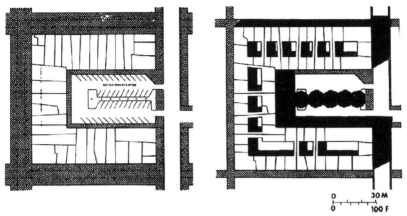

**Figure 2.7** City block design for Habana Vieja proposed by J.L. Sert. *Source*: Wiener, P.L., Sert, J.L., and Schulz, P. (1960) La Havane. Plan Pilote et Directives Génerales. *L'Architecture d'Aujourd hui*, No. 88. Paris (February/March), p. 62

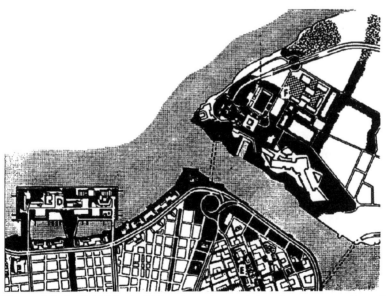

**Figure 2.8** Artificial island with hotels, casinos and shopping centers set just off the Malecón, proposed by J.L. Sert. *Source*: Wiener, P.L., Sert, J.L., and Schulz, P. (1960) La Havane. Plan Pilote et Directives Génerales. *L'Architecture d'Aujourd hui*, No. 88. Paris (February/March), p. 62

Aires (Le Corbusier 1947). Did the island possess symbols like the ones assumed by the Cartesian skyscrapers envisioned by the great Master? Were these ideas born out of imperative functional necessity? These questions were not the real intentions of the design but were, instead, driven by financial gain. Widening the Malecón and creating a marine platform meant driving up land values and padding the personal checking accounts of government officials.

Sert's proposal was certain to have devastated Havana's historic center. Its dialectal homogeneity – recognized much later as a World Heritage Site (designated by UNESCO in 1982) – praised for its narrow streets with modest colonial houses, and pretentious Eclectic buildings that were adorned by the tranquil flavor of its plazas, would have been lost. Although Sert's plan would have conserved a few isolated landmarks, it would have radically altered the profile of Havana. Modern limited-access highways and wide streets with artificial town squares and parking garages were to infringe on the traditional colonial grid. Practically all of the existing construction would have been demolished or radically altered to accommodate this new plan (Wiener *et al.* 1960). With surgical precision, the poor in the old quarters would have been expelled. Industrial satellite towns with workers' housing were envisioned.

A scenic setting for tourist activities had also been included in the design. Along Cuba and Havana Streets – the main thoroughfares of the center of Habana Vieja – were to be high-rise offices, retail and hotel complexes would have replaced the dilapidated colonial blocks. In all, the new design represented a hypothetical Hollywood revival of *portales* and interior patios whose ascetic modernity reflected the Venturian axiom that 'less is a bore'. This was a design with an abstract and reductionist configuration, remote even from the ironic and caustic realism of the masterminds at Disneyland who could have created infinite versions of a 'romantic evening' in Havana.

A perceptive error also existed in Sert's plan regarding the habits and customs of the popular masses of Havana. He had proposed a strip of single-story housing to envelop the city like 'upholstery' as did the original plan for Chimbote, Peru (Donato 1972). In the end, Havana could have been deprived of the extroverted street life typical of Caribbean cities. Lastly, even though they were designed with very different criteria, the Plaza Cívica and Habana del Este projects assumed symbolic and geographical significance.

The negative features of Sert's plan notwithstanding, some of its proposals were consciously or unconsciously included in urban design and planning projects after 1959. The first came in the form of a new shape of the city that would include the bay not just as a boundary, but as a central element of a city that both surrounded and enveloped it. As well, the traditional urban sprawl to the south and west became multidirectional, retaking lands that had been unsettled to the east of the bay. This radial focus required a road network connecting the old areas with newer ones. It entailed the lengthening of the spoke-like road system and some of the proposed beltways, most of which were carried out in the 1960s. Sert's ideas also materialized in the system of green spaces. They possessed a certain flexibility that integrated different neighborhoods and took advantage of open spaces. This made the expensive expropriation of private lands unnecessary. The city's peripheral areas succumbed to planning regulations, not only the road systems but the typologies of orthodox Rationalism, and proposals for low-cost housing.

## Polycentric or eccentric? The urban nodes of Havana

It is difficult to characterize the urban morphology of Havana. On the one hand, it shares few of the features present in North American models of urban structure. The Concentric Zone Model (Burgess 1925), Sector Model (Hoyt 1939) and Multiple Nuclei Model (Ullman and Harris 1945) make certain assumptions about land use that do not apply to Havana. These include the flat topography, equal distribution of transportation and land costs, and the changing nature of suburban transportation in the US city,

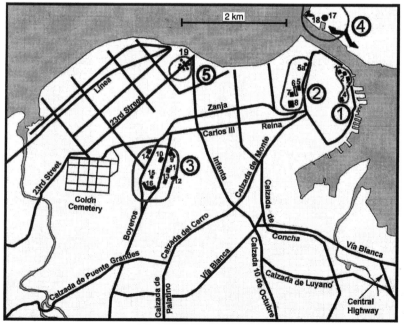

**Figure 2.9** Five functional nodes of Havana.

## 84    Havana

**Table 2.1** The polycentric nature of Havana (numbers correspond to Figure 2.9)

| Center | Sub-center | Functions |
| --- | --- | --- |
| 1. Colonial (1519–1898) | 1. Plaza de la Catedral | Elite residential and religious square |
|  | 2. Plaza de Armas | Political, administrative and military square |
|  | 3. Plaza de San Francisco | Foreign trade |
|  | 4. Plaza Vieja | Retailing and residential square |
| 2. First Republican Center, Central Park, 1902–1930 | 5. Manzana de Gómez | Retailing |
|  | 5a. Presidential Palace |  |
|  | 6. Parque Central | Town square |
|  | 7. Centro Gallego | Former social club |
|  | Teatro de Tacón (García Lorca) | Former theater – opera house |
|  | 8. Capitolio Nacional | Former Capitol Building modeled after Washington, DC's (now a library) |
| 3. Second Republican Center: Plaza Cívica, 1930–1958 | 9.Terminal de Omnibus | Bus station |
|  | 10. Telecommunications Ministry | Government building |
|  | 11. Biblioteca Nacional 'José Martí' | Library |
|  | 12. Oficinas del Estado | Government office buildings |
|  | 13. Municipio de la Habana | City Hall, now a national ministry office (MINFAR) |
|  | 14. Ministerio de Obras Públicas | Public-works ministry |
|  | 15. Monumento a José Martí | José Martí monument |
|  | 16. Palacio de Justicia | Headquarters of Central Committee of Cuban Communist Party |
| 4. New Center Havana del Este | 17. Proposed Presidential Palace (Sert's project) |  |
|  | 18. Ministry buildings |  |
| 5. Complementary Center | 19. 'La Rampa' district within Vedado, loosely defined by L St. and 23rd St. | Social and tourist center in 1950s and today. Includes Coppelia ice-cream parlor and park and such prominent hotels as Havana Hilton (Habana Libre), Capri, St. John, Vedado, and more |

especially the role of the automobile and the highway system joining sub-urbs and downtown. As well, the Latin American urban land-use models by Griffin and Ford (1980) or Bähr and Mertins (1982) fail to capture the non-economic forces that have shaped Havana's nearly 500 years of urbanization.

Figure 2.9 identifies five recognizable nodes or centers in Havana's contemporary landscape: (1) The Colonial Center (1519–1898); (2) First Republican Center (1902–1930); (3) Second Republican Center at the Plaza Cívica (1930–1958); (4) Third Republican Center (1956) proposed by José Luis Sert; and (5) a Complementary Center consisting of residences, hotels, and night clubs. These functional nodes reflect myriad political and economic forces that have left their indelible mark. Throughout this book, we will refer to these polycentric or, perhaps, 'eccentric' centers of Havana, as well as their attendant buildings, landmarks, town squares, and land uses (Table 2.1).

Little survived of Sert's dream for Havana. It was a delirious vision because it contemplated grandeur in a city which, on the one hand, would have held ostentatious casinos, gigantic shopping centers and luxurious skyscrapers. On the other hand, it was also submerged in misery and exploitation. With its population growth held constant, the city preserved the history of its built environment, the semblance of a memory, the rich-ness of its ambiance, and the complexity of its neighborhoods. From 1959 onward, the city's prospect would radically change, and Havana would become the only 'museum' in Latin America's first wave of modernity.

# 3

# The Havana of January

At last, we are in the midst of all the chaos that has come from the breaking up of
Cuba, with all its confusion and sense of inferiority over these last 30 years . . .
On the one hand, fear, surprise, perplexity. On the other, desperation!

José Lezama Lima, *Diario*,
September 11, 1957

When the Revolution triumphed on January 1, 1959, Havana could only
be described as a small 'big' city that had come to dominate an underdeveloped island. Despite Havana's glittering appearance, the rest of
Cuba was not exempt from the external dependency forces that afflicted
Latin America. A single product (sugar) and one principal market for
exports (the United States) characterized the Cuban economy. Extensive
agricultural production split between a *latifundia* system in the eastern
half of the island while the *minifundia* dominated in the west. A well
known litany of underdevelopment traits also besieged Cuba: unemployment, weak industrialization, a deficient infrastructure, low technology,
and poor educational and health indicators (García Pleyán 1986). All these
features were evident in Cuba's towns and cities as well as the internal
structure of Havana.

This profile of underdevelopment stemmed from a fundamental
contradiction between the public and private use of the territory and
resources. Several bipolar development profiles resulted. The original
conflict between Cuba (colony) and Spain (metropolis) continued during
the neocolonial relationship with the United States, and typified the
classic trade imbalance between core and periphery nations (Cardoso and
Faletto 1979). Perhaps the most striking bipolar features were the
geographic schisms between rural and urban, and inner city and subur-

ban. Profit and land speculation drove urban development. Little concern was given to the quality of the natural environment, the rational use of human and material resources, or social and spatial segregation. Public services and infrastructure that did not lend themselves to profitable ventures went underfinanced. In brief, the nation faced weaknesses in infrastructure and structural distortions.

The shining face of Havana and a disproportionate investment in luxury goods masked the harsh economic reality that touched even those lucky enough to hold down a steady job. Uneven access to a relatively deteriorated public-school system produced limited occupational and social mobility for rural workers, small farmers and the chronically unemployed (Barkin 1974, p. 195).

Annual per capita income improved only slightly during the twentieth century. In 1902 it stood at $200 while in 1959 it had crawled up to $374. Disaggregating annual income by workers revealed a dismal mid-1950s figure of just $91 for rural workers (ACU 1957). Income distribution was skewed by the top 10% of wage earners accumulating 38.5% of all income. Geographic disparities were also apparent including the differences between the eastern and western halves of the island as well as between Havana and the rest of the island. Even within Havana income differentials prevailed, as evidenced by the gap between middle and upper-income groups as well as within the 'invisible' city of the proletariat and sub-proletariat (Segre 1978).

Despite these income distribution inequities, Cuba's underdevelopment differed from the rest of the Third World. If the gross national product (GNP), industrialization, and educational levels gave Latin America a higher standard of living when compared with Asia and Africa, then Cuba and Puerto Rico warranted special note within Latin American. Both islands were fairly Europeanized because of Spanish colonial rule which lasted until 1898, almost a century longer than the rest of Spanish America.

Cuba's allure attracted a steady stream of migrants from the Old World after its formal independence from Spain. Between 1902 and 1912, two of three immigrants to Cuba hailed from Europe. Havana maintained levels of European immigrants well above the 30% mark during the first half of this century, even though many migrants ultimately settled in the island's interior during the sugar-boom years. Like Puerto Rico, Cuba displayed strong economic and cultural influences from the United States, dating back to the nineteenth century. This US sway was greater in Cuba than other parts of the world (Manitzas 1974). By 1959, the United States had $1 billion invested and controlled 40% of the island's sugar production, 90% of electric utilities and telephones, and 50% of railroads. It also had significant interests in mining, oil refineries, rubber by-products, livestock, cement, tourism, and a quarter of all bank deposits. Eighty percent of Cuban imports came from the United States. Cuban currency (the peso) established in 1915 was evenly exchanged for US dollars. So common-place was dollar circulation in Havana during the 1950s that people would receive change in dollars when they made minor purchases in pesos.

Cuba obtained 80% of its foreign earnings from exports. As a monocul-tural producer and agro-exporting nation, it remained perennially vul-nerable to external 'shocks', slight market shifts, and natural disasters. That the price of sugar governed Cuba was evidenced by the popular slo-gan 'without sugar, there's no country.' From sugar harvests that aver-aged 5.3 million tons during the 1950s, the United States would purchase 2.8 million tons at above-market prices. Sugar prices varied greatly dur-ing the first half of the twentieth century as did the revenues in the public treasury (Figure 3.1). Oscillating prices made planning difficult. Reliance on a single buyer was made clear by the US sugar quota and a menacing political and military influence that led to two US military interventions in the early twentieth century. As a result of the prevailing role of the United States in Cuban political and economic affairs, there arose a popu-lar saying throughout the island: 'With the Army or without the Army, but not against the Army.' The United States extended its control in the 1950s by allowing the repudiated Batista dictatorship to hold power which later generated public resentment and consolidated support behind the Revolution in the late 1950s. The exodus of upper-class and many middle-class Cubans during the early years of the Castro govern-ment also helped to consolidate the Revolution.

To be sure, sugar was king in the 1950s. It took up half of the arable land and required a quarter of the labor force. As a result, the labor force suffered from seasonal fluctuations during the much feared 'dead time' between planting and harvest, when thousands of workers could not find work. It also meant relying on importing goods that could have been pro-duced in Cuba. Foodstuffs amounted to 22.2% of all imports. Although three-quarters of foodstuffs could have been produced nationally, pres-sures from US producers who sought access to the Cuban market for their products blocked domestic production (Consejo Nacional de Economía 1958). This classic situation of economic dependency (Cardoso and Faletto 1979) led to a trade deficit which by 1958 had reached $43.5 million. Fidel Castro (1984) remarked as early as 1953 that 'except for a handful of food, wood, and textile industries, Cuba is still a raw-material factory' (Castro 1984a, p. 44, our translation).

This monocultural sugar production and bondage of economic depen-

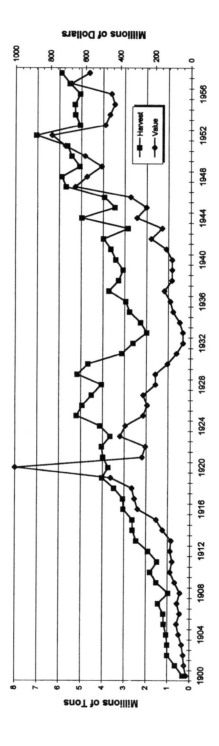

**Figure 3.1** Cuban sugar harvest and value (1900–1958)

dency minimized the chance of 'multiplier effects' or spin-off industries. The work force suffered the most from this malaise. In 1958, the average unemployment rate was 16.4%, to which could be added 30.2% of under-employed workers. The situation worsened at the end of the sugar-cane harvest (*zafra*) when 20.5% of the labor force became completely unem-ployed as opposed to 9.1% unemployment during the peak of the harvest (Consejo Nacional de Economía 1958).

Nevertheless, Cuban monoculture had its own unique features. Sugar production was more capitalist than feudal as noted by the social relations of production among workers (Moreno Fraginals 1978). In the early 1950s, agricultural workers accounted for 63% of the labor force. This made them more 'modern' and their aspirations were distinct. On the one hand, land-ownership consisted of corporate and absentee landlords instead of the nearly feudal patriarchs which reigned elsewhere in Latin America (Manitzas 1974). On the other hand, the Cuban *latifundia* was like any other in Latin America: crops were extensively produced, almost half of the land remained idle, and the 28 largest producers of sugar cane con-trolled a fifth of the arable land.

Local Cuban (*criollo*) industry was small and backwards, not very pro-ductive, and concentrated mainly in manufacturing. In its search for sta-bility, the economy of the nation's capital focused on the real-estate market, or else Cuban capital was invested overseas. Well-known multi-nationals found Havana to be a friendly and profitable market (Figure 3.2). The Cuban government also wielded considerable clout in the econ-omy even though industries were neither nationalized nor created by the state (Manitzas 1974). By the end of the 1950s, 52.8% of Cuba's industrial production had concentrated in Havana and employed a fifth of the eco-nomically active population that worked outside the sugar industry. The sugar industry had its own settlement and production system which included over 150 sugar mills (*centrales*) throughout the island. Among those were the grounds occupied by the sugar mills' sugar plantations, and ancillary installations (*bateyes*) that formed agroindustrial complexes in the middle of the countryside.

These contradictions and inequalities created a unique type of urban system compared to industrialization and urbanization in the North Atlantic countries, but it was fairly common in Latin America. Jorge Hardoy describes the system this way:

> [Cuba was] a fragmented nation . . . that neither understood nor felt its major national problems . . . urbanization, as a process, and the city, as an ecological space, reflected social forces, levels of technical competence, and external ties. In Cuba, like in the rest of Latin America, urbanization did not result from industrialization (Hardoy 1974, p. 286, our translation).

**Figure 3.2**  The Coca-Cola bottling factory at Santa Catalina and Palatino Streets, La Víbora (c. 1955) was one of many multinational light-manufacturing industries locating in the southern suburbs of Havana

Underdevelopment forces notwithstanding, Cuba's GNP ranked among the upper quartile of Latin American countries. Other standard measures attested to Cuba's relative prosperity in the 1950s: the ratio of physicians to population (1:420 in Havana), automobiles (1:20 nationwide), televisions (which arrived in 1949, before many European countries imported them), and other consumer durables. Employed urban workers were relatively well paid compared with rural workers who lacked schooling, medical care, and decent housing. Cuba's level of urbanization, moreover, was high and had been evolving since the nineteenth century. In 1898, 28.5% of all Cubans lived in cities with 20 000 inhabitants or more, while the same figure for the United States was just 23.8% (Hamberg 1986). In 1958, with a population of about 6.5 million, almost one of three Cubans (32%) lived in cities with more than 50 000 people (Various 1971).

The housing rental market was widespread. In 1953, three-fifths of all nuclear families and three-quarters of all Havanans paid rent on their primary residence. Housing conditions in the countryside were deplorable. Many Cubans at that time spent up to a quarter of their wages on rent (UIA 1963). Although tenants' rights legislation existed in Cuba and was fairly progressive for that time, such laws were overlooked or weakened by administrative corruption (Alonso 1950). In short, pre-Revolutionary housing was rife with strong contradictions such as:

drastic differences of living conditions between city and countryside and among social classes and within urban areas, long-standing rent control coexisting with high rents, and an established 'right to occupancy' along with widespread evictions (Hamberg 1986, p. 588).

Underdevelopment was concentrated unevenly in rural areas throughout the island, manifesting itself in various ways. The eastern region was particularly disadvantaged. For example, there was only one physician for every 2550 residents (see Chapter 8 for the contemporary scene). Nationally, four-fifths of all rural dwellings were *bohíos* (huts made of rough planks or canes and thatched with palm leaves); less than 3% had running water, and two-thirds had earthen floors. Even though the majority (87%) of the national urban housing stock had electricity, less than half of all homes was connected to a proper waste-disposal system. As well, less than half of the housing stock was connected to water mains, and even fewer had hook-ups to sewers that were in compliance with the law. In 1958, 1.4 million dwellings were below acceptable standards. Even in Havana – the most prosperous Cuban city – 6% of the population lived in dismal shantytowns (Fernández 1976). Nevertheless, these figures were relatively low compared with other Latin American countries (Hamberg 1990).

## The political framework: antecedents to January's revolution

Dependency in Cuba resulted in part from an irrational use of material and human resources. It generated frustration and irritation in a people who, despite their characteristic nonchalance, had periodically risen up to shake off their oppressors. The military coup d'etat in 1952 unleashed a response that quickly bypassed a traditional political opposition that was demoralized by corruption and the status quo.

Opposition to Batista broadened as it incorporated young people who lacked political-party affiliation. This was the case of the Revolutionary Directorate (*Directorio Revolucionario*) at the University of Havana. The directorate was headed by a young architecture student, José Antonio Echeverría, who was killed in a confrontation with state security forces just outside the campus of the University of Havana after a student-led attack against the Presidential Palace on March 13, 1957.

Other opposition movements disassociated themselves from traditional political parties, as did Fidel Castro when he was a young lawyer. Castro headed a leftist splinter group that broke away from the Orthodox Party, and whose members were inspired by an opposition senator, Eduardo Chibás. Dramatically, the senator committed suicide during a live radio program 1 year before Batista's *coup d'état*. This splinter

movement later took the name *26 de Julio* after the date of the unsuccess-
ful 1953 assault against the Moncada barracks in Santiago de Cuba. The
student movement centered at the University of Havana, a key impetus in
ousting the dictatorship, was significant for many reasons. Two are particularly germane to our discussion of Havana as a world city. One is that
the University of Havana was arguably one of the finest institutions of
higher learning in Latin America. A second reason is that it is located at
one of the highest elevations in Havana ('University Hill' or *Colina
Universitaria*) and since the 1920s had been the site of numerous student
protests. Its central location just a few blocks from the heart of the Vedado
tourist district served to disseminate news reports of violent conflicts
between students and police.

The Moncada attack was the first notable action in a short but whirling
struggle of urban and mountain guerrilla fighters. In both settings, the 26
de Julio movement was at the vanguard and progressively earned the
support of the rest of the country, including such unlikely partners as
members of the upper class and the old Communist Party. The movement
ended triumphantly on January 1, 1959 with the taking of the city of Santa
Clara – strategically important because of its size and location in the middle of the island – and the total collapse of the Batista regime amidst an
impressive explosion of public celebration.

Following this popular victory, there remained a series of social justice
issues with which the Revolutionary government had to address. Perhaps
the most crucial challenge was the critical situation of the poor which
Fidel Castro addressed during his trial for attacking the Moncada. In his
now well celebrated speech, 'History Will Absolve Me', he said:

> The problem of land tenure, the problem of industrialization, the problem of
> housing, the problem of unemployment, the problem of education and the
> problem of health care; we have here six concrete points to which our efforts
> will be directed, with resolve (Castro 1984a, p. 43).

Nevertheless, both critics and sympathizers of the Revolution agree
that Cuba in 1959 – especially Havana – possessed a physical, economic,
and social infrastructure relatively well developed compared with most
socialist movements that would later come to power in Africa and Latin
America. This would support the Revolution immeasurably.

## Havana: structure and infrastructure

Havana City in the twentieth century has always been comprised of counties. In 1959 there were 1.27 million in the city proper and 1.36 million

when adjacent counties (*municipios*) were added to include the metropolitan area. Clearly the primate city of Cuba, Havana was six times larger than the second city of the nation, Santiago de Cuba (Various 1971). The city covered 478 square kilometers (186 square miles). It is still shaped like the fingers of a hand, with radial arteries extending from the western and eastern edges of the bay in the central part of the metropolis. Several of these 'fingers' follow the old routes of *calzadas* and the central highway (Carretera Central) as well as the more recently built bypasses of the 1950s: Calle 100, Vía Monumental and Autopista del Mediodía (see also Fig. 8.8).

## Islands within the city

The coherence of Havana's shape and skyline was affected not only by a poor secondary road network and pockets of speculative subdivisions, but also by natural barriers and large installations which functioned as enclaves within the urban fabric. The port, the city's *raison d'être*, had become an ambiguous element in Havana. It both joined and separated the city functionally and socially. It was a spectacular landscape for tourists as they passed through the narrow strait at the mouth of the bay. The colonial forts of El Morro and La Cabaña cradle the bay as one enters by ship. To the left (eastward) sits the small settlement of Casablanca clinging to the side of a hill which is crowned by the dome of the Observatory. Off to its side sits the enormous white-marble statue, the Christ of Havana, erected in the 1950s. To the right (westward) runs the seaside promenade of Avenida del Puerto designed by the French landscape architect J.C.N. Forestier (see Chapter 2).

Shaped like a bag with the narrow straits forming its top, the bay opens towards the south while the center of Havana falls off in the distance, only to be replaced by another interesting colonial settlement, Regla. Twentieth-century industrial installations surround the town today much as they did in the 1950s (see Chapter 7). The 65 hectare Belot oil refinery that belonged to Esso, Shell and Texaco, and the dockyards are readily apparent. So too are the power plant, Burrus grain towers, and a fertilizer plant. At the southern tip of the old walled city a compact string of docks and warehouses block the view of the water from Havana's first colonial promenade, Alameda de Paula.

This was the heart of the city's trade and industry. Ocean vessels, loading cranes and cargo were among the constant traffic of the ferry boats running between Habana Vieja and Regla and Casablanca. Occasionally, the ferry that transported vehicles and passengers from Key West arrived at Hacendados dock, as did the steamship Florida which regularly sailed between Miami and Havana. Curiously, the Key West–Havana route was the same distance (140 kilometers) separating Havana from the famous and spectacular beaches of Varadero. The human landscape of this 1950s setting included a wide cast of characters: longshoremen, truck drivers, taxi drivers, local residents, tourists, office workers, beggars, sailors and a colorful array of local bar patrons and prostitutes.

If we were to continue along this north–south traverse through Havana Bay in the 1950s, we would find other large industrial complexes, shipyards, rail yards, and roads. In the midst of this lay Cayo Cruz (Cross Key) with its gigantic heap of garbage. The old gas plant Melones (1870), the Tallapiedra power plant (1890) and Paso Superior railroad yards of Vía Blanca were also in full view. Just beside it ran the elevated railroad tracks that led from the great passenger station (1902) that eliminated the possibility of completing a 'green belt' encircling Habana Vieja along the strip where the city walls once stood.

The trade winds blowing through this southern portion of the bay carried factory smoke and the stench of rotting garbage to the nearby poor communities of Luyanó, Atarés and the southern part of Habana Vieja. When the winds blew exceptionally hard, the foul smell and soot even reached Chaple Hill in southern Diez de Octubre, which was settled in the 1920s by middle and upper-middle class families. Ironically, many had chosen these higher elevations for their clean air which helped in treating respiratory ailments. By the 1950s, however, the air had become thick with pollutants.

Air travel became popular and widespread by the 1950s. However, the new look of southern Havana, meant to be viewed from the air, had not been beautified the way that Forestier had envisioned it in the 1920s when most visitors arrived by sea (Laprade 1931). The existing airport at Boyeros in southern Havana was not well connected to the city center. Situated on fertile agricultural lands that were prone to periodic flooding, the area lent itself to other land uses. Moreover, the airport sits on top of the Vento aquifer which is still one of the main sources of water for *habaneros*. Airline traffic endangers the nearby settlements of Boyeros and Calabazar.

Havana's only other airport in the 1950s was Columbia military base, located in the west near the ocean, but it was generally off limits for commercial use. Some commercial activity did, however, take place at Columbia. This was carried out by Aerolíneas Q (Q Airlines), which was associated with contraband activities under the direction of military brass. The Columbia base had been built by US troops earlier this century and was, essentially, the *de facto* center of power in Cuba in the 1950s. This was yet another 'island' in Havana, with its large military and hospital complexes and affiliated military-base centers of privilege. Although in 1959 it was turned into *Ciudad Libertad* (Liberty City) – a large educational complex – Columbia represented the military's intervention between the wealthy and the downtrodden. In practical terms, the Columbia base disrupted the road networks between the old downtown center of Marianao and the nearby upper-class neighborhoods on the strip along the coast.

### Housing and urban structure in the 1950s

By 1959 Havana was a metropolitan area that held two different cities. One was comprised of the inner districts (roughly including the present counties (*municipios*) of Habana Vieja, Centro Habana, and Plaza). The grid pattern gave the area the kind of coherence found in other Spanish-American cities. The cityscape had several nodes such as parks, traffic circles, and landmark buildings. Another city within 1959 Havana contained a seemingly endless number of subdivisions leading out to the southeast, south and west.

The grand axis of the Malecón and Quinta Avenida spectacularly linked the financial and commercial center of Havana with its affluent western neighborhoods where residents could easily slip to downtown Havana – say, Parque Central, for instance – in less than a 20-minute car ride. Upper-class housing in Miramar and adjacent areas initially consisted of Eclectic – and later Neocolonial and modern – *villas* that were adorned with front porches and wonderful tropical gardens. Despite their proximity, working-class neighborhoods to the south were poorly linked by the road network. This is where the rest of the city lived: an array of social classes including lower-middle, working, less-affluent white collar, and the urban poor. This expansion at the city's edge included tiny pockets of the poor and shanties constructed outside the crowded city center.

If the class structure in this southern area was diverse, so too were the types of dwellings. Common house styles were the *petite bourgeoisie* single-family structures of Lawton, Santos Suárez, Víbora, Casino Deportivo, La Sierra, and Almendares, among many others. There were other modest copies of affluent homes that were interspersed among two- to four-story apartment buildings. Alongside this 'presentable' city defined by standards of middle-class decorum, there existed a dismal side of Havana. Substandard and speculative housing was shamefully hidden behind classicist façades and tucked away among the compact blocks of Centro Habana, Cerro and Habana Vieja. These neighborhoods, moreover, had long suffered from land speculation, densification and physical decay. Deterioration was most acute in the living quarters which were formerly occupied by well-off *habaneros*. Although the housing stock was shabby, these districts maintained their traditional retail, financial and historic center functions.

The Havana of 1959 held several types of slum housing. As discussed in Chapter 2, one type was the *cuartería* (a dilapidated rooming house). It evolved from the old Baroque and Neoclassical and Eclectic mansions of Habana Vieja, Centro Habana, Cerro, and Vedado (Chailloux 1945). The other was the *ciudadela*, a tenement house composed of one or two stories of rooms alongside an interior courtyard. This interior space held elementary collective services (laundering, showers, trash bin, access to a spigot) and – by default – social activities like make-shift playgrounds and places for chatting and dancing. Each family – ranging from a few members to several dozen depending on the space of the structure – occupied their own room. Both the *cuartería* and *ciudadela* reflected broader social changes whose qualitative impact modified the image of the inner city.

The *pasaje* was another type of low-income housing scattered about the city center. Literally a 'passage' or 'alley', the *pasaje* was a variant of the *ciudadela* that often intersected with two streets, one at each end. Both the *ciudadela* and the *pasaje* combine another type of housing: the *accesoria*. This arrangement consisted of a one-bedroom apartments in the lower story of the building that could be accessed directly from the street, and was typically followed by a row of rooms found in the *ciudadela*.

Shantytowns formed a part of the pre-Revolutionary Havana landscape. Known locally as *barrios insalubres*, some of the more infamous shanties of 1958 were Las Yaguas, Llega y Pon, and La Cueva del Humo. More often than not, they were prone to flooding, were poorly accessible and steeply sloped, were located next to noxious facilities, or were just plain unhealthy. Shantytowns spawned at the city's edge where Havana grew incrementally, and some were eventually surrounded by formal, legalized construction. These peri-urban shanties became the first points of contact for rural migrants to Havana. They were fed by migratory streams from small towns, villages and the Cuban countryside. Shantytowns symbolized the widening social stratification and quality of life between the Havana elite and the rest of Cuba.

Not all squatters came directly from outside the city. Many found themselves there on the rebound after failing to secure stable work that would allow them to live in more central areas with better services. In that way, the stock of human capital in the shantytowns remained more marginalized than residents in *ciudadelas* and *cuarterías*, and not just spatially. Social and occupational mobility was also limited there, perhaps more than any settlement in Havana.

Altogether, this mass of dispossessed people raises the question of the accuracy of the 1953 census which reported 59.8% of the population working in the tertiary sector (Comité Cubano de Asentamientos Humanos 1976). One reason for the potential undercount is that the 'service' category should have been disaggregated (retail, wholesaling, food services, self-employment, banking, public sector). More significantly, however, is that the employment data failed to reflect part-time work, seasonal labor, underemployment, and what is now widely called the informal sector (de Soto 1989). It was in these tenuous labor markets where most of the shantytown residents earned marginal or substandard livings, which forced them to live in the grim side of the city. Accordingly, the census counted only 6.2% of the city's labor as working in the construction industry. It is likely that this figure did not represent temporary workers and includes what Marx would call the 'reserve army of labor'. This surplus labor kept wages low in what was actually a dynamic sector of the economy. Another 'invisible' segment of the labor force toiled as domestic workers (cooks, maids, chauffeurs, gardeners, handymen, messengers). Informal employment was especially important for poor women whose work choices were limited, and who declined to beg or to prostitute themselves. It was not uncommon that middle- and lower-middle-income families hired one, two or even three maids (*criadas*) for 25 pesos monthly plus meals. This revealed the development of a broad sector of marginal (informal sector) activity. Thus, it is more accurate to speak of a lumpenproletarianization of the city rather than tertiarization (e.g., increase in services) (Various 1973, p. 11). Put another way, the service category represented only one segment of the economy of 1958, and it left out a significant part of the labor force.

### Industrial output and physical structure in the 1950s

The 1950s brought industrial growth to Havana in the form of light industry (including textiles, food processing, and cosmetics) and the vibrant construction sector. The port area and its immediate surroundings are where the shipyards, oil refining, electrical power, and gas generation were concentrated.

Two large axes continued which moved increasingly farther away from elite residential districts. One spread out southeastwards along the Carretera Central and included San Francisco de Paula and Cotorro; a steel mill was located in the latter. This industrial strip extended beyond the metropolitan limit to Cuatro Caminos and, beyond that, to San José de las Lajas. The other concentration included a great southern axis that ran along Calzada de Rancho Boyeros and led to the airport. Both axes departed from an industrial strip, Vía Blanca, that ran along the southern part of the bay and included parts of Cerro. Here, like in Centro Habana and Habana Vieja, small mixed-use tracts of industries, workshops, residences and warehouses also emerged.

The 1957 *Industrial Directory* revealed that 3500 non-sugar mill factories produced more than 10 000 different products. Of that amount, 2340 (69%) factories produced items that the *Industrial Directory* considered to be important because of their vertical or horizontal linkages with other components and products. Only 107 (3.1%) of the factories employed more than 100 workers, 830 (23.7%) factories employed fewer than five workers, and the remaining 937 factories (73.2%) employed between six and 99 workers (Marrero 1981a, p. 311). In line with patterns of industrial location in most Latin American cities (Gwynne 1986), the largest percentage of all industrial plants were located in the province of the capital city.

The current location of industry (discussed in greater detail in Chapter 7) and light manufacturing has not changed considerably since the 1950s because the socialist government has promoted development in provincial towns and the countryside. During the last 5 years of the Batista government three-fourths of the total value of both residential and commercial construction was built in the capital and Havana's neighboring districts. However, only 1% of the new housing was state-built. Data from the Havana Province Institute of Architects (*Colegio Provincial de Arquitectos de La Habana*) which document only those projects directed under their affiliates' charge, reveal that between 1951 and 1955, there were 19 205 licensed construction projects valued at $30.1 million. In 1956, 3841 construction projects were launched which included 7994 housing units worth $60.3 million (Maribona 1957).

**Figure 3.3** Industrial plants by province, 1957
*Source*: Marrero (1981, p. 312)

*Road network*

Two tunnels built during the 1950s under the Almendares River between Vedado and Miramar greatly improved Havana's road network. One tunnel, consisting of two one-way segments, connected Línea Street with Miramar and Marianao in 1953 and the other extended from the Malecón to Quinta Avenida (Fifth Avenue) in 1959. Another tunnel project was completed in 1958 starting from Morro Castle, under the Bay of Havana, to the tip of Habana Vieja near the beginning of the Prado. It hooked up with an excellent highway, the Vía Monumental, which would have given rise to great speculative development of lands east of the city if the Revolution had not triumphed. Instead, large apartment complexes, walk-ups and high-rises, were erected here and in many other areas of socialist Cuba beginning in the 1960s (see Chapters 4 and 6).

At a regional scale, the 1950s saw the connection of Havana with two major coastal highways that connected two important ports: one connected Matanzas 100 kilometers to the east and the other at Mariel, 45 kilometers to the west. Forty kilometers beyond Matanzas was the tourist center of Varadero which would receive considerable investment in tourism. Although Varadero, Trinidad and the Isle of Pines were studied by the brand-new National Planning Board (created in 1955 and discussed in Chapter 2) as possible sites of development, the thrust of development continued to center on Havana.

Other roads, new or expanded, like Avenida 31 in Marianao and the highway, Autopista del Mediodía, lent themselves to upgrading for military purposes because they eased machinery and troop movement to and from the Columbia Military Base and the air base in San Antonio de los Baños. Many streets were repaired and others were widened using the previous lanes of the extensive streetcar network. Electric streetcar transport began in Havana in 1901 and was discontinued in 1952 under the purported benefit of 'modernization' and 'development'. The decision more likely aimed to make way for the sale of automobiles, buses, and fuel than it did to enhance 'modernization and development.' Even though the road network was incomplete, it was one of the few planning projects proposed and carried out by the Batista government.

*Clean and dirty water*

Chapter 1 noted that Havana holds the historic honor of inaugurating in 1592 the first European-built aqueduct in the Americas. The city's water system was further enhanced with the Albear Aqueduct, which won the

Gold Medal at the World Exposition in Paris in 1878 (though it was not officially completed until 1893). These historic landmarks notwithstanding, by the twentieth century Havana's water system had become a nemesis for the city's mayors. In fact, the besieged administration of one municipality led to one mayor's suicide in the 1940s. This dramatic act cautioned the subsequent mayor to mind the city's water problems more closely, and to build the next, so-called 'third aqueduct' that improved the water supply for the middle and southern areas of the city.

In the 1950s several important water mains were finished joining the capital with the new Cuenca Sur (Southern Watershed Basin). As a result, the overall volume of water for Havana increased appreciably even though it had to be drawn from sources each time more remote from the city. Those investments served the ambitious development projects of Havana at the expense of the neglected inner-city areas. The sewage system, inaugurated in 1913, was designed for about 600 000 users but, by the 1950s, had serviced approximately 1 million people in the old municipal limits of Havana. This service area covered the present-day counties of Habana Vieja, Centro Habana, Cerro, Diez de Octubre, Plaza and the oldest section of Miramar. The rest of the metropolis used septic tanks or else discharged runoff and raw sewage directly into rivers, streams and canals.

*Open spaces and recreation*

Despite Havana's tropical location, it was not a very 'green' city by the end of 1958. There was about 1.1 square meters of open space per resident and it was unequally distributed throughout the city. Most of the open spaces were in the well-off neighborhoods of Country Club, Miramar, Vedado and Nuevo Vedado, as well as a few middle-class districts that included Víbora and Santos Suárez. An area as heavily populated as Centro Habana, with its traditional business district, was practically without open spaces in both public and private (courtyards and patios) areas. This produced a textbook case of an urban 'heat island' wherein Centro Habana averaged about 2°F warmer than the rest of the city.

A modification to the Laws of the Indies in 1573 stipulated normative guidelines about the layout of the colonial Spanish-American city. Among its mandates were the use of certain colors to keep temperatures down (i.e., increased albedo levels or solar reflection), and draping narrow streets with canvass to ensure shade; both practices growing out of the Sevillian tradition. In this type of urban pattern, greenery – also inherited from Mudejar tradition – adorned the interior courtyards (*patio*) of the major homes. Shaded galleries gave cool relief to residents doing house-hold chores. While larger traditional homes of the well-to-do had plants, shrubs and trees in the patios, greenery among the poor was reduced to a few flower pots. With the gradual abandonment and subdivision of the old colonial mansions, tenants used patios to build rooms to accommo-date new occupants. Although the growing city continued to follow the same grid plan, the height of buildings increased dramatically, reducing patios to small courtyards that were not much more than simple openings for ventilation.

Outdoor green spaces adjacent to residential neighborhoods first appeared outside the old colonial core in the elegant neighborhood of Cerro built in the first half of the nineteenth century. Aristocratic country houses of the period were called *quintas*. These were Neoclassical *villas* with *portales* and gardens. So lush were these gardens that some really became tropical parks. Even better examples of open areas surfaced in Vedado during the last half of the nineteenth century. One-hundred-meter sided blocks in Vedado were accentuated with *parterres*: tree-lined corri-dors of lawn between the curb and the sidewalk. In front of homes there was a 5-meter wide swath of garden, coupled with a 4-meter deep colon-nade that standardized, broadened and cooled the Vedado landscape. Vedado building regulations instituted rules about the separation of homes and, in doing so, ended the use of the dividing walls that charac-terized Habana Vieja and Centro Habana. Not only were the Vedado lots larger on average than their inner-city counterparts, but zoning regula-tions stipulated that one-third of each lot had to be left uncovered (Montoulieu y de la Torre 1953; Llana 1983). These design features added much to a natural cooling process in the tropical heat.

Miramar replicated many of Vedado's building codes and set-back requirements. Property lots were even larger than in Vedado. In some of the older districts of Miramar, there was a building code that was unique in all of Havana. It required a thin garden between the sidewalk and the property line in addition to the traditional *parterre*. However, this norm did not lead to establishing 'green tunnels' through which pedestrians could walk, protecting themselves from the sweltering heat. It was not that the planners and residents did not believe this was a good idea; they simply acknowledged the fact that most residents did not walk a lot. Moreover, the *nouveau riche* of the district did not wish to obstruct the views of their pretentious homes.

Public open spaces in the colonial districts of Havana were concentra-ted along the *paseos* and plazas, like Alameda de Paula and the Plaza de Armas. The latter, however, was not always tree-covered. Initially, it was an open and dusty expanse designed to accommodate military exercises.

Significant tracts of public open spaces in the 1950s actually consisted of long-standing parks and promenades such as the axis made up of Paseo del Prado (originally called Isabel II), Parque Central (Central Park), the gardens surrounding the Capitolio, the India fountain, and *Parque de la Fraternidad* (Fraternity Square).

One type of influential public space during the first half of the twentieth century, not only in Havana but throughout towns and cities on the island, was the so-called Republican-style park. This consisted of an entire city block adorned with trees and interior sidewalks, two of which, crisscrossed the park diagonally. It also contained lamp posts, cast iron-legged benches and a central element that took many forms: a fountain, commemorative sculpture, kiosk, pergola, or band stand. The Republican Park functioned as a multiple use urban node for children, adults and the elderly, where parties and periodic markets could be held. In short, the Republican Park breached Havana's grid-pattern layout of buildings by providing character, utility, and cool shade to the city's many neighborhoods.

For the most part the unbuilt spaces separating the major thoroughfares that allowed the city to spread were not used to extend vegetative cover throughout the city. Perhaps the only exception was along the banks of the Almendares River, the city's major freshwater stream. Spectacular vegetation consisting of immense *algarrobo* trees (carob tree, *Ceratonia siliqua*) entangled by spectacular vines in a theatrical scenery that resembled a haunted forest, and nurtured by a unique microclimate could be found in *El Bosque de la Habana* (The Forest of Havana) along the west bank of the river, and near two beautiful limestone cliffs separating Kohly from Nuevo Vedado. This was the setting in the 1940s of a colorful mythical character known as 'Tarzan of the Forest.' First land speculation and then a lack of control on how the area was used greatly reduced its acreage. However, in the early 1960s, part of the remaining area was upgraded to become the narrow Almendares Park (see Chapter 8).

Adjacent to Almendares Park and to its south were the gardens of the old Tropical Brewery, *Jardines de la Tropical*, also along the banks of the Almendares River. Even farther south was a rival brewery, Polar, which also boasted beer drinking in a cool park protected by lush riparian vegetation. In the European tradition, the breweries promoted their beers in beautiful beer gardens (Figure 3.4). Not only was the tree canopy of Tropical Gardens a novelty, but it was also well known for its whimsical ferrocement architecture. Pavilions and small structures in the park displayed a strong, early twentieth-century Catalan influence and motifs of sea life and vegetation.

Popular afternoon outings on the evenings of saint's days as well as

**Figure 3.4** Tropical Brewery Park.
*Source*: Habana, Cuba: Ciudad de Encanto. La Habana Edición Jordi (c. 1927)

other celebrations were held at these river parks, always accompanied with lots of beer, and frequently organized by one of the dozens of immigrant associations from different corners of Spain. As discussed in the next section, these Spanish associations were numerous and they afforded their affiliates with a wide array of services in the form of beaches, casinos, schools, home economics courses, hospitalization, and other medical services. Many cemeteries in Havana have pantheons for such groups, and several of the pantheons at Colón Cemetery have considerable artistic value.

### Beaches, casinos and clubs: to each their own

The switch from a Havana heavily influenced by Spain to one of US domination also surfaced in the leisure activities of *habaneros* and their social organizations in the 1950s. The change was not only apparent in the names used (the Spaniards preferred the names '*centro*' and '*casino*' in theirs while those of US influence opted for '*clubs*') but also corresponded to certain nuances among social strata. The inner city of Havana housed large buildings where these social organizations used the gyms, billiard rooms and reading rooms and hosted dances and parties. These functions took place in *ad hoc* Eclectic palaces such as the *Centro Gallego* (1917) and *Centro Asturiano* (1927) in front of *Parque Central*. Paseo del Prado contained the smaller yet impressive palatial structures of the American Club and *Casino Español* as well as facilities of Basque, Catalan and Andalucian associations.

At the beginning of the Malecón (intersection with Prado) was the Unión Club with its stone-carved caryatids along the façades. In the same tradition of social clubs in the heart of the city were the Vedado Tennis Club and the Lyceum Lawn Tennis Club. These three clubs had predominantly Cuban membership. The Vedado Tennis Club, for example, was founded in 1902 and was comprised of patrician members who gave rise to the nickname the 'Marqueses' in the press and sports circles. So prestigious and powerful was the Vedado Tennis Club that it persuaded the public authorities to build a special ocean access for its canoes that went underneath the Malecón in the late 1950s, during the final completion of the seaside promenade.

The gamut of options and social sectors served by clubs was quite broad. Just west of the mouth of the Almendares River was the *Casino Deportivo* (Sporting Club) whose clientele hailed from the middle- and lower-middle classes, and frequented by the wealthy Jewish community of Havana. Farther west was the *Club de Ferreteros* (Hardware Clerk's

Club) for employees in that commercial sector. The *Club de Profesionales* followed with membership from middle- and upper-middle-class backgrounds. Farther along were the *Balneario Universitario* (University Bathing Resort) and the Copacabana, the latter which had both a club house and a hotel, as did the Comodoro. Continuing westward one would find the Miramar Yacht Club whose members were upper-middle class. In the 1950s that club demolished its interesting wooden club house and replaced it with a modern, yet banal building. Moving in the same direction we come across the *Club Cubaneleco*, designated for employees of the *Compañía Cubana de Electricidad* which, despite its name, was a transnational United States company. The Compañía moved its recreational facilities to the former Swimming Club when it sold its old club house in the Vedado to accommodate the huge Focsa building, one of the new 'skyscrapers' of Vedado in the 1950s (Figure 3.5). Finally, this westward string of social clubs was capped off with the *Balneario Hijas de Galicia* (Daughters of Galicia Beach Resort), part of the large Galician colony in Cuba.

Following the Galician facility there was a string of social clubs on the artificial and half-moon shaped beach of Marianao. Always moving westward, the first one was the *Círculo Militar y Naval* that sported a new building thanks to General Batista. Marianao beach also held the pseudo-

**Figure 3.5** View of the Vedado skyscrapers: The Focsa (middle) and Someillán buildings (far left). Photograph by Roberto Segre

Mudejar building of the *Balneario de la Concha* that was not technically a social club as one had to pay for each visit. At the opposite end of the social ladder, yet right next door to the Balneario de la Concha, stood the prestigious Habana Yacht Club. This club, founded in 1886, was the oldest beach resort and club in Cuba. It was also the nation's most exclusive club where new members had to be relatives of a current member.

The Habana Yacht Club was the principal relic of the patrician *criollo* class that managed to withstand the impoverishment inflicted by both the Independence Wars and the Great Depression of the 1930s. Unlike the Vedado Tennis Club, the 'Yacht' (as it was widely called) combined elements of social snobbishness with a more family-like atmosphere enhanced by the allure of the beach. By the 1930s or so, the Yacht had displaced the 'Tennis' as the pillar of social status among Havanan country clubs. The Tennis, on the other hand, had relaxed its admission standards in its quest to draw the best young athletes to its facilities. Over time it took on an ambiguous aura of elegance and corruption.

The *Casino Español* followed the Habana Yacht Club on Marianao's crescent beach. Wealthy Spanish-immigrant merchants, at the insistence of their wives, used the Casino Español to marry their daughters into 'good' families. The beach ended with the *Club Náutico* whose members were high-salaried white-collar workers and homeowners in the neighboring residential subdivision of the same name. Both the subdivision and the beach club had the same owner. South, to the crescent beach of Marianao and, ironically separated by a squatter settlement, was the Country Club de La Habana. The wealthiest Cubans and Americans frequented the club which was surrounded by a beautiful golf course. To the west lay the waterfront properties of the Havana Biltmore Yacht & Country Club also, of course, consisting of upper-class members. Except for the Balneario Universitario and La Concha with their open admission policies, only white people belonged to these country clubs. Because of the loose tropical definition of a 'white person', the more lax a club's position on the racial composition of its members, the less affluent its members tended to be.

The wealthiest *habaneros* belonged to more than one club, using each according to its location and profile. The relative locations of these facilities also provided distinct attributes. The 'Tennis', for instance, with its central location in Vedado, was a great place for a quick game of squash, a shower, and a drink before returning to work in the afternoon. The 'Yacht' was more appropriate for a tranquil weekend outing with the entire family, while the 'Country' was ideal for closing a big business deal with a rich American client. Social prestige was also attached to spending particular holidays at certain clubs: New Year's Eve at 'Tennis', the Tea

Party on Christmas day at the 'Yacht', and the magnificent formal dance, *Baile Rojo*, at 'Country'.

Five of the main social clubs held sporting events. These five – Yacht, Vedado Tennis, Biltmore, Miramar, and Casino Español – formed the 'big five.' Later, they were joined by *Profesionales* to make up the 'big six'. These clubs competed among themselves and with certain American groups such as the dual swimming meet in Atlanta. Physically, Marianao Beach exhibited the futile hypocrisy of class divisions; although the buildings of these clubs were guardedly separate from each other on land, its members shared the same ocean and the same vices. Even when leaving the clubs with their hair still wet, many would cross paths with each other at the roller coaster ride at the Coney Island amusement park, pool halls, bars, and cabarets. Some of the men would run into other club members just by crossing Quinta Avenida where they would sneak off to the *casas de citas* with mistresses or prostitutes.

Contrasts also appeared in other ways. When Batista tried to join the exclusive Yacht Club, he was rejected in the secret, ancient Roman-style voting with white and black marbles. Eventually, the slightly less demanding Biltmore admitted him. In exchange for his membership, Batista gave the Biltmore a splendid marina whose value exceeded all the club's combined assets!

The appropriation of waterfront properties by the elite took place east of the capital as well, but mostly for second homes at a fine, natural beach. In the 1950s there emerged an elegant new subdivision called Santa María del Mar, located west of the small town of Guanabo (a popular free-access beach) and east of the private beach of Tarará. Guanabo existed as a remote vacation spot beginning in the 1930s when, for a middle class family, getting there was a bit like going on a safari expedition. The excursion required taking a street car to the Avenida del Puerto, and then crossing the bay by ferry to Casablanca. From there they would board the old electric train whose rail line was inaugurated in 1916 to connect Havana to the Hershey sugar mill. The family would disembark at the crossroads of a small hamlet, Campo Florido, and from there travel by rickety *fotingos* (1928 Fords) to the beach. Vacationers had to carry or buy enough drinking water to last them several days or even months. Lodging at Guanabo consisted then of a few dozen zinc-roofed cottages. There, in the serenity of the wilderness, a child rising early before dawn could witness the mysterious egg-laying of a giant sea tortoise.

## Havana: sun, sea and sin

Prostitution continued to be a sordid dimension of Havana in the 1950s. Tourism, social inequality, low education levels, machismo, and the deeply ingrained double-standards of the Catholic bourgeoisie sustained the city's sex industry. The cheapest place in the city to secure commercial sex was in the sordid brothels along Pila Street in irascible Atarés. Closer to the city center, though, especially around the port, cheap sex was readily available. San Isidro Street catered largely to sailors and an underworld of shady characters found in most ports, as did Picota, Paula, Conde, and, ironically, Damas (Ladies) Streets. By the 1950s, long gone were the days when San Isidro was the pinnacle of such elegant vice and decadence portrayed by the nostalgia of Alberto Yarini y Ponce de León. The story consists of a well educated young pimp with high-brow last names who was killed in 1910 in a street fight over a French prostitute.

The most notorious district was the strip between Habana Vieja and Centro Habana that adjoined the commercial center. It was framed by the Paseo del Prado, Neptuno, San Lázaro and Galiano. By extension, it was known by the name of the street where the real character of the neighborhood was concentrated: Colón. Another brothel zone adjoined the commercial center, but it was farther south along Zanja Street in *Barrio Chino* (Chinatown). The latter district captured the market of men who would come to and from the pornographic movie house, Shangai. A neighboring city block, the Plaza del Vapor at the end of Galiano Street, was comprised of an entire market where prostitutes were exchanged like any other commodity. The plaza was demolished in 1960.

The neighborhood of La Victoria, so-called because prostitution started there at the end of the Second World War, was located southwest of the Plaza del Vapor around Xifré Street, where Calzada de Infanta met Paseo de Carlos III. This area was near another huge market named after the same Spanish king. Lastly, another well established area of prostitution in the 1950s was situated between Centro Habana and Vedado, very close to La Rampa, along the streets of Marina, Hornos and Vapor. In this area was the notorious house of Marina, considered one of the 'finest' in Havana in the 1950s. Taken in their entirety, these red-light districts occupied about 50 hectares of the central city.

The Havana of the 1950s was marketed as both a tropical paradise and a place to gamble, where the tourist was tempted to 'sin in the sun.' Tourist developers were not timid about marketing Havana's decadence; it was not a mere appendage to the sand-and-beach scene, as the following excerpt from a promotional magazine of the day reveals:

Close your eyes and visualize this scene: Night – a magical night with sky and velvety midnight blue scattered with a thousand glittering stars; low in the east moon, incredibly large and golden.

A warm breeze tantalizingly scented with the intoxicating perfume of strange, exotic tropical flowers.

Music, warm sensuous, entrancing with Latin rhythms which set the blood to stirring and the feet to tapping.

Glamorous, lissome Latin lasses, black-eyed señoritas, languorously, enticingly swaying as they glide over a polished floor in a smooth rumba.

The bright excitement of gaming tables, the whir of the roulette wheel, the age-old chant of the croupier.

A dream you say? A dream that only the rich man can make come true?

How wrong you are! This is the night-time in Havana . . . the 'Paris of the Americas' (cited in Williams 1994, p. 47).

Lurid offers of sex ran the spectrum of price ranges, comfort and discretion. At the low end was quick oral sex in a dark hallway or fornication standing up in a vacant lot whose entrance was often protected by strips of hanging bed sheets. Of course, the conventional *bordello* staffed by numerous women was also an option. Prostitutes working out of their own homes and apartments forced many a neighbor to place signs on their doors which read 'Dont Bother: Family House'. Hustlers, called *fleteras* (runners), worked the streets to direct prospective clients to run-down seedy hotels with which they were affiliated.

At the upper end of the business were bars such as the Mambo Club. These were exclusive and discrete bars, somewhat remote from the city center. Clients could reserve time, space and high-priced women. Another tropical invention was the *posada* where a couple could clandestinely meet for a few hours (an institution still in vogue in Latin America). The cheaper ones were located in the inner city and thus were pedestrian oriented. In the suburbs, a couple could drive up to a discrete facility and disappear behind a garage door. Once inside, they could not be seen by curious customers or even the clerk; transactions would be carried out through a drop box or dumb-waiter system. The full array of 'troops' in the commercial sex industry – street walkers, expensive call girls, pimps, street hustlers, and others – would move into a 'state of alert' when a US war ship arrived in port. To many Cubans, the photographs of drunk sailors hanging from the statue of José Martí in Parque Central served as humiliating memories of those visits. Regrettably, even though these episodes occurred 40 years ago in Havana, the debasing smell of the trafficking of flesh would reappear like an opportunistic virus among the educated and self-employed street hustlers (*jineteras*) of the 1990s.

## Culture, education and health care

Cultural life in Havana showed sustained growth in the 1950s. Since at least the nineteenth century, Cuba had always held within Latin America a rather high level in the arts and humanities. Paradoxically, this profile existed within a country characterized by institutional crisis, public and private corruption, public indifference about 'high culture', and a lack of state support for the arts (Hart 1979; Rodríguez Feo 1994).

Major talents in the fine arts included the painter Wifredo Lam and the novelist Alejo Carpentier. Unfortunately, even they had to emigrate to escape the suffocating setting where they – the island's best and brightest – could not make a living off their artistic and literary forte. The upper class for the most part spent little money on artistic symbols of status, preferring instead bad copies of works bought in Europe as souvenirs, or pretentious portraits made by mediocre local artists. Some departure was noted by upper-class Cubans with notable collections of art such as those held by Oscar Cintas; the Count of Lagunillas, Joaquín Gumá; and the wealthy patrons of the arts, María Luisa Gómez Mena and the Falla-Gutiérrez family. Many national writers subsidized the publication of their own books and poetry and wound up giving them away to friends.

In 1954 Batista made a lame gesture towards reviving the arts. He created the National Institute of Culture, headed by a 'dandy' (a flamboyant socialite), named Guillermo de Zéndegui, whose most notable accomplishment was to eliminate the national subsidy of the world renowned Ballet Nacional de Cuba. A joke that circulated *sotto voce* among the upper class reflected this prophetic association of elitism, superficiality, and uncouthness with the arts. The imaginary setting goes like this: a nervous Batista seeks advice from his brand-new director of the National Institute of Culture about how to behave at an upcoming special exhibit of the Mona Lisa. Looking for an easy way out, de Zéndegui tells the President to pause in front of the painting, take two steps back from the work, and exclaim admiringly: 'Such a face! What an expression!' (*Qué cara! Qué gesto!*). The next day when the exhibit opens, Batista begins his pantomime, but confuses the word 'face' (*cara*) with 'hell' (*carajo*) and exclaims: 'What the hell is this?' (*¿Qué carajo es esto?*).

The lack of institutional support notwithstanding, Cuban art in the 1950s found outlets wherever it could flourish and express itself. The important literary magazine *Orígenes* went out of business, but it was replaced by *Ciclón* and later by *Isla*. The national press also increased the quality and breadth of its coverage of cultural events. In that same decade, a group called *Los Once* (The Group of Eleven), comprised of young artists devoted to abstract expressionism, was founded. Cuban music became celebrated throughout the Americas, and a new style, *filin*, was added to the Cuban repertoire of Mambo, cha-cha-cha, and other popular musical styles. Another organization, *Sociedad Nuestro Tiempo*, covertly allied with the outlawed Communist Party (*Partido Socialista Popular*), labored in promoting theater and classical music. The Havana cultural scene[1] also benefited from painting exhibitions and art cinema at the University of Havana promoted by revolutionary students.

Even though Havana enjoyed a disproportionate concentration of health and educational services compared with the rest of Cuba, public services did not meet the needs of most *habaneros* in terms of both quality and quantity. Politicians and the press frequently commented on the dire situation of public schools, but with little apparent resolve. Nonetheless, the greatest problem was the scarcity and bad condition of the schools themselves. The caliber of the teachers was generally satisfactory. As a consequence of the poor quality of public education, private schools catered not only to the wealthy, but also to the working classes who earned steady incomes. Cuba's large number of parochial schools was noteworthy because unlike most Latin American countries, Catholicism was not deeply rooted in Cuban society though it was far and away the prevailing religion. Catholic schools existed according to purchasing power, religious orders, and, of course, were segregated by gender.

Like the social clubs described previously in this chapter, there was an unspoken social hierarchy of private schools in Havana. For the upper bourgeoisie, for example, there were the all-boys schools such as the Jesuit-run Colegio de Belén where Fidel Castro studied; and the Colegio de La Salle, directed by Brothers of that same order. Nuns ran the all-girl schools of Merici Academy and Sagrado Corazón. Administrators and even teachers of most of these schools were Spaniards, French or Americans, with minor contributions from Cubans and Latin Americans.

Those Cuban families who did not care for a Catholic education, or simply wished to improve their children's English, sent them to private

---

[1]In addition to Lam and Carpentier, a host of stellar personalities occupied the artistic scene, including the writers José Lezama Lima, Nicolás Guillén, Onelio Jorge Cardoso, Enrique Labrador Ruiz, José Z. Tallet, Cintio Vitier, Eliseo Diego, Mirta Aguirre, Jorge Mañach, Lydia Cabrera, and Virgilio Piñera. The visual and graphic arts scene involved René Portocarrero, Carlos Enríquez, Mariano Rodríguez, Amelia Peláez, Agustín Cárdenas and Luis Martínez Pedro. The fields of dance and music contributed the ballerina Alicia Alonso and the musical composers Harold Gramatges, Ernesto Lecuona, Ignacio Villa (*Bola de Nieve*), Benny Moré, Dámaso Pérez Prado, Enrique Jorrín, César Portillo and José Antonio Méndez. Cuban architecture boasted the contributions of Max Borges, Mario Romañach, Frank Martínez, Nicolás Quintana, Miguel Gastón and Antonio Quintana. Historical continuity materialized in the 1960s when many young artists from the previous decade reached their maturity, even though some had worked and lived outside Cuba.

schools such as Ruston or Phillips. The 1950s was also a time when Protestant schools, such as Candler College, which combined religion and English, increased enrollments. The social prestige of these schools was extensive and covered a gamut of social groups and markets. Ungovernable students or those with little talent simply changed from one school to the next, based on the tolerance level and financial need of the receiving institution. With very few exceptions – like the huge complex built *ex profeso* by the Colegio de Belén (today the Instituto Técnico Militar) – most schools, even the finest ones, were located in converted houses. With hindsight, this would suggest that the quality of teaching depends more on the demands and skills of teachers than classroom amenities.

Higher education in Cuba before the Revolution of 1959, like health care and public education, was concentrated in the capital, except for the newly established Universidad de Oriente in Santiago de Cuba and Universidad de Las Villas in Santa Clara. The University of Habana, founded in 1728, had a long tradition of participating in national life, and excelled in the fields of medicine and law. Its campus had been relocated at the turn of the century from Habana Vieja to a commanding location similar to that of the Acropolis. The entire complex was enclosed by a huge wall interrupted by the main entrance of the campus: a grand set of stairs fanning down to the street from a quad of buildings encased by Greco-Roman columns. A statue titled *Alma Mater* anchors the stairs at the top. The design of the monumental stairs is similar to Columbia University in New York City, but is better framed by two strips of smaller, lateral stairs.

At the back of the campus of the University of Havana stood the Calixto García teaching hospital where medical students conducted their residencies. In the 1950s the hospital served as a refuge for students who fled from an invading police force that theoretically could not violate the constitutionally sanctioned right of university autonomy and non-intervention in campus affairs. Surrounding the University of Havana campus stood the administration building (*rectorado*), library, Aula Magna (Great Hall), and the departments of law, natural sciences, chemistry, social sciences, physics, pharmacy, education, electrical and civil engineering, and architecture. Close by the campus one could find the stadium, the Quinta de los Molinos (ex-Spanish governor's summer residence) in which the agronomy department resided as did arts and sciences, philosophy, and the schools of dentistry, medicine and veterinary sciences.

This section of Havana was full of ancillary services and retailing such as cafés, academic preparation and tutoring centers, and student boarding houses to accommodate students from an array of socioeconomic backgrounds and different parts of Cuba. A well known boarding house was the so-called *bombonera* (literally, a candy store) where well-groomed young women from wealthy families lodged. Services spread the influence of the university over a considerable area, ranging from Calzada de Infanta, Paseo de Carlos III, Avenida de los Presidentes and Calle 23, and from San Lázaro turning on L Street as the main axis. In the middle of the 1950s the police dared only to enter this zone in large numbers, readied to engage in combat with students who at that point not only threw back rocks, but fired guns.

The Universidad Católica de Villanueva emerged in the late 1940s in the elegant Biltmore subdivision. It exhibited a clear class spirit that aimed to raise college education to a higher-quality level similar to what had previously occurred in primary and secondary schools. In doing so, its goal was to be both morally and yet socially convenient for the upper classes. It also offered respite from the continuously tumultuous political scene of the University of Havana, beset by closings, demonstrations, and strikes. Despite its intentions, Villanueva carried relatively little weight in the national academic arena, not only because of its high tuition, but also because its faculty and the quality of its students could not match its 200-year old counterpart on University Hill. In 1952, for instance, a graduating student at the Colegio de Belén could be advised by his or her guidance counselor to go study with the lay faculty at the University of Havana instead of the Universidad Católica de Villanueva. Such advice reflected not just objective academic criteria but also the aristocratic disdain of the Spanish Jesuits at Belén, and their dislike of the newly arrived American Augustine faculty at Villanueva.

Medical care mirrored the class-ridden inequities and conflicts present in education. Despite the concentration of medical care personnel and facilities in Havana, there was a great demand for medical care outside the strictly fee-for-payment market. This demand was to a large extent absorbed by mutual-aid societies that were often aligned with regional Spanish immigrant groups (see Chapter 8). In the 1950s, about half of the medical care delivered in the City of Havana was provided by these mutual-aid societies. For the middle class, these societies provided comprehensive medical care for a remarkably low monthly premium. A dense network of neighborhood pharmacies was as widespread as the corner grocer. The poor, though, resorted to charity care or simply did without medical care.

## The growth of the capital

The spread of the metropolitan area during the first half of the twentieth century produced a fragmented array of private subdivisions and properties. Private initiative almost exclusively created this urbanization, without any unifying structure. There was little coordination with neighboring lots or among local jurisdictions. Most architects lacked a deep appreciation for urban design and planning. Suburbanization in the 1950s did not follow the mandates of a master plan. Streets started and ended randomly, and there was little concern about linking subdivisions and municipalities with other parts of the city. Instead, the relationship among different neighborhoods and subdivisions read like an endless list of places and covered very different city-planning attributes and social classes. A good indicator of that was the use of Spanish versus English place names. Older parts of the city drew on the city's traditional, indigenous, and natural landmarks. Generally, the newer and more affluent sections of metropolitan Havana were located in the west. In Marianao and points west, a preponderance of Western, up-scale place names characterized the newer suburbs that prospered in the second quarter of the century. Named after landowners or simply foreign (i.e., non-Spanish) names, these neighborhoods included Kohly, Country Club and Floral Park. Another set of neighborhoods was situated at slightly higher elevations (*Alturas*, meaning Heights, as in Alturas de Belén, Alturas de Coronela, Alturas de Miramar). These communities were a bit remote from the center of town, but they afforded its residents with slightly lower temperatures and more sea breeze in a pre-air-conditioned Havana. Granted, many of these new neighborhoods had 'climate-controlled' homes by the 1950s, but the new subdivisions provided access to resident-owned houses and isolation from the run-down city center. The higher elevations also implied a sense of prestige for being located 'above' the rest of the city. Still other names carried chic or European labels: Havana Biltmore, Alturas del Biltmore, La Playa (Beach), Playa Miramar, and Club Náutico. Others simply carried the name of the owner of the land or the developer, like Embil, De Beche, Parcelación Zayas, or Querejeta.

Havana's crude birth rate in 1958 was fairly high (21.3 live per births per 1000 population) even though it was less than in rural areas (28). High fertility levels in the capital probably resulted from rural and small-town immigrants who were driven by unemployment and misery. Thus, Havana's proportion of the national population rose from 19.8% in 1943 to 20.9% in 1959 (Table 3.1).

The new and growing city of the 1950s had increased 5.7-fold between 1898 (population 240 000) and 1958 (1.36 million in Greater Havana). By the triumph of the Revolution, one of five Cubans lived in Havana. The capital grew in the 1940s and 1950s at the fastest rate in the nation owing to an upgraded road network and improved automobile and bus transportation connecting Havana with the rest of the country. Although pop-

**Table 3.1**  Population growth of Havana and Cuba, 1899–1958

| Year | Havana | Cuba | Havana's percentage |
|------|--------|------|---------------------|
| 1899 | 235 981[a] | 1 572 797[b] | 15.0 |
| 1907 | 302 526[a] | 2 048 980[b] | 14.8 |
| 1919 | 363 506[a] | 2 889 004[b] | 12.6 |
| 1931 | 728 500[c] | 3 962 344[c] | 18.4[c] |
| 1943 | 946 000[c] | 4 778 583[c] | 19.8[c] |
| 1953 | 1 223 900[c] | 5 829 029[c] | 21.0[c] |
| 1958 | 1 361 600[a] | 6 548 300[a] | 20.9 |

*Sources:* [a]*Habana 1* (1971)
   [b]*Anuario Demográfico* (1989)
   [c]*Censo de Población y Viviendas* (1981)
*Note:* Population data for Havana in the 1931, 1943, and 1953 censuses refer to the former municipalities of the present City of Havana (Ciudad de La Habana) and have been adjusted to reflect the present City of Havana. Percentages, where no source is indicated, are calculated by the authors.

ulation growth had been fairly sluggish at about the turn of the century, it shot up with the frenzied high-price sugar years discussed in the last chapter (called 'dance of the millions') until it reached 560 000 residents by 1925. Population growth stabilized during the Great Depression, but then continued in the post-war period. Contributing to this growth was a broadening job market in the metropolitan area, including light industry on the city's outskirts, the construction industry and suburbanization (Segre 1978). Havana experienced an astounding growth of 68% (495 400) between 1931 and 1953. Between 1943 and 1953 it grew by an average annual growth rate of 2.6%, versus the national rate of 2.19%. Between 1953 and 1959, the respective annual growth rates for the capital and nation were 3.0% and 2.3% (Various 1971). Within the capital city, though, population growth at the city's edge was 75% greater during 1953–1959 than in the city center. It was not until 1966 that Havana's overall growth rate would fall below the national level (Various 1973).

Suburban developments spread along the western side of the Almendares River, and southward to the Alturas de Miramar and Kohly. When that prime realty became occupied, newer homes were built to the west in Playa, which shared a boundary with the most affluent areas: Country Club (now Cubanacán), Biltmore (presently, Siboney), and Alturas del Biltmore (presently Atabey). These latter two were completed in the 1950s. During that same decade, land speculation around the Plaza Cívica led to the creation of Nuevo Vedado along the eastern shore of the Almendares River.

High-priced condominium construction increased the density of the central districts. Part of this central-city revitalization by the elite took place in Vedado, which, in the 1950s, still retained its prestige as an elegant neighborhood (Entenza y Jova 1953). In Cerro, however, where elite neoclassical residences sprang up earlier than in Vedado, such residential allure had already disappeared by that time. While westward elite suburbanization ensued, the Condominium Law (*Ley de Propiedad Horizontal*) of 1952 allowed the wealthy to recover parts of the central district (Bugeda Lanzas 1954). Elite housing along the ocean was not new, having begun in the 1920s with the opening up of Miramar. However, the 1952 law did not prohibit structures greater than six stories to be built along the Malecón in Vedado, permanently transforming the city's skyline. These same buildings are still standing along a strip of land from the Malecón in Vedado and inland several blocks.

This type of ocean-front land speculation was bound to deprive the city not only of prime public space and panoramic views, but of cooling sea breezes. This calamity was indirectly avoided by the 1959 Revolution. Further development of this kind would have been disasterous for Havana, but it was pre-empted by the 1959 Revolution. The Revolution also brought to end the plan by José Luis Sert (see Chapter 2) to establish a great artificial island with hotels and casinos just off the shores of Centro Habana. His plans were supported not only by the island's elite, but also by the gangster-driven investment of Meyer Lansky and Santos Trafficante, who were portrayed in Francis Ford Coppola's film, *The Godfather II*.

The city's vocation as a tourist center was too strong not to leave some imprint on the landscape. The 1950s ushered in a new wave of modern-style hotels throughout the bustling La Rampa section of Vedado: Habana Riviera, Havana Hilton[2] (Figure 3.6), Capri, St. John, Vedado, Flamingo, and Colina. Hotels were built in the western edge of the city and extended as far west as Barlovento (today the Hemingway Marina): Comodoro, Copacabana and Chateau Miramar. These facilities, directed mainly at the US tourist market, contrasted with the more stately and elegant hotels of a bygone era: Hotel Nacional (Figure 3.7), Hotel Sevilla and Hotel Plaza. The Hotel Nacional would occupy a prominent role in Havana's landscape because of its premier location on a bluff overlooking the ocean. As Vedado grew and became the premier tourist district of Havana, the Hotel Nacional came to anchor the area around Malecón and L Street. The area is known as La Rampa (literally, 'the slope' because it was one of the few steep hills in the city center).

---

[2]The Havana Hilton has been a major city landmark since it was built in 1958, if only because of its size. It became the Habana Libre in the early years of the Revolution, then the Habana Libre-Guitart (after a Spanish investment group) between 1993 and 1995, and then again the Habana Libre in 1996. Chapter 8 discusses more fully the recent wave of Spanish investment in Havana's tourist industry.

**Figure 3.6** Havana Hilton Hotel (1958) in background was renamed the Habana Libre in the early 1960s with one of the many American cars of the same era that still circulate throughout the city. Photograph by Joseph L. Scarpaci

These hotels supported an extensive network of internationally recognized ancillary services. The Tropicana cabaret was among the most widely recognized tourist haunts, and was satirized in Guillermo Cabrera Infante's celebrated book, Three Trapped Tigers (*Tres Tristes Tigres*). As the story begins, the emcee dutifully recognizes the club's celebrated visitors. After introducing a famous movie star, he then presents a US businessman, first in English, then in Spanish, to the local patrons:

I would like to welcome some old friends to this palace of happiness . . . Less beautiful but as rich and as famous is our very good friend and frequent

**Figure 3.7** Hotel Nacional overlooking the Malecón and the Florida Straits in Vedado. Built in 1930, it was closed for many years but was remodeled and modernized in the early 1990s. Photograph by Joseph L. Scarpaci

guest of Tropicana, the wealthy and healthy (he is an earlier riser) Mr. William Campbell, the notorious soup-fortune heir and world champion indoor golf and indoor tennis (and other not so mentionable indoor sports- ha ha ha!). Mr. Campbell, our favorite playboy! Lights (Thank you Mr. Campbell), lights, lights, lights! Thanks so much, Mr. Campbell! (*Amableypacientepúblicocubanoes Mister Campbell elfamosomillonario herederode- unafortunaensopas.*) (Cabrera Infante 1971, p. 5).

There were restaurants such as Sloppy Joe's Bar, La Bodeguita del Medio, El Floridita and the Terraza de Cojímar whose patrons included Ernest Hemingway and other celebrities (Fuentes 1987). The array of culinary options was indeed surprising for a Caribbean city of such modest size. French, Italian, Basque, Andalucian, Cantonese, Jewish and North American fare were available, not to mention the more modestly priced hamburgers (*fritas*) and oyster kiosks. Popular stands carried the ubiquitous sugar-cane juice, *guarapo*, and Cuban coffee called *tres quilos* (literally 'three cents', its price). A small and attractive theater, Auditorium, featured some of the greatest figures in the world's classical music scene. Auditorium was located in front of Parque Villalón and the elegant café, El Carmelo, on Calzada street. Seedier places existed too, ranging from the questionable bars of Playa de Marianao (where the popular local band El Chori and film-star Marlon Brando could be found) to the squalid pornographic theater, Shangai, located in Havana's Chinatown.

## Havana's built cultural heritage and architecture in the 1950s

The Modern Movement in architecture sheepishly made its appearance in Cuba in the 1940s (Rogers *et al.* 1961). It arrived as Art Deco was waning and it coexisted with the perennial Modern Monumental Movement (Figure 3.8). It was not until the 1950s that the Modern Movement took firm hold in Cuban cities, especially Havana. The rationalist codes of the modernist European masters – Le Corbusier, Gropius, Neutra, Breuer, and most of all, Mies – had arrived in Cuba from the United States in a steady procession. This detour through the north gave the Cuban version

**Figure 3.8** Art Deco-style residence built in the 1940s in Miramar. Photograph by Joseph L. Scarpaci

influences like Wright's organic architecture, the purist minimalist style of the magazine *Arts and Architecture*, and pseudocolonial touches mixed with influences from the Californian Mission Style springing up in American suburbs.

The Latin American vanguard in architecture at the time – mainly contemporary Brazilian and Mexican architects, along with the works of Carlos Raúl Villanueva of Venezuela – had strong influences in Cuba. Latin American styles and movements afforded younger Cuban architects a competing paradigm for shaking off the growing commercialism in Cuba (Segre 1970a,b). This meant synthesizing the international with the Cuban, a process that some Cuban architects had pursued in the 1940s. Not surprisingly, the Modern Movement had a different impact in the United States than in Cuba. In the United States, most projects built in this style were relegated to industrial complexes and prominent downtown office buildings. In Havana, the Modern Movement played a key role in shaping the look of entire residential districts.

Yet most buildings in Cuba built in the 1950s were built without an architect. At one extreme, the poor worked on their homes (self-help construction) while the affluent lived in high-rise condominiums that were designed by builders who would simply find an architect to 'sign off' on the proper paper work. It was not uncommon, for instance, to see such practices take place during a friendly domino game in the *Colegio de Arquitectos* (Institute of Architects).

Perhaps the most striking feature of Havana's built environment in the 1950s was that there was little demolition and substitution of its existing urban fabric. Havana was spared devastating hurricanes for the most part, and it was not exposed to earthquakes which are so prevalent in Mexico, Central America, Peru or Chile (Scarpaci 1994). The net effect was to preserve a valuable stock of buildings that spanned the city's historical periods, architectural styles and social classes. Even though UNESCO declared Habana Vieja and the adjacent fortresses in 1982 as a World Heritage Site, a greater cultural value rests with the enormous stock of twentieth century buildings. A visual appreciation of the different historical periods of construction appears in the three-dimensional model of Havana on display at the *Grupo para el Desarrollo Integral de la Capital* in Miramar whereby distinct periods of construction are represented using a color-coded scheme. The ochre-colored buildings symbolize those which were erected between 1900 and 1958. These buildings which hail mostly from an architectural period called 'lean cow' architecture, are characteristic of eclecticism (Taboada 1987).

The bulk of this construction took place in the first three decades of this century. It is a design much simpler than the ostentatious decorations of the great eclectic architecture found among major single projects. Because this 'minor eclecticism' extended into large sectors of the city, it was more determinant in shaping the look of Cuban cities including Havana than the valuable built heritage composed of pre-Baroque, Baroque and Neoclassical buildings (Coyula 1987). Thus, the cultural heritage of Havana's built environment sets it apart from most Latin American cities. It is unique in its physical and temporal expanse and in the variety of marked architectural styles that survive today. Although many of the city's buildings have deteriorated over four and a half centuries, Havana displays an impressive record of building construction. Its wide array of styles include the important Modern Movement of the 1950s and the introduction of Brutalism at the decade's end. Nevertheless, conservation of this valuable built stock had not been planned and some of it had been abandoned. Before the 1959 Revolution, preservation was limited to a few passionate connoisseurs who concentrated on certain buildings rather than entire neighborhoods. Private patrons sponsored historic preservation but there was no support from the government, the general population or even the average architect.

The financial center of twentieth-century Havana remained in Habana Vieja. Large banks, the stock market (*bolsa de valores*), and attorneys' offices formed a tropical imitation of Wall Street. Modest skyscrapers had appeared by the 1920s that could have easily been found in Chicago or New York. A floating day population of office workers and shoppers filled the district's streets, as did faithful clients from a bygone era who routinely shopped at the once European-like stores along Obispo Street. Those shoppers refused to patronize the growing retail centers nearby which were anchored by US-like department stores on Galiano and San Rafael Streets. The wares of the Jewish merchants along Muralla Street attracted shoppers looking for bargains. Yet alongside this humming retail and service activity, the sordid and progressive degeneration of Habana Vieja could not be hidden.

In the 1940s the main commercial center moved nearby, west of Habana Vieja, along the portico-adorned street of Galiano. Streets intersecting with Galiano such as San Rafael and Neptuno were also important retail centers. The European style of shops and small storefronts were replaced with 'modern', US-style department stores. The new, larger retail outlets catered to as many tastes as income groups, and their products were differentiated by both quality and the social prestige brought by the department store's location. The flashing window displays of El Encanto, a department store that was destroyed in 1961 by arson in support of the imminent Bay of Pigs invasion, contrasted with the modest but well stocked items found in the department stores along Calzada de Monte.

By the 1950s, the 'center' of Havana could no longer be described as either linear or nodal. Instead, it had spread across several commercial subcenters. A common and inexpensive evening activity was to stroll through the streets, window shop, and browse through the stores. The center encapsulated the concept of 'city': to residents who lived fairly close to the city center, to speak about 'going shopping' (*ir de tiendas*) meant 'going to Havana.'[3]

This area of Centro Habana still held the lion's share of the commercial activity of the 1950s despite competition from another new center, La Rampa, located just 2 kilometers west in Vedado. Although La Rampa had very few stores, it contained many restaurants, clubs, cafeterias, and offices. Centro Habana remained the city's commercial district and survived after the Revolution, despite its visual deterioration. By the late 1960s, some shops were haphazardly being converted to housing units while others closed. The overall quality and variety of merchandise dropped quickly, too. Family dwellings originally located over the stores were not kept up and also became run down. These changes notwithstanding, the region characterizes many key features of a city center.

Competition with Centro Habana came from La Rampa. This area developed quickly between 1949 and 1958 as a transition zone between Vedado and Centro Habana. The Rampa was popular because it was close to upper-income homes in Vedado and Miramar. It boasted a distinctive modern flavor and a mixture of functions and land uses: movie houses, theaters, art galleries, restaurants, cafeterias, offices, bars and parks. These locational attributes complemented the cosmopolitan flavor of a large cluster of hotels which Centro Habana sorely lacked.

In the early 1950s construction began on the much contested Plaza Cívica (Civic Center) with its public spaces and monumental buildings which housed only the state bureaucracy (Estévez 1953). To many professionals and ordinary citizens, though, the design carried symbolism that was too obvious and imposing. Building this amorphous and heavy complex, just a kilometer from La Rampa, put an end to Forestier's plan for a land reserve to be part of the proposed Parque Metropolitano. In the end, the *Plaza Cívica* project left only about one quarter of land originally designated for the park.

At least three problems – design, semiotics and contract bidding – plagued the Plaza Cívica project from the outset. The Palacio de Justicia

---

[3]The busy intersection of Galiano and San Rafael streets earned the nickname of 'The Corner of Sin.' 'Respectable' gentlemen would frequent stores where attractive female store clerks worked and, allegedly, the prestige of a store was determined by the attractiveness of its clerks. This district was a popular socializing place for young people in the 1950s.

(Justice Palace, José Pérez Benitoa, architect, 1957), a prominent element in the plan, was a structure of mastodontic proportions. Transformed in the late 1960s as the Palacio de la Revolución, it looked like a criollo rendition of a classic-modern Mussolinesque building in L'EUR 42 (Esposizione Universale di Roma 1942). At its side stood the lamentable monument to Cuba's national hero, José Martí. Ironically, the obelisk from the Martí Monument was a copy of a Schenley Whiskey advertisement that appeared in the 1939 World's Fair in New York. These two structures – the Palacio de Justicia and the Martí Monument – depict the authoritarian and hierarchical view held by the promoters of these plans. Land preparation and contract tendering were mired by dirty back-room deals involving land speculation, kickbacks and payoffs from a corrupt state apparatus. The obvious correlation between this Fascist-like architecture and town planning, on the one hand, with the hundreds of men and women killed and tortured by the Batista regime, on the other, stands as a painful reminder of the dirty side of Havana in the 1950s.

### The inherited city: the dawn of 1959

The Revolution inherited an abnormally large capital city of a small underdeveloped nation. The nation both resented and admired Havana. Cuba was situated relatively high on the Latin American development scale and even more so among the Third World (Ginsberg 1961). Havana was the most important city in the Caribbean basin and among the most attractive in the Americas. Its economy displayed a decidedly tertiary character with a vocation for services, especially tourism. All this was situated in a favorable setting with the bay, shoreline and its expansive eastern beaches.

Havana in 1959 was a sprawling, low-rise city. Urban sprawl had absorbed neighboring settlements which at the same time managed to maintain their character. This cultural patrimony covered the city's architectural history: pre-Baroque, Baroque, Art Noveau, Eclecticism, Art Deco, Modern Monumental, Neocolonial, Rationalism, Organic Architecture, and Brutalism. At the same time, this heritage represented both an important cultural and utilitarian value and highlighted the presence of a broad middle and lower-middle class that aspired to live within the norms of bourgeois decorum.

If Havana was a unique collection of the island's architectural and economic history etched into its built environment, it was also a city of great contradictions. Rich and poor, beautiful and ugly, modern and old, lazy and pragmatic – all these faces were apparent from practically any vantage point. To be sure, Havana was *criolla*, but with a greater Spanish and American influence than other Spanish-American capitals. Social classes were clearly differentiated, but more by their economic status than by birth. Racial discrimination closed access to social and occupational mobility for blacks and created slums. On the other hand, discrimination lessened somewhat in matters of art, music and poetry; most of those media conjured up images of an exotic, dark-skinned tropical sensuality. Miscegenation (*mestizaje*) found a popular outlet for the syncretic Afro-Cuban cults, consensual unions, and vernacular humor (*choteo*).

The central districts of Havana displayed high-population densities and a curious mix of physical and social diversity. High-order services such as banking and tourism at times gave this area a veneer of social integration. But that pretense disappeared in the low population densities and open spaces of elite suburban communities. The cost of a quieter lifestyle meant losing the noisy yet vital mixture of Havana's urban culture. Havana's traditional centers were actually a chain of connected districts that were supported by growing yet well defined secondary centers pushing out towards the city limits.

It was a city of disproportions in the way it looked, its open spaces and work sites, and services. Havana exhibited inequalities between its center and periphery as well as with urban and social decay that had begun in the most congested central areas. It was an attractive, fascinating city while also cynical, a bit laid back, and gullible. Havana awoke expectant that first day of January.

# 4

# Socialist Havana: planning, dreams and reality

> One hears about the end of history, and end of ideology, and even the demise of architecture . . . maybe these outcomes will come about through the miraculous resurrection of a superior man, philosophy, and architecture.
>
> Luis Lápidus, *Patrimonio y Herencia del Siglo XX en Cuba*, Havana, 1995

## The magic of change

The year 1958 ended with a chain of takeovers by the Rebel Army. On December 31 the important city of Santa Clara fell to the July 26 Movement and the *Directorio Revolucionario*. The dictator, Batista, after celebrating the new year with champagne, shamelessly fled in an airplane with a small band of his rogues. More than almost the decade of the 1950s came to an end on January 1, 1959. Cuba, and indeed Havana, had reached a watershed that separated two key periods: that before and after the triumph of the Revolution.

Havana in 1959 started to change in ways unforeseen a decade before. Central districts had increased in density with building subdivisions and the reconstruction of improvised lofts and attics. Curiously, this population became attached to their dilapidated dwellings and neighborhoods because the Revolutionary laws stopped evictions and mandated that residents of tenement houses not pay rent.

The elite corners of the city also changed. Elegant neighborhoods like Miramar were almost completely abandoned by their owners. Bourgeois mansions were converted into schools and dormitories for thousands of children on scholarships who marched in orderly lines along Fifth Avenue, imitating the marches by the light-blue shirted militias. Even the lobby of the old Havana Hilton (renamed Habana Libre), lost its flashy doorman who wore a feathered helmet. In its wake, the lobby had become a sort of bubble-roofed town square '[w]hose vitality and movement shined throughout its rounded area and even became a festive and commemorative symbol of the entire city' (Segre 1989, p. 62, our translation). The most diverse characters rubbed elbows there while the Malecón, just a few blocks from the Habana Libre, was silhouetted by black anti-aircraft guns pointing upwards.

One coffee house, El Carmelo de Calle Calzada, briefly hosted a social mosaic of patrons who flocked to it to enjoy the best ice cream in the city. From this would emerge the famous Coppelia ice-cream parlour discussed in Chapter 8. Former members of the Yacht Club and Vedado Tennis who had still not yet gone into exile would sit at their regular tables. Proud waiters would look pejoratively at the new clients who were dressed in clothing purchased at the low-quality stores along Monte Street. Those shabbily dressed patrons arrived mesmerized at this Havana 'Mecca' of such elegant consumption and *dolce far niente*, located across the street from the most beautiful park in Vedado. This was the setting of Alejo Carpentier's novelette, *El Acoso*. Here too gathered ballet goers who would heatedly comment on the fine points of a ballet *foueté* while they observed with snobbish curiosity the latest vestiges of the Creole class, or become comically alarmed by the extemporaneous nature of a bearded rebel soldier.

The casting of this new collection of social characters was enriched by a group of young readers of the cultural supplement, *Lunes de Revolución*. These youths were ardent fans of the recently created Cinemateca and would sit there discussing a recent poetry recital by the Chilean Pablo Neruda. Only a few tables would separate them from the ballet goers and they might ostensibly turn their backs toward them, for they were deemed silly and superficial. These young intellectuals would be enthralled over the next film of Tomás Gutiérrez Alea, and they would inevitably call him *Titón* (his nickname) to impress those who might be eavesdropping. As the evening progressed, an elite group coming from a midnight concert at the Auditorium Theater would cross the street after having heard the vibrant piano and the hoarse voice of the well-known Bola de Nieve. Seated at yet another table at the café one could find those who might have frequented the Casa de las Américas, including Edmundo Desnoes, Lisandro Otero or Ambrosio Fornet, quietly chatting with the Argentine writer Julio Cortázar or the Peruvian author MarioVargas Llosa.

While the well-known street character *el Caballero de París* (the 'Gentleman from Paris') strolled outside, other famous people also frequented the cafe. The preposterous *Marquesa* aggressively pan-handled while the less money-minded Juan Charrasqueado would guard his alluring figure underneath a large Mexican sombrero, while singing tunes for the legendary *comandante* Efigenio Ameijeiras. Another *comandante*, Rolando Cubelas, displayed his splendid reddish beard in the same place where just 2 years before, a clean-shaven Cubelas had conversed with his friends from Vedado Tennis. This impossible mixture of people, confined to some 300 square meters, encapsulates what Graham Greene had in mind when he said that Havana was a place where anything could happen.

During the first months of the Revolution, crowds who supported the accelerated political changes expressed their gratitude by displaying signs that read, 'Gracias Fidel.' A wide spectrum of citizens shared this exuberance, ranging from a slum dweller in the center of the city, to a public employee in a government ministry, to university students, agricultural workers, waiters, and even the owner of a sugar mill (*Informe Central al XIV Congreso de la Central de Trabajadores de Cuba* 1978).

The euphoria of the post-Revolutionary period, however, was short lived. In the same way in which the democratic-bourgeoisie revolution changed quickly to a socialist revolution, the confiscation of misappropriated goods and property of the *batistianos*, landholders, industrialists, and merchants signaled deep structural changes ahead. According to estimates made by the US Government, the value of North American property confiscated in Cuba amounted to $1.85 billion. Of the 5911 officially received claims made by the United States, 86% of that total value was held by 38 businesses or corporations. If we add to this the property of Cubans who subsequently became US citizens – which was the pretext of the Helms-Burton bill for tightening the US embargo in 1996 – the figure would reach approximately 7 billion dollars more (Pita 1995). Ricardo Alarcón, the current president of the National Assembly, claims that the figure might actually be hundreds of billions of dollars. The enormous discrepancy further underscores the difficulty in sharpening the accuracy of these estimates, and the great weight that those nationalizations had in financing the early social benefits provided of the Revolution.

## The first Revolutionary laws

Law 35 enacted March 10, 1959 lowered rents by 50%. That law transferred from landlords to salaried workers and farmers about 15% of the national income (Chaffee 1992a). In April, land-use regulations were implemented and were complemented on December 23, 1959 by Law 691 (see also Table 6.1). This law, also called *solares yermos* (vacant lots), established a very low and fixed price of four pesos per square meter for urban land. In doing so, land speculation ended (Fernández 1996). In May, 1959 the First Agrarian Reform Law expropriated the holdings of large plantation owners (*latifundistas*). Most of these large landowners were absentee landlords who rented their lands to those who worked them. The new law established a maximum property size of just 402 hectares, a limit which would be further reduced in 1963 to 67.1 hectares by the Second Agrarian Reform Law. As a result, state control increased to 70% of all arable lands (Séneca 1976).

In addition to these measures, other state actions changed the island during the first year of the triumph of the Revolution (Séneca 1976). They included intervention in the Cuban Telephone Company (actually North American), the lowering of electrical utility rates, the creation of National Revolutionary Militias, the opening up of public beaches and private clubs, all of which created a considerable uproar. However, these actions moved in tandem with a campaign of support for national industry and other declarations that reaffirmed the 'Cuban-ness' (*lo cubano*) of the Revolution. A climate of confusion grew among the Cuban bourgeoisie who believed that the United States would ultimately intervene to thwart efforts by the young revolutionaries. By July 1959, however, the important positions of the more conservative Cubans in the government had been marginalized. The very wealthy, preceded by the small Jewish community, began accepting the idea of emigration in hopes that it would be a short one.

The second year of the Revolution would be like the first. In August 1960, 36 sugar mills and North American oil refineries were nationalized. In October of that year banks and more than 300 large firms also suffered the same fate. During this same period, the Committees for the Defense of the Revolution (CDR) were established at the neighborhood levels throughout the island. Private schools were taken over by the State and religious education ended even though the churches were kept open. Some parents, fearing the loss of legal custody of their children, sent them alone to the United States. These youngsters became a part of Operation Peter Pan, and many of them never returned to see their families.

Meanwhile, the climate of internal confrontation escalated. The middle class, ideologically divided, increasingly opted for exile or blended a mixture of anguish and hope that would ultimately carry as much weight as reason. The opposition resorted to help from the United States, hoping to create a base for the invasion of the island. Brigade 2506 invaded the Bay of Pigs (Playa Girón) in April of 1961. Acts of sabotage in the city such as the burning of the famous Havana department store, El Encanto, were tied to the anti-Communist uprising in some rural parts of Cuba, principally in the Escambray mountains in south-central Cuba.

Although we discuss housing in greater detail in Chapter 6, it will be useful to identify briefly its status in the early years of the Revolution, and its relationship with state planning. The Self-Help and Mutual Aid program began in 1960 as a way to find solutions for the 80 000 housing units that were in poor condition. Construction was managed by the Ministry of Public Works while the Ministry of Social Welfare carried out the social research and mobilized the population. This program began with the eradication of the Manzana de Gómez neighborhood in Santiago de Cuba. Officials in the capital eradicated the large shantytowns of Llega y Pon, Las Yaguas, and La Cueva del Humo and also eradicated the notorious Carreño Building just 50 meters away from La Rampa (Menéndez 1992). These residents were relocated in five new complexes in the neighborhoods of Perla, Martí and Zamora. Many families continued being taken care of after their relocation. The new housing complexes contained between 100 and 150 units and included a school and medical clinic. Each family volunteered 24 hours weekly for work and the unemployed received small stipends (Fernández 1976).

This program was quickly abandoned and the Ministry of Social Welfare was dissolved in 1961. Critics of Self-Help and Mutual Aid had charged since the beginning of the program that it maintained social marginality by relocating entire communities, creating little stability, low productivity and poor-quality construction. Data on the number of neighborhoods that were eradicated and housing units built through this means vary among authors: 4700 units would include the eradication of 33 shantytowns with 20 000 residents (Segre 1989). Others (Hamberg 1986) place the figure at 40 neighborhoods; yet another (Fernández 1976) documents some 400 units. The differences in these figures reflect not only the lack of data at a time when the present seemed to last forever, but also because of different foci and opinions among officials and scholars (see also Hamberg 1994). Taken in its entirety, this uncertainty adds even more to the curiosity some 35 years later about what might have occurred had the program continued.

The truth, it would seem, is that this strategy of dealing with Havana's housing and planning problems offered possibilities that were not taken full advantage of because the same measures were not consistently used (Baroni 1994a, b). Planning gave little importance to social work and exaggerated the role of centralized programs that supposedly had solutions that could be repeated and generalized everywhere. Ironically, despite the early evidence given to new technologies, little opportunity was actually given for their experimentation.

If the eradication of Havana's shantytowns are to be commended it is important to note other problems that appeared in their aftermath. Immigrants from the rest of the island as well as those who were displaced within the city of Havana lacked adequate housing. Havana's historic attraction drew to it rebel soldiers, farmers who were welcomed in their homes by *habaneros* as part of a state-sponsored campaign, and others who occupied the homes of those who left the island. Havana also received the families of thousands of Cubans who earned scholarships and who had come from the provinces to study in the city. In this way, neighborhoods such as El Romerillo and La Corbata, located near the Columbia military base, developed. The neighborhood of Atarés located on the slopes of the old colonial castle also attracted immigrants, as did La Güinera located near an important hospital.

## The physical framework and population: change and continuity

The reuse of the elegant newer places such as Country Club, Miramar, Kohly, and Nuevo Vedado – practically vacated by the bourgeoisie – generated a situation of privilege for their new residents. Newcomers to these former elite neighborhoods benefited greatly once these districts were identified as a 'frozen zone'. This meant it served as a housing reserve for high-level government officials, schools and dormitories, dignitaries, foreign experts, and diplomats. What changed the class character most aside from the schools, was the assignment of housing to low-income people (Hamberg 1994). Nonetheless, the level of physical segregation by different socioeconomic groups that the Revolution had inherited slowly dissipated.

Since the 1959 Revolution, the neighborhoods in which the ruling class had resided have lost their charm. Isolation, physical and social deterioration, and difficult accessibility by vehicles plague these neighborhoods. Central city functions have also changed. With the cautious opening of market forces, the Miramar neighborhood is once again adapting itself to major changes. The old boarding houses and shelters derived from mansions that were used for students who had scholarships back in the early years of the Revolution are now being refurbished with hard currencies. Revitalization efforts strive to accommodate new business offices and joint-venture operations even though the traditional commercial center (Centro Habana) shows empty stores and precariously adapted housing in substandard buildings.

Land use in Miramar still includes the presence of embassies, housing for foreigners, and Cuban government officials. However, there is an unprecedented surge in retail outlets for Cuban and foreign shoppers with hard currency (the so-called *diplotiendas*), as well as new joint-venture offices. High-level Cuban government officials and research centers coexist with those who moved into empty dwellings in the 1960s and 1970s. One can still find among this latter group many of the workers and home attendants who worked in the student boarding houses. These include the well known *tías* (literally 'aunts' but actually they were maids) and caretakers who initially occupied the back garages and maid's rooms of their former employers and then eventually took over the entire mansions. Relatives from the countryside also joined them and lived in the many rooms of these spacious homes. In this regard, Miramar has become the Havana neighborhood with the greatest change since the triumph of the Revolution. The beautiful image of Fifth Avenue (Quinta Avenida) has been kept practically the same, although there is much less automobile traffic today than in 1958. While truck and car traffic has declined, an increase in the number of bicyclists who tenaciously pedal through the city on broad, central, and tree-covered routes that could form the best bike-ways of the city, have compensated for this loss on roads adjacent to Fifth Avenue. Although Fifth Avenue is a central promenade and four-lane road, cyclists, public buses and parked cars are forbidden, probably for security reasons as government motorcades often use the road.

## A revolution in stages

Five stages characterize urban and regional planning since the triumph of the Revolution: 1959–1963, from the First to the Second Agrarian Reform Law; 1964–1970, from the Second Agrarian Reform Law to the Great Harvest; 1971–1975, the Great Harvest to the First Five-Year Plan; 1976–1986, the Five-Year Plans; and 1987 until the present, the Process of Correcting Mistakes, and the Special Period. We briefly highlight these stages as they apply to Havana.

### 1959–1963: Nobody's Land, Everybody's Land.

The first stage witnessed the seizure of power by the most radical sectors of the Revolutionary Movement, and the socialization process accelerated through the nationalization of the means of production and the Agrarian Reform Laws. During that period both economic and military aggressions were unleashed against Cuba. Chief among these events were the Bay of Pigs Invasion, the Cuban Missile Crisis, the uprising of anti-Communist guerrillas in the Escambray mountains (that gave rise to the 'cleansing of

Escambray') and other areas, and the North American blockade. Bellicose actions like these spurred investment in Cuba's military and defense assumed a high priority. The suspension of the sugar quota and shipments of petroleum from the United States in retaliation for Cuba's nationalizations were offset by aid and trade from the Soviet Union. This began a profound change in the Cuban economy that would last some 30 years. Not only did this lead to economic and political repercussions throughout the country, it also included cultural changes. Although Spanish names prevailed, many children were named Yuri or Vladimir instead of American names like Frank and Johnny that were common before the Revolution.

Revolutionary Cuba's initial development strategy was profoundly rural oriented. It focused on quickly eliminating the inherent inequality between city and countryside. Development projects during this first stage included the construction of 26 000 units of housing, highway paving in remote areas, and the construction of schools and medical facilities in the countryside. Approximately 150 rural villages were built in the early 1960s, initially by the efforts of the Rebel Army (1959–1960), and later by the Rural Housing Department (*Viviendas Campesinas*) at the National Institute of Agrarian Reform.

National policy during this stage attempted to overcome Cuba's historic dependence on monoculture and a single market. This was to be achieved through a program of agricultural diversification and accelerated industrialization. Both goals were tied to the social objective of eliminating unemployment. However, many of the new jobs were not always in productive activities. That fact, coupled with the effects of centralizing government, created a structural framework that had negative outcomes.

In 1962, the first annual economic plan was enacted and so began the field of physical planning. The initial task of physical planning concentrated on locating agricultural investments and restructuring state farms. Physical planners conducted preliminary studies for creating new regions throughout Cuba. One year later, Havana's first master plan was executed and became the first ever in Revolutionary Cuba.

*1964–1970: Without sugar there is no homeland*

During the second stage, planners attempted to review critically the excessive optimism of the previous phase. Between 1959 and 1963, planning did not take into account the scarcity of materials or financial and human resources. Rising costs in the defense field and the lack of support infrastructure (road networks, ports, warehouses, electrification) had been impediments. As a result, the second stage directed efforts towards creating infrastructure and finding ways to increase development potential. Agricultural production, especially sugar cane, topped the list. It was in this realm that Cuba had historically been the major world exporter. There was no denying the veracity of popular phrase among the bourgeoisie during the Republican period: 'without sugar there is no homeland'. Agricultural and food processing industries entered the state's priority list as did investments for warehouses, energy production, port installations, fertilizers and cement for the building trades.

Despite this sobering realism that supposedly would correct the previous excess of optimism, the second stage was also overwhelmed by the search for quick results. This philosophy was guided by the metaphor of the turnpike model – a limited access beltway – that assumed that the best road to reach a destination is not necessarily the most direct (Hamilton 1992). The 1964–1970 period prompted a great debate about the way to construct socialism: Should it be gradual or in successive stages? Should Cuba follow the theoretical premises derived from the French economist Charles Bettelheim, which were supported in Cuba by orthodox Marxist and Soviet advisors and the countries of Eastern Europe? Bettelheim favored a 'market socialism' based on self-financing state firms as a way to obtain an objective material base that could sustain the social-justice agenda of the Revolution.

A more radical line of action focused on the inequalities that a policy of material rewards in the production system might create. This line of thinking held that the production system could indeed increase in a way that would appeal to the collective interests of Cuban workers through moral incentives. Such a perspective entailed a highly centralized government overseeing a state budget that would allocate resources by a plan and not by following the laws of the market-place. This vision required the creation of 'the new man' espoused by Ché Guevara in his book, *Socialism and Man in Cuba*. Ché's work reflected his interest in the Chinese experience and how it could be interpreted by the revolutionary Cuban vanguard. His treatise also included the realistic conclusion that low economic productivity in Cuba would not create sufficient components to be used as material incentives for workers. In the end, Fidel Castro chose a third path that incorporated some of the ideas of Bettleheim and Guevara (Castro 1965; 1965b; Boorstein 1968; Bettleheim 1969).

In 1968, the Revolutionary Offensive eliminated the rest of commerce and services that still remained in private hands. This was the time of the Agricultural Command Post (*Puestos de Mando de la Agricultura*). In this model, administrators, technicians, workers, housewives, and students dressed in rural workers' clothes would leave Havana to work in the countryside. It was in this setting that the Havana Greenbelt (*Cordón de la Habana*), an ambitious belt of more than 10 000 hectares of fruit trees, pigeon peas and coffee, began. These lands would feed the capital. To carry out the Greenbelt project, lands were purchased from scattered farmers and hundreds of new homes were built for them using Sandino technology (lightweight prefabricated structures with walls of columns and small concrete panels). Each unit was equipped with small self-consumption lots: the micro-plans. This was the epic of 'special plans', 'extra-plans' and 'micro-plans'which became the most important components of the overall development plan. In some cases the new settlements included 30 housing units.

Despite the great promotion of the volunteer project, these efforts did not have proportional outcomes. The pigeon peas, for example, were rejected even by livestock and the enormous green belt project only produced a system of about 30 small reservoirs, a few areas of fruit production, some coffee plants, and an indeterminate amount of 'maybes.' Underlying this Havana Greenbelt development was an implicit anti-urban sentiment. Cities were viewed as parasitic and corrupt places. That view prevailed even in the new rural towns built during the Revolutionary period. The climax of this de-urbanization process was reached when the giant mobilizations of the sugar-cane cutting campaign ensued in the late 1960s. These efforts culminated with the targeted goal of a 10 million ton sugar-cane harvest in 1970. During this massive harvest the cities were practically empty. By 1970, the Cuban economy had become entirely state owned, except for 30% of agricultural land.

The 10 million ton sugar harvest (*La Gran Zafra*) became a symbol with which the faith of the Revolution could be measured. Such a sentiment was expressed with a slogan '10 Million are on Their Way!' (¡*Los Diez Millones Van!*). Those who had discrepancies with the 10 million ton goal were foreign specialists who had analyzed the world sugar market. They had predicted with uncanny precision that the harvest would fall short by some 1.5 million tons. This shortfall had also been predicted by the Cuban Minister of Sugar, Orlando Borrego. Such a precise forecast increased the professional prestige of the experts in the New York firm Czarnikow-Rionda and also brought bitter sweet consolation to one Cuban who soon thereafter became an ex-minister.

*1971–1975: From the great harvest to the First Five-Year Plan*

The third period searched for a harmonious balance between the government and mass organizations. It strengthened the state apparatus through a process of institutionalization. Efforts for economic planning were redoubled as were economic controls that culminated with the First Five-

Year Plan. It also strengthened the role of the Communist Party of Cuba and the nation's unions.

Building efforts received a great impulse with the creation of the Social and Agricultural Development Group (*Grupo de Desarrollo Social y Agropecuario*, DESA) and the Agricultural Development (*Desarrollo Agropecuario*, DAP). The Microbrigade Movement was created by Fidel Castro himself during this time as an alternative mode of building construction that could complement the lack of public housing units. Microbrigadistas also aimed to train and bring back skilled construction workers into the building process and to reduce the excess number of workers at factories and clerical jobs. Groups of employees from a work center would set out for 2 or 3 years to build housing for themselves and for their fellow workers while the center would maintain their salary and the state would supply them with land, material inputs, equipment, tools and provide technical advice (Angotti 1989). From an annual production of only 5000 units built in 1970, the Microbrigade Movement had completed 20 000 new units in 1975. However, the production model of houses employed by state firms remained wedded to the panacea of high-tech solutions, and included IMS technologies (imported from Yugoslavia), a Sliding Scaffolding Model, and the Great Panel 70. The surge in construction produced a marked increase in the Gross Social Product during this period (Table 4.1).

Even though the construction industry's contribution to the gross social product was great, it was difficult to measure the full amount of investment that went into construction. Some experts believed that it was disproportionately large in relation to the end result. It is important to note that the large investment that went into a national network of prefabricated materials plants also created a commitment to use that kind of technology. The results were mixed: not only were the built units rigid and monotonous but they were also costly and dependent on specialized inputs. When ideas were proposed to transfer these projects to remodeling inner city areas, as occurred in the Havana neighborhood of Cayo Hueso, the results were even worse. New big buildings disrupted the layout of the city and interfered with social networks already in place. Central city residents, moreover, had a set of cultural values all their own.

Efforts at centralization required a search for supposedly valid nation-

**Table 4.1** The contribution of building trades to the Gross Social Product

| 1961–1965 | 1966–1970 | 1971–1975 |
|---|---|---|
| 1.9% per year | 3.9% per year | 10.0% per year |

al models that could adapt to the Cuban reality. Construction solutions originally crafted for one situation were repeated and converted into a generalized model. This happened with the Girón prefabrication model. It was used massively in the construction of secondary schools in the countryside (ESBEC, discussed more fully in Chapter 8). About 500 such schools were built during the period. Later, the Girón model was extended to hospitals, hotels and even housing units, and at times were often rather forced solutions. Ironically, the same Microbrigades were rather infatuated with prefabrication without understanding the potential of simpler, local technologies and flexible processes of self-construction that were much more akin to the work of Microbrigades.

Of the 212 000 housing units built in Cuba between 1971 and 1975, only 40% were built by the state. Put another way, about half were erected by the Microbrigades (Hamberg 1986). Planners tried to solve the housing problem through state-directed construction. Conserving the existing housing stock held low priority which resulted in a qualitative, functional and visual deterioration of the central parts of Havana. In cases of severe deterioration, occupants were transferred from buildings on the verge of collapse to sturdier structures.

At the end of the period, the First Congress of the Cuban Communist Party was held in 1975. Preparations for the Congress included beautification efforts in key areas of Havana. These efforts were orchestrated through a program called Urban Revitalization carried out by the Department of Architecture and Urbanism of the City of Havana. The use of large murals, called Super Graphics, and other elements of urban landscape architecture formed key components of this revitalization campaign (Coyula 1985a). The process of institutionalization throughout Cuba would become the most important activity of the subsequent stage and the preparations had already begun.

*1976–1986: the institutionalization of Cuban socialism*

From the outset, the fourth stage concentrated its efforts on the creation of People's Power (*Poder Popular*) organizations, the divisions of the Central Administration of the State (OACE), and the System of Economic Planning and Management (SDPE). A new constitution replaced the one from 1940 which, in its day, was one of the most advanced in the world (Cuba 1976). In the economics sphere the central task became import-substitution industrialization which meant creating exportable funds and satisfying national consumption. During the First Five-Year Plan (1976–1980) state investment reached $11 billion. The emphasis on education that had been instigated in the previous stage also continued. Beginning with the

Second Five-Year Plan (1981–1985), tourism entered as a principal development focus in Havana.

Housing construction increased during this period. To the surprise of many, the XI National Conference on Housing and Urbanism held in Santa María del Mar in 1984 revealed that the production of self-help housing units was practically double that of state firms (Estévez 1984). From an average of 50 000 housing units per year, only 16 400 were built by the state. Eleven years later, one study (Pérez 1995) showed that Havana fared dismally compared with housing construction elsewhere in Cuba.

While state construction efforts continued the multifamily prefabricated mid-rise apartment building designs, self-help efforts received support from local governments and workplaces (especially in the interior parts of the country). At the same time the role of the Microbrigades was reviewed and the sale of construction materials to the general population increased appreciably. Building preservation efforts also rose. For example, between 1973 and 1983 the budget for state companies in charge of housing maintenance increased fivefold while the sale of building materials increased 10-fold. However, the figures distort the frequent diversion of state resources to other prioritized programs. Regarding the sale of building materials to the general population, for example, many materials purchased for repairs were really used to build new housing or expand existing units.

In December of 1984 the General Housing Law was approved. It confirmed and expanded the property of tenants through a rent-payment system. The new law allowed Cubans to rent rooms and it regulated inheritances, swapping (*permutas*), and the sale of homes and lots. The 1984 law also opened the possibility of establishing housing cooperatives to work with self-help housing in construction, remodeling, and expansion. Because the law was approved reluctantly, it fell victim to certain fatal prejudices; some of its stipulations – such as those that pertain to cooperatives – were not well instrumented and still others, such as the ability to sell and sub-lease, were suspended. We explore these and related housing issues in Chapter 6.

**Table 4.2** Housing completion 1959–1990 (in thousands)

|        | State | %  | Self-help | %  | Total | %   |
| ------ | ----- | -- | --------- | -- | ----- | --- |
| Cuba   | 495   | 28 | 1330      | 72 | 1770  | 100 |
| Havana | 99    | 32 | 211       | 68 | 310   | 100 |

The total includes the increase in the housing stock between 1959 and 1990, plus the replacement of dwellings that were lost in that same period. *Source*: Pérez 1995

*1987 – The Correction of Mistakes and the Special Period*

The fifth period corresponds to a crisis in Cuba's socialist model of development and marks a watershed as well as a search for new solutions for the nation's problems. Although normally the 'Correction of Mistakes' and 'Special Period' are analyzed separately, for purposes of brevity we combine them here. Based on the errors made by the eastern European socialist models, the objective of this period was to stabilize the country and the economy. The correction of mistakes, the Cuban response to Russian perestroika, gave greater weight to material incentives and the self-financing of state companies than was the case during the final stage of eastern European socialism in the late 1980s. The effect was to create a generalized dependence and a growing reliance upon the Council of Mutual Economic Assistance (discussed in Chapter 7). The overall well-being of the population increased notably with a state parallel market where one could purchase goods and food in addition to those provided by the state through the ration book. Previously, such items were considered luxury goods. However, this model based on material incentives was quickly modified. Ironically, the harshest critics did not attempt to polish or improve the rewards system but rather opted to abandon them.

Criticisms by technocrats and pessimists came quickly when the state decided to invest in non-productive enterprises. For example, micro-brigade housing and health-care clinics had no economic basis to sustain them. While Perestroika spread in the former USSR, 1987 in Cuba marked a time when moral incentives and conventional directives would be returned to state leadership. The Third Five-Year Plan should have covered 1986–1990 but it was postponed and ultimately eliminated because of the obvious effects brought on by the break-up of the European socialist field and its dire effects on the Cuban economy.

The so-called process of the Correction of Mistakes (*proceso de rectificación de errores*) began turbulently through a series of investments in housing construction and services that overwhelmed the cautious initial forecasts made by economists, who were soon labeled as 'technocrats.' The Microbrigade, accused 10 years earlier of being unproductive, was revitalized and expanded to create the 'social brigade.' It incorporated neighbors from a specific area instead of workers who came from a workplace. From this point on, Microbrigade efforts departed markedly from their performances in the past. The focus turned to building on empty lots in the central city or where buildings have been demolished. No longer were their efforts devoted to the construction of new neighborhoods and towns. Microbrigade efforts were also used largely for the construction of social projects such as hospitals, medical clinics, day care centers, sports and recreational complexes, and the new convention center occupied by ExpoCuba at the city's edge. Their efforts were also used in the construction of facilities for the Pan American Games of 1991 held in Habana del Este and Santiago de Cuba. After the games, though, many of the workers occupied the Villa Panamericana (a common practice in the Cuban building sector through the Microbrigades). For many other Micro-brigadistas, the delay brought by the priority given to this and similar public-works projects proved fatal when combined with the scarcity of building materials, especially when their own buildings remained half built.

One of the most dramatic consequences of Cuba's attempts to balance its economy in the international arena in the early 1990s, after the demise of European socialism, was the appearance of a hard-currency market alongside the national currency. The purchasing power of the Cuban peso, which had long been pegged to the US dollar before 1959, was greatly devaluated in the early 1990s. Inflation skyrocketed and key materials became scarce as pressures mounted to ensure full employment which otherwise had little productive results. This translated into a vicious cycle that was altogether demoralizing. As late as 1989, the Soviet Bloc trading arena had provided Cuba with 85% of its foreign trade, and it did so with favorable prices that were subsidized by the Bloc. The collapse of that market, coupled with Cuba's lack of capital, credit, and energy, sent shock waves throughout the Cuban economy and society. Moreover, it was aggravated by the persistent US blockade. By 1991, imports to Cuba had been cut to almost half of the 1989 level (Figure 4.1), including a drastic reduction in petroleum which was the only source of energy in Cuba. For instance, 13 million tons of imported petroleum in 1989 fell drastically to just 6 million in 1990. Fuel imports plummeted from $12.4 billion in 1989 to $720 million in 1994 (Figure 4.2). In light of this economic downturn, the withdrawal of Soviet aid and trade, and a perception that the United

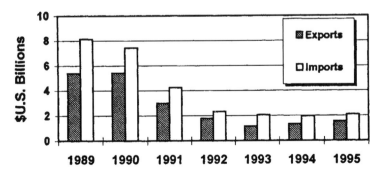

**Figure 4.1** Cuba, Foreign Trade Balance, 1989–1995.
*Data source: Cuba: Handbook of Trade Statistics*, 1995. Washington, DC: CIA, p. iii

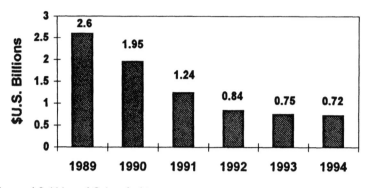

**Figure 4.2** Value of Cuban fuel imports.
*Data source: Cuba: Handbook of Trade Statistics,* 1995. Washington, DC: CIA, p. 11

States will attack the island, the Revolutionary leadership declared in 1990 that Cuba was in its first phase of 'Special Period in a Time of Peace'. Although the economy had improved somewhat by 1996, the label was still in force.

A key strategy for coping with the economic problems of the Special Period has been to allow a gradual opening whereby foreign investors are allowed to participate in joint ventures with the Cuban government. A total of 240 agreements have been signed between the Cuban government and foreign firms as of July 1996. These agreements include 43 nations and span 34 areas of the Cuban economy. An estimated 143 other projects were under negotiation at that time. Despite the passage of the Helms-Burton Law which threatens to prosecute foreign companies doing business in Cuba, 25 new associations were signed in the 3 months following the passage of the law (Prensa Latina 1996).

A second strategy is to encourage the flow of funds from family members abroad which up until that time had been looked down upon. Tourism, biotechnology, and the pharmaceutical industry are now emphasized in Cuba to generate foreign exchange (see also Chapters 7 and 8). All of this takes place in a market in which moral incentives must prevail because few workers share in profits which, instead, accrue to the

---

[1]Throughout Cuba, but especially in Havana, efforts to generate hard currency accentuate differences among Cubans who have access to dollars and those who do not. Scarcity of basic foods, a large portion of which used to come from the Soviet Bloc, began to affect the physical health of the Cuban people. Ironically, this was a realm which had received international acclaim as an accomplishment of the Revolution, even by the most ardent opponents. In 1993, the government was forced to provide massive doses of multivitamins to its 11 million residents to compensate for an unbalanced diet. In the 1990s, and for the first time since the crisis in the beginning of the 1960s, food had displaced housing as the number one social problem among the Cuban people.

state or joint-venture operations. Lacking capital and access to credit from international organisms (partly because of US pressure to discourage such lending), the situation has become increasingly difficult in Cuba and has exacerbated problems of scarcity.[1]

The immediate effects of disinvestment were disastrous. Agriculture and construction were practically paralyzed because of the lack of imported resources such as petroleum, fertilizers, pesticides, fodder, machine repair parts, steel, building components, and semi-assembled products. Lacking such materials exposed the vulnerability of a development model that was very dependent on external resources (IPF 1973). Under the scrutiny of the world market, these vulnerabilities exposed ecological, social, and cultural problems.

Several measures implemented in 1993 tried to arrest the crisis. Central among them was the ability for self-employed workers to earn a living in retail trades. In the agrarian sector, most state lands were turned over to cooperatives in order to create Basic Agricultural Production Units (*Unidades Básicas de Producción Agropecuaria*, UBPC). A highlight of this agricultural reform was the reopening in October 1994 of the Free Farmers' Market (*Mercado Libre Campesino*), which had previously been harshly criticized by Fidel Castro (Castro 1991, pp. 3–6). In its present reincarnation, the new name is the Agricultural Markets (*Mercados Agropecuarios*). Like the industrial markets opened just before them (which included the sale of most items except food), the Agricultural Markets also sell goods at very high prices (see Chapter 7). Problems of scarcity, limited production, and high prices came about as the government attempted to capture circulating hard currency and pesos (Carranza *et al.* 1995). However, the efforts seem to have paid off: since 1994 inflation has fallen and the black market exchange rate of 120–130 pesos to the US dollar had fallen to 20–25 in mid-1996.

Although the major objective of the government's attempt to reinsert Cuba into the global economy has been to provide stability and earn hard currency, much of the Cuban population does fully understand the process. In some cases, the government's actions seem rather *ad hoc*. *Habaneros* coped tenaciously with daily problems such as frequent power outages during the summer of 1993 and the exodus of many northward-bound rafters (*balseros*) in the summer of 1994. Public discontent reached its pinnacle with the first large public demonstration on the Malecón on August 5, 1994, although that may be a single, isolated event.

The state's attempt to improve international and national finances in 1994 has been more coherent. Prices have increased, many goods previously provided free of charge have been eliminated, some taxes have been established, and the time period for repayment of debt has been shortened. At the end of 1994 the Minister of Finances and Prices, José Luis Rodríguez, presented a possible solution to the National Assembly. He proposed the Law for the State Budget of 1995, which compared with 1994 sought to cut the deficit by 69%. This law also entailed a 56% reduction in state central government subsidies for local prices. Such a strategy was hopeful that in some provinces there would be a budget surplus. In 1995 the budget increased by 4.4% in education, 1.9% in health, 5.5% in science and technology, and 4.1% in housing and community services.

Also forecast in 1995 was an alarming increase of 13.1% in social security expenditures, where a deficit of 679.5 billion pesos was expected. Only employers make social security contributions. However, it has become painfully clear that a full employment labor policy and retirement payments maintained throughout 35 years will place great fiscal pressure on the state. Demographic pressures on the aging population will worsen this situation; women can retire at 55 years of age and men at 60. Worker contributions to their own individual retirement funds are now under review. Not much different from the social security debate in the halls of the US Congress in 1995, the idea of increasing individual contribution to their retirement has been controversial in Cuba. Trade unions are especially concerned about having more of their already low wages being diverted to social security payments, especially when many of the self-employed are getting rich.

**Physical planning: A star is born**

Physical planning in Cuba began at the national level in 1962. In 1959 several construction projects were started in new rural communities, cooperatives, and state farms. The projects remodeled quarters for sugar cane workers at the *bateyes* (small settlements around the sugar mills). The Rebel Army Corps of Engineers, directed by Captain Oriente Fernández and later by Commander Julio García Oliveras, was in charge of these early initiatives. Also at that time, the National Institute of Housing and Savings (INAV) built several small suburban neighborhoods as well as the landmark projects at Habana del Este.

The leadership of Urban and Regional Planning in Cuba first emanated from the office of Physical Planning, located in The Ministry of Public Works. It later became the Institute of Physical Planning (IPF) from the Central Planning Board (JUCEPLAN). Initially directed by René Saladrigas, the institute played an important part in reorganizing national territory for state agricultural production. As its offices were in the capital, planners decided to do the planning for Havana Greenbelt (*Habana*), but this was transferred in the late 1960s to the Agricultural Command Outpost located near the village of Nazareno, just south of Havana.

Under the energetic management of Cecilia Menéndez, Nazareno became a teaching center for regional planners[2] in the last 2 years of their studies. An average day's work ended at 7.00 o'clock in the evening for the planners when they were not pulling 'all-nighters.' Among the projects designed by these groups were the new rural communities of Ceiba del Agua and Valle del Perú, designed by Mario González, Mario Coyula, and others.

Planning was directed from the Agricultural Command Outposts, which were frequently visited by Fidel Castro and other revolutionary leaders. These outposts symbolized a rejection of the city and stemmed from the ideology inherent in the rural guerrilla warfare in the Sierra Maestra Mountains. Guerrilla fighters assumed important leadership positions in the new government and, therefore, had a different mentality than the underground. Their rejection of the conventional methods and urban institutions of governance and their disdain for a bureaucracy that was characterized in cartoons mostly by bald headed light skinned men, created conflicts. Employees at the Puesto de Mando would board buses and trucks at cosmopolitan La Rampa in Vedado neighborhood, clad in a 'rural' uniform composed of gray khaki pants and shirts, black boots and shapeless straw hats. On the other hand, high rank officials (*dirigentes*) set off in the same place but in their Alfa Romeos which had been recently imported from Italy to offset the lack of US car imports and keep the state apparatus running.

The IPF laid out in the 1970s a system for siting investments and productive services. These criteria were included in the National Physical Plan, Provincial Plans, Urban Master Plans, and Urban Forecast System and Project Zones for the year 2000 (García Pleyán 1985). By the end of the 1970s, the emphasis had shifted from regional planning for spatially reorganizing rural areas, to urban planning.

With the creation of the People's Powers (*Poderes Populares*) in 1977, that planning structure remained in place until 1995. At the national level, regulatory and locational decisions were made by the IPF in order to balance regional and investment interests. Local-level decision making was made by provincial planning departments (DPPF, *Dirección Provincial de Planificación Física*) which pertained to local governments. Plans and projects for provinces, regions, zones, cities and towns were also overseen by the People's Power committees at the provincial level. Lastly, the municipal offices of Architecture and Urbanism (DAU) exercised control over construction, gathering information and statistics, and adjusting the plans to meet local conditions (García Pleyán 1986). In recent years, these

---

[2]The first urban and regional planners in Cuba were architects, but later included geographers, economists, engineers, and sociologists (demographers).

municipal offices have attempted to decentralize the execution of the master plans and control over local land use. In doing so, it gave considerable agility at the plan-implementation phase but with it came the cost of making important decisions vulnerable to the shortsightedness of local authorities (García Pleyán 1994).

*The First Socialist Master Plan for Havana: 1963–1964*

Under Batista in the 1950s, planning had been bolstered by the work of José Luis Sert, Paul Lester Wiener and Paul Schultz in order to form a team of Cuban architects that contained such well known professionals as Mario Romañach and Nicolás Quintana. This new plan was the first one under the revolution, and was created by architects, the Cuban planner Mario González and the Colombian Luis Espinosa. González also worked on subsequent master plans for the capital and became one of the most recognized planners in the country.

The 1963–1964 plan addressed many of the problems of Havana which until that time had been dealt with by the efforts of six independent municipalities. Each political division had had its own mayor and separate municipal agencies. Planning projects were spotty and idiosyncratic. Broad metropolitan-based planning problems could not be effectively resolved.

Through this plan Havana's political and administrative functions started to be treated as a metropolitan entity. The Master Plan created six regions in order to provide greater physical and social coherence to planning endeavors. Each region had its own center in order to give it an identity and also to reduce commuting. This objective, however, was not carried out despite considerable efforts. Occasionally, persistent political barriers did not allow for some territories to receive uniform services and infrastructure.

This Master Plan took effect when the city had just 1.5 million inhabitants. One of its objectives was to decrease the rate of population growth. In those days the capital city had an annual natural increase of 23 000 residents, as well as 17 000 immigrants from the interior of the country (González 1993). Some planning strategies of the Master Plan redistributed maritime and port activities as well as noxious industries to points elsewhere in Cuba. This shift also carried with it the development of appropriate infrastructure to support those economic activities. Decentralization slowed the rate of Havana's population growth which was exacerbated by environmental, sewage, and transportation problems.

The 1963–1964 Master Plan recommended a reduction in population density in the central areas of Havana. Although this was not achieved, the rate of new housing construction declined and no corrective measures were employed to prevent migration to the capital. The effect was to worsen the quality of the central areas of Havana. Physical deterioration accelerated because of little routine maintenance, especially streets and buildings which needed repair and painting, respectively.

The plan gave considerable importance to the environmental quality of the capital and it examined air pollution originating around Havana Bay: refineries, the gas plant, and the garbage dump at Cayo Cruz. This would be replaced in the early 1970s by a sanitary landfill at a new location near Calle 100, very close to the new Technical University (CUJAE) named after a student martyr killed in 1957, José Antonio Echeverría. The scarcity and poor distribution of green space in the city prompted proposals to increase the pre-Revolutionary ratio from 1 square meter per resident, to 18 square meters per resident. The latter figure was finally achieved in the 1970s. From the First Master Plan arose the idea of the Metropolitan Park (*Parque Metropolitano*). It took advantage of open spaces and tree-covered areas along the banks of the Almendares River. Metropolitan Park connected with the Havana Greenbelt through a network of parks. The most remote of those parks – Lenin, the Botanical and the new zoo – were created in the 1970s. Metropolitan Park, however, was postponed until later even though it was centrally located and of great importance for the city and the Almendares River (see 'Leisure time and green spaces' in Chapter 8).

The delay in creating Metropolitan Park stemmed from the considerable water pollution along the Almendares River and the presence of several noxious industries and shantytowns along its banks. Another factor was the persistence of a policy preference to carry out completely new projects in non-contiguous areas. Therefore, new projects were free of preexisting built environment and social conditions. One result of this strategy was that Havana residents had to travel considerable distances to the parks located along the southern edge of the metropolitan area. A major allure in traveling to the parks was to buy chocolates and cream cheese that could not be bought at the corner grocery.

Because of the delay in starting Metropolitan Park, its lands became threatened by industrial, military and squatter-housing activities. Husillo Dam was partially destroyed in 1990 in order to build a canal for a flood control and drainage system. The demolition seriously affected the historic and environmental value of this area and the canal was never completed. Administrative changes in 1994 brought new hope for completing the park. However, as of 1996 it was still not finished but, when ultimately completed, it will provide a good example of a sustainable landscape

**Table 4.3** Accomplishments of the Master Plan of 1963–1964

---

1. Zones of large-scale housing constuction in Habana del Este (Bahía, Guiteras and especially Alamar); Boyeros (infilling in Altahabana; and to a lesser extent Fontanar, Mulgoba and Panamerican); Central Highway (Cotorro); and La Lisa (Ermita-San Agustín).
2. Industrial zones and warehouses. Habana del Este (Berroa) and La Lisa to the west.
3. The port area (Puerto Pesquero, new terminals of container loading and unloading).
4. Major road networks including beltways.
5. The zone of influence surrounding Plaza de la Revolución.
6. The historic core of Habana Vieja (old walled city). This proposal, conducted with the First National Landmark Commission, was the forerunner of the study which culminated in 1975 with the first master plan for that zone and its subsequent designation as a World Heritage Site in 1982.
7. The location of new cemeteries and garbage dumps.
8. The spatial organization of the city (groups of 1000–2000 inhabitants; microdistricts of 6 000–8 000; districts of 25 000–30 000 and regions of 100 000 and more. Focus influenced by the principles of the International Congress of Modern Architecture (CIAM), British urban planners such as Abercrombie and Korn, as well as from Soviet planners.
9. System of green areas with different levels of parks (metropolitan, regional, district and local) that correspond with new urban spatial organization. A large part of this green area was planted by massive mobilizations, mass organizations, and state workers.
10. New political administrative division which divides metropolitan Havana into a single administrative entity for the entire city, with six regions. The government organized along with those two levels – metropolitan and regional – a smaller unit called the sectional levels. It kept the name of the control and inspection boards (JUCEI) used in the early years of the Revolution. In addition, administrative subdivisions were added: districts and microdistricts, which were used exclusively for planning studies and site plans.

---

where problems are converted into opportunities.

Other important aspects of the plan analyzed the loss of water through the city's poor network of aqueducts and water mains. It also addressed the excessive water consumption by inappropriate technology and deficiencies in the public transportation system. To confront these problems, the Master Plan proposed the creation of functional areas according to zoning principles, which until then had been accepted without any serious questioning (Table 4.3).

Thirty years after the first Master Plan, the principal author (González 1993, p. 15) analyzed some of the main weaknesses of this 1963–1964 Master Plan which included:

- a lack of baseline data

- poor analysis of infrastructure network except for the water mains
- housing located in industrial development zones on top of the Vento water basin
- imprecise delineation of functional zones
- weakness of the proposed road structure
- a lack of team work in settings dominated by architects
- little imagination about the city and not taking advantage of the functional and aesthetic attributes of Havana's more attractive areas

## The Master Plan of 1971

This new plan was prepared by a team of architects in the Institute of Physical Planning that among them included Max Baquero, Eusebio Azcue the Frenchman Jean Piere Garnier, and the Italian Vittorio Garatti (Figure 4.3). This project also included the participation of other specialists such as demographers, sociologists, geographers, and civil engineers. Such professional diversity coupled with what was learned from the previous plan produced a document that had scientific, technical and cultural criteria that were missing from the previous one. It was also influenced by the ideas of Fidel Castro as expressed in the speeches of the day (González 1993). The plan projected that by the year 2010 Havana would have an estimated population of 2.3 million inhabitants. In general the plan kept the principal approaches of the 1963–1964 guide, correcting some of their weaknesses and building on some of their strengths.

The proposed road network was much better organized and incorporated an important element: a transportation node south of the bay that would connect the major passenger and cargo flows to the rest of the city. It was also to include buses and railroads. However, this important node was not developed and the new docks on the southern part of the bay were never completed. The railroad did not receive the priority that was expected. What little investment that was earmarked for the road network, got diverted elsewhere. The 1971 road plan detailed an image of the city with special attention to landscaping roads and major thoroughfares. It was not implemented, however.

Years later, in the beginning of the 1980s, other urban landscape projects took place along major roads and promenades of the city. One of the most important was the arrival of the airport. However, several of these projects were only partially carried out during the late 1980s. An important road was the East–West Highway that would have helped to remove cargo traffic from the center of the city. On the other hand, there was an ambitious program of highway construction. Highway projects were

150

**Figure 4.3** The 1971 Master Plan gave special attention to enhancing the transportation and shipping terminals around Havana Bay. A detail of the proposed design is shown here. In the words of the authors, 'the plan aim[ed] to limit port investment because these activities currently carry too much weight with respect to the rest of the country's ports.' The plan also sought to confine the industrial and cargo functions to a smaller area, allowing the few hills surrounding the bay to encase the industrial functions more naturally along a selected part of the waterfront. Several berths and piers fronting Habana Vieja on the east, and the passenger railroad station on the west of Habana Vieja, would have been taken out of operation. Both functions would have been transferred to the redesigned portion of the Southern bay shown in the figure. Drawing by Vittorio Garratti.
*Source: Arquitectura/Cuba, Vol. 341, No. 1, 1973, p. 67 and facing map insert. Figure courtesy of the Instituto de Planificación Física*

almost always built disproportionately large such as the eight-lane national highway (*Autopista Nacional*). This program was also left unfinished and the national highway never connected with the ring around the port area (see Figure 2.8).

The 1971 plan analyzed the polycentric character of the capital and proposed to reinforce a set of secondary centers. If the Revolutionary Offensive of 1968 against small businesses provided a great boost to the Revolution it also had the unintended outcome of deteriorating the quality of the city's major centers. This occurred when local commercial establishments were readapted as housing units, almost always of an improvised nature and of very low quality. With this came problems of building maintenance in the central areas as well as a dearth of a variety in products and services.

Nonetheless, the range of this planning focus and the new awareness of the city's problems helped give special planning attention to these areas. The 1971 plan emphasized both shopping areas and services as well as workplaces and housing. In particular, the housing program received considerable attention because of the Microbrigades. Another achievement of the plan was the location of housing zones near production, teaching, and research centers. The 1971 plan also maintained the policy of creating special planning districts as outlined in the previous plan and it maintained the concept of creating industrial microdistricts that were compatible with residential areas.

Another activity that received considerable attention in the 1971 plan was the development of the port. As noted above, the southern part of the bay was targeted for the most modern technology for managing ships and maritime cargo. Two proposed terminals, one for containers and another with four piers, were completed, but it was not until late 1995 that an Italian cruise ship company restored a passenger terminal in Habana Vieja. The 1971 planning focus, though, marked an important step towards freeing up and using the traditional dock areas that blocked the view of the water all along the southern half of the old walled city. Although residents of Habana Vieja welcomed these revitalization efforts, planners did not have the power to implement plans.

During this time Habana Vieja became very fashionable because of visits by Fidel Castro and foreign gentry. Throughout the same area there operated as many as six agencies and national commissions dedicated to preserving Havana's built heritage. For example, three branches of the government as well as UNESCO worked to save Plaza Vieja. Perhaps the greatest support for historic preservation and restoration came when in 1982, when UNESCO declared Habana Vieja and the network of colonial forts, a World Heritage Site (see also Chapter 9). That accomplishment not withstanding, efforts continued to be focused on buildings and public spaces that held significance for the country, but were also both costly and time-consuming to preserve. Many of these revitalization efforts produced museums, cultural centers and restored buildings, but they lacked a comprehensive vision to address serious environmental problems and to incorporate the concerns of the local residents.

The principal defect of the 1971 plan was that it did not study Havana's relationship with its hinterland. It also proposed massive housing construction in the southern part of the capital that threatened the Vento Aquifer Basin (González 1993). That aquifer is vital because it supplies about 50% of the capital's current demand for fresh water. Construction of ExpoCuba on top of the aquifer assured visitors prestigious accommodations, but at a site too removed from the center of Havana. As we shall see later, the Special Period took care of that problem in its own way.

## The Master Plan of 1984

This plan had a projection to the year 2030. It was an ambitious work, consisting of 12 volumes of reports that were drafted in the Provincial Physical Planning Office. A team of 67 Cuban professionals and technicians and 14 foreign advisors (mostly Soviet) participated in the project.[3] Both the scope and the depth of the work surpassed previous master plans. In 1984, Havana had a population of 1.9 million residents and a growth rate of 2.3% per year. This plan analyzed the city in relation to the neighboring Province of Havana. It covered aspects such as population, settlement systems, road and transportation networks, agricultural production, recreation, and tourism.

The scope of the plan covered a long period – 45 years – and attempted to assure that the most basic needs of Havana were not overlooked. However, for practical reasons, the plan specified only certain details until the year 2000. The technical basis covered two broad fields: an analysis of current situations and a development forecast and proposal. In time, more detailed planning was carried out.

This 1984 Master Plan studied several alternatives for the capital such as a concentric ring, an east–west alignment, and three variants on these two themes. The east–west alternative posed more problems than the concentric ring in terms of departing from the historic evolution of the city. It

---

[3]The Cuban team was headed by Gina Rey and also included Joel Ballesté, Mario González, Marta Lorenzo, Enrique Fernández, José M. Fernández, Rosa Oliveras, and others. Norald Nercesián headed the group of foreign advisors.

did, however, offer several advantages. These included balancing metro-politan-wide needs but also respecting the traditional centers (a common problem in most cities where the center remains fixed as the city expands), preserving the Vento Watershed Basin, avoiding problems posed by the airport, maintaining the fertile agricultural lands to the south of Havana, and assuring a steady food supply (e.g., truck farming) for the capital. Another advantage of the east–west plan was that expanding towards the east of the city meant that lands not well suited for agriculture would be used. The eastern sector would be 'cleansed' by the prevailing trade winds which would help rid the city of air pollution from points around the bay. Those breezes would also complement the natural beaches along the eastern part of Havana which remained a major recreation source for *habaneros*.

Theoretically, the plan included parallel east–west strips running from the shoreline towards the south that would be devoted to recreation, housing, and light industry, respectively. This idea was similar to the lin-ear-city planning of Soria y Mata for Madrid and Miliutin in Stalingrad. The 1984 plan envisioned a system of central places composed of a major downtown area and five subcenters within five urban regions.

Because of the basic linear structure, three large road networks running parallel to the coast were proposed. One of them, the east–west highway, was outlined in studies before the 1984 plan and construction commenced on the western portion of the road in 1989. A major feature of this plan was to incorporate for the first time in Cuba a system of legal guidelines that had originated from the old Building Codes of 1861. National and provincial government agencies were consulted in addressing environ-mental concerns. For the first time in Cuba, the plan was approved by the Executive Committee of the Council of Ministers in May 1984.

Despite these novel features, important aspects were not sufficiently addressed. This included gathering community input in a few cases but not consistently throughout the entire planning process (Taller 1995). Nor was there a search for a coherent image of Havana. With hindsight, it is safe to say that the plan paid a great deal of attention to how the city would be at the end of the period without spending sufficient attention to the processes that should lead to that form. Similarly, little importance was given to sustainable development principles, the role of the neigh-borhood in a large city, and the creation of 'urban' culture.

---

[4]Personnel from the Physical Planning Department of the province were headed by Aracelis García, Rosa Oliveras and Jorge Carlos Diez.

## The 1990 updating of the Master Plan

This plan was projected to the year 2010 by a team of 37 professionals and technicians.[4] At this time Havana had a population of 2.1 million inhabitants and the scheme anticipated a population of 2.3 million inhabitants. The 1984 plan was thoroughly revised, drawing upon the successes and failures of the plan over the previous 7 years. The new scheme also identified environmental concerns that had traditionally been overlooked. The planners believed that the previous plan had overstated the territorial expansion of the city and therefore chose to 'compact' Havana by filling in open spaces within the city's limits. Smaller service centers received greater attention in the 1990 plan than the previous one where large centers became key functional points. However, despite the rationale of this focus, those subcenters did not materialize, because of the lack of resources as the economy sank into the Special Period (Pérez 1996).

The main causes behind the failure of the 1984 plan were not properly analyzed. The spectacular collapse of the socialist camp, which Fidel Castro called the *desmerengamiento* (dissolution) made clear the intrinsic vulnerability of the model. Havana was dependent upon a budget by the upper echelons of the Cuban government that did not have the proper means for allocating such resources. It also became clear that little attention had been given to land values nor was there balance between material versus moral rewards. Planning had become the victim of top-down decision making and provided few incentives for planners and other technicians.

By 1987 an ambitious construction phase brought on by the 'Process of Correction of Mistakes' (*el proceso de rectificación de errores*) intended to cover up many of Havana's problems. A group of young architects tried to ride on this surge to renovate the ailing Cuban architecture. Their work mostly lacked a proper fitting into local surroundings, and they affiliated themselves with the Postmodern movement that was already falling into disfavor in North America and Europe (Coyula 1993). Their efforts focused on apartments, clinics, and tourist projects, initially with the construction of new hotels and later on with the rehabilitation of existing ones. Another benefit to Havana was the strong growth in the construction of scientific research centers and pharmaceutical plants throughout Havana, especially in the area that came to be known as the 'western pole.'

These programs, like tourism, aimed to generate hard currency in order to keep the country functioning. The actual construction phase, however, belonged to a new organizational form called the *contingentes* (work crews). Unlike the Microbrigades, the *contingentes* were composed of professional builders who worked overtime but were also paid according to their work. Nonetheless, the productivity and quality of their work remained low and their work style was directed more towards meeting deadlines than quality standards.

*First stage of the 1990 updating the Master Plan*

In 1992, the same team that previously had revised the Master Plan, focused its efforts on the first stage and with a more clearly defined territorial focus. What determined this new approach was to consider the circumstances brought on by the Special Period. Thus the first stage worked with the different alternatives proposed for the country to account for the reduction of fuel. The study was much more decentralized than any previous plan. The city was divided among 600 study zones. Considerable importance was given to the 15 county (*municipio*) offices of the Provincial Department of Architecture and Urbanism. In the past, these municipal offices had merely collected data. This new focus, though, placed great emphasis on local potential at a time when 93 Popular Councils (*Consejos Populares*) were created in Havana in 1990, which were later increased to 102. The Popular Councils are government entities with more administrative power than a delegate. This latter representative is elected from a district and serves as an intermediary between the constituents and higher levels of government (see Chapter 5). Significantly, though, these Popular Councils do not have their own funds for making investments.

The premises for updating the Master Plan (Table 4.4) brought a new focus for urban planning in Cuba, one which sought greater sustainable development and public participation. This philosophy began to take

**Table 4.4**  Premises of the first stage of updating Havana's Master Plan

1. Prioritize the most deteriorated areas of the city both for planning as well as for specific action.
2. Emphasize home repair, services and infrastructure.
3. Decentralize planning and building to match local conditions.
4. Execute the work in stages, commencing with the least ambitious ones.
5. Take better advantage of local labor resources.
6. Promote job creation close to where people live.
7. Reintroduce traditional building techniques and materials and in general to favor the use of appropriate technology.
8. Recycle leftover building materials.
9. Encourage the participation of the local population in each stage: planning implementation, construction, and maintenance.

shape among different fields and professions that were influenced by the scarcity brought on by the special period. To that can be added a new appreciation of the spatial, functional, bioclimatic, and cultural patterns of the city as well as traditional materials and techniques used in construction. The movement was initially limited to a few professionals[5] who were dedicated to the theory and practice of architecture and planning and the conservation of national landmarks.

### The Workshops for Neighborhood Change: A Havana experience in participatory planning

The Comprehensive Workshops for Neighborhood Change (TTIB, or *talleres*) were promoted experimentally in 1988 by the Group for the Comprehensive Development of the Capital (*Grupo para el Desarrollo Integral de la Capital*) in three Havana neighborhoods. They targeted areas with dire problems: Atarés and Cayo Hueso in the central zones where most buildings were substandard and overcrowded; and La Güinera in the southern edge of the city, which was a shantytown without streets or roads. The experience continued to grow and by the end of 1996 there were 13 neighborhood workshops. The workshops are comprised of interdisciplinary teams consisting of between three and eight persons who often include architects, sociologists, engineers, and social workers. Usually, a person with organizational abilities who works and lives in the neighborhood is elected. The workshops seek an overall improvement of the physical condition of their neighborhoods as well as the welfare of the residents. Goals are defined after a study of local needs and an inventory are taken of materials installations, offices, housing, and professionals that can be used within the local community.

Even though each workshop has its own goals, there are four general aspects employed by each: (i) to improve the condition of housing; (ii) the development of the local economy; (iii) the education of children and youth; and (iv) development of neighborhood identity. The approach is based upon the principle of not displacing the current population and of finding solutions for current residents. In other words, the decision-making goes from below to above, from the grassroots level to the state. Workshops cooperate with various Cuban and foreign institutions who advise the *Consejo Popular de Barrio* (see Chapter 5) in both the built environment and in the socio-economic sphere. As such, these organizations

---

[5]These professionals included Sergio Baroni, Eliana Cárdenas, Mario Coyula, Carlos García Pleyán, Mario González, Isabel León, Luis Lápidus, Rosendo Mesías, Gina Rey, Isabel Rigol, Eduardo Luis Rodríguez, Angela Rojas, Fernando Salinas, Roberto Segre, among others.

provide much needed support to local government (Coyula *et al.* 1995).

From the start it became evident that the workshops would require their own sources of income for working in the neighborhoods. They experimented with several local initiatives such as the production of building materials and tapping into tourist potential. Other routes included collaboration with foreign non-governmental organizations (NGOs) and even Cuban NGOs,[6] whose resources were used mainly for strengthening the productive and service activities that could help generate revenues for the communities. Ten NGOs have financed projects that provide the workshops with tools and building materials for repairing slum tenements and recycling solid waste (Coyula *et al.* 1995).

In addition to preparing the working document of the *Grupo*, *Estrategia* (Strategy), and collaborating with the workshops, another major task of the *Grupo* has been the building of a large three-dimensional architectural model of the city. This scale model (1:1000) began in 1988 and was opened to the public in June 1995. The model (called the 'City Model' or *Maqueta de la Ciudad*) uses three colors to designate the historical development of Havana: Colonial (sixteenth to nineteenth centuries), Republican (1900–1958), and Revolutionary (1959–present). The scale model is not just a beautiful and interesting artifact for visitors, but a tool that can help cement the relationship between Havana and its residents. It aims to encourage an appreciation for the city's layout, design, and growth, and to promote geographic literacy. Its chief applied use evaluates the impact of new projects around surrounding areas. For example, when large buildings or complexes are proposed, a scaled model of the project can be placed on the larger *maqueta* to assess how well the proposed structures blend in with the surrounding area. As we shall show in Chapter 8, though, a large Spanish joint-venture hotel was built on the Malecón in Vedado. Unfortunately, it was not previously tested on the model to see how well the project would 'fit' into that part of the city.

---

[6]The existence of truly independent NGOs in Cuba is controversial. Gillian Gunn documented what she has identified as numerous NGOs in Cuba. However, the question of true autonomy from the government is not clear. Raul Castro delivered a very controversial report on March 23, 1996, to the Central Committee of the Cuban Communist Party. He emphasized that the Cuban concept of civil society is not the same as that in the United States, and claimed that some foreign NGOs in Cuba 'attempt to undermine the economic, political and social system freely chosen by [the Cuban] people . . . [and] whose only aim is to enslave [Cuba]' (Raul Castro 1996, p. 32). Raul Castro's remarks stem from the official Cuban reaction that many international and Cuban NGOs ideologically undermine the Revolution through the controversial Torricelli Track Two law in the United States.

## Planning: The long and winding road

Planning in socialist Havana has revealed at least five key features. First, the city counts on an abundant supply of trained professionals. Although architects and engineers dominated planning in the 1960s and 1970s, many other professionals now participate. Second, decision-making has slowly moved from high levels of national government to both metropolitan and neighborhood sources. Third, some political goals have derailed the key features of several of Havana's master plans. Implementation of plans in the past decade has been interrupted by the effects of the Special Period. Fourth, the economic viability of local projects and municipal agencies is necessary for local planning projects to be carried out successfully. As we will discuss in Chapter 5, the ability for Havana to generate its own resources – without relying strictly upon funds approved at the national level – is intricately tied to the success of local land use planning, economic development, and zoning (Stretton 1978). Finally, as decision-making slowly devolves from the upper echelons of national government, Havana's municipalities will increasingly face challenges posed by an emerging market. This presents both risks and opportunities for local governments, a point we return to in the concluding chapter.

# 5

# City government and administration: old and new actors

The centralizing project that meant incorporating the entire population within a few institutions was able to work under a model in which goods and services were centrally distributed and with the help of a canon of equity and equality. For a while, at least during part of the Revolution, that was accompanied by a prosperity that produced a sense of shared well-being.

Hugo Azcuy, *Estado y Sociedad Civil en Cuba*, 1995

## Antecedents to city government in Havana

Cuba's colonial and semi-colonial past molded the kind of local government during the republican period that Havana had with independence in 1902, and end with the triumph of the Revolution in 1959. Two constitutions enacted in 1901 and 1940 – the latter considered to be one of the most advanced in the Americas – prescribed an important role to municipal governments. These city administrations were headed by a mayor who was supported by a body of town council members that had deliberative functions. Initially, town council members elected the mayor directly, but beginning in 1908 that charge passed to direct electoral vote by the people for a period of 2 years (Dilla *et al.* 1993). Throughout the twentieth century, Cuba's city governments have faced the same challenges as other Latin American city governments, ie, a high level of dependence on the national government for funding (Scarpaci and Irarrázaval 1994). Such dependence continued during the revolutionary period, which weakened the power of local government vis-à-vis the national government.

The right to vote was manipulated by a corrupt political apparatus. The coup d'etat of 1952 further eroded the already precarious role of municipal governments.[1] Despite the generally subordinate role played by Cuban municipalities, in pre-Revolutionary times the Mayor of Havana had always been considered as the second most important political figure of the country, after the President of the Republic. The distribution and weight of these municipalities was also quite uneven. For example, around 1951 there were 126 municipalities in Cuba, but 26 (21%) of them were located in the province of Havana; the equivalent of one in seven municipalities in the entire country (Dilla *et al.* 1993). Havana Province included all the territories which encompass the current Havana City (created in 1976) and Havana Provinces, minus a small part at the western edge which at that time belonged to Pinar del Río (Figure 5.1).

With the triumph of the Revolution in 1959, the central government named Commissioners provisionally to cover the functions of municipal governments. In 1961, they created the Coordination, Administration, and Inspection Boards (JUCEI) to coordinate and enforce policies and national laws, and to collect and transmit information about their territories to the national government. These boards were established after a meeting with representatives of political and mass organizations, from which a permanent committee was elected. If the Board marked a step toward the decentralization of the island's governance, the provinces benefited more than the municipalities as local governments had little authority over local services. In the Capital, a JUCEI was established in each of the former municipalities, and Havana's counties were reorganized (Table 5.1)

Seeking even more decentralization, the Local Power (*Poder Local*) was established in 1966. According to Fidel Castro, the objective of Local Power was to reinforce the role of mass organizations, especially political organizations (Castro 1977). In 1965, the political institutionalization of the process had been completed, led by the recently formed Communist Party of Cuba (PCC) and its first Central Committee (Castro 1980). *Poder Local* was established in each municipality and was made up of an executive committee, its president, two secretaries, and 10 delegates that were elected in meetings by the population. The delegates were held accountable to their electorate, but the president was elected by members of the

---

[1]The hierarchy of settlements is similar to the United States: in ascending order of size, the normal sequence is towns, cities, municipalities, and provinces (roughly the equivalent of states, but in size only, not in jurisdictional function). We use county and municipality interchangeably. Havana City Province (different from the surrounding Havana Province) consists of 15 municipalities today.

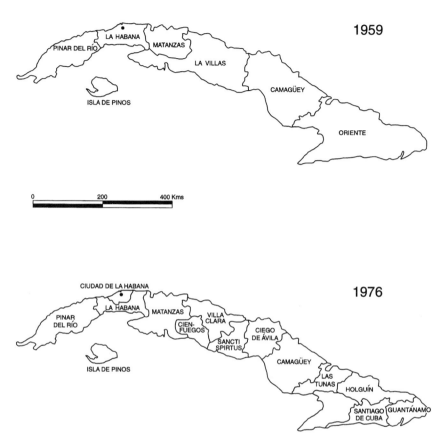

**Figure 5.1.** Jurisdictional reorganization of Cuban provinces, 1959 and 1976

PCC in the area. At the national level, they created the coordination of Local Power.

Also created during this time was the Metropolitan Administration of Havana. As we discussed in the previous chapter, the first Master Plan of Havana (1963–1964) recognized a continuous urban area that had assimilated older municipalities. Subordinate to that Administration were six Regional Administrations, but the territory and name – La Habana, Diez de Octubre, Marianao, Guanabacoa, Boyeros and Habana del Este – changed according to the historic, economic and social features of each municipality.

In the middle of the 1970s Cuba began an open 'complex modernization, decentralization, and democratization process involving the political and governmental system that has been called the *process of institutional-*

**Table 5.1** Reorganization of counties (*municipios*) in pre- and post-Revolutionary Havana

| Pre-1959 name | Post-1959 names |
|---|---|
| La Habana | Habana Vieja |
| | Centro Habana |
| | Plaza |
| | Cerro |
| | Diez de Octubre |
| Marianao | Marianao |
| | La Lisa |
| | Playa |
| Regla[a] | Regla |
| Guanabacoa | Guanabacoa |
| | San Miguel del Padrón |
| | Habana del Este |
| Santa María del Rosario | Cotorro |
| | Arroyo Naranjo (partial) |
| Santiago de las Vegas | Boyeros |
| | Arroyo Naranjo (partial) |

[a]Despite its small size, Regla has a strong tradition of local pride and history that had to be respected when officials tried to change its political boundaries.

*ization*. Such a system was closely related to the implementation of a new plan of placing Cuba favorably in the Soviet economic system' (Dilla *et al.* 1993, p. 29, our translation, original emphasis). That process responded to criticisms of errors produced by a rigid and highly centralized government and planning procedures.

Institutionalization included a new political and administrative division. Stages were identified by the System of Economic Planning and Management (SDPE) to regulate the national economy. A legal socialist framework was created that included the promulgation of the new Constitution in 1976, and a revitalization of political and mass organizations, especially among labor unions (Castro 1978). Institutionalization meant more democratization, with an electoral system of indirect vote at the national, provincial, and municipal levels, and direct vote only at the lower level or constituency level.

Another problem in the capital was the relationship between municipal government and enterprises that were nationally administered and that worked directly with the government ministries. The municipalities looked to the Cuban Communist Party as arbitrator whenever bottle-necks in decision making occurred. In doing so, it isolated municipal governments from their functions as a political and ideological administrative body (González 1995).

A premise in government administration was that information is power and that sharing it also means the beginning of shared power. The lack of information makes it difficult to engender a public debate on issues as is evident in the relationship between grassroots assemblies and higher levels of government. Dialogue such as this is almost always confined to very concrete and immediate issues that rarely enter into the depth of problems, much less their causes.

This weakness threatens municipalities. As Dilla (1995, p. 70) observes, '[municipalities] crudely confront the risk of returning functions without powers, and beneficiaries of a decentralization of poverty . . . the insertion of Cuba in the world market or its integration into regional markets will inevitably produce a fragmentation of national economic space'. On the one hand, powerful state companies hold considerable power. On the other hand, local governments possess few resources and cannot raise their own funds. This creates conflict and resentment. The ongoing tug-of-war occurs in a rapidly changing local context in which the final goals of government planners cannot be well defined. New economic players constantly appear on the scene: cooperatives, self-employed, local economic development projects financed by foreign NGOs, and joint ventures. In this context the popular organizations in Cuba 'should become vehicles of pluralist expression, and not simply transmission fan-belts on a motor that extend from political centers . . . such a relationship assumes mechanisms of negotiation and implementation . . . in order to achieve an effective integration of local society' (Dilla 1995, p. 72, our translation).

Until the constitutional reform of 1992, the municipal assembly elected an executive committee composed of 'professional members' (dedicated full time to public administration) and other non-professionals who held other jobs. Because professional members were each responsible for overseeing different administrative divisions, they gradually turned into virtual representatives and administrators of those agencies. In other words, they served as judge and jury. This duality bound the municipal assembly members into a counterpart for the interest of the electorate and the region to which they served. It also committed them to working with successful programs and, perhaps even more frequently, with the errors and deficiencies of the government agencies.

With a legal reform of 1992, deputies of the National Assembly became elected through direct vote by the population. Although data are scarce, one report by Amnesty International reported that '14 percent of the last election's ballots were ruined, the highest percentage ever, and the only way of showing protest where the voting is obligatory and a single party is running' (Joe 1995). Nonetheless, the reforms also meant keeping a lack of effective territorial representation given that candidates could be elected in places where they did not reside. It also applied the principle of 'closed candidacy' where votes were made in blocks. Actually, those deputies do not represent their territories nor their electorates and often times do not even know them.

With the creation of *Poder Popular*, the capital earned the rank of province, becoming one of 14 that made up the country (in addition to the special municipality of Isla de la Juventud which was the Isle of Pines but had changed its name to Isle of Youth, based on a suggestion of Fidel Castro). At the same time, the provincial assemblies were made up of provincial delegates elected by municipal assemblies on a ratio of one delegate per 10 000 residents (or a fraction greater than 5000) in a municipality. At the time of the July 1995 elections, 29 131 candidates ran for office for some 14 229 delegate seats among the 169 municipalities in Cuba.[2] In Havana, there were 3224 candidates, of which 26.7% were incumbents. The Provincial Assembly of the City of Havana has 215 delegates (Lee 1995a).

If *Poder Local* made greater participation possible in government, it has also had limitations. Provincial governments and other large cities often consume resources and make decisions at the expense of municipalities. The results have been severe in many cases. For instance, in Cuba, the smallest municipality has 7000 residents while half the national population resides in municipalities with more than 100 000 residents (García Pleyán 1995b). In the capital, the municipality of Diez de Octubre has about 240 000 residents, and only two of the 15 municipalities in Havana City Province have less than 100 000 residents. On the other hand, the base delegates serve as communicators of problems without either the resources or the decision making ability to solve them. This has eroded their credibility, a phenomenon which is somewhat unjust if one considers the tremendous amount of effort made by people who are not paid for their work and who must also maintain a regular job on the side.

To address this problem, representatives of administrative agencies were invited to neighborhood meetings (that is, 'rendering account meetings'), but this process became somewhat perfunctory. Over time, it became apparent that agency representatives only infrequently attended meetings, and just like the delegates, rarely had any way to solve problems. In each new electoral process, there has been an effort to reduce the

---

[2]Since 1976, elections are competitive at the local level. By law, there must be at least two candidates and there is no official party slate. Often, party members run against each other, but candidates do not have to be members of the Cuban Communist Party. At least half of the representatives to the national assembly are composed of delegates directly elected to municipal assemblies. This is similar to the notion of 'at large' delegates found in other political systems who represent specific geographic areas.

size of the *circunscripciones* (election districts), which in turn increases the total number of delegates. Improving the delegate to population ratio meant 1600 on average in the capital. In one meeting of the provincial presidents of *Poder Popular* at the end of 1995, the Secretary of the National Assembly called for greater flexibility in provinces in order to professionalize full-time delegates given Cuba's new free-market initiatives (Lee 1995a). But none of these measures got to the root of the problem: the lack of resources and real decision-making power for the delegates.

The initial confusion between elected government and administrative responsibility began to be resolved in 1993 when Executive Committees (*Comités Ejecutivos*) were replaced by the Administrative Councils (*Consejos de Administración*) with clearly defined tasks and relationships. Hence, an attempt was made to delimit the functions of representative government. Nevertheless, resources have continued to be centralized at the national level and budget allocations continue to be quite small at a time when local governments attempt to compete with national priorities in the midst of a terrible economic crisis. In Havana, however, municipalities depend solely on a centrally-allocated budget. In other words, municipal governments respond to the problems without receiving the means for resolving them. At the same time, community participation continues to perform weakly despite the establishment of the Neighborhood Popular Councils (*Consejos Populares de Barrios*) that went from 93 original entities in 1990 to 102 in 1995 in Havana.

Despite its name, therefore, *Poder Popular* in fact has little power and even less community participation. Paradoxically, some attempts by the central government to help them have actually hurt instead. In 1994, in light of the alarming number of problems in the capital such as sanitation removal, a national level commission was created to 'help' the work of local government. The logical solution would have been to transfer resources to systematically pick up more garbage. This style of work merely highlights the weakness of local government. In the end, Havana implements orders from higher levels of government. Unfortunately, the national level of government thinks it is being useful. Gestures of help become diluted until there is a new campaign of activism to carry out another set of directives.

By the early 1990s, it had become widely evident that there were contradictions between the political-administrative structure of Havana City and the needs of the people. In Marxist terms, these contradictions could serve as catalysts to foster necessary changes. Ideological imperatives prevail. Changes should be implemented cautiously so as not to jeopardize the overriding objectives of building socialism, yet occur rapidly enough to avoid economic and moral deterioration to the point of no return.

Authorities also wish to safeguard the achievements reached since 1959. Decentralization and participation seem to be pivotal points for such an ordered transformation. Decentralization, though, should not be confused only with administrative deconcentration (e.g., opening up a local branch of national-level government agency).

Decentralization in many countries has been used to cover up a host of administrative, social, and political problems. Dismantling the welfare state in capitalist societies since the 1960s has been carried out by privatization and deregulation (Scarpaci 1989, p. 11; García Playán 1995b, p. 82). Cuba's challenge is how to carry out decentralization in the Cuban context: Should it merely allow for the economic and political survival of the socialist project? Or, will decentralization turn out to be administrative deconcentration lacking the means for representing the people's and locality's interests? Clearly, city government must tap into local resources and participation. Achieving that goal requires that higher levels of government in Cuba share power. Traditionally, power sharing in Cuba has been viewed suspiciously and as a political concession. However, 'concessions' may be perceived as a loss of credibility among national ministries who traditionally have been identified as the essence of the Revolution (Roca Calderío 1973; De Armas 1975). Power sharing among government agencies that have enjoyed absolute and indisputable political, ideological, military, and administrative enforcement is virtually unknown in revolutionary Cuba. Nevertheless, its implementation cannot come too soon for Havana residents.

Self-governance and the role of civil society will have to be strengthened if Havana is to be decentralized yet retain key features of the socialist project. This will entail creating a new consciousness where 'the decentralization and socialization of power derives from an essential principle for the development of Cuban socialist democracy that includes attaining a pluralism that recognizes the diversity and autonomy of the participants of the decentralization project' (García Pleyán 1995b, p. 143, our translation).

## Neighborhood Popular Councils

Neighborhood Popular Councils (*Los Consejos Populares de Barrio*) began in 1988. They grew out of a need to compensate the reduced number of municipalities following the 1976 political and administrative reorganization of the country. At first, the councils were confined to rural Cuba and had uneven community participation. A few small scattered communities in the City of Havana Province, such as Campo

Florido and Las Guásimas, implemented *Consejos Populares*. Santiago de Cuba and Camagüey provinces installed 'districts' (*distritos*) in urban areas. Unlike the focus of the *Consejos* on community participation, these districts sought to enhance public administration. Positive results among *Consejos* in the capital led to the passage of a law in 1990 that sanctioned *Consejos* in other cities. Article 104 of the Constitution was reformed in July 1992 and stipulated the functions of the *Consejos Populares de Barrio* such that, by 1995, 1454 *Consejos* had been created in 97% of the nation's neighborhood electoral districts (CEA 1995; Lee 1995b).

*Consejos* are composed of delegates from the same neighborhood electoral district who in turn elect a full-time representative to preside over the body. Representatives from grassroots and mass organizations such as the Cuban Federation of Women (FMC) and the Committees for the Defense of the Revolution (CDR) also form part of the local councils. They also include a representative from the Communist Youth Union (*Unión de Jóvenes Comunistas*) but not from the Cuban Communist Party. Representatives from local retailing, manufacturing, and government offices also participate in the *Consejos*, as do representatives from hospitals, schools, and research centers. Sectoral government agencies that are now subordinate to municipal government have membership in the local *Consejo*. These representatives come from housing, education, culture, architecture and urban planning, public works, and other sectors.

Transformations such as those outlined above make the *Consejos*, the newest entity within the system of *Poder Popular*, the ones most in touch with local concerns. In Havana, though, the average size of each area under the jurisdiction of a *Consejo* (about 20 000 people) is still too large for effective dialogue between *Consejo* delegates and local constituents. The area covered by each *Consejo*, moreover, does not always coincide with historic neighborhood boundaries. In the neighborhoods where a Workshop for Comprehensive Neighborhood Change operates (the so-called *Talleres* discussed in Chapter 4), there are reports that *Consejos* benefit from the *Talleres*, but there has been no systematic evaluation of these contributions.

## Land use enforcement in Havana and urban planning discipline

Since the end of the 1980s various criticisms have been put forth about the lack of coordination in the planning and the decision making for Havana's master plans. As described in several chapters throughout the book, this gap between planning and implementation can be seen when the historic image of the city is compared to what is now happening to Havana's built environment. Urban land use regulation links planning to land use implementation. In order to achieve efficient city management of land use, Havana planning authorities require, among other instruments, a clearly defined set of enforceable laws.

Havana's urban planning laws are steeped in the city's rich history and date back to the early period of conquest. The Law of the Indies of 1523 and its reformulation in 1674 allowed hundreds of uneducated soldiers to settle Cuban cities as well as hundreds of cities elsewhere in Latin America (Table 5.2)

Urban land-use regulations in Havana have emanated from more than a hundred government agencies. Since the middle of the nineteenth century regulations were designated as Royal Orders, Laws, Decree Laws, Law Decrees, Resolutions, and Collective and Institutional Resolutions. Between 1859 and 1959, more than eight entities passed laws for Havana, and between 1959 and 1993, another 50 laws and regulations were issued (Fernández 1995). That represents an average of more than one law or regulation per year, of which there have been more than 70 versions.

Havana's 15 municipalities, moreover, have each issued their own Urban Land Use and Zoning Regulations (*Regulaciones Urbanísticas*) (Rodríguez and Cabrera 1995). Although the technical quality of the legal framework that governs city administration in Havana is quite high, the city suffers from major problems. Urban disorder is tolerated as evidenced by inappropriate land uses and unauthorized building projects,

**Table 5.2.** Major urban planning laws in Cuba and Havana, 1523–1985

| Law | Years | Brief description |
| --- | --- | --- |
| *Leyes de Indias* | 1523, 1674 | Regulations about platting new-found settlements |
| *Ordenanzas Municipales* | 1574 | General rules about urban land use |
| *Ordenanzas para la Zona de Extramuros* | 1817 | Land use regulation in areas outside of the Walled City |
| *Ordenanzas y de Policía Urbana* | 1881 | Specified regulatory powers for building and housing inspectors in Havana |
| *Nuevas Ordenanzas de Construcción de la Plaza Cívica* | 1963 | Updated land use and building codes for Havana |
| *Reglamento de Ornato e Higiene de la Ciudad* | 1977, second version in 1989 | Updated public health, sanitation, and waste removal regulations |
| *Regulaciones Urbanísticas* | 1985 | Standardized land use planning regulations and zoning for the 15 municipalities of Havana |

which reflects a lack of citizen compliance. For example, aggressive pruning of the urban tree canopy, historically undervalued, serves as a barometer to the city's problems. Neither residents nor public utility workers respect guidelines for protecting Havana's rich tree cover. The situation becomes even more alarming with the recent arrival of new economic activities, including real-estate market for foreigners. These economic transformations have been ushered in quickly because of the need for foreign capital. Land-use regulations and ordinances ostensibly exist and were created to reconcile discrepancies over land uses (García Pleyán 1995a; Scarpaci 1996). However, they will now have to be reformulated because of the strong foreign presence in order to deal more effectively with outsiders who 'were thought to be forgotten but once again are sneaking around' (Coyula 1995, our translation).

As pressure brought on by unsatisfied needs of *habaneros* increases, the topic of a 'legal residence' has officially entered the government's agenda for action. During his rather acerbic intervention at the National Assembly at the end of 1995, Fidel Castro referred to the 'illegal ones', lamenting the lack of cooperation among Havana residents in denouncing them. Castro remarked:

> Havana receives the punishment it deserves, yes, they and the immense number of Easterners [residents originating from the eastern part of the island] and other provinces that are now here . . . the water network is insufficient, the electrical network, telephones – all of it insufficient. I've heard it said that in the municipality of Havana [there are more than] thirty thousand illegal residents and that isn't one of the largest estimates (Granma, December 30, 1995, p. 3, our translation).

Currently, the annual net gain from migration to the capital is about 11 000 persons, a figure that is almost laughably small considering the situation in other capitals of large cities in Latin America. Nonetheless, that figure masks the fact that annually about 20 000 people leave Havana, many of them young skilled workers, while about 30 000 migrate to Havana, most of them unskilled.

## Urban environment and public participation

Cuba paid little attention to environmental protection for almost 200 years. The enactment of Law 33 on January 10, 1981 marked a first step in environmental regulation. Just 25 pages in length, Law 33 purportedly covers regulations from the 'principles of the Cuban Communist Party concerning the environment.' As such, the law is steeped heavily in rhetoric and ideology and has very little in the way of verifiable policies and procedures. The law even goes so far as to claim that there is 'wise use of natural resources by communist countries versus the indiscriminate use of natural resources by the Capitalistic World' (Barba and Avella 1996, pp. 35–36 our translation). To be sure, environmental problems are grave in Havana and elsewhere in Cuba.

A rapid overview of the major urban-environmental and quality of life problems in Cuba shows natural variation among cities and towns and even similar neighborhoods (Table 5.3). Despite that heterogeneity, the following are some of the main urban-environmental challenges.

Table 5.3 identifies a wide range of urban-environmental problems, and speaks to the ailments that afflict the home, the neighborhoods, and the entire city. It is noteworthy that food procurement is now the number one social problem, dislodging housing as the long-standing number one concern. Housing, however, poses serious challenges because of its generally rundown condition and improvised repairs. Air and noise pollution in Havana are serious problems, although cooling sea breezes tend to alleviate the former problem somewhat. Public transportation runs inadequately and is highly polluting.

Havana has not remained completely idle in the face of these environmental challenges. Public and private solutions surface often. Some are quite innovative and others are more conventional. For example, local building materials and construction techniques have improved in recent years. This means that they are less wasteful and dependent upon fossil fuels inputs and allow for greater resident participation. The massive use of the bicycle has rapidly transformed the urban landscape. As will be noted in Chapter 8, the number of bicycles has increased more than 10-

**Table 5.3** Urban-environmental and quality of life problems

Food and basic article scarcities
Low quality of housing
Poor quality watersheds
Noise pollution
Flooding
Thin vegetative cover
Systematic blackouts and interrupted telephone service
Insufficient public transportation
Scarce household fuel
Poor waste removal service
Heavily littered public spaces
A deficit of public services (now reaching prioritized sector of health and
    education)
Distortions in the urban image of the city

*Source*: Coyula *et al.* (1995)

fold from about 70 000 in 1990. Several bike lanes and bike paths now run through Havana, including an iron bridge (*Puente de Hierro*) over the Almendares River. Related economic activities include mechanical and tire repair, a cycle-bus that takes cyclists from one side of the tunnel under Havana Bay to the other, and accessories such as baskets and racks on bicycles for carrying cargo and passengers. New innovations include the so-called *teteras* which are simple bronze-threaded screws that attach to the rear axle of the bicycle and serve as footrests for passengers on the back seat. Credit for these innovations are divided between public agencies – groping for solutions to major urban problems – and resourceful citizens just trying to survive.

Abandoned lots in Cuban cities, Havana in particular, are increasingly being used as organic and community gardens. Surplus produce may be sold in the open market. The state provides technical assistance to thousands of gardens throughout the city. Animal waste, compost, and other organic inputs help bolster yields. Lands previously considered to be marginal – often at the city edge – have come into production because of the Special Period. Alternatives for garbage pickup now include tractors and carts pulled by animals. Slowly, the mentality of recycling is taking hold among *habaneros* (Hernández 1994). However, this attitude has not been widely supported by personal motivation among residents.

There is still very little environmental culture in Havana both among the citizenry and among the authorities. This lack of concern over the environment bodes poorly for Havana in the near future given that it will confront considerable scarcities. Excuses for not becoming more environmentally aware include a degree of mental inertia and the defense of previous positions. Perhaps even more dangerous is the trend at the end of 1995 among certain official circles – provoked by a real or perceived slight economic recovery – to return to the old ways of doing things in the environmental realm. For instance, there is now some discussion about returning to the old program of new housing made out of large prefabricated panels (see Chapter 6) and of using only petroleum-based chemical fertilizers that require high energy inputs.

Interest in the concept and practice of environmental sustainability has moved beyond academic circles and the initial narrow focus on environmental conservation. Traditional environmental thinking in Cuba has elaborated ideas internationally accepted about the possible existence of sustainability. Widely accepted concepts and practices include a new regard for variety and diversity, the interdependence among elements in a system, the carrying capacity of a particular ecosystem and its regenerative potential, the multiplicity of functions that each element plays, and the idea that various elements in an ecosystem can fulfill the same function. That Cuba is a poor, small, isolated island where most of its population is urban suggests that it is logical to extend these principles of sustainability from the natural to built and social environments.

A perennial challenge in environment defense – and Havana is no exception – is that communities often find it difficult to focus on invisible, short-term goals when other daily needs remain unsatisfied. Cuba, like many other countries, would benefit greatly if it could develop an economic model and a use of the built environment that is viable and rational (Coyula *et al.* 1995, pp. 1–2). Resources required for that kind of development can not only come out of macroeconomic structures, but must also derive from a real and stable family and community economy. The neighborhood can serve as the basic unit of the homeland. In Havana, community participation in the socialist project has been essentially one of mobilization. A variety of new forms of community are evident in Cuba, most of which were practically unheard of just a decade ago (Table 5.4). These new forms of participation reflect both the current economic situation as well as the realization that new options must be employed. Local problems include waste collection, a monotonous diet, scarcity of medications, water shortages, fuel scarcity, the rise in suicides, and prostitution. Entities addressing these problems include *Consejos Populares*, mass organizations, semi-public entities, NGOs, community organizations, and a variety of grassroots units.

### What sustains Havana?

Even though the capital is the most productive place in the country, the income it generates is generally not reinvested back into it in a manner that is proportionate to its level of contribution. One exception is the restoration project of the historic center of Habana Vieja, under the management of the Office of the City Historian (see Chapter 9). That office has a special company, Habanaguex, that turns profits on several businesses that operate in Habana Vieja.

Those special funding arrangements for preservation and conservation in Habana Vieja are unique. The rest of Havana does not have such revenue-generating projects. Instead, it receives its budget and material resources from the national budget which is usually approved, with very few changes, at the end of the year by the National Assembly. The city also receives a corresponding amount of revenue from its 15 municipalities. Revenues cannot be readjusted nor redirected to other areas except when it is explicitly stated by the national government. In 1986, an attempt was made to decentralize municipal budgets in hopes of moving

**Table 5.4** New forms of community participation

| Type of organization | Description |
|---|---|
| *Consejos Populares* | Continues conventional verticalist approach but focuses on a smaller geographical unit with direct feedback by residents. |
| Mass organizations | Although strongly tied to the state contributions from the membership play a greater role. |
| Quasi-state organizations | Examples include Comprehensive Workshops for Neighborhood Change (*Talleres de Transformación Integral de Barrios*). See text. |
| NGOs | Untied Nations, church, and foreign donor-supported groups picking up slack from diminished role of Cuban government. |
| Community organizations | Traditional, private philanthropic organizations that existed in Cuba. Example: Liceo de Regla, created in 1879 and devoted to civic work. |
| Grassroots organizations | Volunteer groups that do not overlap with state agencies or mass organizations. Includes agricultural groups and hog ranchers. |

toward self-financing. This meant giving the municipality a percentage of the taxes that it had collected in its territory, and a greater flexibility to transfer funds between different accounts without altering the total budget. The essence of the problem of housing, for example, is not allowing local governments to generate their own revenues and to receive equitably funds from the national government. In the main, however, the problem is that surpluses cannot usually be used to purchase building materials because there are no materials assigned for this purpose. Municipal governments do not have the autonomy to obtain materials. Pressure brought on by the economic changes in the 1990s forced municipal governments to look for new ways to fill in the gaps left by the withdrawal of centralized planning. One solution is the Inter-Company Cooperation Councils (*Consejos de Cooperación Interempresarial*) that oversee coordination among companies but in the market context (González 1995).

Fixed budgets designated for city and municipal governments in Cuba have always fallen well below the needs of those entities. This situation existed, even during the relatively prosperous bonanza years when trade ties between the eastern European bloc and Cuba were at a high mark.

Even today, the budget allocation to city and municipal governments almost never fulfills budgetary needs. 'Salaries' is the only line item of the budget that is covered 100%.

The budget situation has worsened during the Special Period and is now begrudgingly accepted as given by most of the young people in Cuba who know no other form of government-service delivery. There are two parts to this situation. On the one hand, community participation has lost much of the energy and enthusiasm it held in the 1960s. Many guidelines for promoting community participation have become mechanical and require great effort to implement them. On the other hand, there is a tradition and organizational structure that can mobilize large segments of the population who could yet again become active with clearly identifiable goals for Havana residents (Coyula, González and Vincentelli 1993). Alternatively, these mobilizations could gain greater credibility and take on a protagonist role within civil society; a segment of Cuba that is gradually becoming more empowered in a post-Soviet era (Gunn 1995).

Because Havana depends exclusively on a centrally assigned budget, all items in the national budget are of great importance to the city. In 1993, considered by many to be the most difficult year of the Special Period, a study was conducted that analyzed financial difficulty during two sessions of the National Assembly. In May 1994, the Assembly approved a series of measures to restore the fiscal health of the government. A key component was to reduce the excess of monetary liquidity, which was estimated at 11.9 billion pesos (Lee 1996a). At the end of 1994 they had removed 1.9 billion pesos from circulation, from which 1.7 billion came from an increase in prices and sales. Reductions in the State budget also helped to lower the deficit of 5.05 billion pesos that remained at the end of 1993, which amounted to one-third of the gross domestic product (GDP). That figure was decidedly influenced by the huge amount of subsidies (5.4 billion pesos) directed to inefficient state firms. At the end of fiscal year 1994, the subsidy for losses had fallen to 3.4 billion pesos (a 40% reduction). The budget deficit that was cutback to 1.4 billion pesos, or to 7.4% of the GDP or a 72% reduction from the 1993 level (Lee 1996a).

Any economic recovery must still contend with the national deficit. In 1995 it stood at 775 million pesos and represented 3.6% of the GDP, one-third less than what had been projected. State subsidies for losses by state-owned companies was 1.8 billion pesos less than the 2.15 billion that had been projected (Lee 1996a). Liquidity decreased by about 1.0 billion pesos, only. This resulted from an insufficient supply of goods for sale. The approved 1996 budget forecast 11.6 billion pesos. However, 12.2 billion pesos will be necessary to cover projected expenditures and, of that amount, 7.06 billion will go to social services and other budget items.

State companies will receive 2.67 billion (including 1.6 billion in subsidies for loss and 720 million for price differences) and 300 million will be used to support the basic farmer units of production (*Unidades Básicas de Produccíon Campesina*, UBPC) (Lee 1996a).

Public administration in Havana is now concerned with efficiency as never before since the advent of the Revolution. In order to keep the budget deficit under 580 million pesos, it is necessary to increase the efficiency of state firms which remain the weakest point in the Cuban economy. The government's decision not to shut down state firms that were not profitable was a humane gesture. However, it makes the country's economic recovery more difficult and continues to be the principal reason for excess cash in the economy, contributing to inflation. Many college educated professionals, poorly paid, are earning less now in real terms than they did in 1959 (Chauvin 1996). The government, therefore, is indirectly financing unprofitable state firms. Those same professionals, however, may forget the cost of the education they received as well as the free medical care that all Cubans enjoy. Rising unemployment, moreover, may aggravate the modest gains of the free market and will cast more university graduates into unemployment lines. Instead of dealing with the daunting task of feeding 11 million mouths, it seems more practical to look for a way to find work for 22 million arms so they can feed themselves.

### The arrival of the dollar

Since the arrival of foreign investment, the establishment of a dual economy, and the legalization of the dollar, Havana once again reveals distinct sides. At one extreme are those who have access to dollars or sell goods and services at exorbitant prices in the informal market. In August 1996, 23 money-exchange houses operated in Havana. The new private Cuban corporation, CADECA SA, contemplates opening 200 similar houses throughout Cuba over the next few years. Cuban Vice-President Carlos Lage reported on July 23, 1996 that the Cuban peso had increased its value sixfold in the past 2 years, removing 250 million pesos from circulation during the first semester of 1996 (InterPress 1996b).

At another extreme are those who subsist precariously on fixed salaries and who rely on the meager Cuban peso. Old mansions of the burgeoisie in the 'frozen zones' of Miramar and Vedado are increasingly being converted into offices of joint ventures and state businesses that sell in dollars. The main purpose of these stores is not to increase the options available to *habaneros*, but rather to capture the greatest amount of hard currency in order to finance the continuation of the prevailing system. In fact, that objective is reflected in the name of a chain of stores called TRDs, which stands for 'stores for recovering hard currencies' (*Tiendas de Recuperación de Divisas*). The rather cruel assumption is that the name reflects hard currencies captured by the State at inflated prices (normally at a flat 240% profit margin). That name itself assumes that dollars captured by inflated price (usually 240% above cost) morally belong to the state.

These new dollar-gathering retail activities coexist in the former fancy neighborhoods with embassies, homes of workplace managers, organizational leaders, average citizens and illegal residents. (Many of the latter are remnants of the former caretakers that occupied the homes in the 1960s as discussed in Chapter 3.) Changes in the 1990s rival the transformation of those same neighborhoods in the 1960s. Miramar is still structured along an axis – the famous Quinta Avenida – which retains the same status symbol it did before 1959. Its traditional landscaped green areas, carefully pruned trees, and manicured hedges endure. While the landscape architecture has not varied over these past 40 years, small neon signs which timidly break through this carefully groomed landscape are on the rise. Restaurants, cafés, bars, stores, boutiques, pastry shops, gasoline stations, and a whole spate of foreign firms including Benetton (clothing), Meliá (hotel chain), and ING Bank have recently been installed. This new retail 'glow' symbolizes a kind of rebirth against a backdrop of abandonment and a fading gleam of former bourgeois Havana, pointing to Cuba's timid foray into capitalism.

A new elite occupies the public spaces of Miramar. These new characters do not include elegant yuppies jogging or the nouveau riche speeding along in their BMWs. Instead, one can see the ostentatious new rich of Cuba – *macetas* – riding in their restored 1950s Chevrolets and hearing rock-and-roll or salsa blaring from their car speakers as they drive to the dollar-only shops. Donning only their gaudy tee-shirts, these new rich are unprecedented in socialist Havana. Other new actors in Havana's streets include *jineteras* (prostitutes) and lecherous older Spaniards or Italians driving around in rented Nissans and Toyotas rented from state agencies, and who search for cheap sex. Havana's new 'sexual tourism' is gaining notoriety in Europe especially as it is more accessible than its competition in faraway Thailand.[3]

While these exploits transpire in Miramar, it contrasts with the large traditional stores of Centro Habana. Buildings across town remain underutilized or closed by a lack of merchandise or the advanced stage of deterioration of the buildings, or houses that are precariously adapted to makeshift structures. Miramar, by contrast, seems far removed from the

---

[3]These new sexual exploits are noted on several sites of the World Wide Web.

hard life of other Habaneros. This new investment in Havana is complemented by the ubiquitous ambulant vendors who spring up like mush-
rooms around the city. These self-employed peddle their improvised
products in open-air markets, parks and galleries in the old commercial
districts, and in front of the empty stores.

## Foreign investment and the changing look of Havana

In September 1995 Law 77 passed by the National Assembly broadened
the legal and institutional framework for foreign investment. This law
substituted Decree Law 50, approved by the Cuban–Foreign Economic
Association Law of February, 1982. That law required the Ministry of
Foreign Investment and Economic Collaboration (*Ministerio para la
Inversión Extranjera y la Colaboración Económica*, MINVEC, formally known
as *Comité Estatal para la Colaboración Económica*, or CECE) to engage in
commerce with the USSR and the now defunct socialist countries of
CAME (Council of Mutual Economic Assistance). This government entity
has become the maximum authority in charge of business opportunities
with foreigners. MINVEC monitors business operations and defines the
ways in which foreign investors, both companies as well as individuals,
can do business in Cuba. The law establishes certain guarantees for
investors and defines the authorized ways of investing: joint ventures,
international economic associations, and a completely foreign capital
firm. MINVEC also deals with financial contributions and assessment as
well as the approval and supervision of applications for investment, the
banking system, conditions of import and export, the taxation system,
custom tariffs and accounting, insurance, the monitoring of information,
and the financial registry (Núñez 1996).

Establishing a business in Cuba involves an elaborate chain of
approval and review. MINVEC includes a firm called *Grupo Negociador*
(Business Group) that establishes the conditions between a foreign partner and a Cuban state agency. The firm assesses how to fulfill the terms of
agreement and analyzes future business negotiations established by the
government. The governmental agencies also have their respective business associates and promotional firms that define the scope of a potential
enterprise and the formal details of all proposals. Depending on the
nature of the investment project, business proposals may also be submit-
ted to other agencies such as the Banco Nacional de Cuba, the Minister of
Finances and Prices, the Ministry of Work and Social Security, University
of Havana, and other research centers (Núñez 1996). If the project receives
a positive evaluation by MINVEC then, according to the size of the

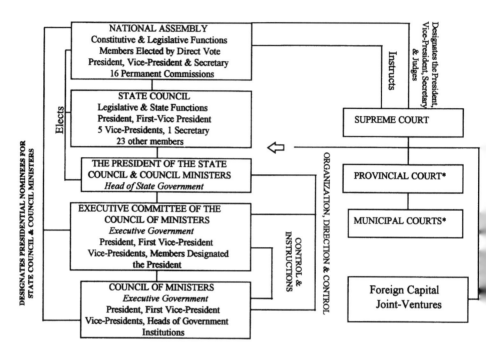

*The presidents, vice-presidents and judges of provincial and municipal courts are elected by the respective assemblies. The 5th article of the Constitution states that the Cuban Communist Party is the supreme force for the direction of the state and civil society.

**Figure 5.2** The New Federalism in Cuba: state, civil society and the market

project, it goes on for review at the Executive Committee of the Council of Ministers or to a special governmental commission for further analysis and final approval. If the project is approved, the Chamber of Commerce inscribes the business in the Register of Economic Associations. The legal framework defines the reach of the businesses as determined by the Law of Foreign Investment, the Tax Law, and the Regulation of Employment and Pay, Tariff Regulations set by customs authorities, and other regulations emitted by ministries and Cuban firms.

There are two predominant forms of associations in practice today: the joint-venture and the International Economic Association. However, the new law of September 1995 allows a Total Foreign Capital Firm to exist without the participation of a Cuban counterpart. The joint venture firm acts as a single company and has a legal status which is different than the participating entities. Both parts put up a certain amount of capital or equity for the new company. Normally, this type of association is a long term agreement (about 20 years). The International Economic Association generally employs works with small projects that are of medium-term duration. This is a contractual form that does not require obtaining legal status in Cuba and all of its legal aspects are established within a contract. Another arrangement used mainly in mineral and oil prospecting is the Risk Investment (*Inversión a Riesgo*). A practice commonly carried out in the tourism sector is the participation of a foreign firm in the administrative management of hotels. There have also been recently created three free-port zones and a network of in-bond warehouses that are not subject to custom tariffs. Among these zones is the large district of warehouses in Habana de Este, known as Havana In-Bond. Officially, the new law excludes foreign investment in areas of national security, health, and education (Núñez 1996).

A system of taxes was approved by Law 73 in 1994 and consists of three elements: flat taxes, tax rates, and payments. For foreign investment, that law established a tax of 30% over net profits, and a 25% tax on the salaries and wages of Cuban workers. Cuban workers employed by foreign companies or joint ventures cannot be contracted directly by a foreign firm, Instead, they must be hired through a state agency called ACOREC, which receives the salary in dollars and then pays the Cuban half that amount in pesos. The foreign firm must pay, in addition, taxes for the right to use land transportation, natural resources, and airports.

Cuba's banking system centers around the Banco Nacional de Cuba which must approve any foreign financial operation in Cuba. Firms or individuals can open accounts in Cuban banks and there are two banks that function with hard currencies: *Banco Financiero Internacional* (BFI) and the *Banco Internacional de Comercio SA* (BICSA). The only foreign bank with a branch office in Cuba is ING Netherlands, but it cannot disburse money. It accepts Visa® and Mastercard® credit cards as long as they are not issued by US banks.

Since the legalization of the dollar in July of 1993, Cubans can now exchange foreign currencies at banks and hotels. The US dollar has become the currency of operation for state enterprises. The dollar circulates in transactions involving a broad range of products and services that are in short supply or else operate within the peso economy. Significantly, this includes food products. The Cuban government operates five chain stores that aim to 'capture' the hard currency: *Tiendas Panamericanas*, *Tiendas Caracol*, operated by the Ministry of Tourism and Hotels; *Tiendas TRD*, operated by the Gaviota tourist group (see Chapter 8); *Tiendas Universal*, operated by Cubanacán, and *Tiendas Cubalse*, run by a corporation of that same name. Foreign companies may distribute their products directly to these five stores. At the end of 1995 there were 212 foreign economic associations operating in Cuba with a total capital of $2.1 billion (about half of all investments in the country) (Núñez 1996).

### New actors in city administration: real-estate laws in Havana

Among the most recent investment opportunities for foreigners is the real-estate market, with special interest in Havana. Cubalse, Habaguanex, and Eproyiv are the Cuban facilities that serve as joint real-estate enterprises. The actors in this real-estate process have changed quickly because of an initial inadequate institutional design. A few years ago, early interest by some real-estate investors was not properly addressed. Given that Cuba was closed to the private market for over 30 years, it was not surprising that Cuban state agencies had little understanding of basic urban, economic, and financial aspects of the real-estate market (Núñez 1996). On several occasions, promises were made with foreign firms without getting prior from Havana's urban planning department (*Planificación Física y Arquitectura*) which enforces urban land use and building permits. Municipal authorities in Havana were also kept out of the decision-making process.

Real-estate investment in Havana – like joint ventures elsewhere in Cuba – tends not to interest Cuban authorities unless they are large projects. This is unfortunate because a myriad of small and medium investments would be more appropriate for Havana as they are kinds of operations that have historically built this world city. They could help the city not only create employment for displaced workers, but also save thousands of local properties, that are on the verge of collapse from an early demise. The new real-estate market could also help provide a central location for the street vendors who – despite the important part they play in satisfying unmet demand in the market-place – nonetheless interfere with traffic, destroy green areas, and introduce visual blight in the urban landscape. On the other hand, a broadened and decentralized revitalization would be more stable and less vulnerable to economic pressures than investment schemes that depend on the whims of a few large foreign investors. In other words, this is related to the need to strengthen the economy from below. Havana's economy requires productive activities other than just self-employed workers. History shows that the city's economy moves slowly between stages of retailing. Hopefully, Havana will not have to wait another few centuries to develop a full range of retail activities (Coyula 1995a, pp. 4–5).

It appears that maintaining a dollar-based real-estate market for Cubans will have to wait until the present demand by diplomats, workers

from foreign companies, business persons residing in Cuba, and other foreigners is satisfied. Havana's urban real-estate market could be broadened in the near future with commercial office space, and hotel-support
facilities for tourism such as marinas. Second homes for retirees who live
abroad might also be considered, including the eventual return of elderly
Cuban-Americans who wish to retire in Havana.

Real-estate activities bring both risks and opportunities. On the one
hand, they might well represent the arrival of much needed capital that
will allow the city to generate wealth that could be reinvested back into it.
On the other hand, a speculative real-estate market could destroy what is
actually the most attractive feature of the city: its non-commercialized
landscape and multilayered built fabric – and convert Havana into just
another tourist spot (Coyula 1995). The title of the very successful anima-
ted feature-length film by Juan Padrón, *Vampires in Havana* (*Vampiros en La
Habana*), could become a portrait of a painful reality if the terrible need for
capital pressures Cuban authorities to do just that. In that case, the city
would become indefensive and succumb to a new form of piracy.

## Havana continues

After his participation in the First Physical Planning Seminar in Havana,
in 1971, the well known US urban designer, Kevin Lynch, formulated
interesting questions in his favorite book, *What time is this place?* Lynch
questions what sort of physical changes could be seen in Havana that
express the deep economic, political, and social changes that had occurred
(Lynch 1972). At that time, new construction in Havana was restricted,
and the buildings that the Revolution inherited seemed to be able to
weather all forms of deterioration. Those transformations were subtle and
perhaps more appropriately labeled as changes in function and of users.
However, Lynch's well-trained eye detected those trends and anticipated
challenges that awaited Havana. As this chapter has shown, these
changes are risky and underscore the new relationship between a highly
centralized form of government, and the new actors on the block: foreign
investment.

In the mid-1980s, investment required for rehabilitating Havana was
estimated at between $10 and $14 billion. The figures were staggering
and inevitably raise the question: how much is this city worth? The capital city represents an enormous investment accumulated over 20 generations. Contributions to the city are material, monetary, energy, and
housing components that translate into great artistic, historical, functional,
and environmental value. Each input has strong economic implications.

The conservation of these values and the development that Havana needs to become a new regional leader seems possible only to the extent that the city itself can finance those changes based on what it can rationally extract from its own resources. Such a perspective requires a fair appraisal of Havana without losing the city to disuse, and without deforming it, selling it, mortgaging it, or giving it away (Coyula 1995).

Havana has survived several critical tests in its long history, and some of them appeared at the time to be fatal. It has been beaten but has retained its composure. Without doubt, complicity for its dilapidated condition must be shared because, layer by layer, a thick web of relations has been sewn that extends beyond the façades of its buildings. The city reaches out to pedestrians hurrying through its streets; they do not have to raise their head to see if the old companion of their dreams is stubbornly there – peeling, crumbling, distorted by salt and water – yet incredibly alive and useful. A city that no longer is what it was, and continues to reinvent itself. Havana always, forever our Havana. *La Habana siempre, siempre nuestra Habana.*

# 6

# The hope and reality of socialist housing

Environment unifies society, individuals, and their surroundings. Life stems from an environmental system that incorporates the past, the present and the future through remembrances, reality and imagination.

Fernando Salinas, 1984

Housing is the social mirror of a city. If monuments define outstanding elements of the cultural landscape, then the residential stock reflects the social contradictions of the city (López Castañeda 1963, 1971). The complexity of habitat stems from the ongoing tensions between affluence and poverty. Flying over any underdeveloped city of the world, one immediately notices the suburban green spaces of the wealthy, or the high rises at the city's edge. Beyond that, there appear ad infinitum the small homes of the middle class and densely settled apartment complexes that derive from speculative housing markets. Scattered through the metropolis, one can see the atomization and the disorder of squatter settlements scattered along the periphery, or buried in the interstices of the inner city. Here lays the clear evidence of the ever-present poverty of the Latin American city.

Havana in the 1950s was no exception to this pattern. The trail of luxurious residences that started at the beginning of the century in Vedado and Miramar continued westward along the coast. There in succession came the neighborhoods of Reparto Náutico, Country Club, Flores, Bittmore, Jaimanitas, Barlovento, and Santa Fé. The housing designs ranged from extended tile roofs covering flowered and California-style chalets, to the first images of the International Style, consisting of light structures and transparent glass surfaces. The industrious middle class and young entrepreneurs occupied the axis along Rancho Boyeros – a road that linked the airport with the city center – with small cottages nestled in green areas. This pattern was evident in the neighborhoods of Santa Catalina and Sevillano, and rose to a greater population density in Alta Habana, gradually tapering off to the remote suburbs of Fontanar and El Wajay. Finally, rather modest and non-descript houses lined up in straight rows along the Central Highway to the southeast. Mantilla, Diezmero, San Francisco de Paula and Cotorro formed this strip of working-class housing, which were mixed in with factories (Figure 6.1).

Once the tunnel under the bay was opened, expansion towards the east – although incipient and controlled by finance and real-estate companies – ensured large-scale developments could not be easily subdivided into small suburban developments. Habana del Este, the largest conceived development in the late 1950s, was of great interest to the US firm Skidmore, Owings & Merill, and the Italian architect Franco Albini. Although these large-scale projects were never executed, in the areas surrounding Habana del Este a few single-family residential structures were built such as in Vía Tunel and Bahía.

This kind of suburbanization contrasted with the traditional Hispanic layout of rectangular blocks along a continuous grid. Comparisons

**Figure 6.1** Traditional wooden bungalows characterized modest housing built in the first half of the twentieth century. This structure is located in Regla. Photograph by Joseph L. Scarpaci

between poor suburban neighborhoods and the middle class show that even among individual housing typologies, the persistence of a few traditional attributes remained. They included the continuous *portal* along the building front. The chalet, on the other hand, was more of an organic design, and was associated with higher income *habaneros* who were eager to capture the romantic realm of nature. In the process of breaking up the city's traditional design and layout, there was also an increase in high-rise apartments in Centro Habana and Vedado (García Vázquez 1968; Garnier 1973; Durán 1992). Beginning with the 1952 Condominium Law, the construction of up-scale high-rises accelerated (Segre 1985a). At that time there was a strong infusion of foreign capital due to the high rates of return in Havana's real-estate market. For instance, between 1941 and 1953 the real-estate market in Havana absorbed 28 million pesos annually, whereas between 1953 and 1958 the figure reached 60 million pesos annually out of a total of 72 million invested nationwide (Acosta and Hardoy 1972). If the foreign housing models from abroad favored individual high-rise structures for the bourgeoisie, then the collective imagination of most *habaneros* clung to the free-standing home and garden.

Speculative investment in the 1950s explains what would appear to be arbitrary suburban subdivisions. They were isolated and mostly disconnected from each other and from Havana's existing street pattern. In some cases these suburban enclaves lacked basic infrastructure such as sewers, lights, electricity, and gas. Moreover, they unnecessarily expanded Havana's metropolitan area. Much of the new suburbanization in the 1950s lay outside the cities, political borders, and therefore exempt from Havana's master plan.

Political corruption permeated real estate. Aesthetic norms or urban design were not used to control development on the outskirts. Fierce speculation and higher land and rental values drove the middle class to suburbs increasingly farther from the downtown areas. Havana's suburbanization had little to do with professional architecture whose parameters were set by professionals. Instead, anonymous builders built homes like any other consumption good.

Small construction companies built the predominant model of 1950s housing: single-family residences. Companies and brand names such as *Gallo* rice; *Colgate* toothpaste; *Candado* soap; *Lavasol, Rina* and *Fab* laundry detergents; and *El País* newspaper sponsored contests that gave homes to lucky consumers who purchased their products. The prototypes of these homes repeatedly surfaced in television spots, newspapers, and magazines which, in turn, molded the popular 'taste' so connected with the image of the ambitious middle-class home. These houses looked like small, pink-colored (flamingo) boxes with their porches in the front, attached garages, and pitched roofs. The suburban Havana 'dream house' created in the 1950s survived several decades of the socialist Revolution and remained present in the minds of many *habaneros* in the 1990s.

## Creativity and innovation in the early housing initiatives of Havana

The housing problem was strongly present in Fidel Castro's well-known Moncada declaration which he presented at his defense for attacking military barracks in 1953 (Castro 1964). Precarious rural living conditions, the rapid increase in tenements, slums and shantytowns in Havana, and the exorbitant rents charged for apartments and houses were a call to enforce the laws of the 1940 Constitution. Although many of these housing laws had been on the 'books' for over a decade, Castro underscored the fact that the constitutional guarantee of housing to every Cuban had not been enforced by the Batista regime (Fernández Núñez 1976).

From January 1, 1959 onward, the Revolutionary government defined three basic principles of its urban and rural housing policy. First, it ended speculation on land and housing. Second, it favored low-income Cubans burdened by high rents. Third, it started building housing for workers and farmers as soon as possible. The first two principles annulled rental payments for those living in substandard housing, and it waived rent for those who could not afford monthly payments. A series of important laws in the first two years radically altered Cuba's housing situation (Table 6.1). Overall, these actions defined housing in socialist Cuba. The state served as an intermediary. Landlords had to sell their rental properties to tenants, and the tenants in turn paid the state. Homeowners could keep their homes no matter how large or well-situated, and even a summer or country home could be kept. All but the biggest landlords received full compensation. However, properties left by those emigrating became state property. The amortization of those former rental dwellings was set between 5 and 20 years. In many cases, rent had been reduced by up to 50% by Law 135. Ten percent of income was charged as rent only for newly assigned units which included newly built dwellings, or those that came into state's hands because of death without heirs or people leaving the country (Hamberg 1994).

Cuba's housing policy in the 1960s was unprecedented in Latin America because for the first time, land speculation and profit making on urban land and housing had ended. The laws also ended the prevailing price structure by fixing a flat rate of four pesos per square meter for all lots, regardless of whether they were in the much coveted downtown areas, or in a distant suburb. By economically leveling the cost of urban

**Table 6.1** Selected housing laws during the first years of the Castro government

| Law No. | Date | Purpose |
|---|---|---|
| 26 | January 26, 1959 | Suspend legal action against those who could not pay rent or mortgages |
| 135 | March 10, 1959 | Lower rents up to 50% |
| 691 | December 23, 1959 | Establish the forced sale of empty lots and their price |
| 892 | October 14, 1960 | Urban Reform Law: a complex doctrine defining the nation's housing policies |

*Data source*: Segre (1989)

space, the private sector gradually lost interest in real estate and housing. In 1960, private construction slowed down considerably, and most building projects underway rested in the state's hands. Although large construction and building materials firms were nationalized in the first few years, private building initiatives continued at a slow pace until 1968. Significantly, all land was not nationalized and there were relatively few 'forced sales' under the housing laws of the 1960s. Small building projects, especially for individual homeowners, continued in Havana during the early to mid-1960s and again in the 1980s.

The new Revolutionary government tackled the problems of racial and social segregation produced by the urban land market of the past, and began mixing different economic and social strata of Havana in order to alter radically the make-up of the city's neighborhoods. Of course, the out-migration by a large Cuban bourgeoisie freed up part of the city's housing stock, thus easing the need for new housing. Slowly, a migrant stream from the eastern provinces consisting of workers, small farmers, and veterans of the fight against Batista began occupying this housing.

Although the Revolutionary government implemented a series of key laws in its early years, there were also signs that it failed to act on other problems in the housing sector. Many of the mansions occupied by those who had emigrated abroad were left to the domestic servants who had previously worked there. These former servants brought friends and family members – many from outside Havana – to live with them. As a result, there were striking cases of neglect and abuse of some of Havana's most symbolic and ornate homes. As population increase and pressure for housing mounted in the city, so too did the rate of self-help housing and state construction (CED 1976; Comité Estatal de Construcción 1977; Coyula 1985a, b). Even though these strategies were conceptually valid for coping with Havana's housing problems, they also had the unintended effect of driving down the environmental quality of certain neighborhoods. Witness, for example, the spontaneous and inadvertent 'ruralization' of the city spawned by self-help housing. Such construction ran against the state's official policy that supported multifamily housing. Even during the last three decades, there has been much anonymous and low-quality construction built simply to provide shelter for those in the former garden suburbs of Havana. It was not until the 1980s that a group of planners and designers in the central government took interest in establishing an urban design and architectural identity for Havana's neighborhoods (GDIC 1991; 1994).

The Revolutionary government directed its housing policies during the first two years towards three fundamental objectives: (i) to eradicate shantytowns; (ii) to construct new housing, giving preference to apartment complexes; and (iii) to devise technical and building solutions to compensate for the lack of building materials resulting from the US embargo against Cuba which was imposed in 1961. This tripartite policy produced results. The largest shantytowns in the central areas of Havana as well as in the suburbs (Plaza de la Revolución, Boyeros, Marianao, Diez de Octubre) were eliminated. Single-story housing complexes were built with lightweight prefabricated walls and roofs, often times erected by the occupants themselves. This production system was called 'self-help and mutual aid' (see also Chapter 4). Self-help housing at that time was increasingly common throughout Latin America (Oliver 1970). Significant legislation in this area consisted of Law 86 (February 17, 1959) which created the National Institute of Savings and Housing (INAV, Instituto Nacional de Ahorro y Vivienda).

INAV was directed by the mythical Pastorita Núñez, a small woman with short hair and large blue eyes that stood out against the olive-green uniform that she regularly wore since the days of armed struggle in the Sierra Maestra. Her demeanor was forged within the Orthodox Party. She inherited the inflexible ethic of the Party's charismatic founder, the opposition senator, Eduardo Chibás. Pastorita quickly created a team of architects headed by Cesáreo Fernández who designed and built several housing complexes. Among them is the well-known Unit No. 1 of Habana del Este (whose name was later changed to Ciudad Camilo Cienfuegos). Within Havana her team also built the subdivisions (repartos) of Capri, Embil, Bahía, Juan Manuel Márquez and Residencial Wajay. Each of these contained groups of multifamily mid-rise buildings such as the complex of four-story buildings (an INAV height limit) located near the Plaza de la Revolución and many other isolated structures that served as in-filling within the city.

Pastorita's success derived from a very simple method that was curiously abandoned later: guarantee the quality of the design without trying to alter the project's technical features. At the same time, various private builders bid on a construction project. The bidding was carefully supervised by young architects, engineers and Pastorita herself. She monitored the amount of building materials they used and the costs of these projects. Taking advantage of her short demeanor, Pastorita would enter the huge concrete tubes stored on the work site and surprise workers who had scatted off to cat-nap. The high quality that came out of these efforts, both in terms of design as in construction, made this a high watermark that has been difficult to surpass in Cuban urbanism.

In just two years of existence, INAV launched enthusiastic and diverse projects in its construction of almost 10 000 housing units throughout the island, 6000 of which were erected in Havana (INAV 1962). New state agencies spearheaded construction along with small private-sector firms which, at that time, were still permitted. INAV awarded contracts to small firms with money that the State obtained from the National Lottery. Building designs included detached or semi-detached houses that were one or two stories high, as well as the typical four-story apartment complex. High-rise structures built in Habana del Este were an exception to this national pattern.

The early years of the Revolution witnessed a short but intense period of housing construction. The establishment of the Board of Technical Research within the Ministry of Public Works brought together the search for practical solutions and the use of local resources. In particular, this included the structural use of brick roof vaults and stackable prefabricated building components (D'Acosta 1964). Even though a large share of this experimental construction was located at the outskirts of Plaza de la Revolución (former Plaza Cívica, or Civic Square), a notable project consisting of three residential structures in 1960 in Tallapiedra neighborhood in Jesús María, was built by Fernando Salinas. This project embodied some of the most important conceptual ideas in Revolutionary housing and architecture at the time. The debate surrounding contextualism had not yet surfaced in Cuba at this time, nor had questions taken hold about CIAM doctrine (which undervalued the link between the traditional layout of the city with new buildings). Salinas argued against the routine and anonymous designs that prevailed during earlier years of the Revolution. He tried, within the limited material means available, to build a new complex in the heart of the older quarters of the city. Salinas wished to take advantage of the curved shape of the road layout and use the traditional patio (interior courtyards) of the older buildings as an interior playground and social space.

## The metaphor of the ideal city

If the essential premises of socialist utopia seek to create improved material and spiritual levels of a society, then one of those premises must be to make that utopia a reality. In such a political project, however, the built environment need not necessarily represent new Revolutionary urban design. Although such utopian designs were apparent in the works of Boullée and Ledoux before the French Revolution and the October Revolution, the situation in Latin America is different. In urban design and architecture, both the Mexican and Cuban revolutions adhered more closely to the traditional heritage cast by the bourgeoisie than the revolutions in Europe.

Three neighborhood units of Habana del Este were proposed but only the first unit was built. Each symbolized the urban utopia of the Cuban Revolution and Units 2 and 1 merit a brief discussion here. Unit 2 expressed dreams far removed from Cuban reality. Designed by Fernando Salinas and Raúl González Romero for 100 000 inhabitants, Unit 2 portrayed the massive scale found in the works of Le Corbusier, the organic styles that had been handed down by Frank Lloyd Wright, and the light exterior shells so typical of the works of Pier Luigi Nervi and Félix Candela. Unit 1, though, differed markedly. Constructed under the auspices of INAV for a capacity of 2300 units and 8000 residents, its inspiration for design came from the blocks of apartment buildings in Vedado.

Salinas and González Romero conceived a residential structure whose symbolic and expressive importance surfaced in public buildings and outdoor spaces. The detailed curvilinear structures and the green areas complemented the monuments that identified a search for a renewed intensity in human relations: the church of 'all religions' or the convention center that serves as the main urban point. Unit 1, the least equipped with social services, did not improve upon pre-Revolutionary architectural design.[1]

With the exception of the area around the Plaza de la Revolución with its four-story height limitations discussed above, INAV built small housing complexes throughout various parts of the city. The population density of Habana del Este played a symbolic role because Cuban society before the Revolution had begun to use urban spaces in the east to prepare

---

[1]The architectural team working on Unit 1 included Roberto Carrazana, Reynaldo Estévez, Mario González, Hugo D'acosta, Eduardo Rodríguez, Mercedes Alvarez, and the engineer Lenin Castro. Unit 1 represented the best examples of sprawling apartment complexes for the middle strata of Havana society. Unit 1's residential composition reflected the leading design principles of the United States and Europe regarding site planning that departed from the existing city grid.

for a suburb for the wealthy. Luxurious homes were to be built there along with shopping centers, hotel complexes, business headquarters, and government buildings, all of which were based on fairly complex and sophisticated engineering, architectural and design principles (see Chapter 3). With the onset of the Revolution, however, a new humanistic perspective in Cuba's housing policies changed the speculative aspect of the housing market in Habana del Este by giving priority to the neediest. This change in thinking was associated with new spaces, new forms of thinking, the availability of resources, the traditional life-styles of the residents, and the expectations of the future residents.

Habana del Este also unified the team work of specialists, architects and engineers. A teamwork approach to housing and planning proved a welcome tonic to the isolated and individualistic method of residential construction building of previous decades. Habana del Este also afforded Cuban professionals a venue for expressing some of the theoretical ideas in vogue in the 1950s.[2] The project revealed some of the essential features espoused by the CIAM (Congress International de Architecture Moderne): alternating between high (10-story) and low (four-story) buildings, green belts that separated housing from major thoroughfares, a hierarchical road system, the separation of pedestrians and vehicles, diverse sites and services, and a wide array of social services (education, culture, arts, public health). These principles were to be employed in a wide range of scales, from the basic neighborhood unit to the community center. Even though there was no significant question about the validity of the neighborhood-unit concept at that time, new complexes fell victim to the segregating functional character such as the 'bedroom community' idea that was a by-product of the functional zoning outlined by the 'Athens Charter' (*Carta de Atenas*).[3]

The high-rise structures of Habana del Este did not go beyond the formal schemes applied in the modernist buildings in the 1950s: the high-rise Focsa building, the Seguro Médico building, or the Naroca building. Low-rise units that reflected the Italian models of those years were more refined than these high rises. The smaller units questioned the reduction-

---

[2]The neighborhood-unit concept outlined by Clarence Perry in the United States, the British New Towns, the satellite cities of Scandinavia, and the post-Second World War experiences in the USSR and eastern Europe all became eligible models from which Cuba could pick and choose. Latin American ideas then available in Cuba included those that appeared in Oscar Niemeyer's magazine *Módulo*. His proposal was validated by the examples displayed at the Fifth International Congress of International Architects held in Moscow in 1958 (UIA 1958).
[3]Valid alternatives in the 1960s included the architects of *Team X* (Peter and Alison Smithson, Giancarlo de Carlo, George Candilis, Aldo Van Eyck, and others). Although the writings of Kevin Lynch, Christopher Alexander and Jane Jacobs also served as potential models for Cuban professionals, that influence came much later, and only influenced a few.

ism of the purist parallelepiped scheme proposed by Ludwig Hilberseimer. Through a design based on 45° angles, the alternating of open and closed areas created a succession of spaces and interior places at a pedestrian scale. Such design was far removed from the Cartesian scheme that had been widespread in earlier decades. Despite some degrees of freedom in design, the uneven training of project leaders and the use of craft construction methods produced incoherence among some of the buildings and grounds.

Expanses of urban spaces and the scale of parking lots (derived from models used in the First World) generated open spaces that were not compensated by sufficient population densities. Because sports complexes were specialized and used occasionally, they failed to engage the community. While providing an important social and political function in the Revolution, sports complexes had little 'personality' and they consumed too much space. Even though Habana del Este became the main paradigm for many years, that model ultimately ceased because of the austere line taken by the Cuban leadership and the economic difficulties in subsequent decades. As Fidel Castro affirmed at the close of the Seventh Congress of the International Union of Architects in 1963: 'You could say that this unit [in Habana del Este] is ideal from our point of view [because of] the construction, the urban housing . . . but also because it is the type of construction that was beyond our economic means . . . And so, naturally, we don't construct those large buildings anymore. We now try to find variety in other forms, but not by erecting tall buildings' (Segre 1970a, p. 110; our translation).

## Dialectical and participatory technology

The flurry of building construction in Havana was short-lived. Upon completion of the large complexes near the Plaza de la Revolución and Habana del Este, the economic pressures from the US blockade impeded the construction of similar structures. An acute awareness developed among the hundreds of architects present at the Seventh Congress of the IUA (UIA 1963) about the economic limitations facing Cuba. This was a time when aid from the socialist bloc did not exist, and the Revolution opted to devote its building resources to cities in the interior and the agricultural sector. Building up provincial towns also aimed to stem the tide of migration to Havana.

Until 1970, state housing construction in Havana was mostly confined to the building of a few prototypes. To some extent, the demographic pressure on Havana was less than in other parts of the country because large numbers of Cubans from the capital emigrated, thus freeing up vacant units. Aid to Havana was not forthcoming because of the decadent reputation of the city created by the former ruling classes, and a sense of disdain they left among the Revolutionary leadership. Volunteers and a large part of the Havana population that had been let go from the Revolutionary Offensive against 'bureaucratism' and small private businesses (1968) was absorbed by the Green Belt (*Cordón de La Habana*) campaign, the agricultural plan for truck and garden farming located in the hinterland of Havana, where sleepy small towns and agricultural communities served hypothetically as a moral alternative to the urban lifestyle (see Chapter 3) (Alvarez-Tabío 1995).

The highly centralized Ministry of Construction in Havana became the locus of technical and design decision making for the entire country. Few architectural designs associated with research and pilot projects were built in the mid-1960s (Machado 1960). Creative and innovative projects existed, but they contrasted sharply with the low-quality construction built by the state and the private sector. Since high-rise construction was halted, Havana's 1950's skyline was hardly altered. Although the character of Havana's neighborhoods was preserved during this time, a process of physical deterioration also began. Paint, building materials, and skilled labor became in short supply.

In conceptual terms, housing policy was based on three premises. One was that construction initiatives were confined to the existing building stock or model rural structures (a rectangular dwelling with a front porch). The second premise was that standardized housing designs of the Ministry of Construction's (MICONS) Urban Housing Department would be confined to four-story apartment complexes or detached, semidetached or row houses for rural areas. A third premise related to the experiments about unique features of the housing unit, building techniques, occupant participation, and site planning (Machado 1969).

The use of the 'cell' panel in Cuba was, to paraphrase Chilean Cristián Fernández Cox (1990), part of the 'appropriate technology' movement. The Venezuelan Fruto Vivas (1983) was inspired by this movement to develop two kinds of lightweight prefabricated panels during his stay in Cuba: the Camilo and Van Troi. Although these panels were easy to handle, MICONS – preoccupied with the unattainable goal of industrialized construction (Bode 1972) – was not fully convinced of their utility. As a result, Fruto Vivas' (1966) plea for a 'construction harvest' of massive housing projects that would draw upon laborers who had finished the sugar-cane harvest, fell on deaf ears. If this idea formulated in 1965 were understood by leaders in the construction industry, it would have avoided the improvised architectural solutions used in the Microbrigade starting in 1970. In the latter, resident participation formed a key ingredient and was supported by Fidel Castro in 1970. At the same time, the ideas put forth by Hugo D'acosta and Mercedes Alvarez were not well received. They had proposed the application of lightweight asbestos-cement materials for flexible-design residential complexes throughout the city (Segre 1989). Significantly, the use of asbestos in Cuba is indiscriminate and is not subject to strict control.

Fernando Salinas was one of the few Cuban professionals who articulated broad design concepts with individual units. As the Program Chairperson of the VII UIA Congress, he knew first-hand the experiences of Third World countries which allowed him to develop a theoretical architectural foundation (Véjar 1994). Departing from the notion that the housing unit is primarily a cultural construct, he defined the dialectical character of a structure according to the changing economic conditions. These factors include its variation and transformation and whether residents participate in both the building and design phases of construction. Salinas also gave special importance to building maintenance, whether carried out by the state or the housing owners; a factor that had so greatly contributed to the precarious image of Havana during the 1960s and 1970s (Segre 1985a).[4]

Salinas built a prototype housing unit in the suburb of Wajay, 18 kilometers southwest of Havana. He employed the Multiflex system which had been developed by his students at the School of Architecture at the University of Havana. At a meeting of architectural schools organized by the UIA in Buenos Aires in 1969, the design earned an award. The Multiflex system consisted of a support structure, formed by a central column, that held up a 6 by 6 meter panel. The simplicity of both elements allowed for the growth of any given structure in all horizontal directions and independence between the structural forms and the interior spaces. The support structure was a key stabilizing factor. It could be made through either traditional artisan methods of pouring concrete on the site, or it could be precast in factories (Figure 6.2). The rest of the housing unit was based on a careful study of each functional element, including the most basic biological needs and the cultural values and habits of each

---

[4]Together with Roberto Segre, Salinas helped refine the concept of 'environmental design' employed in many developing countries. The 'environmental design' concept enlisted some of the ideas of the Bauhaus school of the 1920s. In Europe the developer was able to control for the interaction of different scales of design, but in Latin America, the piecemeal implementation of designs, the impact of complex and diverse cultures, and economic inequality made 'open' solutions difficult or nearly impossible. Because urban housing stems from interactions between professional and popular 'know-how', Salinas and Segre's 'environmental design' approach recognized that urban housing is the product of professional knowledge and spontaneous community initiatives.

**Figure 6.2** Multiflex module designed by Fernando Salinas, in the Havana suburb of Wajay (1969). Photograph by Roberto Segre

family. Equipping the interior of each unit was integrally tied to the exterior panels. It was designed to allow for changes according to a country's economic conditions and those of its occupants. During the first stage of construction the available materials might be, for example, concrete, tile, wood and bagasse. But once new factories were built, the interior panels could be built out of an asbestos–cement mixture with a covering of PVC, steel, enamel steel, or aluminum. All pieces were to be interchangeable and easy to assemble. It was made this way to make it possible for residents to acquire the building materials best suited to their needs. Salinas' prototype in Wajay proved that the dream could become reality; that the creative imagination would have spiritually and materially enriched the daily life of the community. Nevertheless, the model was ultimately scrapped by the Ministry of Construction. In light of the Special Period, there is hope that Salinas' dreams might be used in an uncertain future.

At the end of the 1960s there arose the first attempt to resort to high-rise housing in the central areas of Havana. Along the Vedado waterfront, an area characterized by high-rises built for the bourgeoisie in the 1950s, the architects Antonio Quintana and Alberto Rodríguez built a 17-story experimental prototype based on the precedent set by the buildings of Habana del Este. Two basic premises guided this design. First, structural walls and slabs defined the housing units which were subdivided internally by light elements (*siporex*) that defined functional activities. Second, the continuity of the design had to be ensured. Doing so meant integrating the purist volumes of the apartment complexes into a continuous grid. The banks of elevators and staircases complement the sidewalks and roadways that create the internal traffic system. The model, inspired by the French experiences of Grenoble-Echirolles and Toulouse-le-Mirail and the English cases of Sheffield and Thamesmead, were not applied in subsequent residential high-rises built with the slip mold system.

### The stark utopia of prefabricated housing

From its beginnings, the Cuban socialist economy had aspired to scientific and technical advances (Mesías and Morales 1985). Assumed by political leaders to be an essential tool to move society forward, changing the dire conditions of the masses also entailed the contributions of urban planners and architects. When Vladimir Lenin put forth electrification as a goal of the Soviet state, the pioneers of constructivism (Vesnin, Melnikov, Leonidov, Chernikov, Golossov) created early images about how those socialist images might materialize (Segre 1985b). In the housing sector, these consisted of light metallic structures and thin tensors that braced the building complexes, and which were crowned by antennae on the roofs.

The Cuban Revolution did not escape the illusion of attaining technological progress as one of its loftiest goals and as a means of escaping underdevelopment (Castro 1970). Ernesto 'Ché' Guevara affirmed this sentiment in a well-known talk before Latin American students in 1963 (Segre 1970a). Cuba's technological progress was based in good measure on European models of advanced construction. Cuban housing policies embraced the notion that socialism is equivalent to public housing and prefabrication (Castex 1986).

Even though the aspirations of the socialist revolution in the housing realm were understandable given the unsatisfied needs of a population with limited resources, it turned out that its solutions were unable to satisfy those needs in the short period stipulated by the Cuban leadership. Cuba's post-1959 urban design and architectural history reflects a heightened concern for meeting deadlines, a scarcity of material resources, and a disregard for the immediate past. Both positive and negative factors prevailed in this short history. On the one hand, professionals should have anticipated solutions more suited to Cuban reality in order to, in the words of Fernando Salinas, 'make more with less.' Implementing housing projects received little attention. Bureaucratic and political deadlines to complete housing projects all too often centered around national holidays or artificially defined construction phases. In the end, many of the buildings turned out superficial and shoddy, and were ultimately finished by the more traditional building construction methods than the capital-intensive prefabricated methods originally envisioned.

It was in this context that the unleashing of industrial and prefabricated housing construction succumbed to the same pitfalls found in eastern Europe. Over time, it became abundantly clear that the acritical adoption of foreign technological models was, in many cases, inappropriate to local conditions. Moreover, importing these models stifled the chances for their success because they were often at odds with the proposed design. Manufacturing prefabricated materials not only used local industry, but also meant keeping a careful eye on ensuring a steady flow of building materials, labor and materials (Salinas 1963). All of these ambitious activities related to a First World industrial production system, became insurmountable contradictions in Cuba's own uneven development (Guselnikov 1976).

The US embargo against Cuba in the 1960s was the key factor forcing Cuba to seek a new formula that drew on local resources instead of building methods used before the Revolution. To that end, construction components and techniques had to minimize technical inputs. Housing units made of light shells and vaults sprung up throughout the island. They were used in schools, health care clinics, markets, and sporting complexes in new housing developments (Segre 1989). A second step towards prefabrication coincided with Hurricane Flora in 1963 which inflicted heavy damage on the eastern provinces. The USSR donated a large-panel factory that was built in Santiago. These panels were widely used in the construction of apartment complexes. Housing projects in Santiago's José Martí district built with these panels shortly thereafter were supposed to house 72 000 residents. From that time onward, the Ministry of Construction organized its plans around prefabrication, abandoning traditional craft methods of construction (Bode 1972). This entailed experimenting with a variety of building systems based on European and Canadian construction methods. Those foreign models were reinterpreted somewhat and adapted to local conditions (Table 6.2).

Fidel Castro reaffirmed from the mid-1960s onward that Cuba could be completing 100 000 housing units a year by 1970. His hope was buoyed by the construction of panel factories across the island. Significantly, that was also the same year of the much touted 10 million ton sugar cane harvest (Arrinda 1964; Castro 1978). That goal notwithstanding, the impossibility of carrying out this ambitious housing project produced a major production crisis. By 1970, the state was only completing 4000 housing units a year (Fernández Núñez 1976). Prior to that time, high technology had never been able to outproduce traditional building methods, nor did it surpass self-help housing production. For example, in 1976, prefabricated construction comprised only 23% of all units, while state-directed traditional artisan methods included 50% of all completed units (Estévez 1977).

**Table 6.2** Prefabricated panels used in Cuban construction

| Type | Origin | Building height |
|---|---|---|
| Large Panel IV | Cuban version of large French panels (e.g., Camus, Coignet) | 4 stories |
| IMS (Serbian Materials Institute) | Yugoslavian | Up to 12 stories |
| Slip Mold | Scandinavian | Up to 18 stories |
| Large Panel 70 | Scandinavian | 4–5 stories |
| LH (*losa hueca* or slab core) Technology | Canadian | 4–5 stories |

*Source*: Machado Ventura (1976)

The push toward the 10 million ton sugar cane harvest required all of the nation's available technical, human, and scientific resources. Even though both the sugar and housing goals failed, the 1970s became a time of reaffirming industrial development as a cornerstone of the socialist revolution. In tandem with this push towards industrialization in the housing sector, there was, ironically, also widespread use of traditional artisan construction by the Microbrigades. This alternative method formed part of Cuba's economic planning and its political institutionalization process. The First Congress of the Cuban Communist Party in 1975 affirmed this principle (PCC 1976). The government stated clearly at the congress that it should fill the vacuum in building construction created by the ruralist approach of the 1960s. Housing assumed an important symbolic presence in the city, matching the availability of social services, schools and recreational facilities. Some of the more noteworthy projects were José Antonio Echeverría University campus, the Lenin Vocational School, Lenin Park, and the Botanical Gardens and Zoo, which were located at the city's edge (see Chapter 8). High-rise public housing on the outskirts of Havana not only countered the presence of similar structures in Vedado, but became reference points for the Revolution's modernization efforts in Havana. These high-rise structures spread to the most unlikely and remote corners of the city. Twenty-story high-rise housing in Havana during the first decades of the Revolution paralleled in many ways Stalin's location of seven scrapers in Moscow at the end of the Second World War (Segre 1985b). The enduring nature of Soviet power had been reaffirmed by victory over barbarian Nazi forces. Soviet planning sought to show new features and rights of the unfolding socialist society.

Cuba, too, reaffirmed the equality of land values in the city and rejected the persistent association in capitalist societies between architectural style and social class. The 23 high-rises under construction in Metropolitan

Havana in 1974 were distributed among the municipalities of Centro Habana, Plaza de la Revolución, Habana del Este, and Diez de Octubre. In 1982, the Mayor of Havana proposed to Fidel Castro that 64 buildings be built as part of a special plan for high-rise structures. Euphoria about the perceived economic outlook for the nation's economy influenced the proposal, which had no way of predicting the collapse of the USSR and the restructuring of Cuba's economy. In some cases, these buildings were sited in open areas, with little concern about blending in. In other locations, the unremarkable high-rises aggressively ruptured the flow of nineteenth century *portales* whose distinctive character was accentuated by historicist decorations of the early twentieth century. Perhaps the most dramatic instance of architectural and urban design insensitivity by designers and planners appeared at the intersection of Calzada de Infanta and Calzada de Monte, popularly known as the Tejas corner. There, two modern and nondescript structures (Figure 6.3) arose on what was one of

**Figure 6.3** Modern and anonymous high-rises at Infanta and Monte streets (known as *La Esquina de Tejas*) built in the 1970s, intruding into this historic neighborhood in Cerro. Photograph by Roberto Segre

**Figure 6.4** Twin high-rise apartment towers from before the Revolution in Vedado, just one block off the Malecón. Although each unit has a balcony, the buildings were designed for individual air-conditioning units which have all since been removed. Photograph by Joseph L. Scarpaci

the most significant corners in the city's history (Coyula 1992). Similar buildings appeared elsewhere in Havana in the 1950s (Figure 6.4).

Although prefabricated housing has kept costs down, it disrupted the traditional fabric of the city. In Alamar, the Microbrigades constructed traditional craft or artisan housing. In Vedado, the LH (slab core) housing system was used. Other new housing spread from the Plaza de la Revolución and penetrated older areas such as Cayo Hueso in Centro

Habana. At least two factors account for the cosmopolitan character of these new structures. First, little information existed about the criticisms of these types of buildings, the CIAM theories, and the International Style. Second, there was a short, intense flurry of construction that was out of step with most twentieth century housing. Thus, there was relatively little time for assessing its critical outcomes. Prototypes in Havana were mechanically and faithfully reproduced according to the original European designs. The absence of balconies, awnings, eves, and bright colors contributed to the gray, drab look of Havana's newer housing. This bland appearance is evident in the structures built in the Plaza de la Revolución during the 1970s and 1980s, giving them an anonymous look that disregards any contextual reference. A high degree of abstraction places the structures out of step in both place and time.

Socialist housing in Havana was similar to the many complexes that existed in Prague, Budapest, Sofia, Dresden, Stalingrad and Moscow. The spaciousness of these apartments as built in Cuba made them superior than the speculative housing units built by the bourgeoisie before the Revolution. The technical quality of the prefabricated panels used would have placed the real cost of the final units out of the reach of the occupants had it not been for the low and state-subsidized rent. The gap between the real cost and the low fixed monthly rents (10% of gross income) created a financial deficit that the state was unable to remedy. That the housing model of finance and construction was not financially viable became readily apparent once the Soviet bloc severed aid to the island, and Cuba had to resort to its own (hard currency) resources. Many projects begun in the 1980s had to be halted, remaining unfinished and gradually decaying in the 1990s.

The 200 meter long strip used in housing in the vicinity of the Plaza de la Revolución changed the scale of housing design in Havana. In many respects, it was out of step with the kind of social spaces that drew a community with this level of population together. Also discordant was the lack of attempts to blend traditional architectural styles with large socialist complexes. Clusters of new buildings in Cayo Hueso seemed more like a malignancy rather than a holistic attempt to rebuild deteriorated neighborhoods (Coyula 1991b). Good ideas were not always used. For example, the notion of Le Corbusier's *pilotis* was not fully taken advantage of. This idea places sites and services on the ground floor. Such services might have included bars, cafés, shops and restaurants. Indeed, having included these uses would have energized city life. The area's maintenance was deficient and failed to draw on residents for routine upkeep. Residents were alienated from these new architectural projects because of the educational or class differences among them, as well as the lack of a sense of identification with this state-sponsored property.

## The Microbrigade: precarious design and social content

In the 1970s the housing debate in Latin America centered around two alternative approaches: large housing complexes built by the state and smaller self-help housing (Pradilla 1982). In some countries large housing complexes were still built such as in Mexico, Argentina, Colombia, and Brazil. Successive military regimes in Argentina tried to alleviate the mounting social pressure for adequate shelter. A series of diverse residential housing complexes for low-income residents, including LuganoI/II, Ciudadela, Villa Soldati, and Piedrabuena reflect that need for shelter (Segre *et al.* 1981). At the same time, economists, sociologists, urbanists and architects confronted the problem of 'marginal settlements' as one of the most important elements of the Third World city.

Responses to the housing crisis varied. In Chile, the government of Salvador Allende (1970–1973) began a program for the urban poor who lacked adequate shelter. This program was also associated with a high level of political mobilization among those poor who stood to profit from state housing initiatives (Castells 1974; Scarpaci *et al.* 1988). In other countries (Peru, Venezuela, Colombia) squatter settlements were manipulated in order to distance the housing solution from community participation, which was associated with political and ideological commitments.[5]

The solution put forth by Cuba in the 1970s represented yet another housing alternative in Latin America. Cuba decided to confront its housing demand by using a mixture of state resources and the active participation of the future residents of the new housing units (Coyula 1990, 1991a, b). Several reasons led to this solution. First, prefabricated housing revealed technical differences. Second, prefabrication was costlier than traditional methods (Castex 1986). Third, traditional construction workers were demobilized because in the 1970s they lacked resources. Individual housing solutions, it was felt, created several problems. They increased housing construction and remodeling by users in various parts of Havana which dispersed housing and resources across the city. In this scenario, housing quality and standards could not be ensured, producing an atomization of the state's housing efforts (Herrera 1976; Izquierdo and Liz

---

[5]Local specialists and foreigners (Jorge Enrique Hardoy, Marcos Kaplán, Emilio Pradilla, Jordi Borja, Eduardo Caminos, John F.C. Turner, Charles Abrams, William Mangin) conducted research and issued concrete proposals. In particular, the work by Turner in Lima's *barriadas* served as a hypothetical control model for spontaneous squatter settlements in other Latin American cities (Turner and Fichter 1972).

1984). To offset that outcome, Cuba tried to integrate resources and to draw upon community strengths. Although irregularly produced, by the early 1970s the state had already made heavy investments in cement product factories. This made it easier to distribute building inputs not only among government building projects, but also among people who desire to repair or expand their homes (Junta Central de Planificación 1976).

The state supplied building materials and designated where the units were to be built. Future tenants or users organized themselves in Microbrigades which consisted of 33 workers who built five-story apartment houses with 30 apartments as designed by the architects of the Ministry of Construction (Segre 1984). The Microbrigade was formed within a workplace (e.g., factories, ministries, commerce, education, etc.) which gave them a unique focus (Llanes 1985).

Urban residents in Latin American countries who lack shelter are expected to build their own housing during their free time after the 8-hour work day (Livingston 1990). Sociologists, geographers and economists have criticized this policy by default as a form of double worker exploitation because the free time of laborers should not be used for self-help construction as the state or landowner ultimately will gain ownership (Rodríguez *et al.* 1973). The Cuban proposal, however, solved two problems at the same time. The first was the excess of employees in state companies which lost economic control over profitability and efficiency. It also caused severe problems of bureaucratization that plague socialist governments. A second problem was related to the disappearance of artisan labor skills. The Microbrigade consisted of workers from a given workplace who labored full time on a particular project while the rest of the workers at the original workplace covered the tasks abandoned by their comrades. Thus, activities at the construction site and workplace could be easily coordinated. At the same time, on weekends, all workers could join in 'voluntary work' in order to increase the pace of construction.[6]

Participation in the Microbrigade was voluntary and did not necessarily mean the immediate delivery of housing. The apartments built

---

[6]Two key factors triggered various degrees of enthusiasm for Microbrigades among North American and European scholars such as Tom Angotti, Tony Schumann, Richard Hatch, Jill Hamberg, Kosta Mathéy, and Julián Salas. One point in its favor was that because apartment complexes served as the basic unit in the spatial organization of housing, it could be coordinated by urbanists, architects and builders. This model went against the existing system of suburban expansion and spontaneous single dwellings at the city's edge. As a result, it departed from the long-standing curse of not being able to control the technical or aesthetic dimensions of 'marginal' constructions found in *favelas, callampas, pueblos jovenes, villas miserias*, and other squatter communities found in Latin America. A second attribute was that Microbrigade housing held social and political value.

belonged to the worker collective, factory, or state agency. Once the structure was completed, the workers would then decide how to allocate some of the housing among its unit, and which members should receive priority (Mathéy 1992, p. 189). The government held a firm principle: prioritizing the collective over individual interest. During the 1980s under the Correction of Mistakes Period this very principle led to the creation of social Microbrigades who worked largely at rehabilitating structures. In particular, they focused on schools, hospitals, day-care center, family physician centers, senior citizen centers and other non-residential structures (Hamberg 1994; Mathéy 1994).

In December, 1970, Fidel Castro outlined the structure and organization of Microbrigades in the national meeting of heavy industry. He created the first Microbrigade in Havana, and in the first semester of 1971, defined the various relationships and responsibilities of other organizations that would support this new entity (Castro 1975). That same year, more than 1000 workers were assigned to build 1154 housing units in Plaza de la Revolución, Altahabana, Rancho Boyeros, Alamar, Reparto Bahía, San Agustín, and La Coronela. In just 2 years, a labor force had been consolidated throughout Cuba that included more than 1000 Microbrigades. In 1971, 12 715 workers made up 444 Microbrigades. By 1975, 30 000 workers constituted 1150 Microbrigades that completed 25 600 housing units, in addition to a plethora of non-residential (e.g., social) projects. By 1983, the movement had built 100 000 units nationwide (Hamberg 1986, 1990, 1994). With hindsight, it would have been logical to have built new residences and new workplaces. That was not possible, however, because of the scarcity of available land and because the fragmentation of work projects would have decreased the output of completed units by scattering these initiatives across the city. Co-locating work and residence was also difficult because most households have more than one member working outside the home, and they usually work in different places.

Housing projects in Havana in the 1970s clustered in three large areas and were located in districts that had the greatest number of industrial and service-sector workers. The east Havana area was well endowed with a good road network, as well as sewage and electrical services. As noted above, this is where the bourgeoisie in the 1950s had planned suburban subdivisions. The areas included Alamar (130 000 residents) in Habana del Este municipality; in the south, along an axis with Rancho Boyeros, was Altahabana (110 000 residents); and in the west San Agustín (35 000 residents). The theory underlying the Urban Reform Law (Table 6.1) – the standardization of rent – was carried out in the numerous buildings that proletarianized the edges of the city (Carneado 1962; CEE 1983; Chaline

1987). This notion brought uniformity to the images and streets in Havana's suburbs. It was not by chance that the artist Antonio Eligio Tonel (1991) would create a sculpture – *El Bloqueo* – as a symbol of the urban landscape set on a map of the island made up of cement blocks. The haphazard nature of urban design wiped out the positive aspirations for a social environment with aesthetically meaningful shapes and spaces.

Now that a quarter of a century separates the original Microbrigade initiative from today, there is little doubt that on balance the Microbrigade efforts were positive conceptually and socially. The quality of suburban Havana's apartment complexes is infinitely superior to the self-help housing found elsewhere in Latin America, an even some other apartment complexes in Cuba. For example, these housing units are larger than those in socialist eastern European countries. Suburban Havana apartment complexes also include a generous amount of light and air, as well as large green areas surrounding them (even though the landscaping and maintenance have deteriorated). Clearly, these apartment complexes are a homage to Le Corbusieran precepts.

In planning terms, however, the experience is not considered exemplary in Latin America and the Caribbean because it was divorced from the architectural and design concepts and models in the region. There were no contextualist notions about the traditional city nor was there much concern about the natural landscape surrounding these complexes. In addition, there emerged a debate over the effects of breaking the city up into socialist housing quarters given the strong capitalist inheritance of Havana. Had there been non-polluting light industry and jobs in Alamar that could have drawn a female labor force, it might have changed the singular function of the neighborhood. In essence, the capital continued its 'bedroom communities.'

The early 1970s was a dogmatic period. The Revolutionary government employed rigid institutional structures in architectural projects and cultural life. Varying from the norms or otherwise reinterpreting orders from centralized authority were not permitted. An abstract sense of importance was given to collective interests which made it nearly impossible to present alternative ideas (Castro 1984b). Working in teams was virtually impossible. Unfortunately, this meant that state organizations were not able to share and participate in new urban projects. This may explain why urban spaces in Alamar can best be characterized as depressing. Elements of this poor design remain today and can be noted throughout Havana. Each service such as retail, education, health care, recreation and industry was restricted to a specific and isolated building. Little concern was given to integrating these buildings with others. The presence of almost 100 000 residents in Alamar would have justified the construction of a major civic center, a central space in the community for recreation, cultural functions, and to hold events for the youth of the settlement. Neglecting social spaces for the youth was a particularly glaring oversight because youth represented a large segment of Alamar's population. Instead, isolation created a sort of 'no man's land.' Large expanses of green areas and the impersonal nature of prefabricated structures all so far removed from the dynamism and lively spirit of Cubans. At a time when around the world the rigidity of the International Style and features of the Modern Movement were being criticized and Team X was creating new spaces to promote social interaction, Cuba was replicating tired, old schemes. The end result was a style of construction and housing that was far removed from what a 'real' socialism was capable of producing (Segre 1968b, 1994c; De la Nuez 1990).

As the original impulse brought on by Microbrigades languished in the early 1980s, so too did the pace of construction in Havana. Unlike professionals and practitioners with specialized training in the building trades, key officials in other state agencies had grave doubts about the real benefits of Microbrigade initiatives. A spate of ongoing projects had made it increasingly difficult to distribute resources and technology equitably. From the downturn in the 1980s onward, an uneven rhythm of construction came to a complete halt. Long delays and erratic stops and gos added costs to the final completion of many construction projects. To this must be added the higher salaries of workers' over time. These salaries did not correspond to the actual position of the construction worker but rather to the original workplace to which she or he belonged. Specialized technicians intervened constantly to correct errors made by unqualified workers. In the end, this produced a series of poorly finished buildings.

A lingering Microbrigade problem was retaining experienced workers in construction crews. Upon finishing an apartment complex, many of those same workers occupied them, as was premised in the initial Microbrigade idea. However, despite worker and party organizations encouraging workers to keep on participating in the construction sector after they had secured their own housing, many decided otherwise. Nonetheless, many workers did sacrifice and their adherence to the Revolution's long-term goals came at the expense of immediate material rewards (e.g., housing). Out of a dedicated construction labor force arose 'contingents' (*contingentes*, work crews) that carried out ambitious social projects in the late 1980s and infrastructure works in tourist complexes and places outside Havana.

The dynamism of the 1970s and 1980s produced divergent outcomes in Havana's housing sector. Some professionals struggled for the application of an 'artistic integration in the personalization of mass production'

(Alvarez-Tabío 1994b, p. 18). Attempting to rescue visual and symbolic identity in Cuba's housing complexes, artists and graphic designers creatively painted buildings with large murals, called supergraphics (*supergráficas*) that faded in the Caribbean sun and rain. Construction of schools, houses, factories, agricultural centers and other sites depended on prefabrication and were far removed from high-quality designs. Such structures were based on function without form, and a negation of architecture as a cultural expression. Plans executed by Microbrigades did not take advantage of the implicit possibility of alternatives: 'typical' projects fell victim to facilism, norms found nationwide, and a deeply ingrained bureaucratization of problem solving. In turn, architects became mere construction laborers, without any positive consequences for buildings and designs. Poorly finished buildings reflected little attention to details and technical specifications.

## Back to the traditional city

In the 1980s a generation of painters, writers, artists, sculptors, and architects known as the 'founders' began a new movement. They differed markedly from the utopian and rigid images of the generation before them. Theirs was a world that no longer consisted of issues in 'black and white.' They had witnessed the disintegration of socialism in the former Soviet Union and eastern Europe, from the fervent early years of the Cuban Revolution (Vega Vega 1963), to the downward spiral of the Cuban economy in the 1990s. In the wake of those events stood a unipolar world where market mechanisms had gained unprecedented influence. As the twentieth century ends, a gamut of philosophical and aesthetic ideas has taken hold. The 'founders' verified the existence of a 'real' society that was still far from their ideal. This philosophy allowed room for goals and incomplete projects to coexist. For example, there are now schools in the countryside while *solares* and *cuarterías* in Habana Vieja persist. In debunking the 'myth of the new' (Segre 1994), there is also a rethinking of traditional housing solutions. This new way of thinking could not have emerged had it not been for the fall of the Berlin Wall and the dissolution of the Soviet Union in 1989 which, correctly or not, hurt the Cuban economy.

In the mid-1990s several influences had led to a gradual return of construction in the city.

1. The value of the historic centers and their protection – particularly after UNESCO's declaration of Habana Vieja as a World Heritage Site

– gave salience to conserving the built environments of bygone eras (see Chapter 9).

2. The squalor of social spaces in peripheral settlements oblige inhabitants to use the traditional city centers.

3. There was an ongoing debate at that time among architects about housing complexes and what the future of Havana's center might be. A 1984 conference titled the 'International Seminar of City Architecture and Renewal' set the stage for thinking about these different issues. The thrust of this thinking centered around the fixed and limited number of options available to cities in the 1970s. Those options became limited in the 1990s: the building needs of Havana could no longer be ignored.

4. Economic analyses about the high cost of infrastructure in suburban areas is foremost in planning and design circles. For example, it is now widely accepted that the contiguous areas of Havana should retain pockets of open areas for future construction.

5. Decentralization of economic and political decision-making has brought about greater freedoms and initiatives to provincial and municipal governments (Padrón Lotti and Cuervo Masoné 1991). For architects, decentralization has meant the creation of Architectural Departments (*Direcciones de Arquitectura*) in the municipalities of Havana. These departments include young architects with diverse backgrounds, who differ greatly from their predecessors who were subject to the controls of the Ministry of Construction.

6. The passage of the General Housing Law of 1984 (*Ley General de la Vivienda*) enabled permanent residents of state structures to assume ownership of their units. This law created incentives and a sense of belonging that improved the maintenance of many of Havana's buildings (Dávalos Fernández 1990).

7. The 1986 Correction of Mistakes Period brought not just new housing construction, but also many social projects. In Havana, projects such as day-care centers, schools, clinics, and hospitals stemmed from this initiative (Mathéy 1991).

8. A planning and advising unit in Havana's government, *Grupo para el Desarrollo Integral de la Capital*, provided a new decentralized forum for coping with Havana's housing problems.

9. Havana has been characterized by general deterioration and an overall lack of maintenance. Although the state has been unable to provide all of the necessary building materials, some of this deterioration is due to *ad hoc* building initiatives taken on by residents (Estévez 1977). While self-help housing lacked technical and aesthetic controls, between 1981 and 1983 that sector completed seven units per

1000 inhabitants in Havana versus the state's production of two units per 10000 (Gomila *et al.* 1984).

10. Havana in 1987 exhibited an ailing housing sector even before the Special Period. The city still had 55 000 people in housing that was deemed so precarious that they were slated for the first available housing. Of this group, a few thousand were lodged in shelters (*albergues*, temporary residences for those who had lost their housing). In addition, 213 000 *habaneros* resided in tenement houses (*ciudadelas*) and another 50 000 lived in shantytowns (*barrios insalubres*). In all, some 357 000 lived in substandard housing (Castro 1964, 1987).

Although some of the utopian ideas of the 1970s were criticized because they were not practical and suited to Cuba, some of these same conceptual ideas of that era were successfully employed. The ideas of Fernando Salinas,[7] for instance, were reapplied in university research and the housing construction sector. In the late 1980s and early 1990s, it became quite apparent that the search for creative and scientific housing solutions in the Third World would require some of Salinas' premises. These new housing concepts included: (i) the application of economic principles in building construction; (ii) notions of growth and change; (iii) economic upkeep; (iv) flexibility; (v) variety in housing styles; and (vi) a dialectic vision of nature, philosophy, society and culture to accommodate the architectural forms inherent in the complex reality of the century's end (Salinas 1967).

In the 1980s, housing officials in Havana developed creative ideas and proposals that were not solely focused on the historic district. Architectural designs at the municipal level now used design teams who produce blueprints for new and rehabilitated buildings that blend in with their surroundings. Such an approach is far removed from the formal and pre-conceived ideas of past years, when experimentation was impossible (Baroni 1993). Despite the fact the municipality of Centro Habana was not part of the UNESCO-declared World Heritage Site, it turned out to be one

---

[7]Salinas mentored a cohort of young professionals at the university who came to be known as the 'Generation of the 1980s' (*Generación de los 80*). These professionals (Francisco Bedoya, Daniel Bejerano, Rosendo Mesías, Juan L. Morales, Emma Alvarez-Tabío, Eduardo L. Rodríguez, Raúl Izquierdo, Rafael Fornés, Jorge Tamargo, Emilio Castro, José A. Choy, among others) were responsible for some of the first public housing initiatives. These efforts were developed by the Municipal Popular Power not based on prefabrication, but with the contextual features of local surroundings (Segre 1992b; Alvarez-Tabío 1992). For an example of the work in Atarés, a run-down back-bay neighborhood basically ignored before and after the Revolution, see Ortega (1996).

of the areas of greatest interest among designers. Centro Habana has good environmental quality and potential even though many of its buildings are run down (Bedoya 1992). Only a handful of high-quality rehab and new construction projects occurred in the 1980s.

Other municipalities began projects as well. In Vedado, government authorities questioned the controversial Mario Durán complex which displayed a distinctively Wrightian influence, allegedly because it violated building codes. Such government intervention was ironic in a city where residents had arbitrarily altered the aesthetic coherence of whole neighborhoods. In Marianao, Daniel Bejerano tried to direct the housing units toward the interior of lots. In Diez de Octubre, Oscar Hernández laid out repetitive and geometric styles. A thesis project of Rosa M. Salinas of Nuevo Miramar (1988) became an alternative to the traditional checkerboard street layout. Located on the empty lands of Monte Barreto in Miramar, her project stood directly in the area of hotel and tourist development of the municipality of Playa. It invalidated formalism, not only by the isolated blocks that were acritically used in the city, but by emphasizing social relations and functional uses of neighborhood spaces.

Young architects and designers who embraced postmodernism were harshly criticized by professionals such as Sergio Baroni, Mario Coyula, Ramón Gutiérrez, Carlos González Lobo, and Rogelio Salmona. Postmodernism, a hegemonic model imported from the industrial North Atlantic countries, failed to provide a uniquely adapted alternative for Cuba. Critics contended that architects fell into the trap of trendiness, and were lulled into this style by reading foreign journals and following trends that were alien to Cuba.

The largest two housing projects of the 1980s were Las Arboledas (1984) and Villa Panamericana (1991), the latter embracing the playful mixtures of postmodern designs (Figures 6.5 and 6.6). However, both projects reflected different paths regarding the rigidity of site planning that had prevailed in the Revolution's earlier years. In the case of Las Arboledas, a group of Cuban and North American architects directed by Huck Rorick, and with the initial collaboration of Salvador Gomila, the urban designer Peter Calthorpe, and the landscape architect Ken Kay, designed a microdistrict of 20 000 residents within Altahabana (Rorick and Gomila 1984). Conceived as part of a new kind of apartment complex with formal, construction and spatial variations, this new microdistrict achieved variation by using plazas, winding pedestrian malls, and emphasizing dense tree-covered areas to break up road networks. This kind of project tried to tighten the relationship between rational composition and the natural environment. Works like these were theoretically informed by the ideas of Christopher Alexander and his 'design by

**Figure 6.5** The Villa Panamericana complex completed in 1991 proved to be a costly housing project. Built for the athletic events of the same name, workers who built the project got priority in securing housing there. The low-density neo-traditional and mixed designs of the buildings contrast with public housing built in the early years of the Revolution. Photograph by Joseph L. Scarpaci

patterns' principles.

In contrast, the Villa Panamericana complex closed the stage of large residential complexes in Havana and opted for postmodern formalism to break up the formal layout of buildings. The Villa Panamericana suffers from superficial façades, cornices, and gables. Its site plan was a first attempt to evoke a traditional grid pattern with the use of streets, avenues, parks and town squares. The architect Roberto Caballero and a team of professionals from the Housing Division within the Ministry of Construction projected the image of Havana in an open space on the city's outskirts between the Habana del Este project and Alamar.

Despite the precarious aestheticism and the isolation of the Villa Panamericana from the capital, the complex represents a new part of the city's bedroom communities. It is also a significant improvement in the quality of life for its residents. Although part of the complex is for the sole use of foreign tourists and remains off limits to most Cubans, the presence of *pórticos*, retail activities for pedestrians, and tree-lined axes throughout the center of the complex do facilitate social integration. This remedied a long-standing complaint about the 'cold images' of many housing complexes built during the Revolution. The Villa Panamericana grew out

**Figure 6.6** A broad, tree-lined pedestrian mall accented by playful tile designs runs through the middle of the main street of Villa Panamericana. Photograph by Joseph L. Scarpaci

of the economic, technical and planning forces behind the 1991 Pan-American Games held in Havana and other parts of the island. Moreover, the project was impeded by the disruption of relations between Cuba and eastern Europe which ushered in the Special Period (Castro 1990).

## The depths of the fourth world

As the end of the millennium draws to a close, it has become common-place to identify global problems that create local difficulty. Socialism hypothetically represented a challenge to triumphant neocapitalism. The hopes of that task were dashed with the collapse of the socialist camp which exposed the social and economic problems of a broad strata of the world's populations – problems that are far from being resolved. The reality is most drastic in developing countries where the chance to overcome these problems is hindered by a lack of resources. Increasingly, a wealthy minority distances itself from a poor majority. In Africa, for example, elementary subsistence cannot be achieved for many communities because of drought and famine. Housing deficits plague many other developing countries.

The crisis in Cuba in the 1990s was unexpected and therefore traumatic. Cubans had become accustomed to a gradual increase in their general well-being and expectations. For example, possessing world-class free public health and educational systems came to be badges proudly worn by the Revolution and the Cuban people. A uniform, albeit somewhat bland diet of Cubans of all social strata was actually something formerly associated only with First World countries (Castro 1989). These public social services and food distribution systems, however, had been possible only because of the aid from the more 'developed' socialist countries.

When that support collapsed in 1989 or so, the welfare state fell into crisis, and the state was transformed from an entity that could provide everything to one that could provide little. Cubans had come to expect certain rights and services and felt that the state had specific obligations. During the 1960s and 1970s, few asked about where resources came from that had maintained socialist Cuba at a standard more akin to levels in the developed world rather the penury associated with many Latin American countries (Díaz Acosta and Guerra 1982; Estévez and Pereda 1990). Similarly, few raised concerns about squandering resources on certain imported goods. Perhaps the most important outcome of the Special Period has been the reflection on and analysis of the serious problems created by past mistakes.

Architectural, urban design, and planning fields were also affected. Cuba contained the kind of technocratic bureaucracy common to industrializing countries. As such, it was far removed from local concerns and needs. A schematic and paralyzing dogmatism in Cuba made it impossible to differ from top-down assessments of housing needs and solutions. Instead of soliciting as many solutions as possible to the island's housing needs, options were foreclosed by top authorities and government agencies. That artisan or craft systems never coexisted with prefabrication is evidence of the narrow approach employed in socialist Cuba. Decisions about housing never emphasized the concept of 'dialectics,' so frequently used in the writings of Salinas. This meant that gradual solutions pegged to the resources of housing occupants were not applied. Instead, government officials became obsessed with turnkey projects that entailed turning over spacious, large-scale, and fully equipped housing units (Zschaebitz and Lesta 1990; IPF 1992). Clearly, this was a goal beyond the means of a poor country. While the Revolution resolved the basic housing problems of a majority it also marginalized a significant minority.

Housing construction in Cuba was weakened by the difficulty of oil imports which was an input in the building-materials manufacturing and distribution. Oil shortages paralyzed prefabricated housing production. The building efforts, therefore, shifted to the more deteriorated parts of Havana and drew upon local residents' labor. At the same time, research was conducted on the conditions of *solares* and *cuarterías* in the central areas of the city. The Faculty of Architecture at the University of Havana, in collaboration with the Technical University of Hamburg, Germany, conducted a technical study in Atarés neighborhood (Ortega 1993). Atarés is a poor, predominantly Afro-Cuban neighborhood in the back-bay district of Havana. This project revealed the creativity of residents in finding innovative solutions that catered to household needs. The *barbacoa* – a mezzanine or loft in units with high ceilings used to create a sleeping space or second floor – is used to relieve crowding and open up new living space.

Economic limitations imposed since 1991 have once again eliminated the term 'aesthetics' from the vocabulary of Cuban architects. New problems returning to the forefront of the housing scene consist of making housing less expensive, building 'low-energy' housing that draws on local materials and sun-dried clay bricks that can be assembled manually and without fossil fuels. Herein lie the basic elements of so-called 'sustainable' development. Under this form of building construction, between 1992 and 1994, 17 500 housing units were built nationwide (Bancrofft 1994).

Havana remains one of the most beautiful Latin American cities whose value resides not only in its magnificent landmarks, the homogeneity of its street plan, the exuberance of its parks and plazas, and the transparency of its galleries and colonnades. Because of the persistence of its mixture of styles, Rigau and Stout (1994) have called Havana 'The City of Alchemy.' Even though Havana has been gutted and left unpainted and abandoned, it remains a living testimony of the many societies that inhabited and enriched it. Despite the severe crisis that plagues Havana, the city affords both culture and shelter, and will remain the concrete symbol of daily life.

# 7

## Changing nature of the economy

One has to laugh because [our economists] did not go to Harvard to study capitalist economics but went to the former socialist camp . . . which does not exist any more, and I ask myself what use do we have for socialist economics under the current conditions . . . Now there are 1000 schools of political economy [in Cuba]; whenever three or four economists get together, they found a school and have a formula to solve our problems.

Fidel Castro, Closing speech to the meeting celebrating the 40th anniversary of the attack on Moncada Barracks. *Granma*, July 28, 1993

Consumer societies are not the solution. Political chicanery is not the solution. The capitalist democracy is not the solution. We can adopt some economic measures, but they should not lead us astray . . .

Fidel Castro, in an impromptu interview with reporters. July 1995, cited in *CubaNews*, August 1995, p. 4

One of the most notable changes in the global political economy of the 1990s was the collapse of the socialist camp headed by the USSR. In Cuba, these tectonic shifts in the global political plates created fuel shortages, severe food rationing, power blackouts, transportation crises, and even 'cracks' in the once venerable system of health and education (Stix 1995). We have referred to this economic quagmire throughout the book as the 'Special Period' (*Período Especial en el Tiempo de Paz*), following the official nomenclature used by the Cuban government. The Cuban government has implemented five strategies to address the Special Period.

1. To increase the staple-foods production by shifting displaced workers into agriculture, increasing arable lands, and reducing reliance on chemical fertilizers.
2. To return to the levels of total rationing of consumer goods (food, cloth-

ing, durables) in the 1960s.

3.  To lessen oil consumption through rationing public utilities, scheduled blackouts, and reducing industrial production and the use of tractors, private automobiles, and buses. This includes burning sugar-cane bagasse to run the sugar mills.
4.  To seek out foreign investment through joint projects in order to increase hard currency revenues for the national government.
5.  To implement selected structural reforms and market mechanisms that will reinsert Cuba's economy into the world market and create more market conditions internally. This includes reducing the excess of circulating money (pesos and dollars) and to attract workers into private-sector jobs.

This chapter examines these issues in the context of Havana's changing economy during the Special Period. It begins with a review of trends in the national economy from the mid-1980s until 1994. This serves as a backdrop to understand the 'free-fall' in which the Cuban economy found itself. The latter half of the chapter shifts to the impacts this economic restructuring has had on Havana. The focus is on the emerging free-market private activities within the food and restaurant sectors to illustrate the nature of Havana's changing economy (Rosenberg 1992). The chapter concludes with some reflections on Cuba's transition to socialism and the implications it has for other Third World economies.

### Interpreting the Cuban economy

The centrally planned economy of Cuba is mainly state owned. Since the 1959 Revolution, it has departed little from its dependence on foreign trade and agriculture. Until the Special Period, sugar had traditionally provided nearly three-quarters of total export revenues and, despite the break up of the former USSR, Cuba still exports about half of its sugar crop there. The economic malaise afflicting the island has not always been there. According to macroeconomic indicators, Cuba, like many Latin American countries, showed continuous improvements between 1940 and 1980. In the 1980s, though, Latin America and the Caribbean's overall gross national product (GNP) fell by 8.3%. However, 'among Latin American countries, only Chile, Colombia and Cuba managed to grow' (Gilbert 1994, p. 33). From 1980 to 1985, the real per capita gross domestic product (GDP) in Latin America had fallen at an average annual rate of 1.7% for 19 countries, excluding Cuba. In contrast, the constant price per capita of Cuba's GSP (gross social product; roughly the equivalent of the

GDP), increased annually at an average rate of 6.7%. Zimbalist (1986, p. 24) estimated that real annual Cuban industrial growth between 1965 and 1985 at 6.3 %, a 'very healthy, if not impressive, rate of growth and stands out in sharp relief when compared to the growth experience in the rest of Latin America.' Although there are reasons for skepticism (method of calculation, data comparability, USSR subsidies), the data from the 1980s offer *prima facie* evidence of impressive economic performance. The economic growth is especially noteworthy because the early 1980s marked the beginning of the infamous 'lost decade' in Latin America when the quality of life was quickly being eroded because of inflation and structural readjustment policies (Weil and Scarpaci 1992). Before assessing Havana's economy we must first understand how the performance of the national economy can be measured and tracked over time.

To be sure, there is considerable debate about deciphering Cuban statistics. A number of scholars have questioned whether the Cuban economy is even comprehensible. Others are more sanguine (Brundenius and Zimbalist 1985a–c). They argue that once scholars attempt to understand conventions used by the Council of Mutual Economic Assistance (CMEA), the economic data yield 'fathomable statistics.' Failing to familiarize oneself with CMEA methods can lead to a misinterpretation and distortion of the Cuban economic reality. Worse still, it can leave a *tabula rasa* for imposing political prejudice (Brundenius and Zimbalist 1989, p. 2).

These debates raged well before the Special Period. Today, the island sorely lacks even contemporary socioeconomic figures and other basic information. For example, no telephone directory had been published for Havana between 1982 and 1996, mainly because of the cost of paper. A Mexican joint partner helped in the publication of the 1996 directory. The statistical yearbook (*Anuario Estadístico de Cuba*) was last published in 1989. As a result, much economic data must be garnered from interviews, secondary sources, and surrogate measures of production and commerce. Conventional interpretation is made difficult by this dearth of information.[1]

Analysts working with total output of the Cuban economy use the GSP which differs from the Western GDP in two fundamental ways. The GDP includes value added and nonproductive services while the GSP assesses gross value and excludes nonproductive services. While the conversion of the GSP to GDP for purposes of comparability vary yearly, in the 1980s the GSP of Cuba was about 20% less than the comparable GDP figures for the economy's output (Brundenius and Zimbalist 1989, pp. 12–13).

Since the late 1980s, the economy has declined considerably. In 1990,

---

[1]Unless otherwise noted, sources here stem from our fieldwork and primary data gathered in Havana.

estimates in the decline of Cuba's GSP ranged between 4 and 7%. As the crisis of the Special Period accelerated the following year, so did the range of the estimate in GSP decline; between 15 and 27%, although it narrowed to between 7 and 15% for 1993 (Mesa-Lago 1994, p. 8). The ensuing economic problems stem from at least three factors. One is the de-emphasis of material incentives in the workplace and the abolition of informal produce markets. Although those policies reversed in 1994–1995, it had been attributed to a decade-long drop in economic productivity (Del Aguila 1992). Second, as noted above, the collapse of the former USSR interrupted considerable price subsidies, foreign aid, and an estimated 300-odd industrial and public-works projects that were in production. Third, the continuation of the US blockade has increased the cost of many consumer and industrial goods that could no doubt be secured more cheaply if imported from the United States and not through third countries (Bahamas, Panama, Canada, Jamaica, Mexico and Venezuela). The blockade also deprives the Cuban economy of a lucrative US tourist trade. However, it is expanding its tourist market greatly (see Chapter 8).

For decades CMEA had provided preferential trade agreements among signatory partners, of which Cuba was a member. CMEA was a rather small, isolated market whose 'backbone' was the USSR. Member nations – especially Cuba, Vietnam, and Mongolia – received preferential treatment because of their 'developing nation' status (*The Statesman Yearbook 1982–83*, 1982, p. 52). That meant that the USSR would buy Cuban sugar at prices three times the going rate, and Cuba would receive discounted oil in return. These favorable terms of trade allowed Cuba to satisfy about 90% of its energy needs (Mesa-Lago 1994, p. 1). Cuba had the highest dependency rate of trade among CMEA members (84%), of which 70% alone was with the USSR. In 1989 Cuba received $6 billion in economic assistance, bringing the island's debt to $24 billion. Merchant vessels from the former USSR and eastern Europe carried about 85% of Cuban foreign trade in 1990. Imports from the former USSR plummeted by 70% in 1990 alone (Zimbalist 1993, p. 408). By 1992, vessels from the Cuban merchant marine could handle only 20% of total trade volume; eastern European and Russian vessels now require hard currency for their services (Mesa-Lago 1994, p. 7).

If CMEA dissolution is the proximate cause of Cuba's current predicament, it is unclear how Cuba can arrest its crisis. One consequence of the unraveling of the Soviet bloc is that Cuba is trying to reinsert itself into the global market during the most dire economic period since the 1959 Revolution. Three possible reasons may explain why this has been so difficult for Cuba. First, its sugar harvest has fallen to record lows; from a high of about 9 million tons in the late 1970s to just over 4 million tons in 1995. The ramifications are many as sugar is the primary generator of hard currency. Inability to generate dollars prohibits Cuba from purchasing sufficient oil, fertilizer, machinery, pesticides, and other agricultural inputs. Food production and the quality and quantity of tobacco products have also declined. The externalities derived from the collapse of Soviet aid are multiple and negative: low sugar production and harvest displaced workers in the labor force, many of whom collect unemployment compensation.

Second, those managing the re-emergence of market-driven endeavors in Cuba may not hold the micro- and macroeconomic training required to steer the nation through these difficult times. Political appointments may be a compromise between orthodox 'hard-liners' (*duros*) and reformers.

Third, it is unclear whether the economic reforms outlined in July 1993 (discussed below) will actually propel Cuba to sustainable market reforms. Cuban leaders may not understand market economics and may retain the notion that they can direct the transition to socialism. Alternatively, they may have a good grasp of market mechanisms but may wish to give the impression inside and outside Cuba that the government is still in control of a sustainable socialist project (Mesa-Lago 1994, p. 71; Skidelsky 1996).

The national labor force is estimated to include about 3.5 million workers. Organized labor is affiliated with the only government-approved labor federation: the Workers Central Union of Cuba (CTC). It has 2.9 million members and serves as an umbrella organization for 17 member unions (Del Aguila 1992). In 1989, the overall unemployment rate was pegged at 6%, and 10% for female employment. Unemployment rose during the early 1990s and by May 1996, the Confederation of Cuban Workers estimated at the 17th Congress of their organization that the Special Period had created an employment rate of 7%, which could rise to 13% (*CubaNews*, June 1996, Official says Cuban unemployment is 7%). As the Cuban government downsizes its state bureaucracy, the private sector is expected to absorb displaced workers (Carranza *et al.* 1995).

At this point, it will be useful to recall some of the key features of Cuba's planning system (see Chapter 4) because of its important role in the nation's economic system. Five-year development plans have served as Cuba's economic maps throughout most of the Revolution. They are executed at the national and provincial levels. In keeping with the Revolution's efforts to empower regional governments, the original six provinces of Cuba (Pinar del Río, La Habana, Matanzas, Camagüey, Las Villas, and Oriente) were increased to 14 in 1976[2]. These provinces are Camagüey, Ciego de Avila, Cienfuegos, Ciudad de La Habana, Granma, Guantánamo, Holguín, La Habana, Las Tunas, Matanzas, Pinar del Río,

---

[2]Isle de Juventud (formerly Isle of Pines) is considered a 'special municipality'.

Sancti Spíritus, and Santiago de Cuba. Before the Revolution, higher education, for instance, was confined to Havana; Santiago de Cuba and Santa
Clara were the only other cities with a university. Since the Revolution,
many provinces boast a university and major hospital. The Revolution
has created a kind of hybrid model of regional development that com-
bines elements of Growth Pole Theory (in which secondary regional cities
serve as the 'motors' of development and point of investment around its
designated hinterland) and a commitment to socialist ideals that have
decentralized education and health service into the island's interior. It
was common to find as many as 150 *bateyes* (workers settlements) around
sugar mills before the Revolution (Slater 1982).

Deviations from national and provincial 5-year plans are most apparent by the rise in new foreign investment and the islands of capitalism
they create (Pérez-López 1994a). Although radical for an economy
embracing socialism, these 'reforms,' sanctioned by the Fourth Congress
of the Communist Party in October 1991, are all too common in other
developing countries. The message is simple: Cuba is 'open for business.'
American entrepreneur Lee Iacocca visited Havana in July 1994, and,
according to one journalist, media magnate Ted Turner 'frequently shows
up' there (Bardach 1995). Fidel Castro would welcome US investment
under certain conditions, and has long held that position. Presently,
Cuban officials actively court corporate America. They target consumer
products, manufacturing and tourism companies, and agricultural firms.
Although US firms cannot conduct business with Cuba, many are formu-
lating plans for tapping the Cuban market of 11 million. Havana, for
instance, would profit from investment in biotechnology (Goodrich 1993;
Collis 1995), medical equipment, textiles, asbestos-cement pipes, leather
products, and building restoration (*USA Today*, December 27, 1994).
Although many US companies have signed memorandums of understanding with Cuban government, the passage of the Helms-Burton bill in
1996 will deter any US investment in the near future.

Cubans jest about the 'second conquest' of the island when they refer to
the surge in Spanish investment. Havana is the target for much of this
investment. A Spanish conglomerate refurbished the former Havana
Hilton between 1993 and 1995. The hotel is one of the city's landmarks
that was built in 1958 by Conrad Hilton. Although at least $100 million of
Spanish investment has generated employment in the construction industry in recent years, most building materials, furniture, wiring, glass, and
plaster come from other countries, depriving the city of the usual kinds of
economic multipliers and horizontal integration among the building and
home-furnishing trades. Within the first 90 days of operation, hotel management of the Habana Libre: (i) renamed the hotel the Habana Libre-

Guitart (reflecting the name of the Spanish investment group), and (ii) reduced the hotel's work force from 1200 to 400.

While new investment holds promise, Cuba is still not a sanctuary for 'safe investment'. *The Economist Intelligence Unit* ranked Cuba 116th out of 129 countries regarding investment safety. Tourism, though, remains a reliable commodity the Cubans can market (Espino 1994; see also Chapter 8). Risky investment notwithstanding, companies investing in Cuba are Western Mining (Australia), Sherritt (Canada), ING Bank (Netherlands), Grupo Domos (Mexico), Unilever (UK/Netherlands), Labatt (Canada), and Pernod Ricard (France) (BWR 1995).

## Changes in Havana's economy

Political directives have targeted the countryside and provincial capitals for the bulk of investment since 1959. Rural investment served as a counterweight to the traditional emphasis on Havana (Hardoy 1973). Havana has not held more than 21% of the nation's population since the outset of the Revolution. This stems from a direct policy to avoid urban primacy and resource concentration in the capital city. Fidel Castro stated early in the Revolution that Cuba needed a 'minimum of urbanism and a maximum of ruralism' (Eckstein 1977, p. 443). Reversing the trend of more than 400 years of urbanization was difficult. The 1970 census reported that Havana Province held 38% of the nation's industrial employment, while Oriente held only 23% of all industrial workers, even though its provincial population surpassed Havana's. While these regional disparities are striking, Slater (1982) contends that examining spatial rather than class differences may well obfuscate important structural problems of the Cuban Revolution.

Socialist Cuba deliberately curtailed growth in Havana. Unlike other primate cities in Latin America, Havana has not been the voluntary destination of thousands of rural and secondary-city migrants, thus averting the usual shantytowns and problems of hyper-urbanization associated with this migration stream (although some shanties have existed during the Revolution). For instance, when the Revolutionary government seized office in 1959, Havana and Lima, Peru had populations of comparable size. Since then, Havana's population has doubled while Lima's has increased sevenfold. Notably, Havana lacks the shanties that line the Rimac River in Lima because the few shanties that exist are located in less prominent places. Several reasons account for Havana's unique position as a Latin American primate city. First, the elimination of the private rental market and the illegality of squatting have curbed voluntary migration. Second, housing exchanges in Havana are mostly done with 'For

Swap' signs (*Se Permuta*) and confined mainly to destinations within the city. Third, employment and housing are controlled by the government, although *habeneros* find ways to get around these obstacles. Though government regulation characterizes Cuban housing and employment, unlike the former USSR, residence permits are not required in Cuba. Lastly, and perhaps most importantly, food-ration books are used in local state-run food store (*bodega*) to secure food staples at subsidized prices.

Despite efforts to control population growth in Havana, a recent poll conducted on the island showed that Havana is still the major migration destination. Since 1990 migration to Havana has escalated on par with the worst economic crisis in recent history. In the 1980s, Havana received a steady flow of between 10 000 and 12 000 immigrants annually. By 1993 there were 13 000, which rose to 17 000 in 1995, and an estimated 27 000 immigrants in 1996. The survey, called the National Poll of Internal Migrants and carried out by the Center of Demographic Studies (CEDEM), found several factors producing migration to Havana. Professor Beatriz Erviti of CEDEM remarked that 'the most frequent motive for movement was family related, basically because of marriage or divorce, to improve living conditions and movements due to employment reasons or State made decisions' (Sierra 1996).

As the nation's capital, the city of Havana (population 2.2 million) serves as the major government and service center of the island. In the early 1990s, more than 80% of the nation's imports and exports passed through its ports. The most recently available data show a labor force of 939 400 (Table 7.1), with slightly more than half of the city's labor force working in the productive sphere. Industry, construction and transportation are the largest sectors. Industry (22.6%) concentrates mostly in food processing and pharmaceuticals while construction and transportation each employ 8.7% of the labor force.

These data have probably changed during the Special Period, and they reflect at least two trends.

One trend is that it is likely that the non-productive sphere has increased since 1990, probably surpassing the productive sphere. Fuel shortages and power outages force industry to slow production, as does the lack of hard currency for the purchasing of imported raw materials.

Another unfolding pattern is that in 1997 the construction and transportation industries suffer from fuel shortages; in 1986 buses accounted for 86% of motorized transport, while in contrast automobile trips – never a significant mode of transportation – accounted for just 6%. Roughly 50% of all bus routes have been eliminated, consolidated or cut back, making lengthy waits at crowded bus stops a multi-hour endeavor. Workers in construction and transportation have been displaced elsewhere, remain

**Table 7.1** Havana's labor force by productive and non-productive spheres (c. 1990)

| Sector | Workers (000's) | % |
|---|---|---|
| Agriculture | 90.0 | 0.9 |
| Industry | 211.6 | 22.6 |
| Construction | 82.2 | 8.7 |
| Transportation | 82.2 | 8.7 |
| Commerce | 102.9 | 11.0 |
| Other productive spheres | 13.0 | 1.4 |
| Total productive sphere | 500.9 | 53.3 |
| Services | 45.0 | 4.8 |
| Science and technology | 20.1 | 2.1 |
| Education, culture & art | 105.8 | 11.3 |
| Health, sports & tourism | 67.8 | 7.2 |
| Finance, administration & other | 199.8 | 21.3 |
| Total non-productive sphere | 438.5 | 46.7 |
| Total labor force | 939 400 | 100.0 |

under- or unemployed, or form part of the new self-employed labor pool. In the wake of this transportation crisis has come a huge increase in bicycles. In 1990, *habaneros* used their roughly 70 000 bicycles for recreation and sport. By 1993, there were 700 000 bicycles, mostly purchased from China, which were being used for commuting.

In late 1995 estimates placed the figure at 1 million bicycles (Figure 7.1). The Chinese models *Phoenix* and *Flying Pigeon* sell on installment plans for $60 pesos for students to $120 pesos for workers (Alepuz 1993); in deflated real dollars in 1997 this would range from about $2 to $6 USD. The externalities generated by bicycle imports and use mean: (i) less air pollution in Havana; (ii) greater commuting time for workers; and (iii) a proliferation of private-sector bicycle repair and parking services (Scarpaci and Hall 1995). Increased cycling, however, also carries costs. For example, in 1995, the National Revolutionary Police and the Ministry of Public Health reported 2175 bicycle accidents in Havana alone, and 479 traffic fatalities involving bicycles nationwide (*CubaNews*, Facts & Stats, June 1996).

The proportion of Havana's population working in agriculture has also likely increased (Figure 7.2). Neighborhood gardens have proliferated everywhere but it is difficult to determine whether workers who tend to those gardens would be counted as agriculturists (Roca 1994). Intensification of truck farming has also increased in the southern portions of the municipalities of Boyeros, Arroyo Naranjo and Cotorro (Figure 7.3), departing from a Third World pattern of decreasing peri-urban agriculture (Browder *et al.* 1995). Urban 'husbandry' – once outlawed and subject to stiff fines

**Figure 7.1** Bicycling in Havana. *Top*: rush hour after an early morning rain at the Puente de Hierro bridge over the Almendares River, between Vedado and Miramar; *Bottom*: bus–bicycle transfer point at the Ciclobus which carries cyclists and their bikes through the tunnel under Havana Bay from the northern part of Habana Vieja, and drops them off across the bay. Most continue from there to their homes in Alamar and Habana del Este. Photographs: Joseph L. Scarpaci

and incarceration – now flourishes, and cattle rustlers remove 10 000 animals each year from Cuban farms (Napoles 1996a). Balconies throughout Havana hold chicken coops and goats can be found in yards as can makeshift sties for piglets. For decades pork was unavailable in the City of Havana mainly because of a fever and subsequent infection among swine. A secondary reason was that it was destined for tourist consumption in such typical dishes as roasted pork 'Cuban style' (*lechón asado*) and private livestock has been strictly controlled and even outlawed at various times. Cuban economic development analysts and officials herald the rise in domestic livestock as a sign of local creativity while public health officials fret over the unsanitary conditions (personal interviews, Ministerio de Salud Pública, June 15, 1994). In the main, though, these examples underscore the likely decline in the proportion of workers in the productive sphere. Along with that shift has been a rise in black market (informal) activities and a new urban 'subsistence' economy that is difficult to measure.

While the traditional calculation of the socialist GSP separates wage labor into productive and non-productive spheres, at no time did statisticians or economists envision 'self-employment' as a major category before the 1990s. The Special Period has no doubt cast thousands of *habaneros* into 'services' and 'tourism' (Figure 7.3). Service categories charge in both pesos and dollars and include such low-order retail activities such as beauty shops, shoe repair, massage therapy, spiritual advice, and home restaurants called *paladares*. These food establishments cater to both tourists and local Cubans with dollars (mainly from remittances sent by relatives or revenues from new self-employment). The once clandestine restaurants serve meals perhaps at one-third the rates posted in the city's finest tourist restaurants; a lobster dinner, salad and beer can be purchased for $7 in a *paladar* versus more than $25 in tourist facilities (dis-

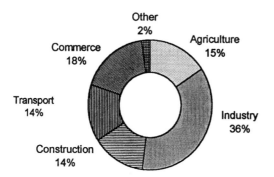

**Figure 7.2** Havana's labor force (1990) productive sphere. *Data source: Ciudad de La Habana. Datos Socioeconómicos, n.d. Havana: Poder Popular*

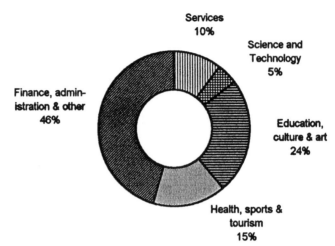

**Figure 7.3** Havana's labor force (1990): non-productive sphere. *Data source: Ciudad de La Habana. Datos Socioecónomicos*, n.d. Havana: *Poder Popular*

cussed in more detail in Chapter 8). Many of the supplies come from pilfering state warehouses or violating fishing laws. Taken in its entirety, the composition of the Havana labor force has increased in the nonproductive sphere as the city enters into a new mixed economy.

### Industrial location in Havana

While we have argued that the 1990 figure showing that 22.8% of Havana's work force labors in industry has probably dropped in the 1990s, the city's industrial infrastructure reveals distinctive patterns of geographic concentration. Although the 'bottoming out' of the Cuban economic free-fall in the mid-1990s is promising, it is still difficult to determine with precision full employment and output data by sector (*Poder Popular* n.d.; Ciudad de La Habana n.d.). In this section, therefore, we identify briefly the major patterns of industrial location in the capital.

Three major concentrations of industrial activity (light manufacturing, petrochemical, and warehousing) characterize Havana's industrial geography (Figure 7.4). First, the back-bay areas of Regla, Luyanó, and Guanabacoa comprise the central area of industry. This is the historic core industrial center, complete with oil refinery and petrochemical industries visible from the eastern edge of Habana Vieja, looking to the south and southeast. Rail yards and a large array of now aging warehouses make up this industrial landscape.

A second industrial cluster is found along the southeastern railroad

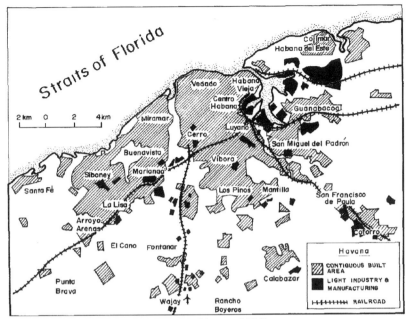

**Figure 7.4** Industry and manufacturing in Havana (1996)

line passing through San Francisco de Paula, Cotorro and Cuatro Caminos. Light industry in the form of food processing, pharmaceutical packing houses, and some light manufacturing is distributed along the railroad corridor and the Central Highway (*Carretera Central*). Buildings and infrastructure here date back to the pre-Revolutionary period, with a few new additions.

A third and less clearly defined concentration of industry in Havana is strewn along a southwestern and western axis running from José Martí International Airport northward into the west-central core of the metropolitan areas. Here too light industry lies adjacent to a major rail line entering from the west and ending at Havana Bay. The concentration is especially strong at the southern edge of Metropolitan Park.

Havana lacks the industrial concentration that characterizes other Latin American capitals such as Mexico City, Buenos Aires, Santiago, and the Lima–Callao metropolitan area. In these cities more than 50% of total national industrial output comes from the capital (Gwynne 1986, p. 82). Cuba's close relationship with the former Soviet Union and eastern bloc nations allowed for a great number of manufactured goods to be imported. Although the concentration of industry in Havana in the 1950s was intense, more than 30 years of attempting to build up provincial industrial production in Matanzas, Santiago de Cuba, Holguín and other secondary cities, has lessened the industrial imprint on Havana. Indeed, the only sign of heavy industry output outside the back-bay area is the utility plant in Tallapiedra and the gas plant at Melones, along the southern rim of the bay. These facilities cast a steady heavy plume across Centro Habana and the Capitolio building. Until the Soviet-initiated construction of a nuclear reactor at Juraguá (outside the south-central city of Cienfuegos) develops cheap energy for industrial production, it is unlikely that Havana's geographic pattern of industrial production will change anytime in the near future (Rohter 1996). A strong residential and service-sector characterize the Cuban capital.

On June 3, 1996, the State Council (*Consejo de Estado*) passed Law Decree 165 which will establish new duty-free zones and industrial parks in the capital, the ports of Cienfuegos and Mariel, and possibly Santiago de Cuba. These duty-free zones consist of territory in Cuba that will not have a resident population. The law will allow duty-free imports and exports to flow through these enclaves. Industrial, business, agricultural, technological, and service activities will be carried out there. In Havana, land next to José Martí International Airport in Rancho Boyeros will be the site of a new duty-free and industrial park (InterPress, *Zonas francas* 1996b).

### Socialist collapse and capitalist promise?

The tenacity of the *habanero* in the face of the city's economic free-fall reveals itself at several levels. Their ability to overcome food shortages, power outages, public transportation problems and other obstacles is evident on each city block. Everyone is trying to survive: bureaucrats, lower-rank party leaders (*dirigentes*), school children, retirees, college professors, manual laborers, and bus drivers. In the daily parlance of the *habanero*, this means *resolviendo* or *solucionando* (problem solving or 'making ends meet'), even if it implies breaking the law. Before July 26, 1993, possession of the dollar was illegal for all Cubans except diplomats. As well, some forms of self-employment existed since 1977. However, the number and types of work have changed. For example, in the 1970s, most men had to be 'disabled' (e.g., get a medical certificate stating they could not hold down their regular jobs) to work in the private sector. 'Moonlighting' had also been permitted in the evenings or on weekends. For the most part though, the private sector was very small before the Special Period.

Even before the 1993 market reforms, many Cubans had stashed away dollars for use on the black market. So desperate was the government for dollars or other convertible hard currencies, that Fidel Castro announced

**Table 7.2** Actions to rehabilitate Cuba's internal finances (1996)

- Graduated hard currency personal income tax
- Graduated local currency personal income tax
- Vessel or property ownership tax
- Tax on earnings from businesses associated with passenger and cargo transportation
- Income taxes for vendors in agricultural markets

in his now famous July 26, 1993 speech the possibility of opening checking accounts in dollars. At the same time, more than 150 types of occupations were operating outside state control by mid-1996, and most can charge in dollars after securing the proper license and remitting the appropriate taxes (Lee 1996a). By August 1996 several taxes had been implemented to rehabilitate Cuba's internal finances (Table 7.2).

Restructuring the economy has brought about deep changes in socialist Cuba. What had been illegal, relatively small, and clandestine until 1993 was suddenly legal and overt. Attendance at work and schools has fallen off from levels of the mid-1980s, although no reliable data exist to assess its magnitude. Street hustlers and money launders (*jineteros*) and prostitutes who work the tourists increased notably. Prior to the Special Period, Cubans approaching tourists for a pen, chewing gum, or a coin would be scolded by passerbys or, worse yet, detained by police if they persisted. State-run stores offered basic wares to the masses, even if they were low-quality products from Czechoslovakia, China, Vietnam, or North Korea. This new 'economic liberty' carries externalities (e.g., non-economic costs) in the forms of delinquency and street crime (cf. Klak 1994), although it pales to the kinds of problems found in US cities, or the rise of organized crime derived from the thawing of communism in Moscow. Havana was heralded during the first decades of the Revolution as being one of the safest cities in the Americas, even by harsh critics of the regime (Mesa-Lago 1994, p. 12). Petty theft and assaults are no longer isolated, random events in Havana. Today, the state-run shops for Cubans are barren and the streets of the city – with their poverty, prostitution, shabby buildings, and begging – increasingly resemble other Latin American cities.

Black market activities proliferate and it is difficult to obtain soap, toothpaste, shoes, spare electrical or automotive parts, extra coffee, or fresh meat and poultry without investing time in going from market to market, house to house, or contact to contact. Almost every household has someone who devotes time checking out black market activity and the new state-sanctioned markets springing up around the city. Figure 7.5 shows the gap in purchasing power between skilled and unskilled labor-

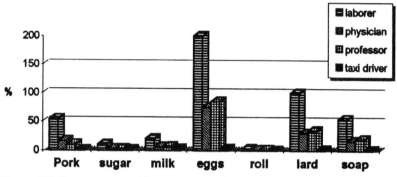

**Figure 7.5** Percentage monthly wages required to purchase black market items, Havana (July 1994)

ers in 1994, and between those who had access to a dollar economy and those who did not. Taxi drivers earning dollar wages had to spend little of their monthly wages on basic foods, lard, cooking oil, or soap. A physician and manual laborer, for example, would spend 16% and 100%, respectively, of their monthly wages for a unit of lard, while a taxi driver would spend about 1%. Although the disparity in purchasing power had narrowed by 1997 because of a drop in the exchange rate between the dollar, the peso and the opening of agricultural markets (Rosenberg 1992), purchasing power remains uneven among *habaneros*.

*Habaneros* are employing new ways of subsistence that fall outside the state's 30-odd year practice of central planning. In the section that follows we examine the food industry as a window to Havana's changing economic base.

## On the new economic geography of Havana's food and *paladar* markets

The nation's economic bind brought on by the Special Period has placed 'food' at the head of the list of Cuban household needs, replacing the long-standing concern over housing (Hamberg 1994). Despite some free-market tinkering with private food markets between 1980 and 1986 (Rosenberg 1986), the Cuban government scuttled market-regulated mechanisms for distributing, selling and preparing food. In 1995, though, numerous food-preparation occupations and restaurants were legalized.

This section examines one segment of the new food market – home restaurants called *paladares*[3] – in an attempt to understand better the emerging market economy in Havana within the context of prevailing research on informal and petty commerce. Divided into four subsections,

it first describes the legal context and brief history of these growing private, neighborhood eateries in Cuba. The second subsection considers the
relationship between food prices on the black market, and the effect
imposed by the recently sanctioned state agricultural markets. We then
turn to some theoretical, ethical and personal observations about the win-
ners and losers in this enterprise. Finally, we conclude with some new
observations about Havana's emerging economic geography and the role
of the *paladares* in Cuba's transition to a new post-socialist economy.

## *Paladares*: the legal framework and problems with state food provision

The state rationing system has been in effect in Cuba since 1961. Over
time, the kinds of goods available have changed, depending on Cuba's
main trading partners and prevailing economic conditions. At present,
most staple food products are covered by the rationing system. Rationing
is documented by the booklet, the *libreta*. Each Cuban household receives
one for buying highly subsidized products at state-owned food stores
(*bodegas*). By law it must be turned in or modified: (i) within 10 days of the
death of a household member; (ii) hospitalization; (iii) old-age institutionalization; (iv) incarceration; or (v) leaving the country.

The *libreta* lists the age composition of the household by the cohorts
< 2, 2–6, 7–13, 14–64, and 65 years and older. Non-food items are sup-
posed to include fuel (kerosene, pre-heated kerosene, liquid gas, charcoal,
firewood), laundry soap, body soap, cigarettes, rum and beer. *Bodegas*
post prices on a chalkboard, along with the period in which the price is
valid, and note whether or not the product is available.

In June 1995 we documented prices at a half dozen *bodegas* in the
municipalities of Plaza de la Revolución, Centro Habana, and Habana
Vieja in the City of Havana. Our aim was to determine which products
had been available most of the time during that calendar year (Table 7.3).
As can be seen, most items were generally unavailable, and the latter were
not products of conspicuous consumption. Naturally, most were allocated
by temporal dimensions and strictly controlled portions because it is a
ration system. For example, each *libreta* allocates 5 lbs of rice and just
under 2 lbs of beans per person monthly (Table 7.3).

---

[3]The term *paladar* literally means 'palate' but comes from a Brazilian soap opera that played
in Cuba in the early 1990s. In this *telenovela*, the protagonist migrates to Rio de Janeiro and
sells sandwiches on the beach. So successful is the venture that she returns to her humble
residence and establishes a restaurant out of her home. Not only is this term used widely
among Cubans, but the actual license granted by Cuban authorities to operate a home-based
diner is called, *Licencia de Paladar*.

**Table 7.3** Products available monthly at selected state-run food stores (*bodegas*) in three municipalities, Havana (1995)

| (A)<br>Generally available | (B)<br>Price of (A) | (C)<br>Generally unavailable |
|---|---|---|
| Rice | 0.24 per lb | Vegetable oil |
| Black beans (*frijoles negros*) | 0.30 per lb | Lard |
| Sugar | 0.14 per lb | Canned tomatoes |
| Baby food (*compota*) | 0.25 per can | Body soap |
| Coffee | 0.12 per two oz | Laundry detergent |
| Cigarettes (strong and mild) | 2/6 pesos pack | Toothpaste |
| Split peas (*chícharos*) | 0.11 per lb | Vinegar |
| Rum | 20 pesos/750 ml | Meat and poultry |

*Data source*: Authors' field notes.

**Table 7.4** Monthly food allocation by household, according to the Cuban *libreta*, selected items (1995)

| Item | Monthly allocation |
|---|---|
| Rice | 5 lbs |
| Black beans | 20 oz |
| Sugar (white) | 3 lbs |
| Sugar (brown) | 3 lbs |
| Chicken | 3 oz |
| Fish (various) | one (6–9 oz) |
| Soy meal (*picadillo de soya*, a chopped meat substitute) | varies |
| Salt | 8 oz |

*Source*: Authors' field notes.

In brief, although the state system of food allocation is heavily subsidized and affordable even for households earning between 120–200 pesos monthly, it lacks variety and regularity (Lee 1996b). This pumps up demand for alternative food sources.

### The rise, fall and then resurrection of the *paladar*

Fidel Castro announced the expansion of private-sector jobs on the 40th anniversary of the attack against the Moncada Barracks. This date, July 26, 1993, marked the first of a series of market liberalizations which, among other reforms, sanctioned the dollar's circulation, and proposed setting up savings and checking accounts in dollars. *Paladares*, part of the self-employed private sector related to food preparation, were also granted legal space to operate and their legal operators now form part of a larger private job sector. In May 1996 it was estimated that there are about 200 000 self-employed workers in Cuba, of which Havana houses the largest number (*CubaNews*, New rules taxes hit self-employed workers, 1996).

However, the first round of *paladares* was short lived. In February 1994, police raided more than 100 *paladares* in the Havana metropolitan area. Allegedly, police raided only certain *paladares* that were operating illegally. These establishments were accused of illicit enrichment. Our interviews with more than a dozen *paladar* operators reveal that most of them had legal permits to operate. They claimed that the police harassed them and then confiscated their wares. The indirect message to the people, according to some restaurateurs, was that many operators were making too much money too fast. Indeed, ostentatious behavior and other conduct deemed to suggest conspicuous consumption is frowned upon (R. Castro 1996). In January, 1996, the National Revolutionary Police assigned 608 new agents trained in criminology, public safety, and other anticrime techniques. Other than breaking up stolen-property rings and handling traffic-related crimes, these new agents will investigate 'influence-peddling' (*CubaNews*, New Police in Havana, February 1996).

Because *paladares* were neighborhood-based operations, the word got out to *habaneros* that conspicuous profiteering among the new entrepreneurial class would not be tolerated by the Cuban state. In May 1994 the penal code was amended to ease the prosecution of 'profiteers', thereby giving the government *ex post facto* powers to confiscate assets and apply sanctions (Pérez-López 1995, p. 27). Those same *paladar* operators stated that they were back in business anywhere from three days to three weeks later.

Minister of Finance Manuel Millares Rodríguez and Minister of Labor and Social Security Salvador Valdés Mesa issued Resolution No. 4/95 on June 8, 1995 which once again 'legalized' *paladares* (*Resolución conjunta . . .* 1995). In doing so, it eliminated the following self-employed occupations: producer of snacks, processor of dairy products, maker of conserves that originated on a farm, and cook. The new law identified the tax payments each self-employed profession in the food-preparation business would make according to the size of the operation and whether or not alcohol was served (Table 7.5). Most of these self-employed occupations pay a flat monthly rate (*cuota fija mensual mínima*). This flat charge is contentious because it requires a market forecast by the entrepreneur to determine whether she or he will in fact generate sufficient revenue to cover the monthly tax. Instead, all *paladar* owners with whom we have spoken would prefer to pay a sales tax that is based on actual sales. Those who charge in dollars must remit monthly quotas to the government in that same currency.

**Table 7.5** Minimum payment criteria for self-employed restaurant owners (*paladares*) as stipulated by Resolution No. 4/95

| Occupation | 1994 minimum monthly quota in pesos | 1996 minimum monthly quota in pesos | 1994 minimum monthly quota in dollars[a] | 1996 minimum monthly quota in dollars[a] |
|---|---|---|---|---|
| (a) Preparer-seller of food products and non-alcoholic drinks at retail level (outside residence) | 100 pesos | 200 pesos | | not applicable |
| (b) Preparer-seller of food products and non-alcoholic drinks (inside residence) | 100 pesos | 200 pesos | 100 US dollars | 200 US dollars |
| (c) Preparer-seller of food products and non-alcoholic beverages through dining services | 400 pesos | 800 pesos | 300 US dollars | 400 US dollars |
| (d) Preparer-seller of food products and alcoholic beverages through dining services | 500 pesos | 1000 pesos | 400 US dollars | 600 US dollars |

[a]The official listing states '*Cuota mínima en moneda libremente convertible cuando proceda su aplicación*' which, for all purposes, is the US dollar.
*Data sources*: modified after '*Resolución conjunta No. 4/95*,' *Granma*, June 14, 1995, p. 2.
*Nuevas disposiciones para el trabajo por cuenta propia. Tribuna de La Habana*, May 5, 1996, p. 1.
See Napoles (1996b) and Lee (1996b).

Our fieldwork shows that most *paladares* cater largely to Cubans, and charge mainly in Cuban pesos. No one we interviewed could identify a *paladar* operator who paid the dollar license fee; although an occasional tourist paying in dollars was always welcome, such revenue would not be reported to government officials. To put these monthly fees in perspective using the purchasing power of an average salary, let us suppose a worker was earning 180 pesos monthly prior to the 1996 tax hikes. The lowest monthly quota required workers to put forth 55% of their monthly pay-check, merely to sell food and drink at the retail level. Most *paladares* fall under category (c) in Table 7.5, 'Preparer-seller of food products and non-alcoholic beverages through dining services'. In that case, they had to place more than 200% of an average monthly wage 'up front,' to operate their family restaurant. The dollar-run *paladar* faced even stiffer start-up costs. If a prospective owner who earns 180 pesos monthly at a current state job wished to secure a $400 license, it would require 4 years of wages (assuming dollars are bought on the black market at 22 pesos per dollar of January 1997). Such an investment, though, would just cover the first month's business tax. To be sure, overtly dollar-run *paladares* need to have direct access to start-up capital in order to operate legally. Most likely, that hard currency comes from overseas remittances by family members.

Other parameters in Resolution No. 4/95 shape the nature of the *paladar* operation. For example, no more than 12 place-settings can exist in any given restaurant. Permanent residents of Cuba can also enter the trade. However, only family labor can be employed and it is illegal to hire by wage or salary non-family members. The kitchen, serving area, and private residences of each *paladar* must pass a sanitation inspection by the local Ministry of Public Health. Once the health inspection is approved and the license is secured, each restaurateur must sign up at the Central Business Register (*Registro Central Comercial*) administered by the Ministry of Internal Commerce. Those preparing food for retail sale are expected to sell their goods at cultural or recreational events, and only in public spaces designated for retail sale. All food providers – regardless of the currency they use or whether they dispense alcoholic beverages – must get their inputs at dollar-run state stores (*diplotiendas*), agricultural markets (*mercados agropecuarios*), or through their own livestock and private gardens. However, 'in all cases [operators] are required to justify to the appropriate authorities the origin of the products used in their enterprise' (Article 7, *Resolución* No. 4/95, our translation). Our sources claim that this is the legal loophole to close down any operator as only dollar stores give receipts for purchases on a regular basis.

*Paladar* owners face other restrictions as well. They are forbidden to sell horse meat, beef, and shellfish (especially lobsters) even though beef and shellfish are easily found. Owners claim that restrictions on horse meat concern problems of hygiene, aesthetics and the likelihood of increasing horse thievery in the countryside. Illegal slaughter of livestock by owners and poachers threatens to decimate livestock. As a result, the state targets beef production for tourism and those who are on special medical diets (sanctioned by physician-approved notations made in the *libreta*). Cuba's yield of beef per head of cattle has deteriorated from 40 to 30 kg between the mid-1970s and 1988; the last date of available data (Figueras 1994, p. 69). Lastly, only milk purchased in dollar stores may be sold, and no food bought from state-run food stores (*bodegas*) or other restaurants[4] may be resold in *paladares*.

---

[4]Restaurants accepting pesos and catering only to Cubans have always existed in Revolutionary Cuba, though they were less common in the early 1990s than they are today. A whole host of small pizza and sandwich kiosks have sprung up in Havana during the past year. However, they require hard currency and are owned by larger joint-venture tourist companies. See Dávalos Fernández (1993) on joint ventures.

## The role of *mercados agropecuarios*, the black market, and their influence on inputs in *paladares*

In the mid-1980s, before the present liberalization of the agricultural and food markets, Cuba had tinkered with private farmer's markets. However, like the *paladares* at the outset, these markets were closed because it was believed that middle-men were acquiring too much wealth, too quickly. Thus, until late 1994, farmers' produce had to be secured through tightly controlled state outlets (Alvarez and Puerta 1994). As of March 1995, there were approximately 1479 agricultural cooperative units in Cuba, of which 486 (one-third) reported a profit (*CubaNews*, 'Facts and Stats', 1995). These cooperatives are permitted to sell their goods to the new *mercados agropecuarios*, although it is likely that two-thirds of those noted above are not making their state quotas (*acopio*) – a prerequisite for selling goods in the private market. For a variety of reasons, therefore, most cooperatives provide few inputs to Havana's legal food markets. *Paladar* operators and other citizens who are unable or unwilling to seek fruits, meat and poultry, and vegetables through that outlet have no recourse but to turn to the black market.

Figure 7.5 shows the purchasing power required to purchase selected commodities that prevailed in mid-1994 when *paladares* were illegal and *mercados agropecuarios* did not exist. We present four income scenarios: manual worker, professor, physician, and taxi driver. Significantly, all workers except the taxi driver are paid in pesos.

The figure reveals considerable variation in purchasing power. Perhaps the most controversial aspect for Cubans and foreign analysts is that the Special Period has placed material incentives on a par with the traditional moral incentives that had been an important motivational factor in the Revolution (Bengelsdorf 1985; Fuller 1985; Zimbalist 1989). A taxi driver, or any other Cuban formally or informally affiliated with the tourist trade (e.g., *jinetera*), has access to a wide array of basic foods and household products because they are either paid in dollars (taxi drivers) or have access to dollars through tourists (*jineteras*). A physician or college professor would have to sacrifice much to buy those items. For example, while a taxi driver would only have to spend about 1% of her/his wage on a pound of pork, a worker would forgo nearly half a month's wage for the same item.

Here lies a deep contradiction in the new market reforms, and one for which Cuban authorities have few facile replies which, in part, reflects the complexity of the matter. Put differently, the Cuban government has commodified basic foods and household staples in a way that is not only unprecedented in the 37 years of the Revolution, but anathema to a social system based on common ownership of the means of production (Forbes and Thrift 1987; Callinicos 1991). The rising of inequality has been acknowledged by Cuban leaders as a major problem stemming mainly from the Special Period.

Recall, however, that the above black market items prevailed before *mercado agropecuarios* were legalized four months later. As a result of this new source of food sales, black-market prices have plummeted. In fact, in June 1995 we were unable to gather any consistent pricing on most of the items shown in Figure 7.5. The only items not regularly sold in the new state markets are soap, milk, and bread products. In brief, the legalization of the *agros* has lowered black-market prices. However, this statement assumes nothing about the general population's ability to acquire these goods. Both the decriminalization of dollars and the legalization of many black-market activities allows the Cuban government to resolve its foreign exchange problems (Pastor and Zimbalist 1995, p. 709).

## Havana's booming food market. Feast or famine?

The *paladar* market is one of several coping strategies employed by *habaneros* during the Special Period. In the daily vernacular of Cubans, people are just *resolviendo* their daily problems. *Paladares* still serve mainly those Cubans who have disposable income, and it is difficult to quantify what proportion of the total population has significant amounts of disposable income. Among their greatest attributes is that they help some consumers who may lack their own fuel, enable those in one part of town to walk a few blocks during a power outage to secure food in a district where the power is on, and they satisfy household needs of the owners.

State-directed efforts in opening up Cuba's economy focus overwhelmingly on large-scale joint ventures. Is this myopic on the part of the government? If the approach employed by Cuba during the Special Period aims to move Cuba closer to socialism and to decentralize production that is guided by macropolicy guidelines, then the *paladares* or similar Cuban-owned small ventures have a natural market niche. One possible context that could scale back state regulation and tap into local resources, has to do with marketing local 'mom & pop' bed-and-breakfasts (B&Bs) to tourists seeking modest accommodations in Havana. On the one hand, one part of the international tourist market would gladly avoid the generic, beach-front, steel-and-glass complexes, so ubiquitous in the Caribbean. On the other, local, urban and suburban B&Bs could keep capital closer to the producers, and employ local residents. The problem from the state's perspective, however, is that capital might slip through the hands of state coffers, or that 'illicit enrichment' might result. As Mesa-Lago (1994) has pointed out, the state has a penchant for either trying to micromanage these new market reforms, or approach these market reforms with considerable timidity.

Carefully managed locally based tourist services could prove to be a source of revenue for Havana's municipal governments; a major policy goal elsewhere in Latin America (Scarpaci and Irarrázaval 1994). Decentralizing economic decision-making in Havana does, at least for Communist Party hard-liners, run the risk of the liberalization of political life and creating a new space for civil society (Pastor and Zimbalist 1995, p. 715). That possibility notwithstanding, Coyula (1991b, p. 49) documents the advantages of bringing production and consumption issues back to the *barrio*, arguing that the 'neighborhood [is] an identifiable, manageable territory whose social, cultural, and productive power has not been exploited.' Foreigners are already visiting the Afro-Cuban neighborhoods such as the back-bay district of Atarés where *santería* services are performed, and back-alley *rumba* parties take place with foreigners and the locals. While the setting is a contrived intercultural experience, there is no doubt that a segment of the tourist market seeks those experiences. Well-connected *paladares* could tap into this tourist market and, perhaps, begin in a small way to narrow the gap between state and civil society.

Is the *paladar* market a feast or famine? There are a series of advantages and disadvantages for *paladar* operators, and they in turn hinge on whether or not the restaurants operate illegally (Table 7.6). Circumstances will vary given the attributes of each entrepreneur. Thus far its multiplier effects are small, constrained in part by the inability of owners to seek out legal wholesalers, to hire staff, or to expand beyond the 12-seat maximum stipulated by law. Advertising is largely by word of mouth although some *paladares* near town squares in Habana Vieja and near the tourist district of Vedado do advertise (*CubaNews*, 'Paladares legalized', July 1995). In fact, one *paladar* in Vedado has prospered simply because it was discussed on a Radio Martí broadcast emanating from the United States. Foreign journalists and tourists now frequent the establishment because of that broadcast. Most *paladares* are not so lucky, and advertising is severely constrained.

Another constraint in expanding Havana's food and restaurant markets is the US trade embargo against Cuba. Politics aside, there is strong evidence that the US food and agricultural exporters would benefit from opening up trade with Cuba. For example, lobbyists at the United States National Pork Producers Council say Cuba would quickly become part of the top 10 export markets for US pork producers (Luxner 1995). Passage of the Cuban Embargo Bill (S. 381 and H.R. 927, AKA Helms-Burton) made such an export market – not to mention a lower-cost input source for small business people – a moot point. In the meantime, *paladares* will continue to provide meaningful employment and independence while also addressing Havana's number one social and economic problem: food.

## The nature of work in today's Havana

The transition to socialism has perennially been plagued by several structural impediments. Marx gave neither a blueprint for socialism nor a description of socialist society when he theorized about how capitalist conditions would engender a transition to socialism. Sandinista Nicaragua showed clearly that the Revolution took hold differently in the Sierra than on the coast (Vilas 1989; Wall 1990). Contemporary Vietnam – with a population six times larger than Cuba's – is aiming to position itself in the global market without abandoning some of its socialist principles. Other lessons about Third World transitions to socialism since post-Second World War are insightful in understanding Havana's economy, and Cuba's present crisis.

First, autarky is not a development option for peripheral Third World economies, especially small socialist ones (Fitzgerald 1986; Stallings 1986). How to combine growth and distribution in such a social transformation (economics) and how to establish representative forms and viable participation (politics) remain perennial questions (Fagen 1986). The recent experiences of Vietnam and China suggest that the inclusion of an important capitalist sector in a mixed economy, whereby the state controls surplus and decisions about accumulation, may be one way the transition

**Table 7.6** Benefits and detriments of the illegality of *paladares*

*Benefits*
Avoiding licensing fees and bureaucratic snares (health inspections)
Less corruption payments to public officials
Evading labor laws
Evading taxes

*Detriments*
Fear of fine and incarceration (social deviant, counter-revolutionary or dangerousness [*peligrosidad*] charges)
Police shakedowns and confiscation of food, beverages and wares (tables, chairs, cassettes, televisions, stereos, etc.)
Inability to advertise widely

to socialism can be accomplished. At the very least, socialist economies would originally guarantee close to full employment, regardless of the fluctuations of the global market. As Fagen (1986, p. 257) noted before the collapse of Soviet aid and trade:

> The more fully the money economy has permeated the society, the more politically unacceptable even a relatively low level of unemployment becomes. This is why policies of (sometimes artificially constructed) full employment make so much sense at the outset of the transition, even though they may violate economic rationality . . . the Cuban revolution is instructive: for more than a decade there was . . . no significant unemployment in Cuba . . . [A]t the outset Cubans (wisely) decided that the political and social costs of open unemployment were greater than the economic costs of full employment.

As noted above, unemployment in early 1996 was officially 7%, but could be much higher.

Second, small internal and regional cooperation markets for most socialist nations (Sandinista Nicaragua, 1979–1989; Cuba; Grenada under Maurice Bishop's New Jewel Movement, 1979–1983; and Chile under the administration of Dr. Salvador Allende, 1970–1973) may prove to be insurmountable obstacles to the transition to socialism (Wall 1990). Cuba aims to replace its former CMEA partners with reorganized Caricom nations. It is among 25 sovereign nations and 15 colonies slated for membership in the Association of Caribbean States (Whitefield 1994).

Third, state-ownership alone cannot define a socialist production model. Centralized planning politicizes the economy. It constrains market signals in the form of prices and seeks to keep producers from being motivated only by self-interest (Brundenius and Zimbalist 1989, p. 141). Deep changes must also take place in the labor process – bringing in worker participation – and in mass participation in forging state policy. However, the Cuban state labor force is targeted for downsizing. In 1996, there were 4.6 million Cubans working in the government, cooperative and private sectors, and about 600 000 to 800 000 of them collect a full salary even while working half-time or less. Pedro Ross, Secretary General of the Cuban Workers' Union (CTC) estimated that in 1995, 60% of the 'surplus' workers let go from the public sector shifted to other jobs, 20% are working in temporary positions, and the balance are collecting 60% of their salary at home. This translates into an official unemployment rate of about 7% (Acosta 1996). The new 'rationalization plan' aims to slash inefficient, state-run industries. Carlos Lage, a major economic decision maker, plans on cutting about one-fifth of all state workers (*The Economist*, 1996). The implications these layoffs portend for Cuba's social relations of production are unclear.

A perennial debate among development scholars and economists is the weight given to 'getting prices right' (Brundenius and Zimbalist 1989; Chowdhury and Kirkpatrick 1994; Pérez-López 1994a; Mesa-Lago 1994). The debate takes different disguises: monetarism versus structuralism; liberalism versus Friedmanism; orthodoxy versus heterodoxy; national-ization versus private enterprise; and so on. Cuba's apparent transition from socialism to points beyond shares many of the structural problems of import-substitution industrialization (ISI) in Latin America from the 1950s through the 1980s. Under ISI, political pressures and union demands led to the extension of tariffs on imported goods from overseas and protectionist laws that stifled competition, innovation and worker productivity (Cardoso and Faletto 1979; Nochteff 1984; Gwynne 1986; Jenkins 1987; Kay 1994). By extension, Cuban dependency on Soviet aid may have led to the kinds of structural problems facing countries that operated under ISI (Mesa-Lago 1988).

On a more practical level, the use of taxation is important and contro-versial in Havana (Table 7. 7). In early 1996, taxes in pesos increased in 144 of 162 private jobs. Some taxes rose more than 100% and even more in 1996. Time will tell if these increases will deter private work in Havana because taxes are too high. To be sure, revenues are needed to run the city's public service and sustain the socialist model.

Cuba's transition to a post-socialist economy not only imposes the sem-blance of market mechanisms and pricing in Havana, but it has led to a drop in morale among workers. No longer do the moral incentives for worker productivity seem as relevant as they once were, and perhaps were more closely tied to material rewards than previously thought. Gone are the halcyon days when altruism, abnegation, sacrifice and discipline produced a 'revolutionary conscientiousness', and when 'critical think-

**Table 7.7** Fixed monthly fees (taxes) for selected private jobs (in pesos)

| Job | Before 2-1-96 | After 2-1-96 |
|---|---|---|
| Hired chauffeur | 100 | 400 |
| Tire tube repairer | 60 | 100 |
| Bicycle and motorcycle parking attendant | 50 | 100 |
| Manicurist | 60 | 100 |
| Hair stylist | 90 | 200 |
| Shoemaker | 45 | 300 |
| Photographer | 100 | 200 |
| Auto body repairer | 45 | 500 |
| Carpenter | 70 | 200 |

Source: Nuevas dispoisiones para el trabajo por cuenta propia. *Tribuna de la Habana*, May 5, 1996, p. 2.

ing' was discouraged (Medin 1990; Fuller 1985; Bengelsdorf 1985). Workers pose an even more basic question: Why go to work at all?

Five fundamental disruptures confront the *habanero* worker.

1. A lack of inputs in the production process. This ranges from books and paper in the office, to raw materials in the factory.
2. Extra hours are needed daily to acquire basic food supplies for the household. Work carries an opportunity cost previously irrelevant in the socialist workplace.
3. Public transportation has been decimated, and the physical cost of cycling takes a toll on worker productivity.
4. The socialist workplace traditionally provides lunch for all workers. But now the lunch meal does not always come. Missing the mid-day meal leads to worker slowdowns, and those who walk and bicycle often leave for home at about 1.30 or 2 p.m. and do not return to work in the afternoon.
5. The Revolution has now stated officially and categorically that it is acceptable to purchase what were formerly labeled 'non-essential consumer goods.' In the best of days, pesos purchased little beyond the mere essentials of needs.

New economic liberties in Cuba brought changes in civil behavior. When a disturbance threatened on Havana's seaside promenade – the Malecón – in August 1994, Fidel Castro entered a crowd 20 000 strong to defuse the setting. The immediate cause of the civil disorder was in response to the prolonged power outages during the summer of 1994. However, it is unclear to what extent it was a reaction to the scarcity of material goods, political repression, human rights abuses, and a loss of civil liberties. It is equally uncertain the ramifications this event could have if the rapid response brigades (*brigadas de respuesta rápida*) had not snuffed it out. Both the public gathering and rise in the black market underscore the power of human agency in questioning and even transforming dogma about how socialism and capitalism are supposed to coexist in Havana. The 1994 demonstration, the first in 35 years of the Revolution, shares a broad parallel with the IMF (i.e., structural adjustment) riots reported by Walton (1987) in other Third World countries. It may have marked the beginning of vocal opposition against the status quo despite the threat of state retaliation. Four consequences of this protest might be expected.

1. A renewed commitment to the Special Period in which rationing is applied more rigorously and police intolerance for civil 'unrest'

increases.
2. Prodding the government sufficiently so that it increases public welfare and creates a more modest political space for limited dissent.
3. Inflation-correcting wage increases for Cubans earning pesos to assuage some of the economic pain.
4. Concessions and new loans from sympathetic nations such as Mexico, Vietnam, Canada, Spain and a handful of western European nations.

### Havana: ¿Adónde va?

Since 1993 a host of private-sector self-employed ventures have proliferated in Havana and elsewhere, albeit with erratic 'stops' and 'gos', as the Cuban government defines and re-defines what can only be described as a new type of *criollo* Keynesian economics. To some Cuban analysts, there is a way out Cuba's quagmire, and its formula sounds much like those drawn from neoclassical economics. One envisions the following:

> a new economic structure [that is] less dependent on a single product, with very active international tourism; hundreds of joint-venture firms and associations and dozens of manufactured goods and agricultural products being exported; this could be Cuba's outlook at the end of the century (Figueras 1994, p. 181; our translation).

While few observers inside and outside Cuba would dispute the value of such a prospect, the economic and policy constraints placed on the simplest of enterprises begs the question about whether such a prospect for the year 2000 is realistic. An increase in government regulation to equalize income distribution may dampen all self-employed enterprises (Alonso 1995; Locay 1995). As Pastor and Zimbalist (1995, p. 705) note, 'the recent spate of halfhearted measures . . . has likely worsened distributional inequities, distorted incentives, and failed to improve the macroeconomy.'

### Work and economy on the eve of the twenty-first century

Distortions in Havana's economy stifle the kinds of multiplier effects we might envision in a less restrictive setting. Taxes, stop-and-go signals about illicit enrichment, and little experience with the private sector constrain the fledgling new market economy. At the national level, Cuba lacks what the Chilean business community calls *transparencia*: clarity about norms, regulation and information that is not controlled by cumbersome laws. Like de Soto's (1989) description of pre-Fujimori Peru, state regulations may hinder more than help Cuba's fledgling cottage industries. Nonetheless, newly expanding private jobs are slated to absorb workers being let go from the public sector.

The template of the city's industrial and manufacturing activities has changed little since the 1950s. Service industries, especially government work and tourism, will likely characterize the nature of work in the Cuban capital well into the twenty-first century. While it is perhaps not surprising that the defining features of a market economy have not yet taken hold, future research should monitor the evolution of the changing nature of work of Havana. For the near future, at least, the nature of work in Havana will continue to reflect the shocks brought about by Cuba's reinsertion into the market. Indeed, the most difficult part of the Special Period may be over.

# 8

## The value of social functions

In this country, all amateurs seek to become professional artists. That is the truth. In addition, everyone wants to become a college graduate. We were forced to impose restrictions on this. Everybody wants to be an intellectual in this country. This is a vice created by the Revolution itself, by the universities.

Fidel Castro, speaking before the Confederation of Cuban Workers, April 30, 1996

### The value of social functions

A variety of measures assess social welfare and the quality of life. With the incorporation of new variables in the index for human development elaborated by the United Nations Development Program (UNPD), Cuba increased its international position in 1995 by ranking 72nd among 174 countries, and classifying among those nations with a 'median level' of human development (EFE 1995). Three fundamental variables produced that index: life expectancy, educational attainment, and gross national product. With a life expectancy of 75.3 years in 1992, Cuba had surpassed even countries considered to have a high index of human development in Latin America (e.g., Argentina, Chile, and Uruguay). Cuba was placed among the 30 most advanced nations in the world in this regard, with the index of 0.84 over a base of 1.0. The literacy rate for adults was 94.9% and a school enrollment rate for people under 24 was 65%. Its real gross domestic product (GDP) per capita was $3412 in 1992, less than Belize ($5619) or Panama ($5164) but more than Peru. Argentina leads Latin America with $8860, which is still quite low compared with the $23 760 figure for the United States (EFE 1995; United Nations 1995a).

The daily per capita consumption of calories in Cuba was 2824 in 1992, making it somewhat less than the base established by the United Nations (2833 calories), but greater than Brazil, Colombia, Panama, Venezuela, Chile, Uruguay, and close to Argentina. Of the 10.8 million Cubans in 1992, 200 000 located in remote rural areas had no access to health care service and a similar number lacked potable water and almost 900 000 had no system for treating human waste. Some 75 000 children less than 5 years of age showed symptoms of malnutrition and 66 000 did not attend schools. On the other hand, infant mortality fell in 1992 from 12 per 1000 live births to 9.7 in 1995, one of the lowest rates in the world, despite the economic hardships brought on by the Special Period. An indicator used by the UNDP study for the first time in 1995 was the Index for the Development of Women. Cuba was placed 47th in this new category, above many other Latin American countries, and it headed the region in income generated by women in the work force at 27.2%. Sweden occupied first place in the world with this indicator at 41.6% (Castro 1995).

Despite this relatively good news about the quality of life in Cuba, some problems – many discussed throughout this book – have recently appeared. A report from the Forensic Medicine Institute of Havana published in March 1995, reported that 2500 Cubans committed suicide in a 1-year period. This incidence of suicide – 225 for each 1 million persons, is twice the US rate (128 per million). Not surprisingly, more young people than old people kill themselves, as do more men than women. Cuba's suicide rate makes it the highest of all countries in the western hemisphere (Aroca 1995). The rapid erosion of the material well-being of the population – brought on by the Special Period – probably plays an important part in explaining this statistic. At the same time, though, it is noteworthy that the accuracy of Cuban statistics is probably greater than other Latin American countries where vital rates registration is not as developed as in Cuba, and Roman Catholic values lead to an under-reporting of suicides.

In this chapter, we examine selected dimensions of the quality of life in Havana. Specifically, we review three facets of services: health, education and leisure. Cuba has staked out a special position in these fields. Few countries in the world have such comprehensive health-care coverage as in Cuba. Before the Revolution, Cuba clearly boasted relatively high levels of life expectancy and literacy, and Havana held world-class tourist attractions. These benefits, though, were not equally enjoyed by all Cubans. Significant gains in life expectancy and literacy have been achieved since 1959.

Divided into five main parts, the chapter begins with a review of the distribution of social functions in Havana. Then we present a brief summary of Cuba's health-care system. Data on the location and utilization of Havana's clinics and hospitals are presented next, followed by a discussion of the city's health-care resources. In the third section we turn to Cuba's and Havana's educational profiles. Special attention is given to the state's policy of building up education services outside the capital city. The fourth section discusses the many venues of tourism in Havana: international, national, health-care, and ecotourism. A final section examines Havana for *habaneros*. We identify Havana's natural and cultural resources that afford its residents with recreational outlets for their leisurely pursuits. Sports in the Revolution is also a key process in the socialization process, and Havana holds a good share of the nation's finer sports facilities.

We begin with an overview of the geographic distribution of selected social functions that characterize Havana.

## The dispersal of social functions

One of the most significant aspects of Havana in the revolutionary era is the emphasis placed on social versus individual concerns. Highly centralized planning determines the location of schools, hospitals, sports complexes, industries and housing. For reasons we have put forth throughout this book, the built environment has been practically unaltered throughout four decades, except for demolitions brought on by natural causes or structural reasons. Despite the prevalence of what has come to be known as the 'myth of the new' (Segre 1994d), most new construction – in the form of gigantic complexes of public housing – has been built outside the traditional fabric in semi-rural and previously unoccupied areas beyond the old city edge.

On the one hand, this pattern of siting public housing at the periphery is typical of the previous 'modernization' plans for Havana.

The plan of Martínez Inclán, the design of Forestier, and the ambitious project of Sert envisioned an expanded city developed around the bay, straddled by equal areas to the east and west (see Chapters 2 and 4). On the other hand, there is a rupture between the 'capitalist' and 'socialist' image of the city. In the capitalist realm, planners prioritized the functional spaces of the bourgeoisie, thereby ignoring the 'gray' areas of the proletariat. In the socialist phase, the operative paradigm sought to dissolve the economic and cultural differences among social groups. Just as Marx and Engels dreamed about joining town and country, Havana would form a seamless urban fabric. Accordingly, it was not by chance that in 1976 the territorial limits of the Province of the City of Havana expanded to include half rural and half urban areas (see Figure 5.1, Jurisdictional Reorganization of Cuban Provinces, 1959 & 1976).

A descriptive summary of the city's education, health, and other services is summarized in Table 8.1. Although the data are from 1989, it provides some insight into the kinds of services that prevailed until the Special Period. Some changes would be evident in the late 1990s if the data were available. For instance, the number of movie theaters and bus routes has diminished (Scarpaci and Hall 1995). In contrast, the number of health clinics has increased from 74 to 79 while the expanse of green areas has remained constant.

One telling trait of Havana is the absence of new symbolic and monumental functions that blight the landscapes of both capitalist and socialist cities. For example, the only large office-building complex is the Ministry of Agriculture on Rancho Boyeros avenue. Sprawling supermarkets, shopping centers and malls do not exist and are, instead, replaced by corner *bodegas* and retail centers at new residential complexes. Aggressive 'socialist realist' monuments, so common in other socialist cities, are not part of Havana.[1] (The only exception is a statue of Vladimir Lenin that is tucked away in the remote Lenin Park, south of the city.) Reducing internal consumption practically emptied the department stores in the city center and deterred an increase in retailing for decades. A surge in the dollar economy and the need to supply foreigners and diplomats living in Cuba created 'segregated' stores in Miramar that, for most *habaneros*, are difficult to reach.

Even though the socialist state created a huge apparatus for administration and control, the empty spaces inherited from the Batista era were sufficient to house the Revolutionary government. For instance, the headquarters of the Cuban Communist Party and most high levels of government reside in the former Justice Palace. Another large share of government offices now occupies former private businesses in the traditional city center. In this sense, comparing Havana with Moscow, Beijing, Hanoi or Bucharest reveals the difference in the referential system of socialism. Havana lacks monuments of revolutionary heroes[2] perched on

---

[1]Busts of José Martí are found throughout Havana and the rest of Cuba's towns and cities. However, our discussion focuses on the modern, social realist architecture that prevailed in eastern Europe and the USSR up until 1989.
[2]There are, though, monuments to nineteenth century independence fighters along the Malecón. We refer to the absence of such revolutionary figures from the 1950s as Fidel Castro, Ernesto 'Ché' Guevara, and Camilo Cienfuegos. This contrasts with numerous Revolutionary monuments of heroes found in the cities of Vietnam or North Korea.

**Table 8.1**  Selected data on services in Havana (c. 1989)

| Service | Components | |
|---|---|---|
| Education | Day-care centers | 405 |
| | Primary schools | 510 |
| | Secondary schools | 165 |
| | Pre-university preparatory centers | 15 |
| | Adult education centers | 71 |
| | Vo-tech high schools | 37 |
| | Higher education | 65 departments/ programs, 68 514 students |
| Health | Hospital beds | 25 000 |
| | Medical research institutes | 12 |
| | Policlinics (primary care) | 74 |
| Culture | Movie theaters | 89 |
| | Museums | 43 |
| | Cultural centers | 25 |
| | Libraries | 25 |
| | Theaters | 16 |
| | Bookstores | 53 |
| Open Space | City parks | 4.11 square meters per inhabitant |
| | Neighborhood parks | 0.88 square meters per inhabitant |
| | City sports areas | 0.16 square meters per inhabitant |
| | Neighborhood sports areas | 1.08 square meters per inhabitant |
| | Total green and sports areas | 10.41 square meters per inhabitant |
| Transportation | City buses | 2200 |
| | Number of routes | 164 |
| | Daily bus passengers | 4 500 000 |
| | Automobile ratio | 36 per 1000 |
| | Kilometers of railway | 293 |
| | Kilometers of streets | 3500 |

*Source*: Grupo para el Desarrollo Integral de la Capital. 1990. *Estrategia*. Havana, p 19.

gigantic pedestals, Herculean, white Greek marble temples, and broad boulevards anchored by Versallean palaces.

Political, social, and economic events gradually eroded the barriers that separated parts of Havana well before state-directed construction projects had begun. Between the Bay of Pigs invasion in April 1961 and the Cuban Missile Crisis a year and half later, US tourism disappeared completely from Cuba as did most of the members of the island's wealthy class. Luxury hotels reduced prices to a minimum which allowed the local population to frequent them. Private hospitals and schools were nationalized and opened to the public free of charge, without regard to race or class. Sophisticated clubs located along the beach (see Chapter 3) became workers' social centers, whose management was turned over to union control. Radical changes produced strong social mobilizations throughout Cuba that broke the traditional segregation of social functions that were class-specific.

The La Rampa district in Vedado exemplifies this change. It had been traditionally characterized by exclusive recreational and hotel facilities. After the Revolution, the area was heavily used by mass organizations, student groups, and workers' organizations (see Chapter 3). Reina Mercedes Hospital once stood on the corner of L and 23rd Street in Vedado. It was leveled with the intention of building a commercial building and in the early years of the Revolution, the Association of Tourist Agents held a convention there. In 1967, though, it was turned into a park and ice-cream parlor called Coppelia (Curtis 1993), which we discuss in greater detail below.

A love–hate relationship with the United States characterized part of the Revolutionary Cuban utopia. Despite the long-standing political antagonism between the two countries, more cultural models adopted in Revolutionary Cuba came from the United States than the USSR. A disproportionate significance has been placed on road transportation in Cuba's transportation network even though the island lacks petroleum reserves and has a dense system of rail lines. The latter network, derived from sugar production, could have easily been refurbished to accommodate passenger travel. Only during the Special Period did the government try to switch from freight to passenger rail service. Eager to join Havana with the rest of the country, to shorten distances, and to overcome the squalid conditions of the Central Highway built in 1930, the Revolutionary government invested heavily in highway construction in the 1970s. Two preliminary highway projects bequeathed to the Revolution – the Monumental Highway to the east and Mediodía Highway to the west – turned out to be too narrow. The outer limit of the southern part of the city was joined along Calle 100 in Boyeros municipality with Monumental Highway in Habana del Este. The highway to Güira de Melena and the Autopista Nacional connected the country to the outer edge of Havana, the latter linking Matanzas and Pinar del Río Provinces, to the east and west, respectively. Who would have imagined in those heady, optimistic years three decades ago that the highways Cuba so sacrificed to build would be empty today? Nonetheless, indestructible Fords and Chevrolets trod steadfastly along the nation's nearly empty highways.

Today, Havana has approximately 2600 kilometers of major roads, many of which are disconnected and narrow (United Nations DESIPA 1995, p. 97). Numerous smaller streets (Table 8.1) accompanied the web of major roads that connected the traditional city with the hinterland. Road building during the early years of the Revolution changed the scale and landscape of Havana. Unlike the linear tourist paths that still prevail today (defined by the axes of Barlovento and Miramar in the west; Vedado and Habana Vieja (central); and the beaches of Brisas del Mar (east), new spaces opened up south of the beaches for recreation and industry. Southeast Havana Province well demonstrated those new land uses: Agricultural Command Posts (*Puestos de Mando de la Agricultura*; see Chapter 3) located in the Nazareno and Menocal hills. Unassuming recreational facilities (camp grounds, really) were built on the shores of dammed lakes in the Province of the City of Havana (La Coca; Zarza in Habana del Este; Bacuranao in Guanabacoa; and Ejército Rebelde in Arroyo Naranjo).

Four major green spaces in the southern and southwestern parts of the city – Metropolitan Park (Parque Metropolitano still in the proposal stage), Lenin Park (Parque Lenin), National Zoo (Zoológico Nacional), and the National Botanical Garden (Jardín Botánico Nacional) – afford *habaneros* outdoor recreation opportunities (Figure 8.1). These green areas are the 'lungs' of the city besides possessing other ornamental and aesthetic functions. Between 1959 and 1984, the ratio of green areas per inhabitant had risen from 1 to 8 square meters (Dirección de Planificación Física 1984).

Coastal areas around Havana still held a privileged position in the 1960s, perhaps because they had been expropriated by the bourgeoisie. Gradually, though, modest tourist complexes for Havana families appeared on the beaches of El Salado, Bacuranao, El Mégano and Arroyo Bermejo. The urbanization of Tarará, formerly a small beach resort with unpretentious single-family homes (see Chapter 3), was converted into a children's recreational center. In a few spots along the coast there arose public housing complexes such as in Habana del Este and, in the west, Reparto Flores in Playa Municipality (adapted for foreign professionals).

By the 1970s, a major planning effort was launched to thin out the population. It entailed using extensive agricultural lands in Arroyo Naranjo and Boyeros municipalities to the south of Havana, and the Havana Greenbelt discussed in previous chapters. Lenin Park, the National Botanical Gardens, and the National Zoo, were clustered within a 1600 hectare strip. Without a doubt, this was the most important plan undertaken during the Revolution in Havana because of the quality of the design, the care taken in integrating it into the natural landscape, and the commitment of both skilled and unskilled labor. The project enlisted the

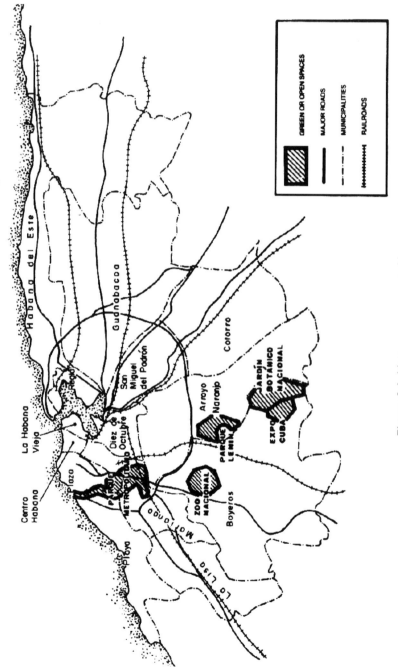

**Figure 8.1** Major green spaces in Havana

help of a prestigious team of specially selected architects.

For two decades, millions of persons have enjoyed these carefully planned installations. Principal among them is the 735 hectares (about 300 acres) of Lenin Park whose works and design began in 1972. It hosts a generous array of services (cafeterias, restaurants, including the luxurious Las Ruinas Restaurant), an amusement park, and cultural and sporting events (González and Cabrera 1996). Lenin Park has been a primary source of weekend recreation for the residents of the capital, although the restaurant charges in dollars and its fare lies beyond the purchasing power of most *habaneros*. In a city that had previously lacked green areas and recreational facilities at a metropolitan scale, these complexes added a new dimension to the available leisure options. Sadly, though, the current economic crisis has greatly curtailed the use of the park because of a lack of fuel for buses and private automobiles. In 1996, it became commonplace to find several tour buses full of Europeans and Canadians waiting outside Las Ruinas restaurant during a week day with few Cubans seated at the tables inside; a rare sight just a few years earlier. That these facilities are now underutilized by *habaneros* speaks to the distance between socialist dreams and concrete reality. The quiet and nearly abandoned Greek Amphitheater in Lenin Park was originally equipped with the most advanced sound and lighting technology of the day, conceived by the sculptor Sandú Darié.

Today, the coastal axis of recreational spaces has again risen to the forefront of leisure activity, with its attendant emphasis on hotel construction in Miramar. The Malecón seaside promenade, originally designed as a limited access thoroughfare, has become the social 'living room' for the city's youth (Pons 1994). It affords teenagers and young people easy bicycle access and the constant beauty of tropical waters.

### Health care

Havana traditionally enjoyed a plethora of health-care services compared with Spain's other holdings. Within the island of Cuba and what was then Spanish-Florida – ceded to England in 1763 – Havana benefited as the largest recipient of hospitals from the establishment of the first hospital in Havana in 1539 (*Hospital Antiguo*), until the nineteenth century (Figure 8.2). The sugar boom of the nineteenth century produced a spate of hospitals elsewhere on the island. In the main, though, Havana held a large concentration of hospitals during its colonial rule.

There is no doubt that pre-Revolutionary Havana possessed a high level of both state and private medical services. Labor union and Spanish

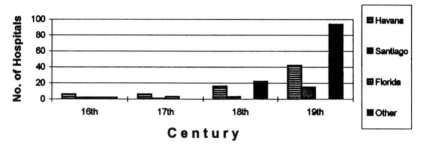

**Figure 8.2** Establishment of Cuban and Spanish hospitals, by region (1519–1989).
*Data source:* Mena and Cobelo (1992)

medical-care institutions had endowed Havana with a broad network of facilities that were called *quintas de salud* in the suburbs; literally, 'health farms', but actually large complexes of buildings – often occupying an entire city block – which were located on old country estates. However, the pre-Revolutionary system failed to include low-income and even some moderate-income *habaneros*. Medical facilities concentrated along the Centro Habana–Vedado–Marianao axis and the *quintas de salud* in Cerro. Medical services that were available to the poor and working classes lacked specialty care. Wealthy Cubans merely traveled to the United States for specialized tertiary care.

Today, Cuba's health-care system is world renown and health ideology is a defining characteristic of the Cuban Revolution (Feinsilver 1993, 1994, 1995). A significant exodus of the nation's medical personnel during the early years of the Revolution prompted the Castro government to prioritize physician training. As a result, Cuba was virtually able to place a physician 'on every block.' Universal health care that is free of charge to all Cubans has helped lower Cuba's mortality and morbidity levels. Before the onset of the Special Period, the state directed about one-quarter of its budget to health care. Health care in Cuba – especially in the capital city – is delivered in hospitals, clinics, schools, and the workplace.

Like most capital cities throughout the world, Havana contains a relative abundance of resources. It has approximately 25 000 hospital beds which is about half of the nation's total stock of 54 028 (Del Aguila 1992). By 1989, Havana had 74 primary health-care clinics (*policlínicos*) and 12 health-care and medical research centers (GDIC 1990, p. 19). Four years later, the number of health-care clinics had increased to 79 (MINSAP 1994), despite the hardship of the Special Period. In 1990, the crude birth rate of Havana was 15.1 per 1000 inhabitants and its crude death rate was 8.2. Life expectancy that year stood at 74 years of age and it remains one of the highest of any Latin American city. By 1984, Cuba had already boasted the greatest life expectancy of any Warsaw Pact nation, and its infant mortality rate was the second lowest (after the former East Germany) (Feinsilver 1993, p. 28). In 1989, Havana's infant mortality rate was 10.7 infant deaths per 1000 live births (GDIC 1990, p. 18). By 1993, Havana's infant mortality rate fell to 9.0 (MINSAP 1994).

Planning measures keep check on runaway rural to urban migration, producing just a net migratory increase of 10 000 per year in Havana while the natural annual growth amounted to 14 000 (GDIC 1990, p. 18). Migration and natural growth added 24 000 new residents in Havana in 1989, for an overall annual rate of growth of 1.16%. Although migration to the capital is controlled by planners, laws and a restrictive housing market (see Chapter 6), in 1995 35% of all Havana residents were born outside the city (*CubaNews* March 1996). The city's low rate of growth is full of implications for planning, housing, and social services, especially compared with other Latin American cities where rates of growth are at least twice as high.

Symbolism in Revolutionary Havana plays a key role in promoting socialism, and health care is a weighty part of that symbolism. Although the well-known symbols of the city include the Martí Monument and the monument to the battleship S.S. Maine on the Malecón, political symbolism related to health care is also front and center. Witness, for example, one of the tallest buildings in the city, the Hermanos Ameijeiras Hospital. It was originally designed to be the *Banco Nacional*, but is now a major tertiary facility. A badge of honor for *habaneros* and Cubans is that 5% of the occupied beds in Ameijeiras Hospital is reserved for non-paying foreigners. These non-Cubans make their requests through Cuban embassies in their countries as well as political parties, peasant organizations, and labor unions. Not all those admitted to the hospital affiliate with socialist or communist parties; the classic example is the eye treatment of the child of a conservative Chilean politician during the hard-line, anti-Communist rule of Brigadier General Agusto Pinochet.

Havana is endowed with a greater number of beds and medical facilities than other Cuban cities because it serves as a national referral center. Hermanos Ameijeiras Hospital reserves up to 70% of its beds for patients from other provinces. Of international renown too is the Center for Genetic Engineering and Biotechnology, reputed to be one of the largest laboratories in the world. A major high-tech research center, it provides the clinical support for a variety of Cuban medical, agricultural, biotechnological, and veterinary products for domestic consumption and export (Los Naranjos 1984). Yet, not all of Havana's health-care infrastructure is high-tech. On the eastern edge of Havana is the José Martí Pioneer City. It is a seaside youth camp capable of housing 10 000 children and between 3000 and 4000 mothers. In 1989, the facility expanded to receive hundreds of children injured by the radiation exposure of the Chernobyl nuclear reactor disaster in the former Soviet Union. This is just one of the medical diplomacy gestures (Feinsilver 1993) and symbols of Havana's 'therapeutic' landscape.

Throughout the past four decades, the policy and practice of hospital care have functioned at several levels in Havana. First, service tries to broaden and improve existing complexes. This policy focused on the *quintas de salud* in Cerro, the Calixto García Teaching Hospital in Vedado, the cluster of hospitals in Plaza de la Revolución, and the subcenters of Marianao-Military Hospital and the National Hospital in Alta Habana. Second, the policy also responded to the massive number of people who frequented the health facilities, and whose care was totally free and available to all residents of Havana. A third objective was to build new facilities or rehabilitate existing structures. As noted above, the 25-story *Banco Nacional* building in Centro Habana was transformed into the Hermanos Ameijeiras Hospital (named after brothers who were martyred in the revolutionary struggle against Batista). Lastly, numerous smaller facilities were built across the city and took advantage of prefabricated construction models that could be assembled relatively quickly.

In the 1980s, the international success that Cuban medicine and 'health tourism' had received led to the construction of highly sophisticated medical services for both nationals and foreigners. Playa Municipality today holds a good share of these newer facilities: the Center for Medical Surgery, the Institute of Tropical Medicine, and the Iberoamerican Center for Regeneration. In Miramar, a prestigious private clinic was converted into a hospital for foreigners: Cira García. South of Miramar, in La Lisa, the orthopedic hospital Frank País was built. It attracts thousands of Latin Americans annually who receive care gratis even though it serves mainly Cubans. In Boyeros, the National Psychiatric Hospital and the rehabilitation hospital Julio Díaz were converted into general hospitals.

During the first two decades of the Revolution, the residents of the city had increasingly used national and provincial hospitals in the city indiscriminately. To rectify that problem, the government tried to tease out the different levels of care more carefully, and to shoulder up preventive care. A concerted effort in the 1970s and 1980s placed health-care clinics (*policlínicos*) in each municipality. Family Physician Clinics (*Consultorio del Médico de la Familia*) were also installed in each neighborhood. By the mid-1990s, Havana City boasted a dense network of health care facilities, ranging from primary care (clinics), secondary care (general hospitals), to tertiary care (specialized medical care facilities) (Figure 8.3 and Table 8.2). Havana also has the most favorable ratio of physicians to population in the entire country (1:250), while Granma Province in eastern Cuba has just 1:569, which although is the lowest, is still quite good compared with

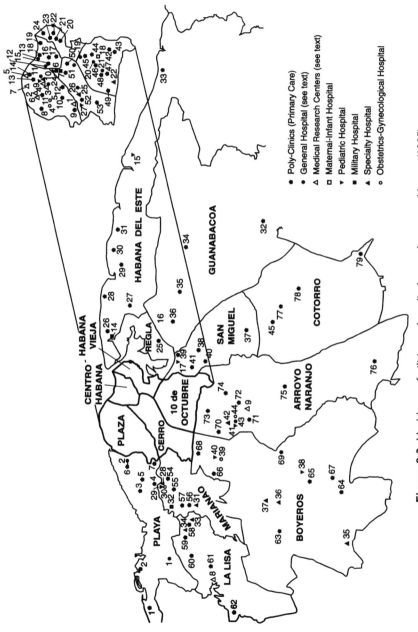

**Figure 8.3** Health care facilities and medical reseach centers, Havana (1995)

**Table 8.2** Key to health care facilities in Havana (1995) (see Figure 8.3)

*Hospitals*
1. Centro de Investigación Médico Quirúgico
2. Cira García
3. Joaquín Albarrán
4. Clodomira Acosta
5. Ramón González Coro
6. Pediátrico Marfán
7. América Arias
8. Manuel Fajardo
9. Pediátrico Pedro Borrás
10. Ortopédico Fructuoso Rodríguez
11. Calixto García
12. Freyre de Andrade
13. Hermanos Ameijeiras
14. Luis Díaz Soto
15. Ciudad Pioneril Tarará
16. Gineco-Obstétrico Guanabacoa
17. Pediátrico San Miguel del Padrón
18. Materno Infantil de 10 de Octubre
19. Miguel Enríquez
20. Santos Suárez
21. Luis de la Puente Uceda
22. Psiquiátrico Isidro de Armas
23. Centro Quirúgico de 10 de Octubre
24. Pediátrico de Centro Habana
25. Salvador Allende
26. Neumológico Benéfico Jurídico
27. Pediátrico del Cerro
28. Oftalmológico Pando Ferrer
29. Pediátrico Juan M. Martínez
30. Eusebio Hernández
31. Psiquiátrico Laura Martínez
32. Carlos J. Finlay
33. Psiquiátrico Gustavo López
34. Ortopédico Frank País
35. Antileproso Hernández Vaquero
36. Psiquiátrico Nacional
37. Rehabilitación Julio Díaz
38. Pediátrico Leonor Pérez
39. Enrique Cabrera
40. Pediátrico William Soler
41. Angel A. Aballí
42. Psiquiátrico 27 de Noviembre
43. Julio Trigo
44. Gineco-Obstétrico Lebredo
45. Psiquiátrico de Soregui

*Free-standing medical research centers*
1. Instituto de Medicina Legal
2. Instituto de Cirugía Cardiovascular
3. Instituto de Neurología
4. Instituto de Oncología y Radiobiología
5. Centro de Retinosis Pigmentaria
6. Instituto de Higiene y Epidemiología
7. Instituto de Higiene de los Alimentos Nutrición
8. Instituto de Medicina Tropical Pedro Kourí
9. Instituto de Medicina del Trabajo

*Primary health-care clinics (Policlínicos)*
1. Santa Fé
2. Manuel Fajardo
3. 26 de Julio
4. Docente de Playa
5. Jorge Ruíz Ramírez
6. Primero de Enero
7. Isidro de Armas
8. 15 y 18
9. Puentes Grandes
10. 19 de Abril
11. Héroes del Moncada
12. Plaza
13. Rampa
14. Héroes del Conrinthia
15. Van Troi
16. Reina
17. Joaquín Albarrán
18. Marcio Manduley
19. Luis Galván
20. Robert Zulueta
21. Antonio Guiteras
22. Diego Tamayo
23. Angel A. Aballí
24. Tomás Romay
25. Regla
26. Camilo Cienfuegos
27. William Santana
28. Cojímar
29. Docente de Alamar
30. 13 de Marzo
31. E. Betancourt Neninger
32. Campo Florido
33. Guanabo
34. Andrés Ortiz
35. Machaco Amejeiras
36. Docente de Guanabacoa
37. Hermanos Ruiz Aboy
38. Bernardo Posse
39. Wilfredo Pérez
40. California
41. Luis Carbó
42. 30 de Noviembre

Table 8.2 Continued

| | | |
|---|---|---|
| 43. Lawton | 55. Ramón González | 67. Mulgoba |
| 44. Luyanó | Coro | 68. Salvador Allende |
| 45. 14 de Junio | 56. 27 de Noviembre | 69. Calabazar |
| 46. Santos Suárez | 57. Carlos J. Finlay | 70. Los Pinos |
| 47. Luis de la Puente | 58. Aleida Fernández | 71. Capri |
| Uceda | 59. Cristóbal Labra | 72. Párraga |
| 48. Luis Pasteur | 60. Elpidio Berovides | 73. Julian Grimau |
| 49. Luis A.Turcios Lima | 61. Pulido Humarán | 74. Mantilla |
| 50. Abel Santamaría | 62. Pedro Fonseca | 75. Reparto Eléctrico |
| 51. Héroes de Girón | 63. Wajay | 76. Managua |
| 52. Cerro | 64. Santiago de las Vegas | 77. Efraín Mayor |
| 53. Antonio Maceo | 65. Rancho Boyeros | 78. Rafael Valdés |
| 54. Portuondo | 66. Capdevila | 79. Cuatro Caminos |

*Data source*: Unpublished materials, Ministerio de Salud Pública, n.d.

other countries.

Health-care specialists are well distributed throughout the nation (*CubaNews*, November 1994). This situation of medical personnel contrasts with other Latin American countries where the capital holds a disproportionate number of specialists (Roemer 1964). Although the distribution of health-care personnel and facilities fares relatively well in several respects, the infrastructure is hampered by shortages of anesthetics, sutures, antibiotics, and even aspirin. At present, bed linens, electric lamps, detergents, and basic custodial cleaning supplies are also scarce. These shortages notwithstanding, the government has established a coordinated system that is integrated with the residential layout of the city. These initiatives have given education and health care a significant presence in the fabric of Havana.

There is perhaps no better measure of the health of a community than the infant mortality rate. This measure portrays the ratio of infant deaths (0–365 days) to every 1000 live births. Havana's mean infant mortality rate was a low 8.73 in 1993. Two notable geographic patterns emerge. First, all but two municipalities have infant mortality rates less than +1 standard deviation of the mean. These outliers – San Miguel and Arroyo Naranjo municipalities – have large rural tracts where the material conditions of the home and the accessibility to health services are less developed than in the urban parts of the province (Figure 8.4). A large pediatrics hospital in San Miguel may also account for higher levels of infant mortality. Another noteworthy feature is the relatively high infant mortality rate in Habana Vieja (+0.06 to +1 standard deviation). The rate reflects the increasingly deteriorated living conditions in this densely settled corner of the city.

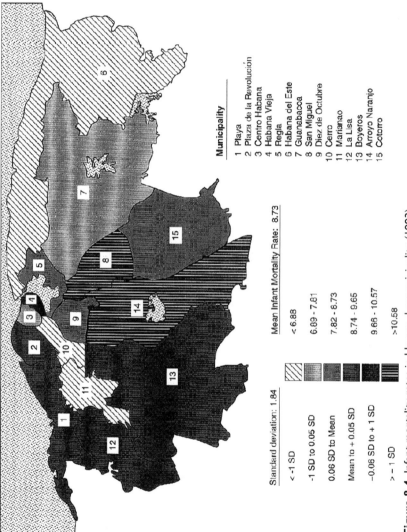

**Figure 8.4** Infant mortality rates in Havana, by municipality (1993)

## Education

Another policy outcome of the Castro government that characterizes its goal of changing the scale of priorities and hierarchies of urban life is the educational system. Nationally, per capita expenditures for education rose from $11 in 1958, to $42 in 1970, and $175 in 1989 (Jiménez 1990). Even during the Special Period in 1991, when funding plummeted to $92 per capita, Cuba remained in second place in Latin America (behind Venezuela at $117 and ahead of Panama at $82) (Cuba Va 1993). Considerable investment has gone into building day-care centers, primary schools, high schools, technological institutes, and pre-university high schools. Most of these new buildings are located in the periphery of Havana as opposed to the traditional centers. Early on in the Revolution, old palaces and mansions abandoned by the bourgeoisie were transformed into schools, as were existing buildings in older areas of the city. Miramar, partly emptied by exile migration, became a large educational space in the city. Thousands of children of peasant farmers from the Sierra Maestra came to Miramar for basic literacy training. The Columbia Military Base in Marianao, a sinister representation of military rule in Cuba that in previous decades controlled the political scene, was transformed into a major educational center. Now called *Ciudad Libertad* (Liberty City), the former barracks contain facilities ranging from primary schools to university classes. Private schools fell under state rule. The huge Catholic school, Belén (or Bethlehem in English, where Fidel Castro studied), previously run by the Jesuits, was turned into the Technical Military Institute. The children of Russian technicians studied at the facilities of the former Colegio de las Ursulinas.

School construction quickened during the early years of the Revolution. Between 1959 and 1961, 671 rural primary schools, 339 urban primary schools, and 99 junior high schools were built. Havana played a key role, often immeasurable in the early educational efforts of the Revolution. For example, thousands of Havana families took in peasants and student boarders who came from eastern Cuba to work or study in the capital. Massive scholarship programs have also brought an 'overflow' of students to the city. The Rebel Army and adults being trained as teachers, artisans, and in other trades also received free, informal lodging in Havana.

Between 1968 and 1973, 475 learning centers of some fashion were built in Cuba. One hundred and ninety Basic Rural Secondary Schools (*Escuelas Secundarias Básicas en el Campo, or* ESBECs) were erected between 1968 and 1973. Each school contained a 500 hectare farm and could hold up to 500 students (Segre 1978). The ESBECs averaged a cost of half million pesos and were clustered around the citric plantations in Ceiba del Agua, Jagüey Grande, and Ciego de Avila. Students boarded there and life was hard for them. Besides carrying a normal course load, they worked in the fields 3 hours daily in their gardens as well as some agricultural production for the nation. Instructors worked there permanently while the student population rotated (back to their home towns) every 3 years. Some schools turned into a rather benign, fenceless prison. Strong kids bullied weaker ones and early sexual activity became a major attraction (including the predominantly young school teachers). Personal belongings were to be kept in open lockers because not only were locks scarce, but officials from the Ministry of Education thought they were unnecessary; every youngster bred by the Revolution was supposed to be honest.

The counterpart of the ESBECs in the cities were the Basic Urban Secondary Schools (*Escuelas Secundarias Básicas Urbanas, or ESBURs*). In terms of design, these complexes usually demanded very large lots and introduced considerable visual blight in the cityscape. Even students in the ESBURs are required to leave for 45 days of agricultural work, usually picking tobacco or coffee. Parents make long, difficult trips on Sundays to see their children and add some extra food to the bland diet.

Two major interventions in the beginning of the 1960s transformed the scale of education in Havana. The first was the creation of small schools that were tied to new housing complexes. The second was a project that portrayed the 'moral objectives' of the Revolution: the college campus of Ciudad Universitaria José Antonio Echeverría (the campus and university are referred to as CUJAE in Cuba) in Marianao municipality, and the National Schools of Art built on the former golf courses of Country Club in Playa municipality. With contrasting architectural images, these two complexes reflected the enthusiasm of young designers by creating both artistic (Schools of Art) and technical (CUJAE) 'cities' (campuses) with environmental and aesthetic qualities that demonstrated the new values imparted by a socialist society.

In the 1970s and 1980s, practically every neighborhood of Havana received some type of educational facility, made possible largely by the Girón method of prefabricated panels of reinforced concrete (see Chapter 6). Originally developed for junior high schools, Girón was later used for day-care centers, high schools, and teacher training centers. The Girón method permitted specialized training centers such as medicine and agronomy to locate in the countryside. Other educational facilities were established throughout the provinces of Havana City and Havana (Table 8.3). The exterior finish on the buildings was often poor due to the uneven surfaces of the panels, especially at joints. Moreover, the designs were

**Table 8.3** New educational facilities placed in and around Havana (1960s–1970s)

| Facility name | Description | Location |
|---|---|---|
| Escuela de Geografía | Geography faculty, University of Havana | Alamar, eastern Havana City Province |
| Instituto de Ciencias Agropecuarias | Agricultural research and training center | San José de las Lajas, Havana Province |
| Centro de Investigaciones de Sanidad Animal (CENSA) | Veterinary science research and training center | San José de las Lajas, Havana Province |
| Escuela Internacional de Cine | Film school | San Antonio de los Baños, Havana Province |
| Instituto Superior de Dirección de la Economía | Economics research center | La Lisa, Havana City Province |
| Instituto Superior de Relaciones Internacionales | Foreign affairs research and training center | Playa, Havana City Province |
| Instituto Superior de Ciencias Médicas | Medical research and training center | Playa, Havana City Province, in former residence of Sagrado Corazón school |
| Escuela Vocacional Lenin | Vo-tech school | Arroyo Naranjo Municipality, Havana City Province |
| Instituto Electrónico | Electronics research and training center | Santiago de las Vegas, Havana City Province |
| Instituto de la Construcción | Building construction research and training center | Santiago de las Vegas, Havana City Province |
| Instituto de Ciencias Agropecuarias | Agricultural research and training center | Santiago de las Vegas, Havana City Province |
| Instituto Superior Pedagógico para la Educación Técnica y Professional | Vo-tech training school | Santiago de las Vegas, Havana City Province |
| Instituto de Economía | Economics research and training center | Cotorro Municipality, Havana City Province |
| Instituto de Geología y Geofísica | Geology research and training center | Cotorro Municipality, Havana City Province |
| Instituto de Transporte Naval | Naval training center | Havana City Province |

simple and relatively low in cost and, as a result, are monotonous and unattractive.

The location of many of these new facilities benefited from the former bourgeoisie's affinity with attractive and bucolic sites. Several biotechnology and genetic engineering research centers were located in the posh residential neighborhoods of Country Club, La Coronela, and San Agustín in the western side of the metropolitan areas. Political parties and workers' organizations also sought the amenities of the countryside. The major labor organization, the *Central de Trabajadores de Cuba*, and the Provincial School of the Cuban Communist Party also opened facilities in these western ex-urban areas. Even the Communist Party's architectural unit 'Ñico López' found a home at Santa Fé beach outside Barlovento, where the yachts of US millionaires used to moor before the Revolution. Lastly, each of these complexes created ancillary facilities such as dormitories, cafeterias, libraries, garages, and related support services. Within the contiguous part of Havana, there were also hundreds of pre-school and day-care facilities built largely in the 1980s, and even within Habana Vieja.

The Cuban government controls all educational institutions since religious and private education has been abolished under the Revolution.[3] In so doing, it has strived to promote access to all facets of education without regard for the ability to pay. School attendance is compulsory through the ninth grade and the state has promoted a wide array of literacy, arts, and cultural programs as part of its increase in public education efforts.

One indelible hallmark left by the Cuban Revolution was the literacy campaign in the 1960s. Volunteers pushed into primarily rural parts of the island and helped to increase the literary rate from 53% in 1953 to 96% in 1988 (Del Aguila 1992). By 1992, the literacy rate had risen to 98.5%, giving Cuba the highest literacy rate in Latin America, followed by Argentina (95.5%), Uruguay (95.4%), and Costa Rica (93.6%) (*CubaNews*, November 1993; *Provincia de la Ciudad de La Habana*, 1992). A museum dedicated to this important grassroots effort – *El Museo de la Alfabetización* in the Marianao district of Havana – displays glimpses of this social movement.

Three public higher education institutions prevailed in 1959: the University of Havana, the Universidad de Las Villas in Santa Clara city, and the Universidad de Oriente in Santiago de Cuba. In 1996, four universities operated in Havana.

### The venues of Cuban tourism

The City of Havana (population 2.2 million) holds several comparative advantages in the South Florida and Caribbean tourist markets. Before the Revolution, Havana always offered low per diem costs for the tourists. Multiplier effects in the 1950s from tourism shared common features with tourism in other Caribbean nations. Rum and tobacco sales as well as a

---

[3]There a few private educational programs offered, although they are sponsored by foreign cultural organizations and embassies. For instance, the Aliance Française offers French classes and adult education.

broad range of artisan industries benefited from the tourist trade. The 1950s was a time when most of the tourist infrastructure was foreign owned. In Cuba, nationalization of tourist facilities increased after 1961. Although joint ventures in Revolutionary Cuba have been permitted since 1982, it would not be until the 1990s that foreign capital would return to the island (Espino 1993).

*A benign climate*

Geography has also dealt the island comparative advantages. Although Havana has a lower latitude than Florida, the Trade Winds produce slightly cooler temperatures in Havana during the summer. In the wintertime, its insular location and a strong maritime influence make it slightly warmer than in Florida (Table 8.4). Proximity to the largest and most affluent international tourist market in the world has not been lost on Cuban governments throughout the twentieth century (Havanatur 1992).

Tourism in Havana has waxed and waned during this century. Before 1920, it was relatively minor. Marrero (1981, p. 316) reported that Cuba grossed $107 million between 1954 and 1956, registering as the third most important source of national wealth behind sugar and tobacco. During pre-Revolutionary times, Havana functioned as one point in a circuit of North American tourist flows along with Las Vegas and Miami. Hotel ownership and gambling operations among the three points were closely coordinated. Short trips across the Straits of Florida by airplane and boat were especially common allures in the Miami–Key West–Havana link. During its peak years of international tourism between Miami and Cuba, hourly scheduled flights operated between dawn and midnight. In the mid-1950s, an average of 260 000 tourists visited Cuba, and Havana was the main destination (Marrero 1981b, p. 322). As we shall discuss below, this figure dropped greatly during the first two decades of the Revolution. Comparable levels would not appear until the onset of the economic crisis brought on by the dissolution of the USSR and the socialist bloc in 1989.

**Table 8.4** Temperature (°C) comparisons between selected Florida cities and Havana

| Cities | Summer | Winter |
| --- | --- | --- |
| Jacksonville | 27.3 | 12.5 |
| Saint Augustine | 28.5 | 14.0 |
| Miami | 27.3 | 19.8 |
| Havana | 26.2 | 22.6 |

*Source*: Marrero (1981b, p. 320).

In the 1960s and 1970s, it was relatively insignificant. Throughout most of the Revolution, Havana's standard tourist fare has been colonial Havana, tourism oriented around the accomplishments of the Revolution, twentieth century architecture, Tropicana Nightclub, and the beaches of Habana del Este.

*The rise and fall of tourism*

The Revolution and the imminent disruption of diplomatic and trade relations with the United States curtailed international tourism in Cuba. In 1957, 304 711 tourists visited Cuba. It would take years to recover pre-Revolutionary levels. Between 1960 and 1975, international tourism practically disappeared in Cuba because the Revolutionary government discouraged it. Revolutionary leaders considered tourism too closely aligned with the capitalist sins of prostitution,[4] drugs, organized crime, and gambling. In 1976, however, the government created the National Institute of Tourism (INTUR, Instituto Nacional de Turismo). As a result, international tourism rose from a mere 8400 visitors in 1974 to 69 500 in 1978 (Espino 1993).

Relative growth of Cuba's tourist trade quickened in the late 1970s, and again in the late 1980s. In the 1980s, the rate of international visitors to Cuba increased at an average annual rate of 9.4%, greater than the Caribbean's rate as a whole. However, in 1988, Cuba had attracted only 3.2% of all Caribbean tourist arrivals, and only 2.1% of the region's tourist receipts (Espino 1991). By 1990, though, approximately 340 000 tourists visited the island, which increased 82% by 1994 (619 000). Figures for 1995 reached 740 000 while for the year 2000 it is forecast that some 2.5 million tourists will vacation in Cuba (Figure 8.5). A strong infusion of Spanish capital and joint ventures has bolstered the island's room capacity. Some of the most recent and notable hotel and tourist complexes include the Meliá Las Américas in Varadero and the Meliá Cohiba in the Vedado district of Havana.

---

[4]Prostitution in Cuba has gained worldwide attention. Regrettably, there are sites on the World Wide Web that explain how and where prostitution operates in Havana, Varadero, Cienfuegos, and other cities. A 1995 survey carried out in the Italian tourist magazine, *Viaggiare*, ranked Cuba as the most popular destination for sex tourists. While prostitution and pimping are not crimes *per se*, they fall under Article 62 of the penal code which classifies 'antisocial' behavior. An April 4, 1996 raid on 400 'bawdy houses' in Havana rounded up residents who worked as prostitutes at 'tunnels, bridges, dens, rooftops and public spaces which served as shelter for those who lived from sexual exploitation'. In June, 1996, *Juventud Rebelde*, a Cuban Communist Party weekly publication, announced that a network of 7000 prostitutes had been destroyed (see Acosta 1996c).

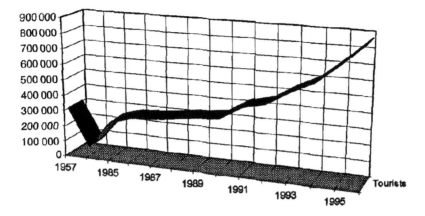

**Figure 8.5**  Tourist arrivals to Cuba (1957–1996) – selected years
*Data sources: Business Tips on Cuba*, May 1995, p. 25; *CubaNews*, Vol. 4, No. 3, March 1996, p. 1; 1996 figure is projected on January–May 1996 count of 435 000, taken from InterPress Service: Cuba-Economy: Cheers as Tourist Numbers Rise, Montevideo: InterPress Third World News Agency

Tourism holds great promise for the island and its capital city. Cuba had 40% more tourist rooms in 1992 than it did in 1991. A recurrent problem is the gap between gross and net revenues from tourism. In 1992, an estimated $400 million in gross receipts yielded just $240 million in net revenues. This amounts to just 1% of the gross social product (GSP). Another obstacle is the relatively low rate of repeat tourism; only 7 or 8% of tourists return to Cuba, versus 20% elsewhere in the Caribbean. One analyst finds that Cuba attracts tourists who spend very little more than their already low-cost vacation packages. In addition, the multipliers are few because of the high rate of imports in the tourist industry (Mesa-Lago 1994, p. 19). For example, Antonio Esquivel, head of the Havana section of the tourism ministry, stated that 'Cuba spends 67 cents of every dollar taken in by tourism – an excessively high proportion' (Napoles 1996e).

Repeat tourism will be the key to Havana's success if the US embargo is lifted. Challenges will also lie ahead after the first wave of curiosity seekers passes through the city's streets. Once a tropical destination is 'discovered' and promoted appropriately, the allure to such a place should create a tourist flow with its own momentum (Stough and Feldman 1984). In truth, there are an unlimited number of sun, sand and sea destinations for the North American and European markets (de Albuquerque and McElroy 1992). Although Cuba at one time had an advantage as a getaway spot for US tourists – and had cultivated experience among tourist industry personnel in the international tourist trade – all that vanished with the strengthening of the Revolution and the US embargo of the island. Lost too was human capital, especially knowledge transferred among generations of tourism workers and business managers.

As Cuba transitions from a fairly 'closed' island to an 'open' one, the surge of tourists poses problems. Host population responses to major tourist influxes elsewhere have ranged from outright hostility to overt euphoria (de Albuquerque and McElroy 1992). The 'mindset' of many Cuban tourism employees must change so that cordiality and attentiveness create repeat tourism. Furthermore, Cuba's eye on the US market would require a special adaptation to Havana's current tourism infrastructure. As de Albuquerque and McElroy (1992, p. 626) note: 'Because of the middle-class Americans' penchant for the familiar, this strong U.S. influence in the Caribbean tourist industry is partly responsible for the observed preference for hotel lodging and the relatively large-scale facilities and shorter stays characteristic of mature destinations,' By 'mature' destinations the authors refer to the highest per capita visitor spending islands in Caribbean islands with fewer than half a million inhabitants (Aruba, Bahamas, Barbados, Bermuda, Curacao, St. Maarten, and the US Virgin Islands).

Havana holds its position as the major tourist destination within Cuba. According to a recent United Nations sponsored publication (*Business Tips on Cuba*, July 1994, p. 20), Havana operates at a 76% hotel-room capacity, compared with 94% in Holguin, 93% in Santiago de Cuba, 62% in Varadero, and 75% in other principal tourist zones in Cuba. Thus, while the Cuban government seeks to expand its tourist infrastructure throughout the island – and not just in Havana – eastern Cuba (Holguin and Santiago de Cuba) approaches maximum capacity while the Havana–Varadero tourist poles have room for growth.

Havana's attraction as an international tourist site stems from the city's architectural beauty and curiosity about the Revolution. Data on the island's performance in recent years bode well for Cuba's new role in tourism. Cuba was placed 14th on the list of the most popular tourist destinations in the western hemisphere, which was up from the 24th spot it held in 1985. During that same time, Cuba rose from 23rd to ninth among nations with the greatest income from tourism (Acosta 1996b).

The state actively promotes tourism abroad, as do a growing number of joint-venture operations. There are 174 Cuban travel representatives outside the country and 38 agencies within Cuba to handle this travel. While Havana is the primary destination, the entire island boasts seven international airports and enlists three Cuban and 35 foreign airlines to handle tourist arrivals (*Business Tips on Cuba*, May, 1995, p. 28). Western Europe is the largest regional market while Canada provides the largest single national contribution to Cuba's international tourist flow (Figure 8.6).

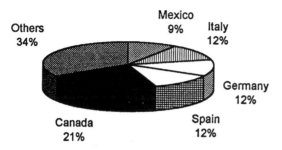

**Figure 8.6** Origins of tourists to Cuba (1994).
*Data source: Business Tips on Cuba, May, 1995, p. 28*

Most Canadians arrive in charter flights departing from the eastern Canadian provinces, and book weekly packages. Varadero's airport, Juan Gualberto Gómez International, is 140 kilometers east of Havana, or 90 minutes by road. Its 60–80 by 3000 meter (197–262 by 9842 ft.) runway can handle large aircraft (*CubaNews* October 1993). Day trips into Havana are common parts of the 'ground packages' provided by these flights. Other than Canadians, Spanish, German, Italian, and Mexican tourists comprise the major visitors to the island.

The Cuban Ministry of Tourism has identified some 67 'tourist poles' along with more than 7000 kilometers of coastline. Figure 8.7 reveals four of those poles within the Province of the City of Havana (Cojímar, Traditional Center, Vedado, and Monte Barreto). Playa Jibacoa, Playas del Este, and Tarará are the most accessible beaches for tourists and residents within Havana City and Havana Provinces (*Business Tips on Cuba*, May, 1995, p. 27). Hemingway Marina, formerly Barlovento, has undergone

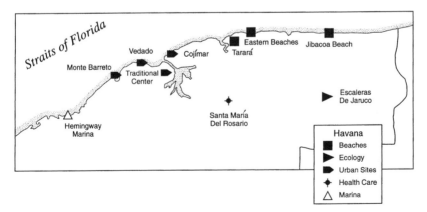

**Figure 8.7** Four tourist 'poles' within Havana City Province

major remodeling and hosts an annual fishing competition. Boats from any country – including the United States – can enter the Marina for recreational purposes and moor there for 72 hours without securing a visa.

*Soldiering and tourism*

If the shift away from the Soviet Union in a post-cold war era has been daunting for Cuba, nowhere has this change been more striking than in the role of the island's armed forces. Long gone are the days of armed struggle in Angola and Mozambique. Cuba indeed has been cashing in on this 'peace dividend' even though it has the second largest army in Latin America (Brazil leads). The Cuban military had worked in endeavors outside military defense well before the onset of the Special Period. Its presence in tourism is strong and growing.

Gaviota (seagull) is the best known company of the armed forces. It gained experience in managing recreational centers for Soviet advisors back in the 1960s. That marked the beginning of what has become a multifaceted presence in Cuba's tourist trade. Gaviota now operates bus tours, marinas, spas, hunting preserves, fishing excursions, and luxury hotels. It also boasts a large fleet of taxis and airline flights. Gaviota pursues horizontal linkages. It taps into tourists' expendable income through the TRD (*tiendas de recaudación de divisas*, or foreign-currency collection stores) Caribe chain of department stores. The Cuban armed forces have reportedly studied China's state-managed economic opening, a process that changed the People's Liberation Army into a major company. Cuba's armed forces have been down-sized by some 25% (from a maximum of 200 000 men and women during its involvement in Africa in the 1980s). The market, though, has brought problems from which even the armed forces are not immune: nepotism and corruption. Despite these problems, the army has produced a well-disciplined cadre of engineers, managers, agronomists and technicians. In the words of economist Julio Carranza, deputy director of the Center for the Study of the Americas in Havana: 'The armed forces are trying to generate foreign exchange so as to be able to sustain themselves as a military force without being a load on the state or a burden on the rest of the economy' (Rohter 1995).

*Health tourism*

As discussed earlier this chapter, principles of equal access to services, an integral approach to health care, and popular participation in health initiatives, guide Cuba's health system (Feinsilver 1993, p. 28). Cuba has generously provided physician and medical care to developing countries in Africa and Asia. It also provides specialized high-tech medical procedures such as cardiac surgery, eye surgery, and cancer treatment at lower costs than those found in the United States, Europe or Latin America.

Cuba's renown system of health care is also available to foreigners provided they purchase services in hard currency. Havana is home to several international tourist hospitals in the Vedado, Miramar, and Centro Habana districts of the city. These facilities provide high-quality, tertiary care services. Foreigners unable to pay for certain specialized care are also treated on an availability basis for specialized services. For example, Frank País Hospital offers rehabilitation services for war casualties from Nicaragua, El Salvador and the former Soviet Union. As well, orthopedic surgical procedures and spinal cord revascularization procedures can be secured there at a fraction of the cost in most advanced industrial countries (Feinsilver 1993, p. 72).

Cuba also promotes other specialized medical procedures under the label *turismo de salud*. A number of small clinics cater largely to foreigners who seek medical procedures that either do not exist in their country, are too expensive there, or have not been approved (i.e., Food and Drug Administration). These include the Center for Placental Histotherapy, Center for Medical Surgery, Cardiology and Cardiovascular Surgery Institute, Gastroenterology Institute, and the Sports Medicine Institute, among others. Foreigners can book complete package trips. Prices include air fare, lodging, ground transportation, nursing and medical care, specified medication and surgical procedures, and designated laboratory work. Patients from the United States can come through third countries (Bahamas, Mexico, Canada, Dominican Republic, Jamaica).

The Center for Placental Histotherapy, for example, has established a track record of evening out skin-coloring among thousands of patients who suffer from a pigmentation disorder called vitiligo. Even though the use of human placenta materials for this treatment is illegal in the United States, Cuban physicians and researchers claim the US embargo and transnational pharmaceutical corporations exert so much pressure that it is difficult to sell Cuban pharmaceutical and biotechnical products outside Cuba. Dr. Carlos Miyares Cao, General Director of the Center of Placental Histotherapy, claims that even foreign medical journals in allegedly 'sympathetic' countries like Mexico succumb to pressure about publishing the clinical results of Cuban researchers (personal communication, Carlos Miyares, June 22, 1995).

*The health tourism experience of a New Jersey mother*

Many 'health tourists' are not daunted by these obstacles. A New Jersey mother, willing to take a risk with Cuba's health tourism and the workings of the Center for Placental Histotherapy, is illustrative. For approximately $2400, the mother and son can fly from Newark, New Jersey to Havana (by way of Cancún, Mexico) for the son's medical care. A week's lodging and treatment for a skin coloration disorder – vitiligo – will identify an appropriate dosage and strength. The boy will bring back two five-gallon containers of the lotion – a year's supply – which are included in the package. He will have to return annually for follow ups and to have the prescription adjusted and refilled. As the mother assessed the health-tourism encounter: 'I could easily run up $2400 in diagnostic work and unproved ultraviolet treatments for the same amount in the Princeton and metropolitan New York areas, without the slightest hope that the vitiligo will dissipate'. While in Cuba she can purchase special lotions for wrinkles, psoriasis, and aging. She will also find a whole line of placenta-based hair products derived from the placenta materials.

Medical tourists like this New Jersey mother, though, comprise a small tourist flow. As Cuban physicians earn just a few dollars a month in real terms, the ratio of labor costs to revenues is fairly low. However, such specialized medical procedures represent years of laboratory work, and the purchase of medical equipment manufactured outside Cuba. The key point is that medical tourism in Cuba has moved well beyond the sunshine, tranquillity, and herbal remedies promoted by health spas, mud baths, and mineral springs in other tropical destinations. As the proportion of household expenditures in the United States devoted to health care and well-being continues to rise, this high-tech medical tourism could bolster tourism in Havana when the economic blockade is lifted.

*Cultural tourism*

The Revolution, with its brigades of volunteers, sugar harvest (*zafra*) campaigns, and international linkages with groups in solidarity with Cuba, receives an undetermined number of 'tourists.' Instead of visiting for the traditional venue of 'sun and sand,' they come out of curiosity or else are ardent supporters of the Cuban Revolution. These visits interject small amounts of hard currency, medicine, and clothing. More importantly, perhaps, they focus international attention on the blockade.

Afro-Cuban culture also attracts thousands to the Havana, and Cubancan, INTUR and other state agencies promote trips that focus on *santería*, the island's African-Catholic belief system. *Santeros* (priests and priestesses) meet with tourists. Short presentations explain the role of deities (*orishas*) that blend Yoruba and Roman Catholic symbols. Musical presentations drawing heavily on rumba and other rhythmic interludes make up another important segment of Cuba's 'cultural tourism'. This is, however, a highly specialized form of tourism. It can easily be accessed in Havana as a primary or complementary activity to the city's many cultural and physical amenities.

*Eco-tourism*

Havana holds little ecological allure for travelers on the eco-tourism beat. Although its population density is one of the lowest of all Latin American capitals, and it holds about 10 square meters of park and green space per resident, it is far from an ecological haven (GDIC 1990). In fact, Havana Bay is one of the most polluted waters in the Caribbean (Collis 1995). Nonetheless, those in search of eco-tourist experiences usually pass through Havana which, in turn, generates multipliers for the Havana tourist market.

In Cuba, 3200 of 6000 species of plants are endemic to the island. The island's flora and fauna richness has prompted UNESCO to identify four biosphere reserves, all of them outside Havana.[5] Traditional outdoor recreation activities, though, abound. Fishing, hunting, diving, and bird-watching side-trips leave Havana regularly and include tourists who come to Cuba chiefly to experience the capital city.

Eco-tourism in Cuba, though, has developed slowly (Collis 1995). Several locations on the island are under consideration for eco-tourism development: Sierra Maestra, Pinares de Mayarí, Tope de Collantes, and Ciénaga de Zapata. One of the closest eco-tourist resorts to Havana is at Las Terrazas, about one hour outside Havana in Pinar del Río Province. An eco-tourist facility opened in 1994 next to a rural 'new town' that was built in the 1960s. Tourists can see some of the island's most varied flora and fauna at Las Terrazas.

At present, it is unclear whether Cuba's search for hard currency will allow for a gradual development of these areas. Cuba's eco-tourism appeal in the realms of flora and fauna sightseeing is that the island is the

---

[5]The four biosphere reserves include the Rosario Sierra at the western edge of the island, a mountainous region known as the Toa River Cuchillas, 970 kilometers from Havana, the Guanahacabibes Peninsula, and Baconao Park, 965 kilometers from the capital (see Napoles 1996f).

Caribbean's largest. These sights will provide 'light recreation' such as hiking, boating, camping, photography and wildlife watching. Although not high on the hard-currency generating scale, they could provide revenue for environmental trusts to protect some of the island's most pristine natural areas.

*Joint ventures*

The new strategy in Cuba's tourist industry relies heavily on joint ventures (Dávalos Fernández 1993). A series of legal reforms since the late 1980s has eased the influx of foreign capital to the island. By August 1996, 240 agreements with investments from 43 countries and in 34 sectors of the economy had been signed (Ministry of Economy and Planning 1996). The primary countries of investment are European (especially Spanish) and Canadian (Table 8.5).

One of the most controversial projects in Havana was the construction of a new five-star hotel. The $70 million Hotel Meliá Cohiba is located next to the famous Hotel Riviera, on the Malecón, in the Vedado district. It employs 450 workers, a significant number in an urban labor market that must absorb workers from downsized state-run enterprises.

Havana's tourism promotions aim at potential visitors from Canada, western Europe (especially Spain and Italy), and Mexico. Sol Hotels in Cuba account for a large share of Havana's tourism promotion (*CubaNews*,

**Table 8.5** Selected joint-venture hotel chains in Cuba (c. 1995)

| Hotel chain | Country of origin | Tourist zone |
| --- | --- | --- |
| Guitart S.A.* | Spain | Cayo Coco, Varadero, Havana, Santiago de Cuba |
| Super-Club | Jamaica | Varadero |
| LTI | Germany | Varadero, Santiago de Cuba |
| Iberostar S.A. | Spain | Havana |
| Sol-Meliá | Spain | Havana, Varadero |
| RUI Hotels, S.A. | Spain | Varadero |
| Raytur | Spain | Santa Lucía |
| Delta | Canada | Santiago de Cuba |
| Commonwealth | Canada | Marea del Portillo |
| Hospitality, LTD | Canada | Granma |
| Kawama Caribbean | Spain | Varadero |
| Hotels (KCH) | Spain | Havana |

*Source*: *Business Tips on Cuba*, July 1994, p. 21.
*Guitart pulled out of Cuba in late 1995.

January 1995, p. 3). The 22-story Meliá Cohiba is a Spanish–Cuban financed complex that offers 462 rooms, which, in 1995 started at $150 per night. Accommodations also include 19 VIP rooms, convention facilities, and 25 presidential suites.

Hotel Meliá Cohiba towers over the surrounding neighborhood. It dwarfs the Hotel Habana Riviera set two blocks back. In the evening, blue-green floodlights cast a powerful glow on the building's modern, gold-colored metal and glass façade. The Meliá Cohiba surpassed the former Hotel Havana Libre (Havana Hilton) as the new symbol of foreign capital in Havana's tourist trade. As discussed in Chapter 7, Cubans euphemistically refer to this new wave of Spanish investment as the 'second conquest' of Cuba.

Another visible building in Havana's 'modern' landscape is the Habana Libre Hotel. Nationalized in the early years of the Revolution, the complex occupies the busiest tourist corner of the city (23rd and L Streets), diagonal to the huge Coppelia ice-cream emporium. Upon its nationalization, the name Havana Hilton became the Habana Libre (literally, 'Free Havana'). In 1993, its name again changed to the Habana Libre-Guitart. The addition reflected the Spanish hotel chain that until October 1995, had also managed Paradiso-Puntarena in Varadero (Matanzas Province) and Cayo Coco Guitart (Camagüey Province), for a total bed capacity of 1500. Guitart had a 50–50 venture with one of Cuba's state tourism companies, Cubancán. However, in October 1995, it withdrew its interests in Cuba and sold its shares to Bank Mora in Andorra for $6.6 million. News reports (*CubaNews* November 1995) claim that the withdrawal has not affected the investment climate in Cuba's tourist industry. Another Spanish chain, Tryp, moved in at Habana Libre.

### Leisure time, green spaces, sports and religion

Havana's climate, briefly described in Chapter 1 and earlier in this chapter, is conducive for year-round outdoor recreation. International appeal derives in good measure from the warm waters (25°C in the winter, 28°C in summer) and beaches within the city limits as well as the world renown beach of Varadero,[6] 145 kilometers east of the capital. A relatively low population density is the product of pockets of open, green areas dotted

---

[6]In 1996 the first toll booths ever during the Revolution opened on the road from Matanzas to Varadero. An estimated 5000 vehicles travel this road daily. Ostensibly, the income from these booths will be used to resurface roads throughout Cuba. Cars pay $2 USD and tourist buses $4 USD. Many say it aims to keep prostitutes out of the exclusive beach resort, as well as other Cubans who may not have any legitimate business there (see Napoles 1996c).

throughout the metropolitan area. Although all beaches and parks in the city are free of charge to both Cubans and foreign nationals, access to certain tourist facilities for most of the Revolution has been limited to foreigners who paid in hard currency. The way some Cubans dress is also used by hotel management to 'screen' out certain individuals. However, it is also true that Cubans share hotels with foreigners, while the former pay in pesos and the latter in dollars. Some hotels also use a 'Cuban menu' for locals and a separate one for tourists.

Because Havana has a relatively low population density and an absence of densely packed apartment buildings, its endowment of green and open areas will come as no surprise. *Habaneros* in 1959 shared only 1 square meter of park space per resident. But by the late 1980s that rate increased 10-fold. Planners are keenly aware of the need to maintain and increase the amount of green areas. Obstacles include a decline in tree nurseries, excessive pruning of trees, a poor maintenance policy, and a need to educate the public about the value of green areas (González 1990, p. 26).

The heart of the metropolitan area contains Parque Metropolitano while the flood plain of the Almendares River, separating Vedado and Miramar, broadens as it passes through the park. The river shapes the linear park into a rich, green area. Although somewhat difficult to reach, the eastern shore of the Bay of Havana constitutes another green area and park. Just across the bay lies the Morro-Cabaña Castles whose lands offer a striking view of the old city.[7] The creation of the 'Greenbelt' around Havana, begun in the 1960s (see Chapters 2 and 3), also provides an abundant 'green' perimeter around the metropolitan area. Green spaces at the city edge can be reached from downtown Havana (*Capitolio*) within 30–45 minutes of driving time

Perhaps the most striking and internationally recognized profiles of Havana includes those paintings, drawings, and photographs that show the Malecón in the foreground and El Morro Castle in the background. To the north of this vista are the tropical waters of the Straits of Florida. While the cultural and recreational importance of the Malecón (Figure 8.9) cannot be overstated, it is important to note other natural look-out points. These points may be forgotten to *habaneros* who have a difficult time securing transportation during the Special Period, and few tourists seek out these vantage points. Nonetheless, the sites noted in Figure 8.10 afford panoramic vistas of the 'Pearl of the Antilles.'

---

[7]Unfortunately, the bay is one of the 10 most polluted bodies of water in the world, according to the United Nations Development Programme (UNDP). An oil refinery on the shore dumped 54 tons of hydrocarbons there in 1993 alone (Napoles 1996d).

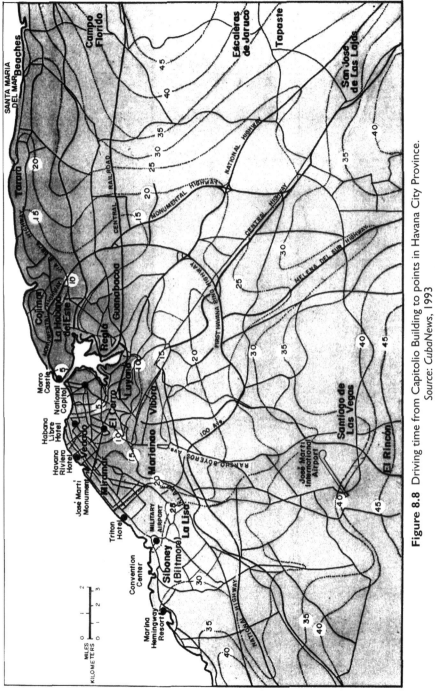

**Figure 8.8** Driving time from Capitolio Building to points in Havana City Province.
*Source: CubaNews,* 1993

**Figure 8.9** The Malecón, Havana's 'social living room' and seaside promenade, with its rhythmic line of *portales* (colonnades); the heart of Centro Habana in the background. Photography by Roberto Segre

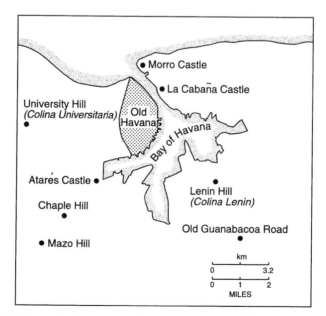

**Figure 8.10** Natural look-out points for panoramic views of Havana

As we briefly mentioned earlier, a celebrated green space in the heart of the city is Coppelia Park at the corner of L and 23rd Street which represents central aspects of the Revolution. Its symbolism is key because the park includes an ice-cream parlor under a huge light-weight concrete structure of modern design. Cuba imported most of its ice-cream from the US mainland prior to the Revolution, and Howard Johnson's 28 flavors was allegedly the brand of choice. Since the imposition of the embargo, a number of products underwent production in Cuba, and ice cream was no exception. *Helado* (ice cream) Coppelia has earned international acclaim on a par with Italian *gelati* and Philippine ice cream (Curtis 1993). Because the city-block occupied by Coppelia is thickly canopied by trees, it is an important place of socialization for Cubans. Open from about 11 a.m. until 2 a.m., it attracts some thousands of visitors daily, most of them *habaneros*.

Parque Coppelia serves as a public space, town square, and point of encounter for the Revolution's *hombre integrado* (new, integrated person). Occupying the center of the block is a two-story restaurant. The facility functions as the typical stand or kiosk one might find in other Latin American plazas. However, this plaza is different. For unlike the Plaza de Armas or Plaza de la Catedral, present or former institutions of importance (i.e., civil government or Roman Catholic Church) are absent. Like public spaces in other socialist countries, it is designed to place greater importance on public rather than private or religious interaction (French and Hamilton 1979). In many ways, it is the ultimate democratic ice-cream emporium because of the social groups drawn there. Here gather dire-hard government officials, soldiers and other *compañeros* of the Revolution, as well as *jineteros* (black marketers), high-school and college students, and a small concentration of homosexuals who have staked out the park as gathering point for that city's minority. This latter image provides the backdrop of the opening scene of Gutiérrez Alea's 1993 film, *Strawberries and Chocolate* (*Fresas y Chocolate*). Coppelia, with its steady line (*cola*) of people waiting for ice cream, is, in the words of Curtis (1993, p. 67) 'a social leveler in that everyone must wait his or her respective turn in the ice cream line.'

Originally built in 1966 on the site of a former hospital, Parque Coppelia's location in the heart of the La Rampa district in Vedado is an important transportation point for the city's buses and taxis that sweep down to the Malecón and to points beyond. The park is surrounded by hotels, airline offices, cafés, cinemas, and government and international agencies. The city block's deep, cool verdant interiors allow for pedestrian circulation to adjacent streets. Even during the Special Period when many services in Havana were cut back, the Coppelia (also a brand name) ice-cream parlors managed to provide service at prices (in Cuban pesos) still within reach of *habaneros*.

Havana also possesses a broad array of cultural attractions that are free or very low cost. A survey in 1992 identified some 262 cultural attractions, including theaters (18), movie houses (80), cultural centers (26), art galleries (29), museums (37), and libraries (25) (*Poder Popular*, n.d.). The Special Period closed many of these facilities in the early 1990s, but by 1997 the network of cultural attractions was returning to normalcy.

Sport installations in Havana were from the outset of the Revolution closely bound to existing recreational facilities. The Castro government aspired to achieve world-class status in sports, an objective that has been achieved in regional, international and Olympic competition. Multiple specialized sports facilities in Havana and throughout the island were required to maintain that level of athletic performance. In the 1960s, the Revolution took advantage of the sports complexes 'inherited' in the form of 'clubs' along the coast and the Ciudad Deportiva (Sports City).

In the 1970s, several sports complexes were scheduled to be built in municipalities that had never had these kinds of facilities. In doing so, the Revolution aimed to provide the same possibilities to all neighborhoods in Havana. Pools and gymnasia were built in Guanabacoa, San Miguel del Padrón, La Lisa, Arroyo Naranjo, and Diez de Octubre (*see* Figure 1.13). A few major projects, such as the Sala Polivalente in San José de las Lajas, were constructed in rural Havana. Perhaps the greatest efforts, though, were directed to the Pan-American Games in 1991. Olympic stadiums, pool, tennis courts and other sports facilities were built along the coast of Habana del Este and Alamar. These sports complexes were carefully integrated with the living quarters and services at the Villa Panamericana which was the last major housing complex built before the current crisis. By 1992, the city contained 1206 sport facilities with a seating capacity for 167 000 spectators (*Poder Popular* n.d.).

Cuba's Special Period has not only created many unanswered economic questions but also spiritual ones. As a result, many Cubans have turned towards different churches for solace. Although religious freedom was never completely outlawed during the Revolution, it contracted greatly and was frowned upon in revolutionary circles. As Malone (1996, p. 5) describes it: 'Harassment of believers at school and limited access to higher education have been the most common complaints. In the past, Cuban children were officially discouraged from believing in God and even mocked for confessing their faith.'

In 1992 and 1993, the Bible was the best-selling title at the Book Fair in Havana. Numerous Protestant denominations are flourishing, and according to one estimate noted in the *Miami Herald*, may include 18% of the Cuban population. Numerous *casas de culto* (house churches) have been established in Havana in recent years and are 'overflowing with new members' (Malone 1996, p. 8). Both the Cuban Communist Parties and Protestant, Roman Catholic and other churches seem to be working towards greater accommodation of each other.

## Whither social functions in the Antillean pearl?

Both residents and tourists highly value the social functions of Havana. The skyline of Havana has changed little since the highlights of 1958. Unlike other Latin American cities that display a system of symbols in the built environment such as modern high-rises, giant shopping centers, banks, insurance companies, luxury hotels, and up-scale condominiums, Havana's exterior is much more modest. In the latter half of the twentieth century, Havana has given priority to indispensable social functions. Instead of disrupting the built form with commercial and civil monuments, continuity has prevailed. And instead of abusing resources, the asceticism of a population that dreamed of the dawn of a real egalitarian society endured (Loomis 1994).

It is clear today that the disruption of the city's economic base has made reality markedly different from some socialist goals. Social functions that are free of charge – sports, outdoor recreation and religious practice – have taken on new meanings during the Special Period. Two facets of Havana – one before and the other after the 1959 Revolution – are clearly stamped on the city's network of social services. The capital city possesses a large stock of historic buildings, hospitals, clinics, universities and schools, parks, and recreational facilities. Its allure is not only unmatched elsewhere on the island, but its social functions are also unique among major world cities. Perhaps the greatest challenge will be maintaining these amenities before they deteriorate further.

# 9

# Habana Vieja: Pearl of the Caribbean

In the back [of the house] is the carriage entrance, small and shaded. In the front, golden-brown brilliance. A floor of broken tile, stained by unmemorable filth. The patio as if it had just been hosed down. Invisible freshness, unexpected clarity.

Antón Arrufat (1981)

## Shaping the urban roots

The handful of men who accompanied Diego Velázquez could have hardly imagined that the tiny *villa* of Havana would someday be so dramatically transformed. From the time of its settlement on November 16, 1519, Havana has shined against its Antillean landscape and has witnessed crucial events in the Americas and the entire world (Roig de Leuchsenring 1964; Segre 1994b). Havana would form part of the illusory utopian dream of Thomas Moore and the first example of an attempt to build a new socialism in the western hemisphere. Poets have praised its luminous aura and diaphanous sky (Arrufat 1981): José Lezama Lima, Alejo Carpentier and Italo Calvino. In what Carpentier (1969) has called the 'will of men', Havana's personality has been molded by the sea, hills and palm groves. Over time, Havana has been shaped by a dialectic of geometric abstraction at one extreme and the persistence of an incredible island landscape at the other (Carpentier 1970, 1974a, b). Christopher Columbus eulogized the island: 'The Admiral has never seen a more lovely place, full of trees clustered along the river, green and beautiful, so different from our own' (Pichardo 1965). As with other Latin American cities, it is difficult to separate the city from its adjacent physical environment; Buenos Aires from the expansive Pampa; Rio de Janeiro from Corcovado and Sugar-Loaf Mountain; Caracas from the Avila Valley; Santiago de Chile from the towering Andes, and Havana from its deep and protected bay which long ago held transparent waters (Segre 1984, 1985b) (Figure 9.1).

Throughout most of its history, government officials, soldiers and sailors, slaves, and merchants circulated throughout Havana's port area, giving the colonial streets and plazas of the port city a clamorous ambiance. Thus, Havana was unlike the typical provincial and introverted urban centers found throughout Latin America. The ebb and flow of world travelers ensured that Cuba's main port would not remain a sleepy backwater (Mediz Bolio 1916). Havana's exuberance reached its annual hiatus with the celebration of pre-Lenten carnival each year. The festivity played a key role in the life of the city because of its changing roles, ambiguous functions, and interjection of new ideas into Havana's culture

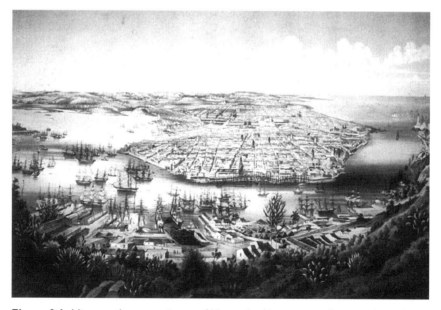

**Figure 9.1** Nineteenth century image of Havana looking westward as seen from the vicinity of what is today Lenin Hill. Regla is in the foreground; El Morro castle and lighthouse at the entrance of the bay (right, middle); Habana Vieja in mid-section followed by Centro Habana; sparsely settled Vedado just before the horizon

(Hernández Busto 1992). In the colonial areas, carnival was a time of 'psychological liberation' for the slaves, and in the Revolutionary period it has symbolized the liberation from socialist harshness.

Churches and convents proliferated in the old city, including Santa Clara, Santo Domingo, San Francisco, Santa Catalina, Paula, and La Merced. These were massive inward-looking structures that housed Havana's religious, educational, and public health functions, not to mention some of the wealthiest women in the city. Despite this clearly defined concentration of wealth and architectural symbolism of power, spatial segregation did not prevail. Lezama Lima's (1970, 1988) poetic description of street life filled with plantation owners, slaves, artisans, nuns, merchants and prostitutes is laced throughout his book, *Paradiso* (Paradise). These characters, in his words, gave Havana 'an enchanting diversity of minstrels', especially during the pre-Lenten celebrations, carnival, and religious processions, and at city markets.

In the second half of the eighteenth century, the city confronted an urban design issue: while neoclassicism was substituting Baroque in Europe, Havana grappled with a search of its own style and design (Fernández Miranda 1985). One response was to introduce subtle decorative details into its classical compositions, provoking José Lezama Lima (1988) to remark: 'that Baroque of ours . . . so firmly friendly to the Enlightenment [of Charles III]'.

The portrait of Havana evident in the Cuban writer Alejo Carpentier's classic book, *El Siglo de las Luces*, joins together three features of colonial Havana. One is the semiregular Medieval layout of its narrow labyrinth of streets that alternate with the crisp geometry of the town's renaissance squares. Adorning the squares are the delicate palaces, with their faintly colored doors and windows. A rhythmic sequence of arcades and exterior porticos as well as shaded courtyards lighten the look of these buildings (Figure 9.2). Shaded courtyards also characterized the formal and spatial continuity of the baroque.

A second feature is the symbiosis among social groups and functions as shown by slaves and colonial masters residing in the same dwelling. The elite residences, called *casa-almacén* (residence-warehouses), contained merchandise on the ground floor such as sacks of sugar or coffee. Slaves or the administrative quarters were placed on the second floor, while the head of the household and his family lived on the *piano nobile* (upper floor; see also Chapter 2). The Havana *casa-almacén* combined the home and the workplace and established a nexus between Baroque style and the Medieval inheritance of multifunctional urban space. Havana's special town design fused together different races and social classes.

**Figure 9.2** Rhythmic sequence of arcades and *portales* facing Plaza Vieja. Photograph by Roberto Segre

A third feature was the concentration of wealth along Havana's narrow streets. A number of buildings remain from that era, including the mansions of the many Spanish royalty.[1]

Local aristocrats and officials from the Spanish Crown aimed to transform the precarious image of the city which, for more than two centuries, lacked any sort of monumental center (Venegas and Núñez Jiménez 1986, 1989). Governor Marquis de la Torre ordered a design for a main town square (*Plaza Mayor*) in 1773. The design was targeted for the space occupied by the Plaza de Armas. It enlisted a continuous stretch of galleries and uniform palaces surrounding the square in a classical rectangular design that symbolized political power (Sánchez Agusti 1984). Despite the Governor's best intentions, only two projects were carried out. One was the Captain-Generals' Palace and the other was the post office (*Segundo Cabo*). Both buildings served as a model for integrating buildings with the adjacent urban setting, which was characteristic of modern urban Baroque. What came to be known as 'environmental Caribbean syncretism' (Segre 1993) would define the uniqueness of this historic core, and would mature and constantly blend artistic and cultural aspects of Havana's built environment.

### The defining limits of the stone wall

In 1982, Habana Vieja joined a select group of world cities declared World

---

[1]These include, Conde (Count) de Casa Bayona, Conde de Casa Barreto, Conde de San Juan de Jaruco, Marquis de Arcos, Marquis de Aguas Claras, and Marquis de la Obrapía (Martín Calvo de la Puerta) (Martín and Rodríguez 1993).

Heritage Sites of Humanity by UNESCO (Mahtar M'Bow 1983). Characterized as a historic center that formed part of a larger metropolitan area (Hardoy and Gutman 1992), the UN appellation set the spatial limits of the historic district. This included the entire area within the walled city, the network of forts throughout Havana, and the segment of Las Murallas neighborhood which was built during the latter half of the nineteenth century (Hart 1982). To some, this delineation was restrictive because it relied upon questionable assumptions about urban culture. UNESCO's identification of historic districts often fails to consider three key questions formulated in conceptual terms by Argan (1983). Applying these notions to Havana reveals the following interrogatives. First, is the mature and expressive period of Havana confined only to an ancient and Medieval relic? Second, is it also characterized by formal and functional attributes of a complex metropolis? Lastly, at what point is there both a qualitative and quantitative break between the historic center and modern city?

Clearly, Havana's historic skyline took shape during the nineteenth century under the architectural and urban-design canons of Neoclassicism (see Chapters 1 and 2). Its formation continued into the early decades of the twentieth century under the figurative and unitary elements of eclectic codes. Despite the encroachment of the modern movement in the city skyline, there appears to be continuity between colonial symbolism (Weiss 1973), and the change of scale and style (Noever 1996). In other words, it makes little sense to speak about a colonial city in Havana in a temporal sense, because time has not been the sole defining feature of the city's old 'look'. Most Latin American cities, for example, began their Republican phase of building construction in the 1820s; clearly, Havana did not (Martín and Múscar 1992).

Perhaps the most important fact about the artificial delineation of UNESCO's historic district is that the area beyond the former location of the old city walls had been incrementally built and blended into the old core area since at least the latter part of the eighteenth century. It is noteworthy that just as it took many years to complete the wall, its destruction was also spread out over many decades. This piecemeal approach deterred any major abrupt changes from taking place. Another important fact that promised a uniform skyline was a series of building codes and land-use regulations that ensured uniformity in building construction in eighteenth and nineteenth century Havana. Thus, in terms of historical periods, the neighborhoods between Paseo del Prado and Infanta were developed before the settlement of the walled city was complete, serving as the last link between 'Old' and 'New' Havana.

The timing of urban planning laws and public intervention in Havana made it difficult, if not impossible, to radically alter the crowded density of the walled city. The Marquis de la Torre, besides his project for the Plaza de Armas, laid out one of the first main boulevards outside the walled city. Originally called the Alameda de Extramuros, this public work was later named Paseo de Isabel II, Paseo del Prado, and ultimately Paseo de Martí. Havana grew from about 100 000 inhabitants in 1800 to nearly a quarter of a million by the end of the century. This population pressure forced city governments to focus on a different scale of urban development. Accordingly, between 1818 and 1862, the urban planning laws (*ordenanzas*) regulated land use and building for new suburban districts (see also Table 5.2; Fernández Simón 1995).

These neighborhoods had to follow the obligatory grid plan. Exceptions were made, however, in some instances. The new streets increased their width from the 6 meters that prevailed in Old Havana, to 14 meters in the suburbs. Outlying neighborhoods also differentiated between traditional thoroughfares (*calzadas*) and new avenues which were characterized by a continuation of portico-covered sidewalks for pedestrian use (Prestamo 1985). Urban growth towards the west increased the use of portico-lined roads of major importance located at five-block intervals: Prado, Galiano, Belascoaín and Infanta. Although conceptualized and laid out in the nineteenth century merely as tree-lined paths, they would become major traffic arteries in the twentieth century (see Figure 1.3).

As noted in the first chapter, Captain General Miguel Tacón began an impressive collection of public-works projects between 1834 and 1838 (Chateloin 1989). The construction and expansion of roadways radically transformed Havana. The east–west axis of Reina-Carlos III and the perpendicular road of Paseo de Isabel II (El Prado) assumed social spaces of the highest prestige within the growing city. Projects like these marked the first-time that urban specialists, especially the engineer Mariano Carrillo de Albornoz (Weiss 1967) and local and foreign designers, craftsman, and artists, linked urban design and planning schema with a concrete project. In 1863, the engineer Manuel Portilla undertook the development of a new neighborhood, Murallas (Walls), which would feature large mansions and house about 900 residents. The sweeping scale of Havana's mid-nineteenth century design eliminated much of the desire and need to enter the 'old' city, especially given the expanding road network. Municipal architect Saturnino García proposed the creation of Serrano Avenue in 1862 to join the port with Príncipe Castle. Buildings between Obispo and O'Reilly streets were destroyed to make way for the new road.

The cultural and aesthetic homogeneity of Havana's landscape is one reason why the UNESCO delineation of the historic district should have been broadened beyond Habana Vieja. As Carpentier (1982, p. 51) described it:

. . . . a casual stroller can move beyond the port fortresses and walk towards the city's outskirts, crossing the entire city center and passing along the old *calzadas* of Monte and Reina, and then beyond Cerro and Jesús del Monte *calzadas*, all the while following a continuous string of columns and archways, in which all types of columns are represented, joined, and blended seamlessly (our translation).

Havana's nineteenth century urban design reflected elements of the international vanguard, despite internal debates between Spanish-born and Creoles, and conflicts over various architectural codes and cultural fads of the day. These debates also surfaced in literature, poetry, music, and sculpture. Classicists and romantics competed with each other to show that their tastes were cosmopolitan and not strictly parochial. They wanted to show that nascent Cuban society was capable of critically adopting elements of modern design. Indeed, Cuba was not merely a static appendage of Spain (Sabbatini 1967). Elements of good taste and international style among the island's elite appeared in several forms: sculpture by the Italian Gaggini (the Lion's Fountain); paintings by the Frenchman Vermay that adorn the Templete monument complemented the scientific thinking of Tomás Romay; the philosophers Félix Varela and José de la Luz y Caballero; and the literary works of Gertrudis Gómez de Avellaneda, Domingo del Monte and José María Heredia (Portuondo 1962; López Segrera 1989).

Social gatherings in the nineteenth century were carried out at splendid new *salones* adorned by Neoclassical columns in the outlying neighborhood of Cerro. The great homes of the Marquis of Pinar del Río, the country estate (*quinta*) of San José, and the home of the Count of Fernandina sponsored 'high culture' gatherings. Other buildings closer to the historic center of town also held such events: monumental structures (*palazzi*) along the 'ring' beyond the old walls such as the Aldama Palace, the home of the Marquis of Villalba and that of the Marquis of Balboa. Along the narrower streets of the walled city we find a few palatial residences of this genre including the homes of José Ricardo O'Farrill, Joaquín Rosí, Joaquín Gómez, and the Marquis of the Royal Proclamation (Pereira 1994).

Another unifying factor of nineteenth century Havana was the expansion of new services and land uses throughout the city. The constraints of the inner-walled city as well as the precariousness of services there made it necessary to spread these services to points beyond. Cemeteries, hospitals, rest homes, markets, leper colonies, parishes, jails, and light industry accompanied Havana's expansion (Rallo 1964). Tobacco factories scattered throughout Murallas neighborhood and precipitated interaction between workers and the elite in the city center (Ortiz 1963). The early introduction

(1837) of the Havana–Bejucal railroad line, with the Villanueva station in Havana and its attendant roads and boulevards, firmly established a pattern of housing, workplaces and services (Le Riverend 1965).

Modernization surfaced yet again in the far corners of nineteenth century Havana, with the construction of Concha railroad station in Marianao and with Cristina station at the western edge of the city. Rail expansion into Havana's agricultural hinterland both facilitated exporting agricultural commodities and created a demand for port warehouses. For the first time, the southwestern shores of the bay could not accommodate this new growth, and warehouse construction sprang up across the bay in the once sleepy suburbs of Regla and Casablanca.

## Modernity's symbiosis and changing morphogenesis[2]

With the advent of the Republic in 1902 that followed four years of United States intervention, the historic center of Havana still remained the most prestigious corner of the city. Despite the new areas of expansion that attracted most nineteenth century construction, many building projects also replaced structures in the old city. Roughly 400 buildings were built in the nineteenth century in the old city, an amount comparable with all the new construction carried out during the previous two centuries (Capablanca 1982; Judget 1989). The scale of new construction was similar to existing buildings, with roughly the same height and building types, thereby ensuring the old city's sober, although sometimes irregular, grid pattern. Neoclassical and decorative refinement replaced the heavy walls and red tile-covered colonial buildings. By that time the 'city of red roofs' had disappeared even though the colorful tiles remained a common feature of many other Latin American city centers (Villanueva 1966).

Old Havana still conserved the aura of Spanish political power and held the city's elegant shops which concentrated along O'Reilly and Obispo streets (De Fuentes 1916). The historic core of Havana was also being equipped with modern infrastructure such as new sewage lines, water, telephone and telegraph lines, gas pipes, and the like. The Spanish-born who ruled Havana had concerned themselves with sources of fresh water to supply the Albear aqueduct. The US Army occupation (1898–1902) improved the quality of the city life by increasing the frequency and coverage of waste removal as well as paving many streets. The US Army

---

[2]This term follows the usage by Peter Eisenman, Jean Nouvel, Rem Koolhaas and others who use 'morphogenesis' in architecture as a process in permanent transformation and renovation. See Rem Koolhaas and Bruce Mau (1995), *Small, Medium, Large, Extra-large*. New York: Monacelli Press, p. 928.

Corps of Engineers expanded Havana's street lighting and telephone system, and replaced the mule-drawn trams with electric streetcars. Modernizing the central city's modern infrastructure worked as a strong 'pull' factor to keep many elite from moving out to Cerro – which had deteriorated during the Independence Wars – and out to the lands opening up in Vedado. Consequently, the new rich located along the borders of the city center, such as the 'ring' area just outside the old walled city and along Paseo del Prado. This latter, tree-lined boulevard and pedestrian promenade included such spectacular residences as the homes of Pérez de la Riva (sugar magnate), Conill (landowner), Dionisio Velasco (Spanish merchant and owner of drug-store chain); and José Miguel Gómez (former general and Cuban president) (Venegas Fornias 1990; Rodríguez and Martín 1994).

In the first two decades of the twentieth century, the image of the historic center changed dramatically. So profound were these changes that during the celebrations of the 400th anniversary of the founding of the city, speakers commented on the hegemony of many 'modern' buildings that 'put an end to the melancholic hue of antiquity that Old Havana had . . . and [gave] it the look of a busy North American city' (Anonymous 1919). Modern was better, and the United States was better still. Nearly 40 buildings were constructed during this same period, including banks, office buildings, and warehouses (Llanes 1987). A construction boom stemmed from *peninsulares* who were concerned about losing their historic comparative advantage in Havana's economy, a massive infusion of US capital, and the desire of a rising class of Cuban-born entrepreneurs to take advantage of this growing post-colonial economy. The built environment of Havana's center bore the mark of each of these new and competing business groups. New construction detracted from the aesthetic appeal of Habana Vieja. A new stock market (*Lonja de Comercio*, 1909) and a custom's house (*Aduana del Puerto*, 1914) developed along the water front.[3] Modernization and an open economy gave rise to new construction on the southern and western side of the old city too: the train station, the shopping galleries of the *Manzana de Gómez* building, (1894–1917), and a series of new government administration buildings.

Increasing US imports required support services and facilities in Havana. Ninety percent of US products came through the port and ample space was devoted to building corporate headquarters, warehouses, office buildings, banks, and related financial services. Some of the older housing stock and building regulations of Habana Vieja were eliminated

---

[3]Both buildings underwent major restoration in 1995 with foreign financial aid as part of broad efforts to revitalize international commerce and selected renovations in Habana Vieja.

in order to satisfy this need for suitable space. Although building heights legally could not exceed five stories, several 10-story structures broke through the city's sleepy skyline within the first decade of the Republic. Tall new buildings stacked along the narrow colonial streets cast deep shadows like dark canyons across the old quarters. 'Efficient' construction companies directed the city's modernization efforts: Purdy & Henderson, Snare & Triest, and Krajewski Pesant, were among a few of the key firms. Prestigious architects from the island and abroad also lent a hand: Rafecas y Toñarely, Luis Dediot, José Toraya, Alberto de Castro, Walker and Gillette, Rafael Goyeneche, Moenck y Quintana, and Leonardo Morales figured in this prominent list (Weiss 1950). As a result of these designers and builders, Havana assumed a bit of the eclectic look found in New York, Madrid and Paris. Notable results of these modernization efforts are visible today: Barraqué Building, Western Union, Metropolitana Building, Banco Nacional de Cuba, Royal Bank of Canada, the National City Bank of New York, The Frank Robins Company Building, Banco Mendoza, Banco Pedroso, and Droguería (Pharmacy) Johnson & Johnson. In tandem with commercial construction arose middle-class apartment buildings and the hotels Ambos Mundos, Cueto and Lafayette.

What impact did this new construction have on the urban fabric of the colonial city? Although the designs were radically different, they did not diminish the sober monumentality of the old city's columns, *pórticos*, cornices, and friezes. The canonical use of classic styles coupled with the adoption of free forms of design coming from the United States, gave a unique quality to the new construction. As well, the use of costly building materials such as precious woods, marble and granite, and sophisticated ironwork accented the new craftsmanship inherent in the designs.

Demolitions in Habana Vieja did not always target structures lacking historical and architectural value. Since the 1920s, several organizations monitored urban 'revitalization' efforts in the old city. The School of Engineering and Architecture at the University of Havana, certain parts of the press, and professional associations often spoke out when particular projects threatened the city's cultural heritage. For example, the architects, Emilio de Soto, Félix Cabarrocas, Pedro Martínez Inclán, and Luis Bay Sevilla lashed out against the speculators Zaldo and Salmón. Real-estate investors destroyed the Santo Domingo convent at the site of the first university in the city. In the 1950s in its place rose a banal office building with a useless heliport (the city's first) on its roof. Other atrocities occurred, such as the demolition of Santa Catalina de Siena convent in order to make way for a bank. As the spire crumbled atop the old Tacón jail, designs were underway to build the Palace of Justice (designed by Luis Bay Sevilla but never built).

Fortunately, Santa Clara convent was saved (even though it was turned into the Ministry of Public Works headquarters), thanks to the Protest of the Thirteen.[4] The area occupied by the old Tacón jail was sold off piecemeal in a public auction, just as was done with the San Francisco convent (which was used as the Main Post Office). Old structures such as these were not maintained and eventually deteriorated. Greed on the part of municipal authorities may account for the deterioration of other public spaces. At least three major design and planning calamities remain indelibly marked in Havana's historic center: the underground parking garage beneath Plaza Vieja (Figures 9.3 and 9.4), which altered the scale of the square by raising it 1 meter above street level (demolished in 1995 by order of Eusebio Leal Spengler, City Historian); the Neocolonial fortress of the National Police on land of the artillery school; and the apartment buildings constructed next to the Cathedral.

The dream of a modern, Antillean metropolis preoccupied the government of Gerardo Machado (1925–1933). Havana would have its historic district transformed to meet this objective, and the plan of J.C.N. Forestier was pivotal in this regard. Forestier's plan included landscape modification such as lining Teniente Rey street with palm trees to enhance the view of the Capitolio building, but that project was never implemented. Buildings were, however, restored around the Plaza de Armas and Plaza de la Catedral.

Historic preservation techniques intended to restore structures to their original state, as envisioned by Viollet-le-Duc, were enlisted. The search for natural building materials, as postulated by John Ruskin, and the persistence of a classical design, ran counter to the natural image of Havana's classic landmarks. For example, the fragile limestone and crushed seashell walls of many old buildings were removed to show the stone beneath it, as it was considered more 'European.' Architects Evelio Govantes and Félix Cabarrocas restored the Templete monument on the Plaza de Armas in 1928–1930 as well as adjacent mansions (Hernández *et al.* 1990). Their work highlighted the stark and sober gray walls which contrasted with the traditional color schema of the city as described by historians, chroniclers, and as painted by René Portocarrero and Amelia Peláez. Enrique Gil and Luis Bay Sevilla used a similar approach in their restorations of the homes belonging to the Count of Casa Bayona and the Marquis of Arcos on the Plaza de la Catedral. Taken in its entirety, this concept lent a certain mystery to the history and environment of the colonial city (Capablanca 1982; Cohen 1991; Cirules 1993). It was challenged

---

[4]This group consisted of intellectuals headed by Rubén Martínez Villena who, in 1923, had also denounced the corrupt practices of governments in power (Le Riverend 1966).

**Figure 9.3** The underground parking garage at Plaza Vieja as it looked until its demolition in 1995. Photograph by Roberto Segre

by some of the most prestigious specialists of the era such as Manuel Pérez-Beato (1946) and Pedro Martínez Inclán. These restoration efforts ran contrary to a major premise of historic architecture: restore a painting by not painting; 'restore a sculpture without sculpting; and restore a building without building' (Martínez Inclán 1946).

Despite the bustle of building construction and minor restoration projects during the first decades of the twentieth century, a progressive deterioration of the historic center was visible by the 1930s. Hardly any conservation or restoration had taken place. Colonial buildings were especially run down. This trend reversed slightly in the 1940s and 1950s because of the efforts of philanthropists, artists, journalists, historians and architects. Headed by the official City Historian Emilio Roig de Leuchsenring (1889–1964) – an indefatigable defender of historic preservation – a team of scholars and celebrities fought to preserve the old city.[5]

In 1928, during the Second Municipal Conference (*Segundo Congreso de*

---

[5]This cadre of luminous figures which included Emilio Vasconcelos, Joaquín Weiss, José Bens Arrarte, Domingo Ravenet, Juan José Sicre, Luis Bay Sevilla, Pedro Martínez Inclán, among others, sought to save the historic city. A force of younger activists also joined the preservationist movement, including Eugenio Batista, Mario Romañach, Nicolás Quintana, Emilio de Junco, Ricardo Porro, Reynaldo Estévez, and Manuel de Tapia Ruano.

**Figure 9.4.** The elevated, treeless, flat slab of concrete on top of the garage served as the new plaza. Here a baseball game with neighborhood kids. Photograph by Joseph L. Scarpaci

*Municipios*), the Plaza de Armas and the Plaza de la Catedral were declared National Historic Monuments. The Constitution of 1940 displayed a progressive streak by promulgating Article 58 which referred to the preservation of cultural and artistic heritage sites such as national monuments and landmarks. That same year the mayor approved Roig de Leuchsenring's creation of the Commission on Landmarks, Buildings, Historic Places.

Professional organizations that brought together the youthful vanguard gave new impetus to the preservation of colonial architecture. Pedro Martínez Inclán created the professional forum, *Patronato Pro-Urbanismo* (Urban Patronage) in 1942, and developed courses in Urban Studies within the School of Architecture at the University of Havana. Urban studies examined the design and cultural components of the plazas of Havana. The journal *Arquitectura* published by the Institute of Architects of Havana Province (*Colegio Provincial de Arquitectos*) published articles almost monthly by Latin American historians and preservationists.[6] These works greatly influenced generations of Cuban architects and planners (Gutiérrez 1992).

The transformation of Havana's commercial base did not alter the essence of Habana Vieja in the early twentieth century. Even though modern department stores opened in Centro Habana, and offices, hotels, and government buildings gradually moved out to Vedado, Habana Vieja kept its dynamism and multiple land uses. It maintained its rich colonial stock of buildings and diversity of social classes which, in literary terms, has been depicted by Cuban writers. Lezama Lima, for instance, presents the nuances and character of streets and places that come with a long-standing familiarity with the place, while the works of Guillermo Cabrera Infante, especially *Tres Tristes Tigres* (Three Trapped Tigers) and *La Habana para un Infante Difunto* highlight the decadent and superficial aspects of Habana Vieja (Damade 1994).

Havana took on several contrasting realities. The dock areas had bars and small cafés along San Pedro and Desamparados as well as nightclubs for prostitutes and sailors. In the southern part of Habana Vieja – Merced, Paula, San Isidro streets – lay the crowded quarters of poor laborers. Old mansions converted into *ciudadelas* clustered around the small town squares (*plazoletas*) of Belén and Cristo. Ethnic neighborhoods (comprised of Turks, Poles, and Arabs, Jews and others) concentrated around the retail and wholesale district of Muralla, Teniente Rey, Luz and Sol Streets. Amid these very different neighborhoods of Habana Vieja survived the elegant shops on Obispo and O'Reilly Streets. These were located next to banks and offices, and frequented perhaps more by intellectuals and waning aristocrats than the new bourgeoisie; the latter were too far removed in their protected suburbs. This part of the city was characterized by noise and bitter smells from the stoves of local residents that had survived since the time when Baron von Humboldt described Havana nearly a century before (Alvarez-Tabío 1994a; Seguí 1994).

In the 1940s and 1950s Habana Vieja continued as a meeting place and

---

[6]Contributors included many well-known professionals such as the German-Dominican Erwin Walter Palm, the Peruvian Emilo Hart-Terré, and Argentines Angel Guido and Mario Buschiazzo.

a place of surprise, pleasure, tourists, Hollywood stars, and artists who mixed with drug traffickers, gamblers, pimps, prostitutes, bohemians, and working class families. This potpourri of colorful characters formed part of the literary recreations by Severo Sarduy (1967). Celebrities helped give the old city its cosmopolitan flavor. For example, Graham Greene and Ernest Hemingway frequented the Ambos Mundos hotel for brief 'encounters' and consumed the celebrated local drinks *mojitos* and daiquiris at the Bodeguita del Medio and Floridita restaurants. This depiction of the old city as a place of incredible street life and a wide cast of characters forms part of the human scale that the writer Lezama Lima portrays in his silent characters who wander through the narrow streets slowly and enigmatically.

By mid-century, the Habana Vieja of the past had changed considerably. Its characteristic form, carved out by the distinct shapes of its military architecture and exclusionary social spaces of iron, wood and crystal changed, was in decline. In its place stood long shaded streets that gave refuge from a menacing world beyond where the old walls stood. Buicks and Cadillacs, neon signs for night clubs, casinos, and beaches, all expressing another side of the city, were displayed throughout Habana Vieja. Areas of Havana's 'rum and sun' scene, cheap sex, and the Tropicana were dominated by repression and corrupt police terror. Law enforcement waited at the beck and call of politicians and members of organized crime. As discussed in Chapters 2 and 3, the 1950s was replete with contradictions. Havana had become a time bomb whose imminent explosion would chart a new history that would destroy an immediate past in order to search for a renewed future (Fornet 1967; Chaline 1987; Choay 1992; Damade 1994).

## Salvation and amnesia of the past

Images of Havana in the 1950s, sensationalized by travel agencies and the unforgettable last scene of *Godfather II* with Al Pacino, would be replaced with revolutionary values. These new values included, perhaps, an overvaluing of manual labor and a desire to compensate those who had suffered hardship and sacrificed under the Batista dictatorship. During the period of Revolutionary insurrection (1957–1958), Cuba was clearly a highly segregated nation. Magazines and the social pages of daily newspapers carried pictures of cocktail parties, receptions, balls, and dances; drama that was remote from the lives of most Cubans. The massive presence of US tourists and businessmen also portrayed a different view of Cuban reality.

The Revolution was going to create a 'new' man (to paraphrase Ché Guevara), whose place would not be in the cities of Cuba, but instead in the countryside and mountains where the struggle for freedom was forged (Lagache 1992; Cabrera Infante 1994). With the benefit of hindsight, viewing Cuba as a schism between city and countryside oversimplified the complexity of social classes and was reductionist. Equally complex was the cultural and economic makeup of the city. Thus, a 'ruralist' planning perspective (Baroni 1989) would, in the end, provide little benefit to Havana and its residents.

The inherent features of the formerly walled old city were not promising for a modern city. In the early 1960s, approximately 70 000 residents were crowded into a mere 142.5 hectares laid out in 180 city blocks. As a result, Habana Vieja had a population density ranging from 500 to 1000 persons per hectare in the early 1980s (Capablanca 1982). In the mid-1990s, planners estimated that about 80 000 residents currently lived there when, ideally, the area should only house about half that number. Crowding is a major problem and the population density of Habana Vieja is one of the highest in all of Latin America.

At the time of the Revolution, only 500 out of roughly 3000 buildings were in good condition. Of that total, 900 possessed historical value. In the 1950s, 131 buildings had been transformed into ruinous *ciudadelas* (Fernández 1989). The precarious housing conditions carried over well into the late 1970s when there arose several water-related epidemics in the area. Although at one time Habana Vieja had a water-supply system that was so sophisticated that it had earned a prize at the World Exposition in Paris in 1878, a lack of maintenance and an excessively large consumer population had rendered the system problematic. In addition, systems of gas, electricity, sewage and other infrastructure had not been adequately upgraded or maintained during the Republican period (1902–1958). Public and private motor transport choked the narrow streets of the colonial core. Residents of Habana Vieja had low levels of formal education: 57% had graduated from primary school, 40% from high school, and 3% had some post-secondary training. Black Cubans were in the majority, and they suffered from high unemployment (Judget 1989). With the exception of a few projects already noted, there were no historic restoration plans for buildings in the old city (Segre 1985a). Moreover, the overcrowded buildings housed low-income residents as well as private and public enterprises that invested little in building maintenance. The 'natural' deterioration of these structures was aggravated by the annual torrential rains and tropical storms.

Soon after the nationalization of large companies and US banks (1960), the severance of diplomatic relations with the United States (1961) and the beginning of the US blockade against Cuba, the life of the city – especially the center – began declining quickly. The shelves of merchandise in department stores along the popular streets of Muralla and Teniente Rey became bare, as did the more elegant stores on Obispo and O'Reilly. Office buildings increased their vacancy rates and branch offices of internationally renown banks began closing. Tourism ended abruptly, and only La Bodeguita del Medio and the Floridita restaurants survived which, today, are frequented by tourists and those few Cubans with dollars (Paolini 1994).

Erroneous economic decisions also aggravated the deterioration of the historic center. The so-called 'Revolutionary Offensive' began in 1968 and marked the elimination of all private businesses. Like the historic center of many other Latin American cities (De Tercin 1989; Martín and Múscar 1992), Habana Vieja had attracted a large percentage of self-employed merchants, artists, and painters, whose elimination had a negative effect on the historic center (Segre 1992a). Eliminating small entrepreneurs also coincided with a fight against the bureaucracy of city government (Garnier 1971, p. 1973), which remained in effect until the early 1990s.

For a short time in the late 1970s and early 1980s, Habana Vieja reactivated its functional role as the historic and artistic center (Rivero 1981). The memorable 'Saturdays in the plaza' entailed the authorized selling of artwork and handicrafts by talented artists in two improvised markets located in the Plaza de Armas and Plaza de la Catedral. Within a short time, however, the crafts fair was abruptly shut down by the government[7] because of 'illicit enrichment' on the part of the artists and craftspersons. In 1993, in the old governor's summer home – Quinta de los Molinos – in Vedado, just below the University of Havana, the same artisan fair was reinstated. By 1996, street vendors of old books, popular art, and handicrafts had once again saturated the Plaza de Armas and the Plaza de la Catedral.[8]

At the same time, the demise of the old city meant a gradual loss in the old building trades which, since colonial times, had achieved high levels of craftsmanship (Coyula 1991b). Not only did masons, stone cutters, carpenters, blacksmiths, and bricklayers disappear, but a whole generation of young apprentices was interrupted, creating a huge in gap in the transfer of traditional building techniques. The myth surrounding prefabrica-

---

[7]A similar theme was reflected with biting humor in Guitérrez Alea's film, *Death of a Bureaucrat*.

[8]It is generally believed that the merchandise in the 1990s is of lesser quality than in the previous era. Also, in the 1970s and 1980s, there were few tourists in these markets, and the sales were almost entirely in pesos. In the 1990s, tourists are the main clients and they pay in dollars.

tion – long considered to be a universal panacea – also surfaced in the historic core in the form of buildings with standardized designs such as schools and health clinics (De la Nuez 1991; Segre 1994b).

## Dreaming of the future form of Habana Vieja

Urban and regional planning strategies worked in tandem to achieve their respective goals. As identified in Chapter 3, a clear manifestation of that coordination appeared in the 1968 'Greenbelt' (*Plan del Cordón de La Habana*), which had three goals. First, it sought to integrate *habaneros* into the agricultural push towards the unattained 1970 sugar harvest goal of 10 million tons. Second, the ring or 'Greenbelt' would enable Havana to become self-sufficient in food (Gutelman 1967). Third, the new farm belt at the city's edge would absorb idle labor stemming from the drastic reduction in small businesses from the revolutionary offensive and clerical workers in the antibureaucracy campaign. Although the plan included the construction of several dams and agricultural-worker settlements, it ultimately failed because it neither achieved its agricultural goals nor attracted the volunteer workers to farms in the adjacent hinterland. Priority given to rural productive infrastructure throughout Cuba left few resources available for urban housing initiatives (Segre 1985a).

The housing shortage in the historic center forced the government to allow local residents to convert vacant stores into apartments. Such commercial-to-residential conversion was a radical measure that made it difficult to reactivate retail activity in the streets of the old city while also disrupting the look of the place. In the absence of building code enforcement, new occupants adapted these new spaces as they pleased, which many times resulted in radically changing the façade of buildings, and arbitrarily replacing stained glass and other windows with bricks, drywall, or concrete blocks. At the same time, the high ceilings of the old residences made it possible for the new occupants to build a loft-style mezzanine (called *barbacoa*) to maximize the number of occupants per dwelling. However, the weight of these makeshift lofts and the furniture they held often weakened the load-bearing walls of these old structures. Prefabricated panels that separated the iron grillwork around the windows from the walls changed the exterior of these nineteenth century buildings (Coyula 1985a, b; Mathéy 1994).

The two master plans elaborated for Havana during the 1960s (see Chapter 4) did not make special reference to Habana Vieja (Casal and Sánchez 1984). Even though a good deal of attention was placed on the road network and industrial complexes at the city's edge, the plans revealed concern about returning to some of the roots of the historic center in a way that clearly emanated from the ideas of the CIAM (*Congrés Internationale d'Architecture Moderne*).

These master plans emphasized the role of the pedestrian and sought to revive functions of the city center that would include workplaces which drew upon local labor markets. Cultural activities also held a priority in the new plans as did a concern over reducing population densities and increasing the amount of open spaces in Havana. In essence, these strategies sought to push the city beyond its original compact layout, and towards a more dispersed metropolis. Without a doubt, though, the most significant proposal of the master plan regarding Habana Vieja focused on land use around the port, and the elimination of the warehouses in order to open up the view of the bay from the old colonial streets (Padrón Lotti and Cuervo Masoné 1988).[9] In doing so, the port could still be modernized with container systems for sea–land transfer and break-in-bulk points. However, the new container facilities would lie in the back bay, to the south and west of the old city. The relocation of the warehouses and siting of the new container facilities would free up the original shoreline along the bay to accommodate the shipping of non-containerized merchandise, the circulation of heavy vehicles along the waterfront, and the habitual disorder caused by the movement of ships, trains and trucks. Most of this initiative, however, including plans for cleaning up the highly polluted bay, was postponed because of its high cost, and then later the progressive decline in public resources made the port's revitalization efforts virtually impossible.

It was not easy in the early years of the Revolution to pay a great deal of attention to architectural and historic preservation. Only Alejo Carpentier (1979), in his book *La Consagración de la Primavera*, saw the necessity within the Revolution for young and creative architects to restore colonial structures. A small team called the National Landmarks Commission formed within the National Council of Culture in 1963. Its charge was to develop a national plan for restoring Cuba's principal landmarks (López-Castañeda 1971). Scant resources available for these endeavors led them to concentrate on efforts around Catedral, Armas and San Francisco plazas because of their coherent and homogeneous nature. Of particular importance was increasing sensitivity about preserving the city's built cultural heritage. This was further strengthened through international connections Cuba began making with both western and eastern

---

[9]This was the vision of Martínez Inclán in the 1930s, and the way the road running along the Bay of Havana and the eastern edge of the old city – Alameda de Paula – had existed originally.

Europe during the 1960s and 1970s. Historic preservation and the safe-keeping of national landmarks received great impetus after the dissemi-nation of the 1964 Venice Charter (*Carta de Venecia*) and the 1965 meeting in Warsaw, Poland of the International Council of Monuments and Sites (ICOMOS) (López-Castañeda 1963; Rigol 1978).

The exodus of the Cuban bourgeoisie also meant the loss of the city's concern with urban architecture. A growing political class in Cuba con-sisting of the urban proletariat and farmers gave the Revolution a prag-matic approach. One concerned more about satisfying immediate needs and less about inheriting contaminated bourgeoisie values, including architectural ones. During the so-called 'hard years' (Sánchez 1989), the Department of Demolitions had more power in carrying out their annual goals than did those who tried to restore national landmarks. Political leaders suddenly thrust in decision-making positions often made seem-ingly random decisions about the built environment, without having the faintest ideas about criteria used by trained professionals. Not surpris-ingly, some decisions were positive while others were not. On the one hand, the former Aldama Palace was restored to its original condition, a task complicated because it had been converted into a tobacco factory. On the other hand, the architectural integrity of the Segundo Cabo palace on the Plaza de Armas – one the best examples of Cuban colonial architecture – was marred by a modern-style top floor. A similar incident occurred in 1995 with the Lonja de Comercio (stock market building) where a modern steel and glass structure was installed around the original cupola as part of a Spanish joint-venture's efforts to convert the building into a modern office complex.

Despite its emphasis on technical studies, the School of Architecture at the University of Havana played an important part in the struggle to save the city's cultural heritage. Young professors and students of architec-tural history revived the writings and ideas of Joaquin Weiss and Pedro Martínez Inclán which led them to undertake studies of building restora-tion in Habana Vieja. In the 1970s, a team called the Architecture and Urban Studies Historic Research Group (GIHAU, *Grupo de Investigaciones Históricas de la Arquitectura y el Urbanismo*), directed by Roberto Segre, organized a series of studies, including drawing the façades of every building in the old city.

## The historic roots syndrome

The new socialist constitution of 1975 ushered in a new stage in the life of Cuban institutions. It greatly strengthened provincial and local powers.

These new local institutions reduced the excessive and centralized powers of many government functions. Key elements of the 1940 constitution addressing historic districts were embraced. In 1977, the National Assembly of People's Power (*Poder Popular*) passed two executive laws that embraced the principles of the new constitution: the Cultural Heritage Protection Law and the National and Local Landmark Protection Law. Since 1978 the legislation has protected 57 historic urban centers, sites and buildings throughout the country, including the seven original *villas* of Baracoa, Bayamo, Santiago de Cuba, Camagüey, Sancti Spiritus, Trinidad and La Habana. In 1980, two entities were given direct responsibility for aspects in the old city: the National Center for Conservation, Restoration, and Museum Studies (CENCREM) which is sponsored by the National Ministry of Culture; and the City Historian's Department of Architecture office which is part of the City Museum and Havana's local government. Lastly, the *Grupo para el Desarrollo Integral de la Capital* was created in 1987 to strengthen a singular vision of the city.

The master plan of Habana Vieja includes two levels of action: transforming the district's social and economic functions, and architectural and urban planning projects. An essential premise behind government actions is community participation and raising people's awareness about the cultural value of Habana Vieja. Eusebio Leal Spengler, the City Historian, has acted as a major catalyst in disseminating information about the city's rich history. In 1995, the Council of the State Law granted him absolute power over the decisions and initiatives over many aspects of the historic district (Leal 1986, 1988). In the early 1990s, he created Habaguanex,[10] a joint-venture for-profit firm. Habaguanex attracts hard currency for historic preservation (Pattullo 1996, p. 192–194). The company brought in $4 million dollars in the first year of operation (Luis 1995, p. 38). By using conferences, workshops, street fairs, mass media, and the City Museum, Leal Spengler educated both the local community and politicians about the value of Habana Vieja. Revitalization efforts by local residents have also counted on a blend of specialists who serve as technical advisors, and local 'sweat equity' by the residents. Combining local residents with outside experts ensures that gentrification will not displace the local popula-

---

[10]Habaguanex S.A. (whose corporate slogan in English is 'The future world of Old Havana') is probably the most powerful state agency in the old city today. This new state firm seeks to generate hard currency through tourism and related services in Habana Vieja, and then use those funds for purposes of historic preservation. Among its many tasks, the firm operates and manages a series of restaurants in and around the area including El Patio, La Mina, Hostal Valencia, Don Giovanni, La Zaragozana, Hanoi, La Torre de Marfil, Al Medina, Puerto de Sagua and Castillo de Farnés. They also negotiate with foreign investors who wish to invest in Habana Vieja.

tion from their old housing stock. Although population displacement because of urban revitalization are common in other Latin American historic districts such as Old San Juan, Puerto Rico, it has been policy in Havana to avoid such outcomes.

The vision for reducing population densities in Habana Vieja relied on voluntary actions among residents who would be attracted by better living and work conditions than elsewhere in the city (Capablanca 1982). Increasing jobs in Habana Vieja have benefited women, who have found employment in services, non-polluting light industry, crafts, and artisan workshops. However, the existing social problems of Habana Vieja were not fully taken into account. Such problems included lower levels of schooling, unemployment, crime, and delinquency. Moreover, these social problems were especially aggravated by overcrowding and *solares* and *cuarterías*. Pockets of these residents were not factored into redevelopment efforts, and they differed markedly from artists and intellectuals in the old quarters. Although the inclusion of these latter two groups formed a key component in eastern Europe, they did not automatically increase the standard of living in Habana Vieja. Planning directives also failed to implement measures to improve gradually run-down housing or provide relief for thousands of residents (Figure 9.5). With the benefit of hindsight, an incremental approach to housing improvement would have been more effective given the impossibility of completely restoring the entire historic district all at once.

State ownership of land and the disappearance of private property made it impossible for the costly restoration operation to be profitable. If other Latin American cities relied on investors who could recuperate their investment by charging higher rents once restoration has been completed, comparable investments in Havana went into a 'black hole' because issues of social justice and equity outweighed services, and rents paid by residents of restored buildings represented a minimal portion of real costs.

Resource availability from a variety of government agencies and local and foreign firms enabled the government to financially support various project in the historic center. For example, the Spanish bank, Grupo Argentaria, financed the restoration of the Lonja de Comercio for renting office spaces at a cost of $20 million. Costa Line, an Italian shipping company, restored the Customs Piers, for $35 million. When the pier opened in 1995, it marked the first time since the early years of the Revolution that foreign cruise liners dock in Havana Bay.

Strengthening of tourism through hotels and restaurants and the location of cultural institutions in Habana Vieja helped to rejuvenate the old city partially. Habana Vieja hosts a wide array of tourist attractions and government offices that bring a distinct vibrancy to these quarters (Table 9.1).

**Figure 9.5** Modern buildings built in Habana Vieja in the late 1980s respected the low skyline of most buildings. The structures relied heavily on precise geometric features but still contrasted with the more traditional structures adjacent to them. Photograph by Joseph L. Scarpaci

What is the contemporary land use of the old city? In 1992, one of the authors directed a research project that documented the ground level land use of 4747 buildings and lots in Habana Vieja. The purpose of the land-use survey, part of a larger comparative land-use study of 11 other Latin historic inner-city neighborhoods, was to document land uses, building height and building conditions (Scarpaci and Gutman, in press). *Land uses* included residences, parks, restaurants and grocery stores (*bodegas*, in Havana), institutional buildings (government and religious), parks, parking garages or lots, and demolished or abandoned lots and buildings.

**Table 9.1** Tourist and public facilities in restored buildings of Habana Vieja

| |
|---|
| La Fuerza fortress/Ceramics Museum |
| The House of the Count of Casa Bayona |
| Colonial Art Museum |
| The Oficios and Obrapía Palace |
| Valencia Hostal |
| The House of Juana Carvajal/The Archeological Cabinet of the City Historian |
| The House of the Conde of San Juan de Jaruco/Cuban Fund for Cultural Works (*Fondo Cubano de Bienes Culturales*) |
| House of the Conde de Casa Barreto/Provincial Center of Art and Design |
| Santa Clara Convent (headquarters of CENCREM) |
| Mateo Pedroso Palace/Crafts Palace |
| Segundo Cabo Palace/Cuban Book Institute |
| House of the Count of Casa Lombillo/Education Museum |
| House of the Cardenas Sisters/Center for the Development of Visual Arts of the Ministry of Culture |

*Source*: Martínez and Rodríguez (1993).

*Building height* was measured by the number of floors, and building condition by a curb-side assignment of the façade and entrance (as 'poor', 'fair', and 'good'). The 1992 survey of Habana Vieja found that three of four street-level land uses were residential, giving it a higher residential profile than either Montevideo or Buenos Aires (other cities in the study with more than 1 million inhabitants). The second defining land use was 'institutional,' attesting to Habana Vieja's large number of government buildings, offices, and most of all, warehouses used for food and other goods. The small circulation of automobiles in Havana produces a low percentage of urban space devoted to garages and parking lots (Figure 9.6). In the old quarters, just 1% of the lots and buildings were used for parking (versus 5% in Buenos Aires and 3% each in Montevideo (Uruguay), Cuenca (Ecuador), and Santa Fé de Bogotá). In short, these land uses characterize the highly pedestrian and residential nature of Habana Vieja which seems to be frozen in time.

### Innovation and tradition

Ambitious plans coming with Havana's designation as a World Heritage Site carried a hefty price tag. As a result, restoration efforts were initially confined to a few streets, plazas, buildings, and interiors of city blocks. In the 1980s, emphasis was placed on historic areas as opposed to building-specific projects that characterized the previous decade. A series of 'development axes' guided restoration efforts. These axes centered on the streets of Oficios and Mercaderes and Obispo and O'Reilly as well as the plazas of Catedral, Armas, Cristo and Vieja (Figures 9.7 and 9.8).

## Havana *(Habana Vieja)*
### Land Use, 1992, *n* = 4747

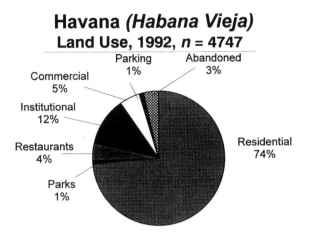

**Figure 9.6** Land uses in Old Havana (Habana Vieja) (1992)

Until the 1980s, the predominant policy approach in historic preservation was the so-called 'passive' one. This meant reviving, restoring, and recycling valuable old buildings, retaining the open spaces left by building demolitions in order to open up the tightly-packed center, and not building new structures. Key features of the passive policy approach were relaxed because of the need for social services and housing. New terms of the preservation debate centered around aesthetic and design principles such as a 'constructive management' policy of urban renewal (Hardoy and Gutman 1992).

The debate between the 'old' and the 'new', such as that which arose in the 1950s, resurfaced in the 1980s. State agencies represented the traditional essentials approach that argued for a strict and faithful compliance with the formal and decorative features of the past. Public agencies and individuals embracing this position included the Cultural Heritage Office (Marta Arjona and Antonio Núñez Jiménez), the City Historian (Eusebio Leal), and CENCREM (Center for Conservation, Restoration, and Museum Studies, led by Isabel Rigol and Luis Lápidus). Embracing this strict adherence to past design required the reproduction of complex details which was often done with shabby 'modern materials.' Architects and designers soon discovered that they had forgotten the teachings of the great Italian masters such as Franco Albini, Carlo Scarpa and Ernesto N. Rogers. The young design professionals of the so-called 'Generation of the 1980s' promoted innovations and novel applications of formal codes of interior design and the filling in of empty lots with structures that blended harmoniously with their settings.[11]

The myth that the planning and design practices could solve many of

**Figure 9.7.** The insertion of some new buildings in Habana Vieja, such as this apartment complex designed by Emma Alvarez-Tabío in the late 1980s, blend harmoniously with surrounding façades, yet are clearly modern. Photograph by Roberto Segre

**Figure 9.8** Restored buildings on Calle Obispo, Habana Vieja. Photograph by Roberto Segre

Havana's problems shifted radically from the bureaucratic paradigm of the Revolution (dealing with widespread urban problems) to myths about colonial architecture (González Mínguez 1991; Segre 1994d). Several factors accounted for this paradigmatic shift. One was the collapse of the socialist world which, in turn, created greater political isolation for Cuba. Another was the dire economic rut in which Cuba finds itself in the 1990s. And yet another stems from an insecurity about the future. Taken in their entirety, these factors help explain why officials have looked back in time for planning and design solutions. History lent a sense of legitimization and social order in a system that, in Choay's (1992, p. 188) words, 'cannot overcome its own changes nor the acceleration of those changes.' The heritage-site syndrome and narcissism of historic preservation move in tandem with the 'mummification and fetishization of architecture' (Dorfles 1965). In other words, the acritical reproduction of historic landscapes meant reviving some buildings which, to paraphrase Filarete and Mario Botta, really should have been 'helped to die.' Brilliant forms and spaces derive from these restoration efforts, with their modern pastel colors that lack historic meanings (Rodríguez 1991, 1992, 1994). Images from the mass media zoomed in immediately on the new 'colonial' restoration, especially the film industry. Nevertheless, the problem was not only one of color, but concerned issues of historic veracity given that such banal and picturesque perfection never registered in the collective memory of *habaneros* (Herrera Ysla 1991). An example of this thinking is the proposal to turn back the clock and demolish the present Ministry of Education building and replace it with a replica of the Santo Domingo convent.

New housing in Habana Vieja is established in three ways: (i) converting large mansions into apartments, such as the compact units proposed by Carlos Dunn in the Plaza Vieja; (ii) the official use of the 'loft' (*barbacoa*) as put forth by Rafael González de la Peñas in the units at 402 Oficios street; and (iii) the use of flat roofs for building new living spaces in the old city. Juan Luis Morales, Rosendo Mesías, Teresa Ayuso and Lourdes León earned a prize in the Third Iberoamerican Competition at the Torroja Institute in Madrid. This award-winning design included the use of characteristic designs and the participation of the residents.

---

[11]Advocates of this approach were Eduardo Luis Rodríguez, Emma Alvarez-Tabío, Felicia Chateloin, Patricia Rodríguez Alomá, Abel Rodríguez, Ricardo Fernández, Emilio Castro, Rafael Fornés, Francisco Bedoya, Juan Luis Morales, Rosendo Mesías, and Jorge Tamargo. Despite the 'generation gap', the ideas of these young professionals found support among certain older government officials (Mario Coyula, Director of Architecture, *Poder Popular*) and well-established professionals who were identified with the postulates of the modern movement (Sergio Baroni, Roberto Gottardi, Antonio Quintana, Fernando Salinas, Roberto Segre).

Four-story apartment complexes arose in the empty lots of the old city. They had unique façades and included traditional inner courtyards and patios. Good examples of these apartments can be found in the structure designed by Emma Alvarez-Tabío on Oficios street, Eduardo Luis Rodríguez's work on Velasco, and Francisco Bedoya's structure attached to the Aldama Palace. One might imagine that the innovators triumphed over the 'essentialists' in this design and planning polemic. However, the cityscape revealed evidence to the contrary. Several projects were greatly exaggerated and of low quality in the formal sense. Others built by poorly trained Microbrigade workers with low levels of technical training had extremely poor finishings. Therefore, some 'modern' structures aged prematurely in striking contrast to the detailed perfection of the older ones. In some cases, veteran work crews had to be brought back to rescue some of the Microbrigade projects.

The disintegration of the socialist world in 1989 and the ensuing Special Period in Cuba curtailed restoration efforts in Habana Vieja (Figure 9.9). Funds destined for restoring national landmarks dried up. In 1994, the San Francisco Convent opened a historic preservation school and the following year a new wing of the restored Santa Clara Convent was inaugurated as a post-graduate center. Perhaps the most painful fact is realizing that it will be nearly impossible to create a multifunctional space in the heart of the colonial city (Segre 1992b). Except for a few celebrated restaurants, the decline in commercial activity and deterioration of food services have made the narrow streets and plazas silent once nightfall sets in (Paolini 1994).

Private spaces have replaced public spaces as meeting places and community exchange in Habana Vieja. Individual activities prevail over gatherings of friends around restaurant tables. Recently, the home restaurants (*paladares*) in the living rooms and small kitchens have become the new 'public' gathering points. Only tourists in Habana Vieja wander in search of urban history, trying to decipher in the old stones the enigmas of the present and future. The new uses of buildings and private spaces reflect the changing economic conditions. Magnificent exterior balconies, for instance, which once looked 'like elegant chariots in the air' (García 1992, p. 93), have lost their splendor. Far off in the distance of 'ruralized' Habana Vieja today, one hears the cackling of caged roosters and hens that now own the balconies and rooftops. 'And suddenly you realize that the roosters don't call the families together, dispersed as they are by a Biblical wind, and that there are no longer dogs in the streets nor flying cockroaches' (Alvarez-Tabío 1994a, p. 16). Habana Vieja continues to exist, although it is a bit more lethargic than in the past. Its residents remain hopeful that the future will both heal its wounds and revive the glories of the past.

**Figure 9.9** The need for simple building maintenance and historic preservation existed well before the Special Period and remains in parts of Habana Vieja. Here a Microbrigade project on Mercaderes Street photographed in 1992 remained idle, and part of the scaffolding had deteriorated. Photograph by Joseph L. Scarpaci

# 10

## Havana's future:
## risks and opportunities

It's beautiful to be a communist, even though it gives you lots of headaches. And
the thing is that communist headaches are supposed to be historical, that is to
say, they don't go away with aspirins, but only by creating paradise on earth . . .
Under capitalism our heads ache and they decapitate us. In the struggle for the
revolution the head is a time bomb . . . Communism will be, among other things,
an aspirin the size of the sun.

Roque Dalton, *On Headaches*

If the Cuban Revolution thwarted efforts to change Havana into just
another Antillean Miami, the events after 1959 should be assessed according to what might have occurred had an unfettered market prevailed. This
closing chapter considers such a scenario. The tension surrounding the
city's uncertain future permeates daily life, and the chapter begins with
an overview of those anxieties and uncertainties. We then summarize
some of the key features, risks, and opportunities in different aspects of
city life (population, housing, social services, education, communications,
transport, road network, water supply, energy and household fuel).
Lastly, we address the trade-offs that exist between rescuing the city from
its economic quagmire, and radically transforming its built environment
in the twenty-first century.

## Saving Havana: anxieties and uncertainties for the 'Pearl of the Caribbean'

Havana is facing its most pressing problems of the century. Like other metropoli, its 'urban kingdom' (Mongin 1995), with its sprawling territory, has definitively replaced the concept of the compact city which has been 'blown to pieces' (Fernández Galiano 1994). Change in urban structure in many cities is attributable not only to the now universally diffused US suburban model, but also because of warfare, terrorism, and civil strife. These conflicts have ranged from Berlin, Stalingrad, Nagasaki and Hiroshima, to Hanoi, Sarajevo, Beirut, Grozny, Los Angeles and Oklahoma City (Lang 1995; Enzensberger 1995). In Latin America, guerrilla conflict hurt city residents more than it changed the make up of the city. Repression against Tupamaros, Montoneros and Sendero Luminoso (Shining Path) inflicted the greatest toll against individuals as opposed to buildings.

Modernity and markets have also threatened the great world cities. Since the 1950s explosion in real-estate speculation, Latin American cities have changed in profound ways. Little remains of the colonial heritage of Buenos Aires, Montevideo, Rio de Janeiro or Caracas. Similarly, Mexico City and São Paulo today retain few of the monumental Eclectic places that once graced their historic centers. Some Art Deco or Rationalist designs still remain in Santo Domingo, La Paz or Quito. A yearning for the modernity of glass-wrapped skyscrapers, sumptuous apartment buildings, and giant shopping centers has replaced this historic memory (Rama 1985; Sarlo 1994).

Havana is an anomaly in contemporary urban history. Its image in the 1950s as an Antillean metropolis that was destined to become another nexus in the Las Vegas and Miami triangle of gambling and tourism was frozen in time on January 1, 1959 (Benítez Rojo 1989; Michner and Kings 1989). This event derailed multimillion dollar investments by tourist companies and organized crime. Nevertheless, the Revolution also benefited from expensive projects started by the local bourgeoisie and foreign investors. Buildings as well as the city layout have withstood the encroachment of urbanization until today, despite the 'macondian' rains (García Márquez 1979), hurricanes, obsolescence, and lack of maintenance that have beaten the city for nearly four decades.

Prioritizing provincial capital investment meant fewer resources for Havana. Practically nothing of significance was built in the inner city since 1959 because of the elimination of the private sector and the evening out of land values. On average, the commercial value of the city was reduced to $4 per square meter. Revolutionary ideology gave Havana a predictable character through the construction of houses, schools, hospitals, hotels, and shops at the edge of the traditional city. For decades, the 'myth of the new' prevailed (Segre 1995). Havana's architectural heritage reflects several styles, ranging from the colonial to the International Style and a whole array of paradigms within each design. Like a 'rusty oasis' (Fernández Alba 1995) that has heroically withstood the march of time, this variety of design stands out within the squalid extension of the urban fabric.

Cuba lost its solid economic support with the collapse of the Soviet world, and with it went the possibility of giving its residents the quality of education, medical care and housing found in the First World. Since the onset of the Special Period in 1989, daily living has slipped to conditions found in the Fourth World. Havana became the main victim of this situation. Power blackouts darkened the city's streets into irregular and dangerous tunnels while the gasoline shortage precipitated ecology correct and sweaty bicycle travel. City services suffered, especially street cleaning and waste removal. Strict food rationing and shortages ended the few bars and restaurants which had previously graced Havana's streets. State construction projects and the overworked Microbrigade efforts also came to a grinding halt. Residents, already cramped into smaller quarters, could do little to preserve or repair their dwellings. City government fell into fiscal straits, unable to provide even a modicum of services. As dire as these symptoms may be, urban planners and administrators around the world confront growth management, urban policy and scale, and privatization daily (Kirby 1995). Havana, alas, is not immune.

As we have documented throughout this book, the gravity of the economic quagmire opened doors to foreign investment. Ironically, the development of joint-venture tourist installations has brought negative consequences; mainly the frantic search for the dollar (once the persecuted and prohibited symbol of *yanqui* domination) which circulates freely throughout Cuba. A new free-market wave prevails in Havana. It includes farmers' markets, the sale of craft goods, and the private in-house *paladar* restaurant. Piecemeal initiatives have partially renewed urban life but in different ways. Social relations, for instance, once concentrated in public spaces are now confined to the private spaces of homes or garages. Not to be outdone, the state jumped into the market frenzy by opening numerous dollar-run stores, changing the tranquil residential flavor of Miramar into a string of retail outlets.

The rush of new opportunity is everywhere and with it comes a challenge to urban design and planning in Havana. Foreign investment ushers in tourists, a few cruise ships are now docking in Havana Bay, and new hotels are springing up across the city. Together, they represent hope for Havana as well as a serious threat to the architectural treasures of the city. A genuine concern over the city's safeguarding is evident even in, Miamai, where the prestigious Cuban-American architect Andrés Duany, among others, make up the Cuban National Heritage organization in Miami. This group is dedicated to the preservation of the built environment of Havana, and has expressed concern about the need for a uniform planning law that would regulate zoning in this new frenzy of foreign investment. A 1996 *New York Times* article highlighted the activities and hopes of these Cuban Americans in South Florida (Wise 1996).

The passion of these expatriates and their desire to preserve the city's historic heritage is laudable. Pumping public and private investment into former Communist countries is a policy goal argued by many. The argument rests on the premise that the collapse of Communism affords a special opportunity for liberal and capitalist nations to reassert their leadership (Skidelsky 1996). Nonetheless, two distorted points come through in the case of the Cuban expatriates wish to save Havana's built form. In their stating that 'Things are falling down, everything is disappearing', one might assume that the socialist government did little in the past few decades to protect the city. In fact, scarce resources and considerable personal sacrifice went into the creation and maintenance of the Landmarks Commission, the Center for Restoration, Conservation and Museum Science, and the Office of the City Historian. At the same time, a recent show of love for the city appeared with the creation of the *Grupo para el Desarrollo Integral de la Capital* in 1987. Solidarity for Havana's well-being also comes from UNESCO and governments in Europe, Mexico, Venezuela and Argentina. These countries have financed numerous building, restoration, and conservation efforts in the historic center. Spain in particular has played a key role in this regard. In Barcelona, the ETSAB (*Escuela Técnica Superior de Arquitectura Barcelona*) is compiling a collection of drawings of the Eclectic buildings constructed at the turn of this century. The provincial government of Andalucia published a seminal guide to colonial architecture in Havana. In Asturias, an architectural organization (*Colegio de Arquitectos del Principado de Asturias*) is joining efforts with Havana to restore the Malecón and is preparing an exhaustive work on the modern architecture of Havana.

The rather apocalyptic remarks by the Cuban National Heritage group must be tempered and placed into context. It is also important to note that had the socialist project not ended the development efforts of the 1950s, even less might be left today of Habana Vieja, the residences of Vedado, or the Art Deco in Víbora or Marianao. Would Habana Vieja have qualified as a World Heritage Site if the Master Plan of José Luis Sert had been implemented? And would the Malecón, despite its dilapidated state, still retain that look so identified with the beginning of the century, or would it rather be dominated by high-rise condominiums and hotels?

It would appear, then, that the 'Little Red Ridinghood' syndrome has taken hold of some Miami architects. Behind a seemingly innocent cultural vocation hides the hairy ear of the 'Big Bad Wolf.' Speculators, builders, real-estate moguls, and others have been anxiously waiting for 40 years to retake the Havana, and to restore the lost value of the city's property. As a recent conference on global cities sponsored by the Lincoln Institute of Land Policy concluded, spatial planning techniques in market economies are increasingly rendered powerless. In their wake arise 'new rules of property and politics that de facto makes city governments subordinate to powers outside their control' (Lincoln Institute of Land Policy 1996, p. 7).

Will Havana succumb to this same fate? Leading Cuban economists still argue that social property is the *sine qua non* of a socialist project (Carranza *et al.* 1995, p. 9). Without a command economy, social property, and the state's control over the means of production, the term 'socialism' loses its original meaning (Przeworski 1989, 1992). Classical socialist models have tried to allocate resources through an economic system in which central planning was absolute. While the prevailing economic paradigm in Cuba contends that 'the construction of socialism does not require the elimination of the market but the suppression of the hegemony of capital, which is different' (Carranza *et al.* 1995, p. 14, our translation), it is unclear whether such a goal is possible, or whether the conceptual premises are sharply elucidated. As this chapter suggests, there is good reason to question the romantic notion of Havana as it withers before us. Instead, there may be a middle course that is both prudent and possible.

### Arresting urban decline: a sectoral assessment

What future direction should the city take? Which of the two faces of this beautiful Antillean metropolis should shine more brightly in the twenty-first century? The living museum of the past, or a ubiquitous, modern and placeless skyline? As one of us commented in a *New York Times* article about Cuban-Americans in South Florida who wish 'to safeguard the Cuban National Heritage . . . which has been threatened by an accelerating process of deterioration' (CNH, n.d.): 'What people [in Havana] resent is to think of Cuban-Americans sitting in Miami, putting in pins [in maps] and placing Burger Kings and McDonalds in Havana' (Wise 1996). To be sure, the Revolution stopped the 'Miamization' of Havana's water front and made both Cuba and Havana 'a different America' (Chaffee and Prevost 1989). However, it also overlooked important gaps in the financ-

**Table 10.1** Sectoral assessment of Havana's physical and human resources (1997)

| Sector | Characteristics | Risks | Opportunities |
|---|---|---|---|
| Population | • low population density<br>• life expectancy of 74 years<br>• growth below fertility replacement level<br>• 56% of population is working age | • down-sizing (*compactación*) state firms will increase unemployment<br>• top-heavy state bureaucracy will impede citizen participation | • many mass organizations can be used to mobilize community projects<br>• no threat of 'hyper-urbanization' |
| Housing | • 60% of the nation's precarious housing stock is in Havana<br>• 100 000 uninhabitable housing units<br>• half of city's stock is in average or poor condition<br>• irregular and low pace of construction | • further deterioration<br>• potential displacement of residents through joint ventures or foreign investment | • good original construction quality favors conservation<br>• self-employment complements state provisions and allows individuals, not the state, to make repairs |
| Social services | • central planning, lack of individual incentives and full employment have produced shortages, long lines, high prices and poor services<br>• high-quality health care and educational services<br>• state strives to maintain socialist establishment | • widening gap in quality of services between center and suburbs<br>• worsening of physical condition of schools and health-care facilities<br>• access to dollars producing dual-class system and dual markets | • Special Period can be used to phase in adequate tax policies to nurture entrepreneurs yet finance essential social services |

**Table 10.1** cont.

| Sector | Characteristics | Risks | Opportunities |
|---|---|---|---|
| Education | • 10 billion pesos invested nationally in higher education since 1959<br>• high concentration of skilled workers in Havana labor force<br>• rote memorization of facts in high schools despite good texts | • rising unemployment for high-school and college graduates<br>• disparity between formal education and gainful employment | • good potential for retraining skilled laborers who have been displaced from downsizing public agencies |
| Culture | • high concentration of theaters, art galleries, and internationally renown artists and events | • continued closing or irregular scheduling of small galleries, theaters and museums<br>• deterioration of national landmarks and monuments<br>• low cultural values of hustlers (*macetas*) are becoming a success model; they promote local culture in sordid or inauthentic way | • neighborhood-based music, theater, cultural or dance events hold potential small businesses and local tourism<br>• small bed-and-breakfast establishment potential in city's neighborhoods could tap into local cultural allures |
| Transport | • bus system is main transportation mode in absence of metro or streetcar system<br>• 1 million bicycles (about one for every two *habeneros*)<br>• transfers for precarious roads (i.e., tunnel under bay) | • return to high consumption of fossil fuels and discontinuance of conservation practices once Special Period ends<br>• poor integration of bicycle lanes and safety measures and lack of shaded bicycle routes<br>• must improve taxi and jitney services | • unprecedented introduction of conservation practices and the creation of a culture of bicycling have produced a 'greening' of the city<br>• revive and improve sad service connections between city center, suburbs and inter-provincial points |

**Table 10.1** cont.

| Sector | Characteristics | Risks | Opportunities |
|---|---|---|---|
| Road network | • dense network of primary and secondary arteries with major sectors in need of repair<br>• ramps for elderly, invalids baby carriages and bicycles as well as bike lanes in short supply | • continuation of spotty and low-quality road repairs will prove costly in long term unless public works commence soon<br>• economic recovery may revive private automobile and taxi travel and increase noise and air pollution and greater demand for parking facilities | • development of pedestrian malls could be modeled after existing samples (San Rafael, Obispo, Prado)<br>• circular cement speed bumps separating cars from cyclists permanent part of road system |
| Water supply | • ample water reserves exist to meet present and future demands<br>• over half of pumped water is lost through leakage<br>• low water pressure requires electric pumps for building cisterns | • leakage threatens road and building foundations by dissolving limestone rock<br>• salt water intrusion in aquifer<br>• decline in chlorinization and treatment of drinking water increases intestinal ailments | • technical aspects of water problems concerning treatment and distribution well known to professional personnel (problem is lack of money for solving problems) |

**Table 10.1** cont.

| Sector | Characteristics | Risks | Opportunities |
|---|---|---|---|
| Communications | • telephone service deficient because of obsolete and damaged technology; overloaded switchboards in poor condition<br>• one of lowest telephone indexes in Latin America (12.5 per 100 inhabitants)<br>• rains disrupt phone service<br>• tightly controlled access to the use of fax, Internet, e-mail, and World Wide Web | • continued neglect of telecommunications system will lead to greater deterioration and greater costs when/if ultimately repaired<br>• non-digital dialing is incompatible with many telephone, FAX, Local Area Network (LAN) systems | • new foreign investment will improve broad gamut of hardware services<br>• educated population capable of using Internet resources for education and small business |
| Energy and household fuels | • scheduled and non-scheduled power blackouts peaked in 1993 but by 1996 were less common<br>• high sulfur and polluting petroleum for power plants is purchased on spot market | • public street lighting insufficient and some dates back to 1890s; needs repair and maintenance<br>• obsolete and highly polluting thermoelectric plants pose health and environmental risks<br>• household fuel sources expensive, unevenly distributed, and polluting | • *habaneros* now well schooled in energy conservation<br>• thousands of neighborhood vegetable gardens exist, and potential exists to expand community gardens which use mainly organic inputs |

*Data source:* Authors' fieldwork

ing of urban services and the maintenance of its built environment.

An opportunity to identify what *habaneros* perceive as the city's major challenges arose when Havana became a member of the Ibero-American Strategic Development Center (CIDEU). CIDEU tried to stimulate the development of strategic urban plans that counted on a participatory methodology and a sensitivity to local culture. As such, it sought to integrate citizen, public, and private initiatives for harmonious urban development and to promote the exchange of experiences in economic and trade cooperation among city members. All of this took place as part of certain initiatives that commenced in the 1980s, and in which cities participated in the kind of strategic planning characteristic of large companies and corporations that function in a competitive market-place.

Havana's risks and opportunities vary across sectors. Population, housing, social services, education, culture, transportation, road networks, water supply, communications, and energy and household fuel all pose distinct challenges (Table 10.1). At the same time, however, underlying each problem is a basis for improvement and lessons to be learned about Havana's future.

### Lessons learned, lessons forgotten

Havana's two faces have vacillated from a free-market economy, to central planning, and now back to a moderate mixed economy. Radical changes like these suggest that there are models to be copied, and lessons to be learned. The experience of the former Soviet Union and eastern bloc nations should be telling in the case of Cuba and Havana. Havana's micro-enterprises must cope with pricing, advertising, return business, buying in bulk, and access to credit. A new business class plots along, building their firms, and incrementally improving their entrepreneurial learning curve. *Paladar* owners welcome their new-found occupational independence, and may desire less of what the government wishes to impose over all self-employed: 'greater discipline and control' (Granma, *Si de cuenta propia se trata*...1995; our translation). Perhaps the only obstacle in their horizon will be a battery of new government guidelines and taxes in the event that *paladares* – as past experience has shown – should prove to be too profitable in the eyes of Cuban authorities.

Recent structural changes in Havana's political economy raise more questions about the nature of the socialist state than our theoretical tools can answer. Many theorists have long been disenchanted with the nature of the state in eastern Europe, the former USSR and Cuba before the socialist camp collapsed. Far from withering away in those societies as envisioned by Marx, the state took on an almost Orwellian role in its management of everyday life. Today, though, new free-market regulations provide minute detail about who can become self-employed. *Perestroika* and *glasnost* in the former USSR ushered in rapid change as have market liberalization reforms in post-Mao China. As Kay (1994, p. 208) posited: 'Whether these herald a new phase in the transition to socialism or a new variant of capitalism only time will tell.' The unanswered theoretical question is whether the introduction of the dollar has derailed the Revolution and, if so, whether it can get back on track.

The sudden shift towards limited capital accumulation in Havana – historically a process confined to the capitalist mode of production – is changing Cuba's transition to socialism. No longer is socialism the anti-systemic force theorists once considered it to be (Polanyi 1977; Taylor 1985). While the eastern Europe experience shows that it is not alarming to find inequalities under state socialism (Szelenyi 1982), we can only hope that the Cuban experience can avoid the pitfalls that have plagued the former socialist alliance (Tismaneanu 1992; Clawson 1992; Murrell 1992; Ickes and Ryterman 1992). Because of 38 years of socialism, Havana is ill-prepared to easily support a market economy. Socialist Budapest, Prague, Warsaw, and other eastern European nations permitted limited private ownership of businesses, self-employment in certain services, and farmers' markets alongside their centrally planned economies (Pérez-López 1994b, p. 249). To many Cubans and students of development studies around the globe, Cuba was going to provide a missing ingredient in Marx's incomplete theory of the state's role in making a transition to socialism.

### An ambiguous destiny

As we have attempted to show throughout this book, Havana is unique among Latin American cities for several reasons. Its population is small compared with other capitals, and its growth rate is among the lowest in the region, having increased its population from just over 1 million residents in 1959 to 2.2 million in the mid-1990s, and with little immigration. Its skyline changed little and the neighborhoods, streets, blocks, and houses have not significantly altered the look of the capital since 1959. Nevertheless, a visitor returning to Havana after an absence of nearly half a century will find changes in the people and the land uses of the city. The façades of many buildings are tired, streets are dark, potholes are large, and neighborhoods are quiet except for the sound of passing bicyclists. But that same visitor would be struck by the persistence of the city and the tenacity of its urban heritage. Everything, or almost everything, remains in the same place. Despite the steady pounding of salt spray, rains, hurricanes, little maintenance, and a poor national economy, Havana survives (*pa'lante* in local vernacular), albeit more run down than ever before.

The city is also exceptional in Latin America because the old colonial homes and the Eclectic palaces built by the sugar aristocracy ('sugarocracy' as Moreno Fraginals called them) remain, as do the creative Art Deco buildings and the modest and widespread examples of the Modern Movement. It is remarkable that the street layout of Habana Vieja remains relatively unchanged over these past centuries. Moving westward comes Centro Habana, which despite its debilitated state, has held on to the continuous protection afforded by its famous *portales*. Adjacent Vedado retains a dense tree canopy over its streets and its majestic Beaux Arts mansions. West of Vedado is Miramar. Although it is rapidly becoming a major retail center for up-scale stores and foreign residents, it has not lost its residential charm and is still home to many working-class *habaneros*. South of the city center is Lawton and Víbora where one can easily see the creative interior subdivisions and remodeling of homes, gardens, and *portales* built by a middle class decades before.

Let us imagine what might have happened had the Revolution of January 1, 1959 not arrived. To be sure, the proposals of José Luis Sert and his Harvard associates would have been carried out by the National Planning Board. Havana today would easily have 3 or 4 million residents. A strip of high-rise luxury hotels, country clubs, condominiums, and offices would form a waterfront barrier from Guanabo in the east to Santa Fé in the west: a 40 kilometer ribbon of steel-and-glass towers. Havana's shoreline would resemble nothing more novel than parts of Miami Beach, Isla Verde in San Juan, Puerto Rico, or Copacabana and Botafogo in Rio de Janeiro. Real-estate speculation would have boomed in two clusters: apartments and offices in the central areas (Habana Vieja, Centro Habana and Vedado) and a suburban extension of high-income neighborhoods to the west, in Country Club, Biltmore, and La Coronela. This kind of suburbanization would have brought shopping malls and large supermarkets along with private universities and schools. The road axis along Rancho Boyeros might have spurred 'garden' neighborhoods. Along the Central Highway we could easily envision improvised shanties and the small homes of manual laborers. Vacant lots dotted throughout the city would be occupied by squatters and low-income residents; these would be the 'gray areas' of the city, so common in the 1950s, and so ripe for the rise of *solares* and *cuarterías* created by a speculative real-estate market and, most likely, the home of the urban poor and newly arrived migrants from the *campo*.

Habana Vieja, Centro Habana, and Vedado would have lost their original shape. It may have been revived by new administrative functions and stores, but it would also have included the visual blight of the large plastic signs and icons of McDonalds, Pizza Hut and Burger King. Concentrating retail activity along the main roads and central places: Prado, Parque Central, Reina, Galiano, Belascoaín, Infanta, La Rampa and Zanja. Sert's plan to widen all these roads would have been carried out with limited-access roads. They would have criss-crossed the fabric of the city, reaching even into the depths of Habana Vieja as discussed in Chapter 9.

We would find a different Havana. Surely it would be brighter – colored by neon lights and illuminated billboards – and better painted, cleaner, and well maintained. The scarcity of building materials in socialist Cuba is well known. It has arrested architectural development as surely as Vesuvius arrested Pompeii (Livingston 1996). Nonetheless, *habaneros* wait patiently for the chance to improve their homes. Cristina García (1992, pp. 38–39) captures this sentiment in her fictitious account of contemporary Havana:

> Last fall, the line at the hardware store snaked around the block for the surplus paint, left over from a hospital project on the other side of Havana. Felicia bought the maximum amount allowed, eight gallons, and spent two Sundays painting the house with borrowed brushes and ladders . . .'After all', she said, 'you could die waiting for the right shade of blue.'

Shiny buildings would tower over the city, designed, no doubt, by internationally renowned architects. Yet those same structures would have dismissed the cultural glimmer of the past, the traces of history etched into its landscape, as well as the amenities that make Havana a special place. The questions to be asked are: How can a vibrant future be achieved without losing all that has been conserved? How can we balance the changes that are soon to come with the urban heritage maintained so laboriously despite the absence of resources to execute such a Herculean task? Can the wishes of the Cuban National Heritage in Miami be accommodated with the aspirations of the *Grupo para el Desarrollo Integral de la Capital* in Havana, and with the rapid real-estate and speculation boom that would transform Havana? Is it possible to reconcile the dreams of many 90 miles away, with those who sleep in the city every night? With a rush by some to make up for more than 40 years of 'lost' time, the end result will be a series of buildings that look more like the Cohiba Meliá Hotel next to the Hotel Habana Riviera on the Malecón, than a more balanced approach to urban growth might reveal. Other Miami–Havana ties are more subtle, but just as real, nonetheless. There is even rising interest in burying Cuban-Americans, now entombed in south Florida, in Cuba, once legal barriers dissolve (de Córdoba 1996).

The incipient challenge facing Havana is how to handle changes that will prepare the city for a competitive economic market so as not to jeopardize the notability of its built environment or undermine its social accomplishments. Even the business-minded British publication *The Economist* (April 6, 1996, p. 12) devoted a special supplement to Havana, noting:

> Old Havana, if it can be rescued before it crumbles, is a jewel of Spanish colonial architecture, and has a certain risqué chic spiced up with smoking and sex. Cuba has a highly educated work force and a sophisticated consumer market. And, most tantalising of all, Americans are debarred from trading there.

While substituting the traditional rigid nature of city government for other forces could be advantageous, it is important not to succumb to other extremes. Such a perilous situation might result when, for instance, the power of money overshadows the collective will of *habaneros* who would be removed from participating in how the city is administered. Having said that, we are acutely aware that current government administrative problems plague the city (see Chapter 5). A vibrant city, we contend, must take into account the wishes of its citizens.

The only way to obtain the $10–$14 billion dollars necessary to restore Havana is to act swiftly at both macro and micro levels (Coyula 1995). At one level, careful attention must be given to establishing guidelines about new investment, settlements, and economic activities. At another level, community participation should be encouraged that will help restore public spaces, buildings, and empty shops in starting small firms and other initiatives. Havana's streets, stores, plazas and colonnades need to be revived in a way that integrates the present, albeit cautious, drive towards a market economy with ways of the past, and with the social accomplishments of the Revolution.

These goals are not incompatible. As the exiled Cuban poet René Vázquez (born 1952, in Caibarién) observed at a conference on Cuban 'bipolarity' in Stockholm, which included Cuban writers from the island and in exile, "It"s time to start forgiving and understanding ourselves, or at least to tolerate and acknowledge the other's rights to exist as a Cuban . . . Nothing is more similar jto a Cuban Communist than a Cuban anti-Communist. Our call [to this meeting] appealed to moderation, analysis, prudence and respect for the true protagonist of this meeting: the suffering Cuban people (Vázquez 1994, pp. 7–8, original emphasis, our translation). At the same conference Miguel Barnet (born 1940, in La

Habana) remarked: "Only those who transcend the limits of time shall win the battle, no matter in which pole they are . . . the journey will be forever if it is committed to eternity. The dialogue between us cannot suffer from cracks or divergence. We can live with them, even if they are painful . . . One way or another, we are the heirs of a nation forged in its own contradictions . . . Time will erase personal discrepancies . . . I see everyone in Cuba because a Cuban cannot be assimilated and because no one has really left, whether in a dream or in a nightmare' (Barnet 1994, p. 20).

Two faces emerge in the Antillean skyline of San Cristóbal de la Havana after nearly 500 years of urbanization: one before the Revolution – with colonial relics, twentieth century housing stock, and ostentatious high-rises of the 1950s – and one after the Revolution that directed construction to public housing and schools. Time and neglect are etched into both faces. The utopian ideal of restoring Havana will not only depend on life-saving foreign investment, real-estate developers, multinational corporations, or joint ventures. It will take more than skyscrapers, shiny hotels, and luxurious condominiums to revive a lackluster Havana and to restore its original radiance. Only by reviving the economy, guaranteeing modest levels of individual well-being, and orchestrating some aspect of the city's new private initiatives towards a common goal, will the shining face of Havana's streets and plazas reappear. When every house can be repaired, painted and rejuvenated by its occupants, Havana will become the 'Antillean Pearl' it longs to be.

# Bibliography

Acosta, D. 1996a. Labour-Cuba: Change of attitudes needed along with reforms. Montevideo: InterPress Service. Worldwide distribution via the APC networks. April 29.

Acosta, D. 1996b. Cuba: Public and private spheres must come to grips on tourism. Montevideo: InterPress Service. Worldwide distribution via the APC networks. June 26.

Acosta, D. 1996c. Cuba: Pimps and prostitutes expelled from 'Blue Paradise.' Montevideo: InterPress Service. Worldwide distribution via the APC networks. June 11.

Acosta, M. 1995. Entrevista con Carlos Lage en el NTV. *Granma*, December 22, p. 4.

Acosta León, M. and Hardoy, J.E. 1971. *Reforma urbana en Cuba revolucionaria*. Caracas: Síntesis Dosmil.

Acosta León, M. and Hardoy, J.E. 1972. La urbanización en Cuba. *Demografía y Economía* (Mexico City) **6**: 41–59.

ACU (Agrupación Católica Universitaria). 1957. *¿Por qué la reforma agraria?* Havana: Universidad Católica.

Alepuz, M. 1993. Bicycles overtake bus travel in Cuba. *Urban Age* **2**: 16–17.

Alonso, A. 1950. La injusticia y el privilegio. *Propiedad Urbana* (Havana). No. 166: 9.

Alonso, Y. 1995. Castro only wishes embargo was the problem. *Houston Chronicle*, July 25, p. 17.

Alvarez Estévez, R. 1988. *Azúcar e inmigración, 1900–1940*. Havana: Ciencias Sociales.

Alvarez-Tabío, E. 1989. *Vida, mansión y muerte de la burguesia cubana*. Havana: Letras Cubanas.

Alvarez-Tabío, E. 1992. Cocina al minuto. Acerca de la alquimia, la gula y la improvisación. *Arquitectura Cuba* **41**: 3–5, Havana.

Alvarez-Tabío, E. 1994a. La Habana hablada a tres. *3ZU* **3**: 16–21 (ETSAB, Barcelona).

Alvarez-Tabío, E. 1994b. El sueño después. In C. Véjar Pérez-Rubio, Ed., *Y el perro ladra y la luna enfría. Fernando Salinas: diseño, ambiente y esperanza*. Mexico City: Universidad Autónoma de México, pp. 15–20.

Amaral, A. 1994. Editor. *Arquitectura neocolonial. América Latina, Caribe, Estados Unidos.* Mexico City: Fondo de Cultura Económica.

Análisis del Mercado de la Vivienda 1955. *Propiedad Urbana* (Havana) **254**: 21.

Angotti, T. 1989. Microbrigades and the spirit of rectification. *Frontline* (Oakland, CA) **6** (14): 13.

Anónimo, 1919. *La Habana y sus grandes edificios modernos, obra conmemorativa del IV Centenario de su fundación.* Havana: Pernas y Figueroa.

Aranda, S. 1968. *La revolución agraria cubana.* Mexico: Siglo XXI.

Argan, G.C. 1983. *Storia dell'arte come storia della cittá.* Rome: Editori Riuniti.

Aroca, S. 1995. 2,500 Cubans a year kill selves; rate called highest in hemisphere. *The Miami Herald,* 31 May, page 10–A.

Arrate, J.M.F. 1762. *Llave del nuevo mundo. Antemural de las indias occidentales. La habana descrita: noticias de su fundación, monumentos y estados.* Havana 1830.

Arrinda, A. 1964. El problema de la vivienda en Cuba. *Cuba Socialista* **40**: 11.

Arrufat, A. 1981. La ciudad que heredamos. *Revolución y Cultura* **107**: 10–19 (July).

Aruca, L. 1985. Los portales de La Habana. *Arquitectura y Urbanismo* 3–85: 24–29

Aymonino, C. 1965. *Origini e sviluppo della cittá moderna.* Padua: Marsilio.

Bähr, J. and Mertins, G. 1982. A model of the spatial differentiation of Latin American metropolitan cities. *Applied Geography and Development* **19**: 22–45.

Bancrofft, R. 1994. Alternative building materials and technologies for housing construction in Kuba. In K. Mathéy, Ed., *Phänomen Cuba. Alternative Wege in Architektur Städtentwicklung und Ökologie.* Karlsruhe: Lehrstuhl für Städtebau und Entwerfen, pp. 196–202.

Barba, R. and Avella, A.E. 1996. Cuba's environmental law. *Association for the Study of the Cuban Economy Newsletter* **Winter** Issue, pp. 35–36.

Barclay, J. 1993. *Havana: Portrait of a city.* London: Cassel.

Bardach, A. L. 1995. Letter from Havana: Casablanca on the Caribbean. *Vanity Fair* **March**, 56–72.

Barkin, D. 1974. La redistribución del consumo. In D. Barkin and N. Manitzas, Eds, *Cuba: Camino abierto.* Mexico: Siglo XXI, pp. 186–223.

Barnet, M. 1994. Estocolmo 1994. In R. Vázquez, Ed., *Bipolaridad de la cultura cubana.* Stockholm: The Olof Palme International Center, pp. 19–21.

Barnou, P. 1951. *Breve historia de Holanda.* Buenos Aires: España-Calpe.

Baroni, S. 1989. Territorio y modo de vida. *Planificación Física.* **2**: 5 (Havana).

Baroni, S. 1993. Rapporto dall' Avana. *Zodiac* **8**: *Rivista Internazionale di Architettura* (Milan) **September 1992–February 1993**: 161–177.

Baroni, S. 1994a. Report from Havana. *Phänomen Kuba. Alternative Wege in Architektur. Stadtentwicklung und Ökologie,* Karlsruhe Stadtebauliche Schriften, Karlsruher, K. Mathéy: 21–30.

Baroni, S. 1994b. La Habana y su país (en sus tres tiempos). *Carta de La Habana* No. 5, Havana: Grupo para el Desarrollo Integral de la Capital.

Bastlund, K. 1967. *J.L. Sert: Architecture, city planning, urban design.* London: Thames and Hudson.

Bay Sevilla, L. 1924. *La vivienda del pobre.* Havana: Imprenta Montalvo. Cardenas y Cía.

Bedoya, F. 1992. Edificio de comercio, servicios y viviendas en Reina y Aguila, Centro Habana. Primer premio concurso Poder Popular, Habana 1989. *Arquitectura Cuba* **375**: 22.

Bejerano, D. 1992. Conjunto habitacional 'Buen Retiroí', calle 45 entre 106 y 108. Marianao. *Arquitectura Cuba* **375**: 24.

Bengelsdorf, C. 1985. Between vision and reality: democracy in socialist theory and practice. Ph.D. dissertation, Massachusetts Institute of Technology.

Benítez Rojo, A. 1989. *La isla que se repite. El Caribe y la perspectiva posmoderna.* Hanover: Ediciones del Norte.

Benjamin, W. 1962. *Saggi e frammenti: Angelus Novus.* Turin: Einaudi.

Bens Arrate, J.M. 1931. La grande Habana de 1950. *Colegio de Arquitectos* **5**. XV(May): 18. Havana.

Bens Arrate, J.M. 1956. La Habana republicana. Desarollo urbanístico. *Revista Nacional de la Propiedad Urbana* **274** (February): 14. Havana.

Bens Arrate, J.M. 1959. Las oportunidades de La Habana. *Revista Nacional de la Propiedad Urbana* **300** (February): 10. Havana.

Bens Arrate, J.M. 1960a. La grande Habana de 1980. *Arquitectura Cuba* **322** (May): 273. Havana.

Bens Arrate, J.M. 1960b. La grande Habana. Los problemas de la zonificación. *Arquitectura Cuba* **322** (July): 323–324. Havana.

Bens Arrate, J.M. 1960c. La evolución de la ciudad de La Habana desde mediados del siglo XIX hasta las primeras décadas del XX. *Arquitectura Cuba* **322**: 327–329, 437. Havana.

Bergad, L.W. 1989. The economic viability of sugar production based on slave labor in Cuba, 1859–1878. *Latin American Research Review* **24**: 95–114.

Bettleheim, C. 1969. On the transition between capitalism and socialism. *Monthly Review* (**March**), p. 9.

Bode, G. 1972. *Hacia la industrialización del sector de la construcción.* Havana: Ciencia y Técnica. Instituto Cubano del Libro.

Boorstein, E. 1968. *The economic transformation of Cuba.* New York: Monthly Review Press.

Browder, J., Bohland, J. and Scarpaci, J. 1995. Patterns of development on the metropolitan Fringe: Peri-urban expansion in Jakarta, Bangkok and Santiago. *Journal of the American Planning Association* **61**: 310–327.

Brundenius, C. and Zimbalist, A. 1985a. Recent studies on Cuban economic growth: A review: *Comparative Economic Studies* **27**: 1 (Spring).

Brundenius, C. and Zimbalist, A. 1985b. Cuban economic growth one more time: A response to Imbrogolios. *Comparative Economic Studies* **27**: 3 (Spring).

Brundenius, C. and Zimbalist, A. 1985c. Cuban growth: A final word. *Comparative Economic Studies* **27**: 4 (Winter).

Brundenius, C. and Zimbalist, A. 1989. *The Cuban economy: measurement and analysis of socialist performance.* Baltimore and London: Johns Hopkins University Press.

Bugeda Lanzas, J. 1954. *La propiedad horizontal.* Havana: Cultural.

Bühler-Oppenheim, K. 1949. *Datos Históricos sobre el tabaco.* Havana: Actas Ciba.

Burgess, E.W. 1925. The growth of the city: An introduction to a research project. In R.E. Park, E.W. Burgess and R.D. McKenzie, Eds, *The city.* Chicago: University of Chicago Press, pp. 47–62.

*Business Tips on Cuba.* 1994. Growth in tourism. (July), **1:5**. Havana: Oficina Nacional de TIPS en Cuba.

*Business Tips on Cuba.* 1995. *Tourism* (May). Havana: Oficina Nacional de TIPS on Cuba, p. 28.

BWR 1995. Business Wine Report (BWR), January 26. Cuba is opening for business (on the Internet).

Cabrera Infante, G. 1971. *Three trapped tigers* (Translated from the Cuban novel *Tres Tristes Tigres* by Donald Gardner and Suzanne Jill Levine in collaboration with the author). New York: Harper & Row, Publishers.

Cabrera Infante, G. 1985. *La Havane pour une Infante défunt.* Paris: Seuil.

Cabrera Infante, G. 1992. La Habana para los fieles difuntos. In *Mea Cuba.* Barcelona: Plaza & Janés.

Cabrera Infante, G. 1994. *Mea Cuba,* Barcelona: Plaza & Janés.

Callinicos, A. 1991. *The revenge of history: Marxism and the East European revolutions.* Oxford: Polity Press.

Capablanca, E. 1982. Habana Vieja. Anteproyecto de restauración. *Arquitectura Cuba* **353/354**: 4.

Capablanca, E. 1983. La Plaza Vieja. Propuesta de restauración. *Arquitectura Cuba* **354**: 355–356.

Cárdenas, E. 1991. *En la búsqueda de una Arquitectura Nacional.* Havana: Editorial Letras Cubanas.

Cardoso, H. and Faleto, E. 1979. *Dependency and development in Latin America.* Berkeley: University of California Press.

Carneado, J.F. 1962. El problema de la vivienda y la Ley de Reforma Urbana. *Cuba Socialista* **14**: 10–30.

Carpentier, A. 1970. *La ciudad de las columnas.* Barcelona: Editorial Lumen.

Carpentier, A. 1974a. *El siglo de las luces.* Havana: Editorial Arte y Literatura.

Carpentier, A. 1974b. Problemática de la actual novela latinoamericana. In *Tientos y diferencias,* Havana: UNEAC (Unión de Escritores y Artistas de Cuba).

Carpentier, A. 1979. *La consagración de la primavera.* Havana: Editorial Letras Cubanas.

Carpentier, A. 1982. *La ciudad de las columnas, fotografías de Grandal.* Havana: Editorial de Letras Cubanas.

Carranza, J., Gutiérrez, L. and Monreal, P. 1995. *Cuba: La restructuración de la economía.* Havana: Editorial de Ciencias Sociales.

Casal, F.T. and Sánchez, M. 1984. Planes directores de la Ciudad de Havana: análisis post-revolucionario. *Universidad de La Habana* **222** (January/September): 289.

Castells, M. 1974. *Estructura de clases y política urbana en América latina.* Buenos Aires: SIAP.

Castex, P. 1986. *La politique de production-distribution du logement à Cuba.* Paris: Groupe de Recherche et d'Echanges Technologiques.

Castro, F. 1964. *La Historia me absolverá.* Havana: Editora Política.

Castro, F. 1965a. Discurso del Comandante Fidel Castro en la Reunión de los Secretarios de los Servicios Generales de las 25 Sindicatos Nacionales (21/01). In Roberto Segre, Ed., *Cronología de la Revolución Cubana referida a la arquitectura (1953–1969). Ensayos sobre arquitectura e ideologia en cuba revolucionaria.* Havana: Universidad de la Habana, 1970, p. 122.

Castro, F. 1965b. Constitución del Partido Comunista de Cuba. Speeches from September 30 and October 1, 1965. *Cuba Socialista* **51**.

Castro, F. 1970. Discruso (speech). Clausura Congreso U.I.A. (September–October 1963) In Roberto Segre, Ed., *Ensayos sobre arquitectura e ideología en cuba revolucionaria.* Havana: Centro de Información Científico-Técnica, University of Havana, pp. 104–110.

Castro, F. 1975. Informe Central al Primer Congreso del Partido Comunista de Cuba. *Granma* (December 20), p. 2.

Castro, F. 1977. Discurso (speech). Clausura en el segundo período de la Asamblea Nacional del Poder Popular (December 24) *Bohemia* **52** (30 December). Havana, p. 2.

Castro, F. 1978. Discuros (speech). Clausura del XIV Congreso de la Central de Trabajadores de Cuba (December 2) *Granma* (December 4). Havana, p. 2.

Castro, F. 1980. Informe Central al Segundo Congreso del Partido Comunista. *Bohemia* 52 (26 December). Havana, p. 2.

Castro, F. 1984a. *La historia me absolverá*. Havana: Editorial Política.

Castro, F. 1984b. Discurso (speech). Clausra del Primer Fórum Nacional de Energía. (December 4). *Granma* (December 6). Havana, p. 2.

Castro, F. 1987. Pleno extraordinario del Partido Comunista de Cuba en la Ciudad de La Habana. *Granma* (15 June). Havana, p. 3.

Castro, F. 1989. Discurso (speech). En teatro 'Karl Marx'. *Granma* (October 2). Havana, p. 3.

Castro, F. 1990. Discurso (speech). 26 de julio. *Bohemia* (August 3). Havana, p. 50.

Castro, F. 1995. Seguimos creyendo en los enormes beneficios del socialismo. *Granma*, December 30.

Castro, R. 1996. Maintaining revolutionary purity. Excerpts from a report presented by the General of the Army, Raul Castro to the Central Committee of the Communist Party of Cuba, March 23, 1996. Reprinted from *Granma* (Havana), March 27, 1996. Cited in *Cuba: Political pilgrims and cultural wars*. Washington, D.C.: The Free Cuba Center of Freedom House, pp. 31–37.

CEA (Centro de Estudios de las Américas). 1995. *Los Consejos Populares, La gestión de desarrollo y la participación popular en Cuba. Conclusiones Preliminares*. Havana: CEA.

Centro de Estudios Demográficos (CED). 1976. *La población de Cuba*. Havana: Ciencias Sociales.

CEE (Comité Estatal de Estadísticas). 1983. *Censo de población y viviendas de 1981. Evolución de la urbanización en Cuba. 1907–1981*. Havana: Instituto de Demografía y Censos.

Chaffee, W., editor. 1992. Cuba: a background. In *Cuba—a different America*. Lanham, MD: Rowan & Littlefield.

Chailloux, J.M. 1945. *Síntesis histórica de la vivienda popular (los horrores del solar habanero)*. Havana: Editorial J. Montero.

Chaline, C. 1987. La Havane: urbanisme de rupture ou de rattrapage? *Les Annales de Géographie* **534**: 171–185. Paris.

Chateloin, F. 1989. *La Habana de Tacón*. Havana: Editorial Letras Cubanas.

Chauvin, L.O. 1996. The many struggles of Cuban academics. *The Chronicle of Higher Education*, **May 31**, p. A–33, 35.

Choay, F. 1992. *L'Allegorie du patrimoine*. Paris: Editions du Seuil.

Chomsky, 1994. Recent historiography of Cuba. *Latin American Research Review* **29** (3): 220–236.

Chowdury, A. and Kirkpatrick, C. 1994. *Development policy and planning*. London: Routledge.

Cirules, E. 1993. *El Imperio de La Habana*. Havana: Casa de las Américas.

Ciudad de La Habana. n.d. Datos Socioeconomicos. Havana: Poder Popular, Ciudad de la Habana (pamphlet).

Clawson, P. 1992. Understanding the post-Soviet wasteland. In Vladimir Tismaneanu and Patrick Clawson, Eds, *Uprooting Leninism, cultivating liberty*. Lanham, MD: University Press of America and Foreign Policy Research Institute, pp. 49–58.

Cohen, J.L. 1991. Sulle traccie di Henard. *Casabella*. **34**: 531–532. Milan.

Collis, D. 1995. Environmental implications of Cuba's economic crisis. *Cuba Briefing Paper Series* No. 8 (July), Washington, D.C.: Georgetown University, The Cuban Project, Center for Latin American Studies.

Comité Cubano de asentamientos humanos. 1976. *Los Asentamientos Humanos en Cuba.* Havana: Editorial de Ciencias Sociales.

Comité Estatal de Construcción 1977. *La vivienda y su desarrollo en Cuba. Seminario Internacional de Arquitectura. 6 al 18 de noviembre.* Havana: Ministerio de la Construcción, CEDITEC.

Comité Estatal de Construcción 1978. *Arquitectura y desarrollo nacional, Cuba, 1978.* Havana: Ministerio de Construcción, CEDITEC

Consejo Nacional de Economía. 1958. *El empleo, el subempleo y el desempleo.* Havana: Consejo Nacional de Economía.

Coyula, M. 1985a. Housing, urban renovation, and Popular Power. Some aspects concerning Havana. *Trialog* **6**: 35. Darmstadt.

Coyula, M. 1985b. Vivienda, renovación urbana, y Poder Popular: La Habana (primera parte). *Arquitectura y Urbanismo* 7(2), 12.

Coyula, M. 1987. Materia y espíritu de lo ecléctico urbano. *Arquitectura y Urbanismo* 1: 38–43.

Coyula, M. 1990. Planning Havana's future: an interview with Mario Coyula. *Cuba Update* 4 **(XI)**: 22. New York.

Coyula, M. 1991a. Al reencuentro de la ciudad perdida. *Arquitectura y Urbanismo* **91** (1): 23–31.

Coyula, M. 1991b. Dándole taller al barrio. *Casa de las Américas* **185** (October/December): 132–140. Havana.

Coyula, M. 1992. El veril entre dos siglos. Tradición e innovación para un desarrollo sustentable. *Casa de las Américas* **189** (October/December): 94–101. Havana.

Coyula, M. 1993. Para aprender del pasado: una guía de La Habana. *Guía de Arquitectura. La Habana colonial 1598–1898*: Seville: Junta de Andalucía, pp. 11–14.

Coyula, M. 1995. La Habana siempre, siempre La Habana. *ArquiAméricA II.* San José, Costa Rica.

Coyula, M., González, G. and Vincentelli, A.T. 1993. *Participación popular y desarrollo en los municipios.* Havana: CEA.

Coyula, M., Cabrera, M. and Oliveras, R. 1995. *Los Talleres de Transformación Integral de Barrios: Una experiencia de planeamiento participativo en La Habana.* Havana: Grupo para el Desarrollo Integral de la Capital.

Cuba 1968. Supplement to *Statistical Abstract of Latin America.* Los Angeles: Latin American Center, University of California at Los Angeles.

Cuba. 1976. *Constitución de la República de Cuba.* Havana: Ministerio de Justicia, Editorial Orbe.

*Cuba Va.* 1993. Coordinadora Estatal de Solidaridad con Cuba. *Cuba Va* **5,** (December) Havana: Coordinador Estatal de Solidadarid con Cuba.

*CubaNews.* 1993a (October). Infrastructure, p. 9. Miami: The Miami Herald Publishing Company.

*CubaNews.* 1993b (October). Approximate driving times in the Havana area, p. 6. Miami: The Miami Herald Publishing Company.

*CubaNews.* 1993 (November). Demographics: Cuba's Education Levels, p. 14. Miami: The Miami Herald Publishing Company.

*CubaNews.* 1994 (November). Cuba's health system: tested in hard times, p. 11. Miami: The Miami Herald Publishing Company.

*CubaNews*. 1995a (January). New five-star hotel, p. 3. Miami: The Miami Herald Publishing Company.

*CubaNews*. 1995b (April). Cuba's water resources, p. 9. Miami: The Miami Herald Publishing Company.

*CubaNews*. 1995c (July). Paladares legalized, p. 5. Miami: The Miami Herald Publishing Company.

*CubaNews*. 1995d (November). Tourism: Guitart Out of Cuba, p. 4. Miami: The Miami Herald Publishing Company.

*CubaNews*. 1996a (February). New police in Havana, p. 3. Miami: The Miami Herald Publishing Company.

*CubaNews*. 1996b (March). Facts & Stats, p. 4. Miami: The Miami Herald Publishing Company.

*CubaNews*. 1996c (June). Official says Cuban unemployment is 7 percent, p. 2. Miami: The Miami Herald Publishing Company.

*CubaNews*. 1996d (June). New rules, taxes hit self-employed workers, p. 2. Miami: The Miami Herald Publishing Company.

*CubaNews*. 1996e (June). Facts and Stats, p. 4. Miami: The Miami Herald Publishing Company.

Curtis, James. 1993. Havana's Parque Coppelia: Public space traditions in socialist Cuba. *Places* **8** (3), 62–69.

D'Acosta, H. 1964. La investigación y el desarrollo técnico en las construcciones de Cuba, después de la revolución. *Arquitectura Cuba* **332** (April–May–June), p. 37.

Damade, J. 1994. Les villes de La Havane. En Jacobo Machover. *La Havane 1952–1961. D'un dictateur à l'autre: explosion des sens et morale révolutionnaire*. Paris: Serie Memoires 31, Editions Autrement, pp. 42–48.

Dávalos Fernández, R. 1990. *La nueva Ley General de la Vivienda*. Havana: Editorial Ciencias Sociales.

Dávalos Fernández, R. 1993. *Las empresas mixtas: Regulación jurídica*. Havana: Consultoria Jurídica Internacional.

de Albuquerque, K. and McElroy, J.L. 1992. Caribbean small-island tourism styles and sustainable strategies. *Environmental Management* **16**: 619–632.

De Armas, M. and Robert, M. 1975. *Vivienda de los estratos populares en la seudo-república*. Thesis. Escuela de Arquitectura, Facultad de Tecnología. Universidad de La Habana.

De Armas, R. 1975. *La revolución pospuesta*. Havana: Ciencias Sociales.

De Fuentes, W. 1916. *Por el arte. Arquitectura, pintura, escultura*. Havana: La Moderna Poesía.

De la Nuez, I. 1990. La arquitectura posible. *La Gaceta de Cuba*, **2** (February): 10. La Habana.

De la Nuez, I. 1991. El espejo cubano de la posmodernidad. Más allá del bien y del mal. *Plural* **238 (July)**: 21. Mexico.

De las Cuevas Toraya, J. 1993. *La industria cubana de materiales de construcción*. Havana: Ministerio de la industria de materiales de construcción.

De Córdoba, J. 1996. Grave issue: Exiles, even in death, seek to return to Cuba. *The Wall Street Journal*, March 26, pp. 1 and 9.

De Soto, H. 1989. *The other path: the invisible revolution in the Third World*. New York: Harper & Row.

De Terán, F., Editor. 1989. *La ciudad hispanoamericana. El sueño de un orden*. Madrid: CEHOPU.

Del Aguila, J. 1992. Cuba. *The Software Toolworks Multimedia Encyclopedia*. Novato, CA: The Software Toolworks.

Díaz Acosta, A. and Guerra, S. 1982. *Panorama histórico literario de nuestro América, 1900–1943*. Havana: Casa de Las Américas.

Díaz Briquets, S. 1994. Cuba. In M.G. Greenfield, Ed., *Latin American urbanization: Historical profiles of major cities*. Westport CT and London: Greenwood Press, pp. 173–187.

Dilla, H. 1995. Los municipios cubanos y los retos del futuro. *Comunidad* **4**: 69–72. Havana: Instituto de Planficación Física.

Dilla, H., González, G. and Vincentelli, A.T. 1993. *Participación popular y desarrollo en los municipios cubanos*. Havana: Centro de Estudios sobre América.

Dirección de Planificación Física, 1984. *Plan Director* (map). Havana: Instituto de Planificación Física.

Donato, E. 1972. Sert, 1929–1959. *Cuadernos de Arquitectura y Urbanismo* **93**: 2. Barcelona.

Dorfles, G. 1965. *Nuovi miti, nuovi riti*. Turin: Einaudi.

Durán, M. 1992. Edificio de apartamentos en calle 11 entre 4 y 6, Vedado. *Arquitectura Cuba* **375**: 30.

Duverger, H. 1993a. Los orígenes: la villa de San Cristóbal de La Habana. In M.E., Martín and E.L. Rodríguez, Eds, *Guía de arquitectura. La Habana colonial (1519–1898)*. Seville and Havana: Junta de Andalucía, p. 17.

Duverger, H. 1993b. Acápite. In M.E. Martín and E.L. Rodríguez, Eds, *Guía de arquitectura. La Habana colonial (1519–1898)*. Seville and Havana: Junta de Andalucía, pp. 15–32.

Duverger, H. 1994. El maestro francés del urbanismo criollo para La Habana. In Bénédicte Leclerc, Ed., *Jean Claude Nicolas Forestier (1861–1930): Du jardin au paysage urbain*. Paris: Picard Editeur, pp. 221–240.

Eckstein, S. 1977. The debourgeoisement of Cuban cities. In I. L. Horowitz, Ed., *Cuban Communism*. New Brunswick, NJ: Transaction Books, pp. 443–474.

*Economist*. 6 April 1996. *Survey: Havana*. Special Supplement.

Eliash, H. and Moreno, M. 1989. *Arquitectura y modernidad en Chile, 1925–1965*. Santiago de Chile: Universidad Católica de Chile.

Entenza y Jova, P. 1953. Algunas consideraciones sobre la legislación de alquileres. *Propiedad Urbana* **230**: 11.

Enzensberger, H.M. 1995. *Guerra Civil*. São Paulo: Companhia das Letras.

Espino, D. 1991. International tourism in Cuba. Paper presented at the First Annual Meeting of the Association for the Study of the Cuban Economy. Miami, Florida, 15–17 August.

Espino, D. 1993. Tourism in socialist Cuba. In D.J. Gayle and J.N. Goodrich, Eds., *Tourism marketing and management in the Caribbean*. London and New York: Routledge, pp. 111–119.

Espino, M.D. (1994). Tourism in Cuba: a development strategy for the 1990s. In J. Perez-Lopez, Ed., *Cuba at a crossroads: Political and economics after the Fourth Party Congress*. Gainsville, FL: University of Florida Presses, pp. 147–166.

Estévez, R. 1953. El Forum del Colegio de Arquitectos sobre la Plaza Cívica y Monumento de Martí. *Espacio* **9(II)**: 36. La Habana.

Estévez, R. 1977. Los Poderes Populares y el Plan de Viviendas. Formas de ampliar los recursos para incrementar la construccion de viviendas. *VII Seminario de Viviendas y Urbanismo*. Havana: CEDITEC.

Estévez, R. 1984. Análisis de la realizaciones de viviendas en Cuba y en otros paises socialistas. Paper presented at the XI Seminario de Vivienda y Urbanismo, Havana, March (mimeo).

Estévez, R. and Pereda, J.A. 1990. Situación, demanda, y política de vivienda y urbanización en Cuba desde 1959. Ciudad '4, *IV Congreso Iberoamericano de Urbanismo*, Havana: Congreso Iberoamericano de Urbanismo, pp. 117–118.

Fagen, R. 1986. The politics of transition. In R. Fagen, C.D. Deere and J.L. Coraggio, Eds, *Transition and development*. New York: Monthly Review Press, pp. 249–263.

Feinsilver, J. 1993. *Healing the masses: Cuban health politics at home and abroad*. Berkeley and Los Angeles: University of California Press.

Feinsilver, J. 1994. Cuban biotechnology: A first world approach to development. In J.F. Pérez-López, Ed., *Cuba at a crossroads: politics and economics after the Fourth Party Congress*. Gainesville: University of Florida Presses, pp. 167–189.

Feinsilver, J. 1995. From healing the masses to healing the classes: Scenarios for the reform of the Cuban health sector. Paper presented at *Toward a new Cuba? Revolutionary legacy and market imperative in the age of globalization*, Princeton University, April 7–8, 1995.

Fernández, E. 1990. Las zonas residenciales en Ciudad de La Habana. Ciudad '4. IV. *Congreso Iberoamericano de Urbanismo, Comisión 2. Renovación Urbana*. Havana: IV Congreso Iberamericano de Urbanismo, p. 155.

Fernández, J.M. (1976). *La Vivienda en Cuba*. Havana: Editorial Arte y Literatura.

Fernández, J.M. 1995. Sobre la necesidad del establecimiento de un sistema jurídico sobre el ordenamiento urbano en Cuba. *Comunidad* 4/95. Havana: Instituto de Planificación Física.

Fernández, J.M. 1996. *Regulaciones y desarrollo urbano en la Ciudad de La Habana*. Havana: Grupo para el Desarrollo Integral de la Capital.

Fernández, O. 1981. La Habana Vieja. Renace una ciudad. *Cuba Internacional* **1** (January) 33. La Habana.

Fernández, P. 1987. La vivienda obrera durante el machadato: el Reparto Ludgarita. In P. Fernández and L. Merino, Eds, *Arte: Cuba, república*. Havana: Universidad de La Habana, Colección de lecturas, Facultad de Artes y Letras. 125.

Fernández Alba, A. 1995. Metrópolis de oasis oxidados. *Astrálago* **2**: 3–7 (March) Madrid.

Fernández Cox, C. 1990. Hacia una modernidad apropiada. Obstáculos y tareas internas. In A. Toca, Ed., *Nueva arquitectura en América Latina: Presente y futuro*. México: G. Gili, pp. 71–79.

Fernández Galiano, L. 1994. Metrópolis. *Arquitectura Viva* **35**: 3 (March/April).

Fernández Miranda, M. 1985. *La Habana, ciudad de América, La Habana Vieja: Mapas y planos en los archivos de España*. Madrid: Ministerio de Cultura de España.

Fernández Núñez, J.M. 1976. *La vivienda en Cuba*. Havana: Arte y Literatura.

Fernández Simón, A. 1950. *Memoria histórica técnica de los acueductos de la Ciudad de La Habana*. Havana: Colegio Provincial de Arquitectos.

Fernández Simón, A. 1959. Los distintos tipos de urbanizaciones que fueron establecidos en la ciudad de La Habana en su época colonial. *Revista de la Propiedad Urbana* (**February**): 39. Havana.

Fernández Simón, A. 1995. Los distintos tipos de urbanizaciones que fueron establecidas en la Ciudad de la Habana durante su época colonial. In F.J. Préstamo Hernández, Ed., *Cuba: Arquitectura y Urbanismo*. Miami: Ediciones Universal, pp. 163–180.

Figueras, M.A. 1994. *Aspectos estructurales de la economía cubana*. Havana: Editorial de Ciencias Sociales.

Fitzgerald, E.V. 1986. Notes on the analysis of the small underdeveloped economy. In R. Fagen, C.D. Deere and J.L. Coraggio, Eds, *Transition and development*. New York: Monthly Review Press, pp. 28–53.

Forbes, D. and Thrift, N. 1987. *The socialist third world: urban development and territorial planning.* Oxford: Blackwell.

Forestier, J.C.N. 1928. *Gardens. A note-book of Plans and Sketches.* New York: Charles Scribner and Sons.

Fornet, A. 1967. *En blanco y negro.* Havana: Instituto del Libro.

Freixa, J. 1973. *José Luis Sert.* Barcelona: G. Gili.

French, R. and Hamilton, F. E. 1979. *The socialist city.* Chichester: John Wiley and Sons.

Fuentes, N. 1987. *Ernest Hemingway Retrouvé.* Paris: Gallimard.

Fuller, L. 1985. *The politics of workers' control in Cuba, 1959–1983.* Ph.D. dissertation, University of California, Berkeley.

García, C. 1992. *Dreaming in Cuban.* New York: Ballentine Books.

García Márquez, G. 1979. *Cien años de soledad.* Bogota: La Oveja Negra.

García Pleyán, C. 1986. *La transformación de la estructura de las ciudades principales de Cuba.* Havana: Instituto de Planificación Física and Instituto Superior Politécnico José Antonio Echeverría.

García Pleyán, C. 1994. *Convocatoria al simposio sobre planeamiento y gestión territorial en los municipios cubanos.* Havana: Instituto de Planificación Física (October).

García Pleyán, C. 1995a. Gestión del suelo y disciplina urbanística: resultados del primer taller de derecho urbanístico. *Comunidad* **4/95**. Havana. Instituto de Planificación Física.

García Pleyán, C. 1995b. Planeamiento urbano y gestión local en los municipios cubanos: Desafíos y perspectivas en un contexto cambiante. *Comunidad* **4/95**. Havana: Instituto de Planificación Física.

García-Saíz, M.C. 1990. Antillas: Audiencia de Santo Domingo. In Francisco de Solano, Ed., *Historia urbana de iberoamérica. La ciudad barroca, análisis regionales, 1573/1750.* Vol. II–2. Madrid: Consejo Superior de Colegios de Arquitectura de España, Comisión Nacional Quinto Centenario, Junta de Andalucia, Consejería de Obras Públicas y Transportes..

García Vázquez, F.J. 1968. *Aspectos del planeamiento y la vivienda en Cuba.* Buenos Aires: Editorial Jorge Alvarez.

Garnier, J.P. 1971. Une ville et une révolution. La Havane. *Espaces et Sociètés* **3** (July): 147. Paris.

Garnier, J.P. 1973. *Une ville, une revolution: La Havane, de l'urbain à la politique.* Paris: Editions Anthropos.

GDIC (Grupo para el Desarrollo Integral de la Capital). 1990. *Estrategia.* Havana: Ediciones Plaza Vieja.

GDIC. 1991. *Problemática de las urbanizaciones en las zonas de desarrollo de viviendas en la Ciudad de La Habana.* Havana: Grupo para el Desarrollo Integral de la Capital.

GDIC. 1994. *Prediagnóstico.* Havana: Grupo para el Desarrollo Integral de la Capital (October).

Gelabert-Navia, J.A. 1994. Havana in the 1920s. In Kosta Mathéy, Ed., *Phänomen Kuba. Alternative Wege in Architektur. Städtentwicklung und Ökologie.* Karlsruhe: Karlsruher Stadtbauliche Schriften, p. 43.

Gilbert, A. 1994. *Latin America.* London: Routledge.

Ginsberg, N. 1961. *Atlas of economic development.* Chicago: University of Chicago Press.

Gobierno de Cuba. 1899. *Censo de población.* Havana: Gobierno de Cuba.

Gomila, S., Portuondo, J., López, M. and Estévez, R. 1984. Intervención del Centro Técnico de la Vivienda y el Urbanismo en el Seminario Internacional de Arquitectura y Remodelación de Ciudades (mimeo). Havana, p. 363.

González, G. 1995. Cambios económicos y descentralización municipal en Cuba: Los retos del futuro. *Comunidad* **4/95**. Havana: Instituto de Planificación Fisica.

González, M. 1990. Sobre áreas verdes en la capital. *Boletín Informativo* **7**: 18–26 (Havana: Centro de Documentación, Poder Popular).

González, M. 1993. *Sobre planos, esquemas y planes directores de la Ciudad de La Habana.* Havana: Grupo para el Desarrollo Integral de la Capital.

González, P. and Cabrera, E. 1996. Todas las tonalidades del arco iris: Parque Lenin, convergen naturaleza, cultura y recreación. *Sol y Son* (Havana: La Revista Internacional de Cubana de Aviación **36** (3): 39–42

González Manet, E. 1976. El Vedado: Anatomía de un barrio. *Boletín de la Comisión Nacional Cubana de la UNESCO* **64**: 16. Havana.

González Manet, E. 1983. Historia y presencia de la vieja Habana. *Boletín de la Comisión Cubana de la UNESCO* **91**: 22. Havana.

González Mínguez, N. 1991. La ciudad cubana en 1990: perspectivas. *Ciudad y Territorio* **86/87**: 9. Madrid.

Goodrich, J.N. 1993. Socialist Cuba: A study of health tourism. *Journal of Travel Research* (**Summer**): 36–41.

*Granma*. 1995. Si de cuenta propia se trata. June 15, p. 2.

*Granma*. 30 December 1995. Seguimos creyendo en los enormes beneficios del socialismo, p. 3. (Speech given by Fidel Castro at the National Assembly.)

Griffin, L. and Ford, L. 1980. A model of Latin American city structure. *Geographical Review* **37**: 397–422.

Gunn, G. 1995. *Cuba's NGOs: Government puppets or seeds of a civil society?* Washington, D.C: Cuba Briefing Papers Series, Georgetown University.

Guselnikov, V. 1976. *Economía de la construcción.* Havana: CEDITEC.

Gutelman, M. 1967. *L'agriculture socialiste á Cuba.* Paris: F. Maspero.

Gutierrez, R. 1983. *Arquitectura y urbanismo en Iberoamérica.* Madrid: Ediciones Cátedra.

Gutierrez, R. 1992. *Buenos Aires. Evolución histórica.* Buenos Aires: Fondo Editorial Escala.

Gwynne, R. 1986. *Industrialization and urbanization in Latin America.* Baltimore and London: Johns Hopkins University Press.

Hamberg, J. 1986. *Under construction: housing policy in revolutionary Cuba.* New York: Center for Cuban Studies.

Hamberg, J. 1990. Cuba. In Kosta Mathéy, Ed., *Housing policies in the socialist Third World.* London: Mansell, pp. 35–70.

Hamberg, J. 1994. The Dynamics of Cuban Housing Policy. Doctoral dissertation. Columbia University, New York, NY.

Hamilton, N. 1992. The Cuban economy: dilemmas of socialist construction. In W. A. Chaffee and G. Prevost, Eds. *Cuba, a different America.* Totowa, NJ: Rowan & Littlefield.

Hardoy, J.E. 1974. Estructura espacial y propiedad. In D. Barkin and N. Manitzas, Eds, *Cuba: Camino abierto.* Mexico: Siglo XXI, pp. 274–311 (second edition).

Hardoy, J.E. 1992. Theory and practice of urban planning in Europe. In J.E. Hardoy and R. Morse, Eds., *Rethinking the Latin American City.* London and Baltimore: Johns Hopkins University Press, pp. 20–49.

Hardoy, J.E. and Aranovich, C. 1969. Urbanización en América hispánica entre 1580 y 1630. *Boletín del Centro de Investigaciones Históricas y Estéticas* **11(May)**: 35. Caracas.

Hardoy, J.E. and Gutman, M. 1992. *Impacto de la urbanización en los centros históricos de Iberoamérica*. Madrid: Mapfre.

Hart, A. 1979. Discurso pronunciado en la cuarta conferencia intergubernamental sobre políticas culturales en Latinoamérica y el Caribe, auspiciada por la UNESCO (Bogotá, 11/1/1978). Del Trabajo cultural. Selección de discursos Editorial de Ciencias Sociales: 309. La Habana.

Hart, A. 1982. La declaración de La Habana Vieja como Patrimonio de la Humanidad es un reconocimiento a la defensa del patrimonio cultural de Cuba. *Granma* (December 16), p. 4.

Hart, A. Sociedad civil y organizaciones no gubernamentales. Granma August 23 (part one); *Granma* August 24 (part two). Havana.

Havanatur. 1992. *Cuba: Body and soul. Technical information for tourism professionals.* Panama: Creative Printing.

Heine, J. 1991. Habana Vieja. La ciudad de las columnas. *Mundo* **10B(IX)**: 16. Santiago de Chile.

Hernández, E. 1994. Sustentable, alternativo, progresivo...bajo consumo. *Carta de La Habana. No. 5.* Havana: Grupo para el Desarrollo Integral de la Capital, p. 2.

Hernández, T., Lores, R. and Méndez, L. 1990. *La nueva Habana Vieja.* Lima: Cambio y Desarrollo, Instituto de Investigaciones.

Hernández Busto, E. 1992. Los otros signos de la Isla. *Plural* **250** (July): 22. México.

Herrera, L. 1976. Plan de normalización para la Construcción. *Revista Normalización* (January–March) **111**: 3.

Herrera Ysla, N. 1991. La Habana de mi corazón. *Excelsior* (Sección Metropolitana, 2/3): 1. Mexico City.

Herring, H. 1966. *The history of Latin America.* New York: Knopf.

Hoyt, H. 1939. The pattern of movement of residential rental neighborhoods. In *The structure and growth of residential neighborhoods in American cities.* Washington, D.C.: Federal Housing Administration, pp. 114–122.

Ibarra, J. 1985. *Un análisis psicosocial del cubano: 1898–1925.* La Habana, Ciencias Sociales.

Ibarra, J. 1992. *Cuba: 1898–1921. Partidos políticos y clases sociales.* Havana: Ciencias Sociales.

ICGC (Instituto Cubano de Geodesia y Cartografía) 1979. *Atlas demográfico de Cuba.* Havana: ICGC.

Ickes, B. and Rytergman, R. 1992. Credit should flow to entrepreneurs. In Vladimir Tismaneanu and Patrick Clawson, Eds, *Uprooting Leninism, cultivating liberty*, Lanham, MD: University Press of America and Foreign Policy Research Institute, pp. 69–84.

INAV (Instituto Nacional de Ahorro y Vivienda) 1962. *Presencia del INAV en la revolución cubana.* Havana: INAV.

Informe Central al XIV Congreso de la Central de Trabajadores de Cuba. 1978. *Granma* (December 2), Havana, p. 3.

InterPress. 1996a. Cuba: Peso gana terreno al dólar en casas de cambio. Montevideo: InterPress Third World News Agency (IPS) Service, distributed electronically through the APC network, August 21.

InterPress. 1996b. Cuba: Zonas francas, nuevo paso en apertura al capital extranjero. InterPress Third World News Agency (IPS) Service, distributed electronically through the APC network, September 13.

IPF (Instituto de Planificación Física) 1973. La Habana Metropolitana, un instrumento para el desarrollo de Cuba socialista. *Arquitectura Cuba* **341/2(XXVI)**: 3. La Habana.

IPF 1992. El problema de la vivienda en cuba: algunas consideraciones para su solución (July), Havana: IPF (mimeograph).

Izquierdo, R. and Liz, M. 1984. Vivienda en La Habana. Paper presented before the meetings of Remodelación de Ciudades, Havana (November). Havana: UNAICC.

Izquierdo, T. and Quevedo, M. 1972. *Elementos para la historia de un barrio residencial habanero*. Tesis de Grado. Havana: Escuela de Arquitectura, Facultad de Tecnología, Universidad de La Habana.

James, P. 1959. *Latin America*. London: Cassell.

Jenkins, R. 1987. *Transnational corporations and the Latin American automobile industry*. Pittsburgh: University of Pittsburgh Press

Jiménez, G. 1990. 29 años sin analfabetismo. *Granma*, 1 March, p. 2.

Joe, B.E. 1995. Yndamiro Restano: Recently released POC Thanks AI, plans to return to Cuba. Amnesty International (mimeo, November).

Johnson, W.F. 1920. *The history of Cuba*. New York: Freedom Publishers.

*Journal of Decorative and Propaganda Arts, 1875–1945*. 1996. No. **22**. (Theme Issue on Cuba). Miami: Wolfson Foundation of the Decorative and Propagana Arts, Inc.

Judget, J. 1989. The many lives of Old Havana. *National Geographic* (**August**) 1: 278–300. Washington, D.C.

Junta Central de Planificación. 1976. *La situación de vivienda en Cuba en 1970 y su evolución perspectiva*. Junta Central de Planificación, Dirección Central de Estadística. Havana: Orbe.

Kavafis, K. 1978. *Poesías completas*. Madrid: Ediciones Peralta.

Kay, C. 1994. *Latin American theories of development and underdevelopment*. London: Routledge.

Kirby, A. 1995. A research agenda for the close of the century. *Cities* **12**: 5–11.

Klak, T. 1994. Havana and Kingston: Mass media and empirical observations of two Caribbean cities in crisis. *Urban Geography* **15**: 318–344.

Kuethe, A.J. 1986. *Cuba, 1753–1853: Crown, military and society*. Knoxville, TN: University of Tennessee Press.

Labatut, J. 1957. Experiencias en la práctica y la enseñanza de la planificación urbana. *Arquitectura* **290 (XXV)**: 446. La Habana.

Lagache, E. 1992. La Havane expectative. *Lumières de la Ville* **5** (June): 177. Paris.

Lang, P. 1995. *Mortal city*. New York: Princeton Architectural Press.

Laprade, A. 1931. Parques y jardines de J.C.N. Forestier. *Colegio de Arquitectos de la Habana* **3** (XV): 9. Havana.

Leal, E. 1986. *Reqresar en el Tiempo*. Havana: Editorial Letras Cubanas.

Leal, E. 1988. *La Habana, ciudad antiqua*. Havana: Editorial Letras Cubanas.

Le Corbusier. 1947. Plan Director de Buenos Aires. *Número Monográfico de la Arquitectura de Hoy* **4**. Buenos Aires.

Le Riverend, J. 1960. *La Habana. Biografía de una provincia*. Havana: Academia de la Historia de Cuba.

Le Riverend, J. 1965. *Historia económica de Cuba*. Havana: Editora Universitaria.

Le Riverend, J. 1966. *La República. Dependencia y revolución*. Havana: Editora Universitaria.

Le Riverend, J. 1992. *La Habana, espacio y vida*. Madrid: Mapfre.

Lee, S. 1994. Entrevista a Carlos Lage. *Granma*. October 31.

Lee, S. 1995a. Se presentarán 29,131 candidatos para los 14,229 escaños municipales. *Granma*, June 27.

Lee, S. 1995b. Batallas priorizadas: Ordenar el trabajo por cuenta propia, garantizar el cobro de impuestos y eliminar toda ilegalidad. *Granma*. December 28.

Lee, S. 1996a. A comienzos del 96: Hablemos de presupuesto y de impuesto. *Granma*, January 5.

Lee, S. 1996b. La ayuda familiar y otras respuestas. *Granma*, May 23, p. 2

Levine, R. 1993. *Tropical diaspora: The Jewish experience in Cuba*. Gainesville: University of Florida Presses.

Lezama Lima, J. 1970. *La ciudad hechizada*. Havana: UNEAC (Unión Nacional de Escritores y Actores de Cuba).

Lezama Lima, J. 1988. *Confluencias. Selección de ensayos*. Prólogo, Abel Prieto. Havana: Editorial Letras Cubanas.

Lincoln Institute of Land Policy. 1996. Global city regions: Searching for common ground. *Landlines* **8**: 1, 1–7 (Cambridge, MA: Newsletter of the Lincoln Institute of Land Policy).

Livingston, M. 1996. Houses that dream in Cuban: The crumbling of Habana Vieja. University of Tennessee, Department of Architecture (mimeo).

Livingston, R. 1990. *Cirugía de casas*. Buenos Aires: Editorial CP 67.

Llana, M.E. 1983. *Casas del Vedado*. Havana: Letras Cubanas.

Llanes, L. 1978. Los marginados de la arquitectura (1902–1919). *Universidad de La Habana* **207** (January/March): 89–100.

Llanes, L. 1985. *Apuntes para una historia sobre los constructores cubanos*. Havana: Letras Cubanas.

Llanes, L. 1987. Las actividades comerciales y financieras y su influencia sobre las construcciones. In P. Fernández and L. Merino, Eds, *Arte. Cuba, república*, Havana: Facultad de Artes y Letras, Universidad de La Habana, Havana, pp. 49–53.

Llanes, L. 1993. 1898–1921: La transformación de La Habana a través de su arquitectura. *Letras Cubanas*, p. 86

Locay, L. (1995). *Institutional requirements for successful market reforms*. Paper presented at the 'Cuba in Transition Workshop'. Shaw, Pittman, Potts & Trowbridge. Washington, DC, April 10, 1995.

Loomis, J.A. 1994. Architecture or revolution: The Cuban experiment. *Design Book Review* **32/33** (Spring/Summer): 71–80.

López, A. 1987. Las obras oficiales durante el período de gobierno de Ramón Grau San Martín (1944–1948). In P. Fernández and L. Merino, Eds, *Arte: Cuba república*. Havana: Colección de lecturas, Facultad de Artes y Letras, Universidad de La Habana, p. 269.

López Castañeda, F. 1963. Labor de restauración realizada por la Comisión Nacional de Monumentos durante el año 1963. *Arquitectura Cuba* **332 (XXX):** 6–17.

López Castañeda, F. 1971. Conservación y restauración de monumentos. *Constructores* **1** (January) 19–25. La Habana.

López Rangel, R. and Segre, R. 1986. *Tendencias arquitectónicas y caos urbano en América Latina*. Mexico: G. Gili.

López Segrera, F. 1989. *Cuba: Cultura y sociedad 1510–1985*. Havana: Editorial Letras Cubanas.

López Segrera, F. 1972. *Cuba: Capitalismo dependiente y subdesarollo (1510–1959)*. Havana: Casa de las Américas.

López Segrera, F. 1980. *Raíces históricas de la revolución cubana (1868–1959)*. Havana: Ediciones Unión.

Los Naranjos. 1984. *Creación y desarrollo de una empresa pecuaria genética modelo. empresa pecuaria genética 'Los Naranjos'*. Havana: Editorial Científico-Técnica.

Luis, R. 1995. ¿Se salvará La Habana? *Prisma* **271**. Año 21, pp. 33–38, (September/October). Havana.

Luxner, L. 1995. Cuba as future client and competitor. *CubaNews* (June). Miami: The Miami Herald Publishing Company, p. 8.

Lynch, K. 1972. *What time is this place?* Cambridge: The MIT Press.

Machado, O. 1960. *Comunidades pesqueras*. Havana: Departamento de Desarrollo Social.

Machado, O. 1969. Discurso (speech). *Clausura al Seminario de Viviendas* (March). Havana: Ministerio de la Construcción.

Machado, O. 1976. La Habana: DESA. La industrialilzación de la construcción de la vivienda. El sistema I.M.S. en Cuba (mimeo).

Mahtar M'Bow, A. 1983. *La Plaza Vieja*, Ministerio de Cultura. Havana: Ediciones Plaza Vieja.

Malone, S.T. 1996. Conflict, coexistence, and cooperation: Church–State Relations in Cuba. *Cuba Briefing Paper Series* Number 10. Washington D.C.: The Cuba Project, Center for Latin American Studies, Georgetown University (August).

Manitzas, N. 1974. El marco de la Revolución. In D. Barkin and N. Manitzas, Eds, *Cuba: Camino abierto*. Mexico City: Siglo XXI, pp. 13–59 (second edition).

Maribona, A. 1957. El fantástico crecimiento de la propiedad urbana en La Gran Habana. *Diario de la Marina. Siglo y Cuarto* (Special Supplement). Havana, pp. 78–82.

Marrero, L. 1956. *Historia económica de cuba: Guía de estudio y documentación*. Havana: Universidad de Havana: Instituto Superior de Estudios e Investigaciones Económicas.

Marrero, L. 1975a. *Cuba: Economía y sociedad*: El siglo XVII (I). Madrid: Editorial Playor, S.A.

Marrero, L. 1975b. *Cuba: Economía y sociedad*: El siglo XVII (II). Madrid: Editorial Playor, S.A.

Marrero, L. 1976. *Cuba: Economía y sociedad*: El siglo XVII (III). Madrid: Editorial Playor, S.A.

Marrero, L. 1981a. *Geografía de Cuba*. San Juan, Puerto Rico: Editorial San Juan

Marrero, L. 1981b. *Cuba: Economía y sociedad*. San Juan, Puerto Rico: Editorial San Juan.

Martín, M.E. and Rodríguez, E.L. 1992. *La Habana. Map & guide to 337 significant architectural monuments in the Cuban capital and surroundings*. Darmstadt: Trialog.

Martín, M.E. and Múscar, E. 1992. *Proceso de urbanización en América del Sur*. Madrid: Mapfre.

Martín, M.E. and Rodríguez, E.L. 1993. *Guía de arquitectura. La Habana colonial (1519–1898)*. Seville: Selección y Catálogo, Junta de Andalucia.

Martínez Inclán, P. 1925. *La Habana actual. Estudio de la capital de Cuba desde el punto de vista de la arquitectura de ciudades*. Havana: Imprenta P. Fernández.

Martínez Inclán, P. 1946. *Alqunas nociones de estética urbana*. Havana: Imprenta P. Fernández.

Martínez Inclán, P. 1949. *Código de Urbanismo. Carta de Atenas, Carta de La Habana*. Havana: Imprenta P. Fernández.

Mathéy, K. 1991. Self-help housing policies and practices in Cuba. In K. Mathéy, Ed., *Beyond Self-Help Housing*. London: Mansell, pp. 181–216.

Mathéy, K. 1994. Informal and substandard neighbourhoods in revolutionary Cuba. In K. Mathéy, Ed., *Phänomen Kuba. Alternative Weqe in Architektur. Städtentwicklung und Ökoloqie.* Karlsruher Stadtebauliche Schriften, Karlsruhe, pp. 123–132.

Mediz Bolio, A. 1916. *Palabras al viento. Crónicas de Cuba.* Mexico: Ateneo Peninsular.

Medin, T. 1990. *Cuba: The shaping of revolutionary consciousness.* Boulder: Lynee Rienner.

Mena, C. and Cobelo, A. 1992. *Historia de la medicina en Cuba: Hospitales y centros benéficos en Cuba colonial.* Miami: Ediciones Universal.

Menéndez, M. 1992. Entrevista con Nisia Agüero. In M. Coyula, Ed., *El desarrollo del país y las políticas urbanas.* Havana: Instituto Superior Politécnico José Antonio Echeverría, pp. 17–22.

Mesa-Lago, C. 1988. The Cuban economy in the 1980s. In S. Roca, Ed., *Cuba: Past interpretations and future challenges.* Boulder: Westview Press.

Mesa-Lago, C. 1994. *Are economic reforms propelling Cuba to the market?* Coral Gables: University of Miami, North–South Center.

Mesías, R. and Morales, J.L. 1985. Arquitectura al servicio del usuario. Creadores de su Vivienda. XI Seminario de Vivienda y Urbanismo (mimeo). Havana: Centro Técnico de la Vivienda y el Urbanismo.

Michener, J. A. and Kings, J. 1989. *Six days in Havana.* Austin: University of Texas Press.

Ministry of Economy and Planning. 1996. *Cuba Economic Report. First Semester, 1996.* Havana: Ministry of Economy and Planning.

MINSAP (Ministerio de Salud Pública). 1994. Unpublished health, morbidity and mortality data gathered by the Geography Section, MINSAP, Vedado, Havana City.

Mongin, O. 1995. *Vers la Troisième Ville?* Paris: Hachette.

Montoulieu y de la Torre, E. 1953. El crecimiento de La Habana y su regularización (1923). *Ingeniería Civil.* **8 (IV)**: 567. Havana.

Moreno Fraginals, M. 1964. *El Ingenio. El complejo económico social cubano del azúcar, Vol. 1. 1760–1860.* Havana: Comisión Nacional Cubana de la UNESCO.

Moreno Fraginals, M. 1976. *The sugar mill: The socioeconomic complex of sugar in Cuba, 1760–1860.* New York and London: Monthly Review Press.

Murrell, P. 1992. Privatization versus the fresh start. In Vladimir Tismaneanu and Patrick Clawson, Eds, *Uprooting Leninism, cultivating liberty,* Lanham, MD: University Press of America and Foreign Policy Research Institute, pp. 59–68.

Nápoles, R. 1996a. Cuba: Cattle rustlers and illicit butchers devastate herds. InterPress Service. Worldwide distribution via the APC networks. May 17.

Nápoles, R. 1996b. Cuba: Government limits private profit making. InterPress Service. Worldwide distribution via the APC networks. June 6.

Nápoles, R. 1996c. Cuba-economy: Taxes hit free market sales. InterPress Service. Worldwide distribution via the APC networks. May 7.

Nápoles, R. 1996d. Cuba-Environment. Havana Bay – The island's most polluted ecosystem. InterPress Service. Worldwide distribution via the APC networks. May 30.

Niddrie, D. 1971. The Caribbean. In H. Blakemore and C.T. Smith, Eds, *Latin America: Geographical perspectives.* London: Methuen, pp. 73–120.

Noceda, J.M. 1984. *Las formulaciones teóricas del Movimiento Moderno en la arquitectura y el urbanismo en Cuba: 1928–1958.* Thesis. Havana: Escuela de Arquitectura, ISPJAE; Facultad de Artes y Letras, Universidad de La Habana.

Nochteff, H. 1984. *Desindustrialización y retroceso en Argentina, 1976–1982: La industrial electronica de consumo*. Buenos Aires: Facultad Latinoamericana de Ciencias.

Noever, P. 1996. Editor. *The Havana project: Architecture again*. Vienna and Los Angeles: Prestel.

Novick, A. 1991. Arbitros, pares, socios. Técnicos locales y extranjeros en la génesis del urbanismo porteño. *Arquitectura Sur* 4 (II): 44. Mar del Plata, Argentina.

Núñez, R. 1996. *Land planning & development in Havana City: Two study cases. The new investment context regarding land*. Havana: Grupo para el Desarrollo Integral de la Capital.

Oliver, P. 1970. *Shelter and society*. London: Cresset Press.

Ortega, L. 1993. Junto al barrio: Rehabilitación de Atarés. *Arquitectura y Urbanismo* 14: 9–14.

Ortega, L., *et al*. 1996. Barrio de Atarés. In H. Harms, W. Ludeña and P. Pfeiffer, Eds, *Vivir en el 'centro.' Vivienda e inquilinato en los barrios céntricos de las metrópolis de América Latina*. Hamburg–Harburg: Technische Univerität, pp. 95–134.

Ortiz, F. 1963. *Contrapunteo cubano del tabaco y el azúcar*. Havana: Consejo Nacional de Cultura.

Otero, R. 1940. Obras de embellecimiento que proyectaba J.C.N. Forestier para La Habana. *Arquitectura*. 86 (VIII): 208. La Habana.

Padrón L., M. and Cuervo M., H. 1988. La Ciudad de La Habana: Una nueva voluntad urbanística en marcha. Paper delivered at the III Congreso Iberoamericano de Urbanismo. Barcelona and Havana: JUCEPLAN and IPF.

Padrón L., M. and Cuervo M., H. 1991. La ciudad de La Habana: Una nueva voluntad urbanística. *Ciudad y Territorio* (Madrid) 86–87: 107.

Palm, E.W. 1955. *Los monumentos arquitectónicos de La Española*. Santo Domingo: Universidad de Santo Domingo.

Paolini, R. 1994. La Habana Vieja: víctima de la guerra fría. *El Diario de Caracas*, May 29, p. 30. Caracas.

Park, R.E., Burgess, W.W. and McKensie, R.D. 1925. *The city*. Chicago: University of Chicago Press.

Partido Comunista de Cuba. 1976. *Plataforma programática del Partido Comunista de Cuba*. Havana: Departamento de Orientación Revolucionaria del Comité del Partido Comunista de Cuba.

Pastor, M.A. and Zimbalist, A. 1995. Waiting for change: Adjustment and return in Cuba. *World Development* 23: 705–720.

Pattullo, P. 1996. *Last Resorts: The cost of tourism in the Caribbean*. London: Cassell and Latin American Bureau.

Payne, S. 1995. Cubais garden revolution. *Permaculture International Journal* 54: 14–14.

Pendle, G. 1978. *A history of Latin America*. New York: Pendle.

Pereira, M.A. 1985. El monumento a José Martí en la Plaza de la Revolución. In *Memorias del 3er simposio de la cultura en la Ciudad de La Habana*. Dirección Provincial de la Cultura, Poder Popular, 20, Havana.

Pereira, M.A. 1994. *La producción monumentaria conmemorativa en Cuba 1959–1993*, Havana: Docotoral thesis, Facultad de Artes y Letras, Universidad de La Habana.

Pérez, F. and Fernández, M. 1996. *A strategy to improve water supply and sanitation in Havana*. Havana: Grupo para el Desarrollo Integral de la Capital.

Pérez, H. 1975. *El subdesarollo y la vía del desarollo*. Havana: Ciencias Sociales.

Pérez, L. 1988. *Cuba: Between reform and revolution.* New York: Oxford University Press.

Pérez, M. 1995. *Condición y estructura de la vivienda en La Habana.* Havana: Grupo para el Desarrollo Integral de la Ciudad.

Pérez, M. 1996. *Hacia una política local de mejoramiento ambiental con participación comunitaria.* Havana: Grupo para el Desarrollo Integral de la Capital.

Pérez Beato, M. 1936. *Habana antigua. Apuntes históricos.* Havana: Fernández y Co.

Pérez de la Riva, J. 1946. *Origen y régimen de la propiedad horizontal.* Havana: Moderna Poesía.

Pérez de la Riva, J. 1963. *Correspondencia reservada del Capitán General don Miguel Tacón con el Gobierno de Madrid: 1834–1836.* Havana: Departamento de Colección Cubana, Biblioteca Nacional 'José Marti'

Pérez de la Riva, J. 1965. Desarrollo de la población habanera. *Bohemia,* 12 (November): 100. La Habana.

Pérez de la Riva, J. 1975. Los recursos de Cuba al comenzar el siglo: inmmigración, economía y nacionalidad (1899–1906). *La república neocolonial. Anuario de Estudios Cubanos.* Volume 1. Havana: Ciencias Sociales, 5–35.

Pérez-López, J. 1994a. Islands of capitalism in an ocean of socialism: Joint ventures and Cuba's development strategy. In J. Pérez-López, Ed., *Cuba at a crossroads: politics and economics after the Fourth Party Congress.* Gainesville: University Presses of Florida, pp. 190–219.

Pérez-López, J. 1994b. Economic reform in Cuba: Lessons from Eastern Europe. In J. Pérez-López, Ed., *Cuba at a crossroads: politics and economics after the Fourth Party Congress.* Gainesville: University of Florida Presses, pp. 238–263.

Pérez-López, J. 1995. *Cuba's second economy.* New Brunswick, NJ: Transaction Books.

Personal communication, Dr. Carlos M. Miyares, General Manager, Centro de Histoterapia Placentaria, Miramar, June 28, 1995.

Peyrerea, C. 1929. *Las huellas de los conquistadores.* Madrid: Aguilar.

Pezuela, J. 1868. *Historia de Cuba.* Volume 1. Madrid.

Pichardo, H. 1965. *Documentos para la historia de Cuba época colonial.* Havana: Editorial Nacional de Cuba.

Pichardo Moya, F. 1943. La edad media cubana. *Revista Cuba* (Havana).

Pino Santos, O. 1973. *El asalto a Cuba por la oligarquía financiera yanqui.* Havana: Casa de las Américas.

Pita, F. 1995. Las propiedades confiscadas hay que reclamarlas aquí. *Granma,* **29** April, p. 4.

Poder Popular. n.d. Datos Socioeconómicos. Ciudad de La Habana. Havana: Poder Popular.

Polanyi, N. The problem of the capitalist state. *Review* **1**: 9–20.

Pons, P. 1994. La Habana. ¡Abajo con el Malecón! *Ajoblanco* **69**: 38–41 (December) Barcelona.

Portela, A. 1994. Oil search. *CubaNews,* April, p. 7. Miami: The Miami Herald Publishing Company

Portuondo, F. 1965. *Historia de Cuba, 1492–1898.* Havana: Editorial Pueblo y Educación.

Portuondo, J.A. 1962. *Bosquejo histórico de las letras cubanas,* Havana: Editora del Ministerio de Educación.

Poumier, M. 1975. *Apuntes sobre la vida cotidiana en Cuba en 1898.* Havana: Ciencias Sociales.

Pradilla, E. 1982. *Ensayos sobre el problema de la vivienda en américa latina*. Mexico City: Unidad Xochimilco.

Prensa Latina. 1996. Cuba: Economic Report, First Semester, 1996, Ministry of Economy and Planning. Electronic posting from prensal@blythe.org, July 24.

Presno, P.R. 1952. Factor de progreso para la república ha sido y es la colonia española. *Album del cinquentenario de la asociación de reportero de La Habana. 1902–1952*. Havana: Editorial Lex, 109.

Préstamo, F. 1995. *Cuba y su arquitectura*. Miami: Ediciones Universal.

Provincia de Ciudad de La Habana. 1992. *Características generales de la Ciudad de La Habana*. Havana.

Przeworski, A. 1989. Class, production and politics. A reply to Burawoy. *Socialist Review* **19** (2): 87–112.

Przeworski, A. 1992. *Democracy and markets: Political and economic reforms in Eastern Europe and Latin America*. Cambridge: Cambridge University Press.

Quintana, N. 1974. Evolución histórica de la arquitectura en Cuba. *Enciclopedia de Cuba*. Tomo 5. Madrid: Playor, 91.

Rallo, J. 1964. Transformación de La Habana desde 1762 hasta 1830. *Cuba en la UNESCO* **3/4/5 (March)**: 6. La Habana.

Rallo, J. and Segre, R. 1978. *Evolución histórica de las estructuras territoriales y urbanas de Cuba. 1519–1959*. Havana: Facultad de Arquitectura, Instituto Superior Politécnico José Antonio Echeverría.

Rama, A. 1985. La ciudad letrada. In R. Morse and J.E. Hardoy, Eds, *Cultura urbana latinoamericana*. Buenos Aires: CLACSO 5, pp. 12–29.

Resolución conjunta. 1995. No. 3/95 de los Ministerios de Finanzas y Precios y de Seguridad Social sobre actividades y oficios por cuenta propia. *Granma*, **13** June, p. 2.

Ramón, F. 1967. *Miseria de la ideología urbanística*. Madrid: Ciencias Sociales.

Ramón, F. 1991. La Habana: Por una ciudad más humana, bella, y funcional. *Actas del XVI Congreso Anual de la Asociación de Estudios del Caribe*. Havana: Asociación de Estudios del Caribe.

Rigau, J. and Stout, N. 1994. *Havana*. New York: Rizzoli.

Rigol, I. 1978. Protección de monumentos. *Arquitectura Cuba* **347/348**: 90. La Habana.

Rivero, A. 1981. Una vieja ciudad rejuvenece. *Revolución y Cultura* **107** (July): 76. La Habana.

Rivero, N. 1994. Cuba's oil predicament. *CubaNews*, April, p. 7. Miami: The Miami Herald Publishing Company.

Roberts, W.A. 1953. *Havana: The portrait of a city*. New York: Coward-McMann, Inc.

Roca, S.G. 1994. Reflections on economic policy: Cuba's food program. In J.F. Pérez-López, Ed., *Cuba at a crossroads: politics and economics after the Fourth Party Congress*. Gainesville: University of Florida Presses, pp. 94–117.

Roca Calderío, B. 1973. Prólogo. *Seis leyes de la revolución*. Havana: Editorial de Ciencias Sociales, p. 12.

Rodríguez, A.A. and Cabrera, F. 1995. La problemática de la legislación urbanística en la capital. *Comunidad* **(April)**, pp. 95–97. Havana: Instituto de Planificación Física.

Rodríguez, E.L. 1991. Arquitectura joven cubana: solamente una propuesta. *Excelsior*, Sección Metropolitana, **14**(12): 1. México.

Rodríguez, E.L. 1992. Hacia una realización alternativa o el arquitecto en crisis. *Arquitectura Cuba* **375 (XLI)**: 64–71. La Habana.

Rodríguez, E.L. 1994. Entrevista. *El Nuevo Herald*, **6** (7): 1–2. Miami.

Rodríguez, E.L. 1996. The architectural avante-garde: from Art Deco to Modern Regionalism. *The Journal of Decorative and Propaganda Arts, 1975–1945.* **22**: 255–276.

Rodríguez, A., Riofrio, G. and Welsh, E. 1973. *Segregación y desmemorización política: El caso de Lima.* Buenos Aires: SIAP.

Rodríguez Feo, J. 1994. Carta desde La Habana. *Gazeta de Cuba* **1**: 94.

Roemer, M. 1964. *Medical Care in Latin America.* Washington, D.C.: Pan American Health Union.

Rogers, E. N., Sert, J.L. and Tyrwhitt, J. 1961. *El corazón de la ciudad. Para una vida más humana de la comunidad (CIAM).* Barcelona: Editora Científico Médica.

Rohter, R. 1995. In Cuba, Army takes on party jobs, and may be only thing that works. *The New York Times,* June 8, p. A–12.

Rohter, R. 1996. Cuba's nuclear plant project worries Washington. *The New York Times,* February 25, p. A–18.

Roig de Leuchsenring, E. 1952. Transformación de La Habana en medio siglo, 1902–1952. In *Album del cincuentenario de la asociación de reporteros de La Habana. 1902–1952.* Havana: Editorial Lex, 163.

Roig de Leuchsenring, E. (1964). *La Habana, apuntes históricos,* Vols II and III. Havana: Consejo Nacional de Cultura.

Rorick, H. and Gomila, S. 1984. *Las Arboledas sketchbook. Design for a new community in Cuba.* Havana: Centro Técnico de la Vivienda y el Urbanismo and Groundwork Institute.

Rosenberg, R. 1992. Cuba's free-market experiment: Los mercados libres campesinos, 1980–1986. *Latin American Research Review* **27** (3): 51–89.

Rossi, A. 1966. *L'architettura della cittá.* Padua: Marsilio.

Sabbatini, M. 1967. La formazione della societá neocoloniale cubana. Rome: *Ideologie* **1**: 54.

Salinas, F. 1963a. La industrialización de la vivienda: Una proposición. *Arquitectura Cuba* **336**: 33.

Salinas, F. 1963b. Informe del Relator General, 'La arquitectura en los países en vias de desarrollo' (mimeo), VII Congreso de la Unión Internacional de Arquitectos. Havana, September, p. 29.

Salinas, F. 1967. La arquitectura revolucionaria del Tercer Mundo. *Tricontinental* **1** (July–August), Havana, pp. 93–102.

Salinas, F. 1971. Descolonización de la ciudad. *Arquitectura Cuba* **340 (XXIV)**: 2–3.

Salinas, F. 1988. *La Cultura de la vivienda Cubana. De la arquitectura y el urbanismo a la cultura ambiental.* Guayaquil, Ecuador: Facultad de Arquitectura Universidad de Guayaquil.

San Martín, J. 1947. *Memoria del plan de obras del gobierno del Dr. Ramón Grau San Martín.* Havana: Ministerio de Obras Públicas.

Sánchez, O. 1989. Tras el rastro de los fundadores: un panorama de la plástica cubana, *Cuba. Trajectoire Cubaine,* Centre d'Art Contemporain, CAC, Corbeil Essones, 8–17.

Sánchez Agusti, M. 1984. *Edificios públicos de La Habana en el siglo XVIII.* Valladolid: Universidad de Valladolid.

Sánchez-Albornoz, N. 1974. *The population of Latin America.* Berkeley: University of California Press.

Santovenia, E. 1943. *Historia de Cuba.* Volume II. Havana: Trópico.

Santovenia, E. and Shelton, R. 1964. *Cuba y su historia.* Miami: Rema Press.

Sapieha N. 1990. *Old Havana, Cuba.* London: Tauris Parke Books.

Sarduy, S. 1967. *Ecrit en dansant.* Paris: Seuil.

Sarlo, B.A. 1994. Cidade Real, Cidade Imaginária, Cidade Reformada. *Revista do Patrimônio Histórico e Artístico Nacional* **23**: 167–177. Rio de Janeiro.

Sartor, M. 1993. La cittá latinoamericana tra antecedenti precolombiani, leggi di fondazione e tradizione. *Zodiac* **8**, *Rivista Internazionale di Architettura.* September 1992/February 1993, Vol. **93**, p. 15 (Milan).

Scarpaci, J. 1989. Theory and practice of privatization. In J.L. Scarpaci, Ed., *Health services privatization in industrial societies.* New Brunswick, NJ: Rutgers University Press, pp. 1–24.

Scarpaci, J. 1994. Chile. In Gerald Greenfield, Ed., *International handbook of Latin American urbanization*, Westport, CT: Greenwood Press, pp. 37–69.

Scarpaci, J. 1996. Industrial analysis: Havana's real estate. *CubaNews*, December, p. 9. Miami: The Miami Herald Publishing Company.

Scarpaci, J, Gaete, A. and Infante, R. 1988. Planning residential segregation. The case of Santiago de Chile. *Urban Geography* **9**: 19–36.

Scarpaci, J. and Gutman, M. forthcoming. *Plazas and Skyscrapers: The Transformation of the Latin American Historic City Center.* Tucson: University of Arizona Press.

Scarpaci, J. and Hall, A.Z. 1995. Havana peddles through hard times. *Sustainable Transport*. **4** (Winter): 4–5 and 15.

Scarpaci, J. and Irarrázaval, I. 1994. Decentralizing a centralized state: Local government finance in Chile within the Latin American context. *Public Budgeting and Finance* **14** (4): 120–136.

Segre, R. 1968a. Significación de Cuba en la evolución tipológica de las fortificaciones coloniales de América. In Roberto Segre, Ed., *Lectura crítica del entorno cubano.* Havana: Editorial Letras Cubanas 1990, pp. 23–65.

Segre, R. 1968b. Vivienda y prefabricación en Cuba. *AUCA* (Santiago, Chile): 44.

Segre, R. 1970a. Cronología de la Revolución cubana referida a la arquitectura 1953–1969. In Roberto Segre, Ed., *Ensayos sobre arquitectura e ideología en Cuba revolucionaria.* Havana: Universidad de La Habana, Centro de Información Científico y Técnico, pp. 67–155.

Segre, R. 1970b. *Diez años de arquitectura en Cuba revolucionaria.* Havana: Ediciones Unión.

Segre, R. 1974. *Transformación urbana en Cuba.* Barcelona: Gili.

Segre, R. 1975. Contenido de clase en la arquitectura cubana de los años 50. *Revista de la Biblioteca Nacional José Martí* **3** (September–December), p. 97.

Segre, R. 1978. Las transformaciones ambientales en Cuba. In Roberto Segre, Ed., *Las estructuras ambientales en América Latina.* Havana: Departamento de Cultura, Universidad de La Habana, pp. 217–281.

Segre, R. 1984. Architecture in the revolution. In R. Hatch, Ed., *The scope of social architecture.* New York: Van Nostrand Reinhold, pp. 349–360.

Segre, R. 1985a. *La vivienda en Cuba: República y revolución.* Havana: Departamento de Actividades Culturales, Universidad de La Habana.

Segre, R. 1985b. *Historia de la arquitectura y el urbanismo. Países desarollados. Siglos XIX y XX.* Madrid: Instituto de Estudios de Administración Local.

Segre, R. 1989. *Arquitectura y urbanismo de la revolución cubana.* Havana: Pueblo y Educación.

Segre, R. 1990. *Lectura crítica del entorno cubano.* Havana: Letras Cubanas.

Segre, R. 1992a. La Plaza de Armas: simbolismo originario y figuras del poder. *DANA* (Documentos de Arquitectura Nacional y Americana) **31/32**: 113–116. (Resistencia, Argentina: Instituto Argentino de Investigación de Historia de la Arquitectura y del Urbanismo).

Segre, R. 1992b. Savia nueva en odres viejos: la continuidad del talento. *Arquitectura Cuba* **375**: 7–14.

Segre, R. 1993. Sincretismo en la arquitectura centroamericana: trayectoria de Bruno Stagno. *Revolución y Cultura* **1**: 43–47.

Segre, R. 1994a. Preludio a la modernidad: convergencias y divergencias en el contexto caribeño (1900–1950). In A. Amaral, Ed., *Arquitectura neocolonial. América Latina, Caribe, Estados Unidos, Memorial.* San Pablo, Mexico: Fondo de Cultura Económica, 95.

Segre, R. 1994b. Architektur und Städtebau im revolutionären Kuba. Das historische Erbe und der Mythos des Neuen. In K. Mathéy, Ed., *Phänomen Kuba. Alternative Wege in Architektur, Städtentwicklung und Ökologie,* Karlsruher Stadtebauliche Schriften, Karlsruhe, pp. 1–19.

Segre, R. 1994c. *Arquitectura antillana del Siglo XX.* Xochimilco: Universidad Autonóma de Mexico.

Segre, R. 1994d. Tres décadas de arquitectura cubana: la herencia histórica y el mito de lo nuevo. *Revolución y Cultura* **33**: 36–45 (May/June). Havana.

Segre, R. and López Rangel, R. 1982. *Architettura e territorio nell'America Latina.* Milan: Electa Editrice.

Segre, R., Cárdenas, E. and Aruca, L. 1981. *Historia de la arquitectura y el Urbanismo: América Latina y Cuba.* Havana: Pueblo y Educación.

Segui G. 1994. Les odeurs de la rue. In Jacobo Machover, Ed., *La Havane 1952–1961. D'un dictateur à l'autre: explosion des sens et morale révolutionnaire.* Paris: Série Mémoires **31**, Editions Autrement, 27–38.

Séneca, J.C. 1976. *Ordenamiento urbano.* Havana: Instituto de Planificación Física.

Sierra, R. 1996. *Who migrates and why.* Montevideo. Interpress Service.

Skidelsky, R. 1996. *The road from serfdom: The economic and political consequences of the end of Communism.* New York: Allen Lane, Penguin Press.

Slater, D. 1982. State and territory in postrevolutionary Cuba: Some critical reflections on the development of spatial policy. *International Journal of Urban and Regional Research* **6**: 1–33.

Soto, L. 1977. *La revolución del 33.* Tomos I/II/III. La Habana. Ciencias Sociales.

Stallings, B. 1986. External finance and the transition to socialism in small peripheral societies. In R. Fagen, C.D. Deere and J.L. Coraggio, Eds., *Transition and development.* New York: Monthly Review Press, pp. 54–78.

*Statesman's Yearbook 1982–83.* 19th Edition. New York: St. Martin's Press.

Stough, R. and Feldman, M. 1984. Tourism development models: Public policy management implications. Paper presented at the Caribbean Studies Association Meetings, 30 June–2 May, St. Kitts, West Indies (mimeo).

Stretton, H. 1978. *Urban planning in rich and poor countries.* Oxford: Oxford University Press.

Szelenyi, I. 1982. *Urban inequities under state socialism.* Oxford: Oxford University Press.

Taboada, D. (1987). La arquitectura de las vacas flacas. *Arquitectura y Urbanismo* **87**: 1.

Tabares del Real, J.A. 1971. *La revolución del 30: Sus Dos Ultimos Años.* Havana: Arte y Literatura.

Taller. 1995. *Los Consejos Populares, la gestión de desarrollo y la participación Popular en Cuba. Conclusiones preliminares.* Havana: Centro de Estudios de América.

Taylor, P. 1985. *Political geography: World-economy, nation-state and locality.* London: Longman.

Tejeira-Davis, E. 1987. *Roots of Modern Latin American Architecture*. Heidelberg: University of Heidelberg.

Tingle, V.R. and Montenegro, A. 1923. *La gran vía de La Habana*. Havana: J.E. Barlow.

Tismaneanu, V. 1992. Between liberation and freedom. In Vladimir Tismaneanu and Patrick Clawson, Eds, *Uprooting Leninism, cultivating liberty*, Lanham, MD: University Press of America and Foreign Policy Research Institute, pp. 1–48.

Turner, J.F. and Fichter, R. 1972. *Freedom to build: Dweller control of the housing process*. New York: Macmillan.

UIA (Unión Internacional de Arquitetos) (Cuban Section) 1963. *Informe de Cuba al VII Congreso de la UIA*. Havana: UIA.

Ullman, C.D. and Harris, E.L. 1945. The nature of cities. *Annals of the American Aademy of Political and Social Sciences* 242: 7–17.

United Nations. 1995a. Havana. In *The challenge of urbanization: The world's large cities*. New York: United Nations, Department for Economic and Social Information and Policy Analysis, Population Division, pp. 96–98.

United Nations. 1995b. *United Nations Development Survey, 1995*. New York: United Nations.

Valladares y Morales, A. 1947. *Urbanismo y construcción*. Havana: P. Fernández y Cia.

Various. 1971. Habana 1. *Arquitectura Cuba* **340**.

Various, 1973. Habana 2. *Arquitectura Cuba* **341–342**.

Vázquez, R. 1994. Prólogo. In R. Vázquez, Ed., *Bipolaridad de la cultura Cubana*. Stockholm: The Olof Palme International Center, pp. 7–18.

Vázquez Raña, M. 1993. Entrevista con Carlos Lage. El Sol de México. *Bohemia*. Havana, June 11.

Vega Vega, J. 1963. *La reforma urbana de cuba y otras leyes en relación a la vivienda*. Havana: Ministerio de la Construcción.

Véjar, C. 1994. *Y el perro ladra y la luna enfría. Fernando Salinas: diseño, ambiente y esperanza*. Mexico City: Universidad Autónoma de México.

Venegas, C. 1989. Las fábricas de tabaco habaneras. *Arquitectura y Urbanismo* 3 **(X)**: 14. La Habana.

Venegas, C. 1990. *La urbanización de las murallas: Dependencia y modernidad*. Havana: Letras Cubanas.

Venegas, C. and Núñez Jiménez, A. (1990). *La Habana: Fotografias de Manuel Méndez Guerrero*. Madrid: Instituto de Cooperación Iberoamericana.

Vilas, C.M. 1989. *State, class and ethnicity in Nicaragua: Capitalist modernization and revolutionary change on the Atlantic coast*. Boulder: Lynne Reinner.

Villanueva, C.R. 1966. *Caracas en tres tiempos*. Caracas: Ediciones Comisión Asuntos Culturales del Cuatricentenario de Caracas.

Violich, F. 1987. *Urban planning for Latin America*. Boston: Oelgeschlager, Gunn & Hain.

Vivas, F. 1966. Hacia una arquitectura de masas. *Boletín de la Escuela de Arquitectura* (Havana) **5–6**: 4–8.

Vivas, F. 1983. *Reflexiones para un Mundo Mejor*. Caracas: Edición del Autor.

Walker, P.G. 1996. Challenges facing the Cuban military. Washington, D.C: *Cuba Briefing Papers Series*, No. 12, Georgetown University

Wall, D. 1990. The political economy of industrialization in Sandinista Nicaragua. Ph.D. dissertation, University of Iowa.

Walton, J. 1987. Urban protest and the global political economy. The IMF Riots. In M.P. Smith and J.R. Feagin, Eds, *The capitalist city*. London: Basil Blackwell, pp. 364–386.

Weil, C. and Scarpaci, J. 1992. *Health and health care in Latin America during the 'lost decade': insights for the 1990s.* Minneapolis: Prisma Institute, University of Minnesota Press.

Weiss, J. 1947. *Arquitectura cubana contemporanea.* Colegio Nacional de Arquitectos. Havana: Letras Cubanas.

Weiss, J. 1950. *Medio siglo de arquitectura Cuba.* Havana: Universidad de La Habana, Facultad de Arquitectura, Imprenta Universitaria.

Weiss, J. 1966. *La arquitectura colonial cubana: Siglos xvi al xix.* Havana and Seville: Instituto Cubano del Libro and Junta de Andalucía.

Weiss, J. 1967. Un urbanista olvidado. *Arquitectura Cuba* **337**: 69.

Weiss, J. 1972. *La arquitectura colonial cubana.* Siglos XVI/XVII. Havana: Editorial de Arte y Literatura.

Weiss, J. 1973. *La arquitectura colonial cubana,* Tomo I. Havana: Siglos XVI/XVII, Editorial de Arte y Literatura.

Weiss, J. 1978. *Techos coloniales cubanos.* Havana: Editorial Arte y Literatura.

Wernstedt, F. 1961. *World climatic data: Latin America and the Caribbean.* Ann Arbor, Michigan: Edwards Brothers, Inc.

West, R. and Augelli, J. 1966. *Middle America: Its lands and peoples.* Englewood Cliffs, NJ: Prentice-Hall.

White, T. 1898. *Our war with Spain for Cuba's freedom.* New York: Freedom Publishers.

Whitefield, M. 1994. Cuba may be able to dance around the trade embargo. *The Fort Worth Star-Telegraph,* April 22, p. 3

Wiener, P.L., Sert, J.L. and Schulz, P. 1960. La Havane. Plan pilote et directives générales. *L'architecture d'aujourd'hui* **88**: 62 (Paris).

Williams, S. 1994. *Cuba: the land, the history, the people, the culture.* Philadelphia: Running Press.

Wise, M.Z. 1996. The challenge of a crumbling Havana. *The New York Times,* January 15, p. 38–H.

Wright, I.A. 1916a. *Los orígenes de la minería en Cuba.* Havana.

Wright, I.A. 1916b. *The early history of Cuba.* New York: Macmillan.

Wright, I.A. 1927. *Historia documentada de San Cristóbal de La Habana en el siqlo XVI.* Havana: Imprenta El Siglo XX.

Zimbalist, A. 1989. Incentives and planning Cuba. *Latin American Research Review* **24**: 65–94.

Zimbalist, A. 1993. Teetering on the brink: Cuba's current economic and political crisis. *Latin American Studies* **24**: 407–418.

Zschaebitz, U. and Lesta, F. 1990. *Actas de Atarés. Rehabilitación urbana de barrios en La Habana, Cuba.* Hamburg, Germany: Hamburg Technical University.

# Index